An Ideal Wine

An Ideal Wine

One Generation's Pursuit of Perfection—and Profit—in California

DAVID DARLINGTON

HARPER

An Imprint of HarperCollinsPublishers
www.harpercollins.com

Portions of this book originally appeared, in slightly different form, in the *New York Times Magazine* and *Wine & Spirits Magazine*.

HarperCollins books may be purchased for educational, business, or sales promotional use. For information, please write: Special Markets Department, HarperCollins Publishers, 10 East 53rd Street, New York, NY 10022.

FIRST EDITION

Designed by Fritz Metsch

Library of Congress Cataloging-in-Publication Data has been applied for.

ISBN 978-0-06-170423-9

11 12 13 14 15   OV/RRD   10 9 8 7 6 5 4 3 2 1

*This book is for two people,
without either of whom it would not have been possible:
Bill Strachan and Joel Peterson.*

The wine is juicy, vines are wood,
The wooden table gives wine as good.
Profound insight! Now you perceive
A miracle; only believe!

—MEPHISTOPHELES, Goethe's *Faust*
(Walter Kaufmann translation)

Author's Note

AS THIS BOOK was going to press (what an old-fashioned term), a bombshell burst over the world of wine when Robert M. Parker Jr., founder and preeminent voice of the *Wine Advocate,* announced that, as of February 2011, he would no longer review California wine. Though he'll continue to critique older vintages, as well as new wines from Bordeaux and the Rhône, Parker said he was turning over the contemporary California duties to Antonio Galloni, who also evaluates Italy, Champagne, Burgundy, and Chablis for the *Advocate.*

In other words, Parker's 100-point scoring system will continue to dangle over the heads of American winemakers, though at this point it's hard to envision Galloni (or the less personal authority of the *Advocate*) carrying the same weight wielded by the creator's notorious surname. Hence, the change has been heralded as the "end of an era"—an epoch that happens to be chronicled in this book.

In that light, readers holding half-empty wineglasses might be tempted to regard parts of *An Ideal Wine* as passé. Au contraire. To a large extent, this is a work of history—a portrait of a place and time. Now even its present-day scenes, which would inevitably have come to seem dated, have acquired the same hindsight that characterizes the more plainly retrospective parts, circumscribing the whole as a window on a well-defined period. If, as the saying goes, journalism is the first draft of history, Parker's exit imposed an unanticipated deadline, closing the book on a much-declaimed chapter in California wine.

That said, it would be folly to suggest that, with his departure, American vintners are now free to pursue the muse unfettered.

Regardless of Parker's priorities, the *Wine Advocate*, *Wine Spectator*, *Wine & Spirits*, *Wine Enthusiast*, and numerous other point-wielding publications will continue to affect winemakers' sleep, no matter which regions feel the heat of the "papal" palate most directly. All of which calls into service another trusty proviso: The story you're about to read is true. Only the names of some of the characters may have been changed.

AN IDEAL WINE

LATE SEPTEMBER: THE autumnal equinox. A predictably perfect Northern California autumn afternoon—sunny, warm, windless, and crowned by a clear blue sky. Thanks to a premature spring that inspired grapevines to bud out early, the wine harvest is already winding down—even cabernet sauvignon, one of the last varieties to ripen, has mostly vanished from the vines.

With the smooth-jazz trumpet of Chris Botti on his CD player, Leo McCloskey pilots his Mercedes C230 north into Napa Valley. Wearing his customary warm-weather wardrobe—loose-fitting pants, shoes sans laces, short-sleeved shirt unconfined by a belt—he's on his way to Chappellet, a 25,000-case winery on the Valley's eastern edge.

Flipping open his cell phone as he drives, McCloskey calls a client in neighboring Sonoma Valley. "I'm looking at your numbers," he says. "They're pretty beefy. You need at least 50 percent as a Four; if you have that at midferm, you're already there. I think drain-down sweet is the name of the game this year. Let's do what they do at Lafite— come out of the fermenter shy of tannin, and later we'll add tannin. We can also see what happens if we play with the oak treatment on one of the wines. I want to encourage you to move more aggressively than you normally would. That's my job."

The winemaker on the other end tells McCloskey that one of the winery's cabernet vineyards still hasn't been picked. "Are you tasting the velvety characters that happen just before raisining?" McCloskey asks. "That's good! You know how you're looking for those ripe, plummy flavors? You're getting them by delaying."

He listens for a few seconds more. "You're golden," McCloskey says. "Beautiful—you got a statue in the quad. Hey, I gotta fly."

He pushes the red button on his phone. "If you're in Sonoma and your benchmark is Napa or Bordeaux, you have to rearrange Mother Nature," McCloskey explains. "You have to adapt your winemaking to match the beauty of Napa and Bordeaux. Napa cabernet is the only New World wine ruler that's being used internationally—it wins price, volume, and scores. The reason it's the market winner is because the word *Napa* is a brand. Sonoma is an also-ran."

McCloskey turns left on the Silverado Trail, entering the Stag's Leap growing district, one of Napa Valley's most prestigious appellations. "They picked too early," McCloskey says, gazing at acres of grapeless vines receding from both sides of the road. "We have a weekly online bulletin that tells people when to pick. On September thirteenth we said not to, and people who picked anyway drained down at 87.1. We said, 'We told you so.'"

This advice was based on grape samples that customers had sent to McCloskey's company, Enologix. Upon receiving the fruit, the lab staff treated the juice with solvents and, using a high-performance liquid chromatograph, measured a selection of its secondary chemical compounds. The resulting figures were entered into a computer that, using software that McCloskey developed, compared the projected wines' chemistry with that of an "ideal" digital cabernet. The outcome was a "quality index" that translated into a critical score of 87.1 (on a 100-point scale) if all the grapes were picked that week.

"My system divides wines into two tiers," McCloskey says. "Either you're across the 90-point line or you're not. Last year the average picking date was September twenty-fifth, but we predicted that the 90-point break wouldn't be crossed until October twenty-first. Jim Laube [California critic for the *Wine Spectator*] just reviewed that vintage; he called it spotty, like '98. But my customers had flavors that turned from herbal to plummy. They made fabulous wine."

McCloskey turns right onto California Highway 128, heading east into the oak- and pine-covered hills. "The conventional wisdom makes 85-point wine," he says. "My thinking is in tune with Laube, Robert

Parker [of the *Wine Advocate*], and [the noted winemaking consultant] Helen Turley. It's gratifying to see that we're all on the same page."

Some might suggest that this book has too-few pages. Such curmudgeons would observe that—owing especially to the influence of Parker, who has been called the planet's most powerful critic of any kind, in any field—wines all over the world have been getting more and more homogenous, merging into a plummy, velvety "International Style," free of the astringent tannins that can make wine taste tough or bitter, but devoid of a sense of *terroir* or regional distinctiveness, the most celebrated goal of winemaking. Other than his penchant for superripe grapes (hence, high-alcohol wine), Parker's most lamented influence is his popularization of the 100-point rating system now employed by most magazines and other wine-evaluation organs—most prominently the *Wine Spectator*, Parker's comaven in market molding. The so-called Score has been called America's main contribution to the wine business: a democratic, no-nonsense way of slicing through the elitist jargon that obscures quality from the consumer. It's also maligned as an insidious influence that makes mindless puppets of wine buyers, enables anointed wineries to command prices that only the rich can afford, and turns vintners into sycophants seeking the favor of kings Parker and Laube. At the upper end of the market, a thumbs-up or thumbs-down from the *Spectator* or *Advocate* can make a big difference in the price of a bottle; at the boutique-start-up level, it can spell survival or oblivion.

None of which fazes Leo McCloskey. "When the consumer score got inside the wineries, that upset the industry," he acknowledges. "But when the dominant market metric is deep inside your value chain, that's when you know you're in business. The wine world is so big today that without ratings it would be chaos. When wine cost five dollars a bottle we could all be sports and bohemians. But at fifty dollars it's too much of a risk."

The road rises and bends to the right, traversing the southern edge of Lake Hennessey, water supply for the city of Napa.

"In the seventies there were no rulers," McCloskey recalls. "California was a Belle Frontière—the covered wagons came over the hill, and a guy jumped out and started a winery. People could be into high concepts like 'character' or 'terroir,' which are like saying you're against abortion if you're a Republican—it's just name-dropping that means you're morally right. Sophisticated French terms are supposed to trump everything else in the wine business, but today the ruler for luxury goods is the consumer—and the consumer doesn't need to know about terroir. All he wants to know is whether a wine is worth twenty-eight dollars, or whatever he's paying for it."

Across from a boat ramp on the eastern shore of the lake, Mc-Closkey turns onto a pristinely paved driveway that leads uphill into a moss-draped forest. "Throw away the old rulers from the seventies," he advises. "They were hearsay. Today the fine-wine business has graduated to the world stage, where success is driven by metrics. If the consumer says 100 points is absolute, that's it, baby—it's a dog-eat-dog world, and the fastest way to achieve success is to accept some rulers and measure your success against them."

Enologix exists to facilitate this goal. Solely through chemical analysis, McCloskey maintains, he can enable wineries to create a commercially successful product. But he goes further than that, asserting that this isn't merely a matter of taste or trendiness. McCloskey insists that high-scoring wines can be scientifically proved to be the best wines on the market.

"Leo is saying that the consumer value chain is legitimate," Mc-Closkey says of himself, passing the turnoff for Bryant Family Vineyard, producer of a 100-point, $500 cabernet. "Winemakers need to say, 'Hey, bring it on. Let me feel the pressure of the consumer.' That's what Ralph Nader, and Robert Parker, and the *Wine Spectator* are about. That's the front of the curve."

TRANSCENDING THE FOG that engulfs the coast, Randall Grahm pilots his red 1972 DS21 Citroën up Empire Grade, the fifteen-mile-long road that leads along the spine of the Santa Cruz Mountains from the University of California campus. Just past the Waldorf school where his daughter is a student—the school, like the biodynamic system of farming that Grahm adopted a few years ago, is based on the teachings of the early-twentieth-century "spiritual philosopher" Rudolf Steiner—Grahm turns off the pavement, winding through a dark redwood forest on a gravel track, eventually emerging into a clearing with a sloping one-acre vineyard on its northern edge. Dandelions grow between the vine rows, and each of the rusted steel posts that support the horizontal trellis wires is capped by an inverted red plastic cup to prevent ripping the netting that protects the fruit from birds. The white netting looks like cobwebs, promoting a kind of Halloween atmosphere, or—in light of its alternative resemblance to fake snow—a Christmas tree farm. The canes that emerge from the woody arms of each vine are trained to grow straight upward, maximizing the leaves' exposure to sunlight; called VSP for "vertical shoot positioning" (now the predominant system of grape growing worldwide), the visual effect is that of a series of wall-like green curtains with the fruit—in this case, dark blue bunches of pinot noir grapes—hanging along the bottom, about a foot off the ground.

"This vineyard has too many structural flaws to make great wine," Grahm announces as he gets out of the car. "The vines are way too far apart; the clones are oldfangled, not particularly sexy; and it has some disease. I pruned it twenty-five years ago, when it was mostly chardonnay. This is only my second year using it for pinot noir; on the first vintage, the pH got away from me a little bit—it's a nice wine, but it didn't have deep color."

After pausing to look at his iPhone—at this writing, Grahm has more than 370,000 followers on Twitter—he approaches the vines at his characteristic gait: vaguely tense and preoccupied, arms slightly bent, hands forming loose fists just behind his torso. His attire—dirty, well-worn jeans with a pair of red-handled pruning shears protruding from the back pocket, below a T-shirt advertising TURTLE'S LIQUORS OF GLENWOOD SPRINGS, COLORADO—might seem to indicate a more relaxed personality. One of Grahm's longtime trademarks, a bushy ponytail, covers the back of his neck, though his hair is now getting gray and disappearing from the top of his head.

"We had crummy weather in the spring," Grahm reports as he enters the vineyard. "It was wet and cold—there were a lot of shot berries,* and the grapes didn't pollinate very well. I'll be surprised if there's a half ton per acre." The fruit is composed of loose, skimpy bunches with individual grapes varying widely in size. Grapevines typically yield at least three tons of fruit an acre, depending on the age of the plants and the way in which they're managed; half a ton makes only one barrel of wine, or twenty-five cases. "I'm not going to sell it," Grahm demurs. "I'll taste it, drink it, show it off, and give it away. I'm just doing this to keep my hand in—to meditate on it, so as to someday do it on a manageable scale. It's my psychotherapy—I like being in the vineyard, and this one is very close to home."

In other words, Grahm does not own this vineyard. Although his winery is identified with the Santa Cruz Mountains (it was originally located in the hamlet of Bonny Doon, about three miles from where he now stands), he hasn't grown any of his own grapes in the area since the early 1990s, when his estate vineyard died of Pierce's disease. The only grapevines that Grahm now owns are a hundred miles to the south, near the town of Soledad in the Salinas Valley, a

---

* Undeveloped grapes, owing to inadequate fertilization during the blooming period.

region traditionally associated more with lettuce than with wine. The vineyard he is now addressing belongs to a University of California Santa Cruz biology professor, but since contracting to buy the fruit, Grahm has been taking care of it himself: pruning, suckering, shoot thinning—tasks typically performed by Hispanic workers. Now, with a new vintage imminent, he's here to check on the ripeness of the grapes.

Dropping onto his hands and knees, Grahm pulls back the netting to reach the low-hanging fruit. He sets about scissoring grapes from the vines, tossing bunches into a plastic bucket that will be transported back to his winery, where a lab assistant will analyze the "primary" chemistry—pH, total acidity, and degrees Brix, an approximation of grape sugar. The longer unpicked grapes remain on the vines, the more intense and fruity their flavor, although their acidity—which helps to impart a sensation of "structure" and promotes aging—does the opposite, causing wine to taste flat and "flabby."

"I just made one of the grievous errors of sampling," Grahm announces. "I picked grapes from an outer row. Those vines have deeper roots and get more water, so they'll have more leaf canopy, and they won't get the stress signal to start ripening as soon as these other guys. The inner rows will be sweeter." The vineyard is conspicuously lacking in irrigation hoses. Adhering to the Old World model, in which artificial watering of vines is illegal, Grahm is an advocate of dry farming, which provides plants only the H_2O that they receive from rain and groundwater—a necessary (if not sufficient) criterion, he believes, for a vineyard that truly represents its place on Earth. "It is a non sequitur to talk about the terroir of an irrigated vineyard, rather like trying to accurately describe the natural history of an animal by observing its behavior in a zoo," he once wrote in an essay titled "In Search of a Great Growth in the New World." Among the qualities that Grahm extols in wine is the sense of minerality, which he thinks is obtainable only from vines forced to root deep for natural water sources.

"Irrigation is the biggest systemic error that we do in California," he says. "To have a distinctive site, you have to grow vines in a certain way to give them cues to respond the right way. If you want a *vin de terroir,* you need to be able to dry farm—but for that you need the right kind of soil. You need more water-holding capacity, for one thing, and it needs to be held so it's available all season long. In California, vines grow overabundantly in spring when they have a lot of water, but if the soil gives up water too quickly, they run out of steam. One of the things that's brilliant about Bordeaux is its receding water table: It lowers as the season progresses, so plants are always getting a measured amount of water." By contrast, California's "Mediterranean" climate—which typically receives no precipitation at all between April and October—tends to deprive grapes of moisture late in the growing season, causing their sugar concentration (aka "physiological maturity") to outpace their flavor development (phenolic—or, considered another way, psychological—maturity). Since sugar is converted to alcohol during fermentation, this is sometimes said to be the main reason for the recent trend toward high-alcohol wines.

"I'd say 22.3 or 22.4," Grahm guesses, randomly popping berries into his mouth and perceiving a level of ripeness substantially below the current fashion. "I like the acidity, and the color's nice; there's not a lot of flavor, I have to say, but the paradox is that if you wait for flavor, you could wait forever. You have to sort of extrapolate. Presumably, if the flavor is beginning to develop, it will continue to develop by Monday, when I'd like to pick. But frankly I'm talking out of my ass, because I'm not a pinot noir maven."

There is some wistfulness to this admission, though it doesn't exactly qualify as news. In the wine industry at large, Grahm is still widely known as the Rhone Ranger, a title he secured in the 1980s by popularizing the grapes of France's Rhône River valley—syrah, grenache, mourvedre, roussanne, marsanne, viognier, et al.—in California, whose climate he found better suited to those varieties than to pinot noir or cabernet sauvignon, the totemic grapes of Burgundy and Bordeaux (which have cold winters with rainfall dispersed throughout the year). Under this mantle, Grahm styled himself the "junk dealer" of American vintners, buying grape varieties that nobody (then) wanted and turning out wonderful wines along the lines of Gigondas and Châteauneuf-du-Pape. Combining his talents for winemaking and marketing—the latter expressed in clever names, fanciful labels, witty newsletters, and outlandish PR stunts, all orchestrated by a mischievous mind with a hyperliterate sense of humor—he built one of the world's most recognizable wine brands, known for such products as Le Cigare Volant (Flying Cigar, inspired by the real-life village of Châteauneuf-du-Pape, which once passed an ordinance barring UFOs from landing), Old Telegram (after the stone-filled vineyards of Domaine du Vieux Télégraphe, itself named for an eighteenth-century communications tower connecting Paris and Marseille), and Vin Gris de Cigare (a pink rosé similar to those produced in Tavel and Provence). Along the way, Grahm pioneered the cartoonlike graphics that now pervade the industry to a fault and was an early champion of screw caps, declaring such hitherto déclassé closures superior to traditional corks. In sum, he was the leading iconoclast of California wine, making fun of everything from Robert "Moldavi" (in his modern folktale "Don Quijones") to T. S. Eliot ("The Love Song of J. Alfred Rootstock") to *Ten Ways to Know You've Met a Real Wine Geek* ("He has brought his own food to the restaurant"), most of which waggery was unveiled in his semiannual Bonny Doon newsletter.

All of this occurred, however, after Grahm failed in his first ambition: to make great pinot noir. "The great pinots are the greatest wines," he still contends. "They're captivating—they have depth, seductiveness, fragrance, complexity. . . . There's nothing like them—they're unrivaled. But pinot noir needs a cool climate, absurdly low yields, high humidity, and special soils, none of which we generally have here. Our conditions are much friendlier for Rhône grapes, which is why I did it—because I wanted to succeed and not beat my head against the wall forever. But at a certain point you realize that sooner or later you're going to die and there are certain things you still want to do. Remember when you were young and seized by a pretty face? Pinot is like the girl you never kissed but wanted to. Is she intrinsically more captivating than grenache or syrah? Probably not; it's just a construct, based on nothing—a madness. I think my desire to produce pinot noir probably has to do with an elevated testosterone titer. There is absolutely no reason to produce a second-rate pinot noir, or even a first-rate Burgundian wannabe. Why not just buy some land in Burgundy? The whole idea now is to do something original."

Which explains not only why Grahm is fooling around with this little pinot noir vineyard (as he put it, rehearsing how "to do it on a manageable scale") but also why he is back in the Santa Cruz Mountains. In 2006, with Bonny Doon positioned as the twenty-seventh biggest winery in the United States—producing some 450,000 cases a year, most of it under the low-priced Big House label, named for a maximum-security prison in Soledad—Grahm again took the wine world by surprise, selling off his two most successful brands (Big House and Cardinal Zin), downsizing production by 90 percent, and declaring his intention to refocus on "original" wines expressive of terroir.

"There are chess masters who can play fifteen or twenty games simultaneously and succeed at all of them," Grahm says. "I'm not one of those people. I was overly ambitious—I tried to do too many things, and I had a basic philosophical and spiritual problem: I was no longer making wines I believed in or had any real feeling for. When you commit to a high-volume brand, you have to keep feeding it or it dies—your cost of production goes down, but so does your profitability, because you're pushing through tighter and tighter channels. I didn't have any money left over for more interesting and important projects, like planting vineyards. I was on a rocket ship and couldn't get off."

Grahm acknowledges that his sense of urgency—even desperation—was connected to turning fifty, becoming a father, and surviving a life-threatening infection. Coincident with this midlife crisis was his embrace of biodynamic farming—the eccentric, organic agricultural system marked by such notably nonmainstream practices as homeopathic soil treatments timed in accordance with celestial movements. *Biodynamie* (loosely translated as "life force") defines a farm as an organism that should be able to flourish—to grow, replenish, sustain, and cleanse itself—without artificial inputs; the better to express its individuality, it should have its own pastures for livestock, habitat for "good" insects to control injurious pests, and means of capturing its own waste stream and recycling it into nutrients. After being exposed to such thinking, Grahm came to consider it the best means of enabling a vineyard to express terroir—a concept that, in the 1990s, he had defined as "the *soul* of the vineyard, the soul of the wine, remaining pure and immutable," even as his Bonny Doon products increasingly represented blends of various vineyards from different places. Although Grahm had since converted his Soledad property to biodynamic practices, he still felt that, unlike the great sites of Europe, it didn't possess the requisite "intelligence" for the kind of wine he aspired to make; hence he announced that some of the proceeds of the sell-off would go toward purchasing property for new vineyards—one devoted to Rhône grapes (the wife who had been so good to him, and whom he admittedly still loved), but another for the long-desired mistress, pinot noir.

"I don't know if I'll succeed or fail, but I'm going back to my original idealism—the feeling that anything was possible," Grahm says. "I'm ready. I'm excited. And I'm scared witless."

I FIRST MET RANDALL GRAHM and Leo McCloskey in the late 1980s. Grahm, still on an ascending arc in the most admired phase of his career (recently anointed a "genius" and "national treasure" by Robert M. Parker Jr.), was a fellow guest at a dinner party given by some of my neighbors in Berkeley. Our host, a wine merchant, served a lamb roast studded with little light-colored things I later learned were truffles; I contributed a zinfandel nouveau that I'd made in my garage across the street. When Grahm innocuously called my wine "nice," I pressed him for what he *really* thought, prompting a throat-clearing observation that it was "a little high in VA." (Volatile acidity, which is activated by excess oxygen and can turn wine into vinegar, is a common problem for inattentive home vintners, although lab tests later showed mine to be *low* in VA.) After we went on to sample various other wines with dinner, Grahm asked, "Would this be more amusing?" and pulled a bottle of Château Figeac, a highly regarded Bordeaux, out of a case he had stashed below the table. Not long afterward he fell asleep on the couch, leaving the remaining social duties to Bonny Doon's general manager Patrice Boyle, who was then occupying a dual role as Grahm's girlfriend.

Over the next several years, I encountered Grahm intermittently at wine events. Despite (or because of) his notoriety, he usually struck me as restless and distracted, exuding the impression that he was there only temporarily, en route to somewhere else—a circumstance that's always true of everyone, but which in his case somehow seemed especially palpable. One night at the Bay Wolf in Oakland, during a festive Rhône-themed dinner that featured four winemakers rotating among the rooms of the restaurant talking to paying guests (exactly the kind of "Meet the Winemaker Dinner" that Grahm liked to lampoon in his newsletter), he used his time at my table to talk about the Chinese meditation practice chi gong; another time, addressing the annual Hospice du Rhône conference in Paso Robles on the subject of matching grapes to their environments, he told the audience, "You have to figure out who you are, and then *be* who you are." When I told him later that I'd enjoyed the talk, he commented with a faraway look, "Now if only I could put it into practice." Viewed with the hindsight that his sprawling business was then slipping slowly out of his control, today Grahm's distraction seems understandable; on the other hand, this tendency toward ADD may have been at the root of some of his business problems.

When I first met McCloskey, he was working at Ridge Vineyards in the Santa Cruz Mountains, where I was doing research for my book *Angels' Visits* (later retitled *Zin*). Coming in and out of a room alongside the winery lab, I noted, was "a sandy-haired man in his late thirties, wearing blue jeans and hiking boots," alternately printing out data on a computer and injecting wine samples into a high-performance liquid chromatograph—a device that, he eagerly explained, "cracked" wines into their flavor and pigment components so as to obtain "chemical snapshots" of them.

"Wine is basically a synthesis of chemical flavors from the skin, pulp, and seeds of the grape," McCloskey told me. "It's a group of molecules—you can measure it, and you can tell during harvest whether the grapes that year are going to have high levels of it." While traditional wine science concerns itself mainly with "primary" chemicals—things like sugar, alcohol, and acidity, which play a metabolic role in plants and determine basic standards of acceptability in wine— McCloskey was instead looking at secondary "flavonoids" such as tannins, terpenes, phenols, and anthocyanins, which affect texture, aroma, taste, and color—the foundations of what we call quality. "We need more chemical information about what makes wines 'good' and 'bad,'" McCloskey said. "If you measure the primary chemistry in wines from good and bad years—or, say, in Ridge cabernet versus some jug cabernet from the Central Valley—they're very similar. So the puzzle remains: What is 'good' about one and 'bad' about the other?"

McCloskey clearly believed himself to be on the verge of something big. "We're trying to measure, for the first time in California, the secondary chemicals that are in red wine," he proclaimed. "We believe we've found the class of compounds that distinguish wines in good years and bad years." He added that his ultimate goal was linking the chemical compounds to wine's economic value—and, over the next decade, he proceeded to do exactly that. A few years after I met him, McCloskey founded Enologix, a business offering "metrics that assist winemakers in improving wine quality and boosting average national critics' scores"—an approach that, in due course, would garner McCloskey considerable attention and criticism. After all, if *de gustibus non est disputandum* is the credo of even the connoisseur, how can something as individual as wine taste (or any taste, for that matter) be quantified? By declaring that there *is* accounting for it, McCloskey inspired one magazine to characterize him as "radioactive," another to define his aim as "reducing love to an algorithm." In the wine world he was commonly characterized as a mad scientist, in the same way that Randall Grahm was tagged a mad hatter or court jester.

"Leo is the id of the wine business," Grahm himself told me not long ago. "He's not some strange alien force; he's us. On its face, [Enologix] seems like a rational idea: Everybody needs to increase sales to survive; we want to figure out how to get high-scoring wines, so in that sense Leo is providing a service. But while it may be good for individuals, it's not good for the wine business in general, because it discourages creativity, individuality, personality, and a soulful connection between the winemaker and the wine. When his wine becomes an expression of the will of the people rather than of himself, the winemaker becomes hyper-self-conscious and loses his moral and aesthetic compass—and when that happens, everything is lost."

This wasn't a bad way of expressing how, by the early 2000s, Grahm had come to feel in general about the wine business—an industry that, in the decade after I'd met him, underwent a sea change in its basic assumptions, practices, and philosophies. Helped along by *60 Minutes'* 1991 exploration of the "French paradox" touting its salubrious health benefits, wine had come to rival beer as adult Americans' beverage of choice, and as the stock market experienced a twenty-year climb, the number of U.S. wineries exploded, as did the volume of low-priced, highly drinkable imports from places like Argentina, Chile, South Africa, New Zealand, and Australia. Today, foreign-made wines account for more than a quarter of U.S. wine sales (twice the share occupied by imports in 1990), and in the past twenty years, the number of bonded California wineries has more than tripled, from 800 to 2,800. With increasing corporate consolidation, however, 80 percent of this production is now controlled by a number of companies—Constellation, Beringer Blass, Brown-Forman, Kendall-Jackson, Allied Domecq, Diageo, the Wine Group, E. & J. Gallo, et al.—that can be counted on two hands.

In this ever-more bottom-line-oriented atmosphere, wineries are desperate for any tool offering an edge on the competition. The primary leg up is a 90+ score, especially when conferred by Parker or the *Spectator*. And since this target is too crucial to be left to chance, an arsenal of aids—reverse osmosis, micro-oxygenation, spinning cone, artificial oak chips, cultured yeasts, commercial enzymes, superconcentrated colorants—is now available to enable winemakers to spin silk from dross, searching for a sweet spot in the public palate. Yet romance remains the industry's stock-in-trade, with the result that vintners have come to resemble delusional sidewalk barkers, committed to convincing consumers and themselves that they're doing one thing (gently shepherding nature's urges in products that express a sense of place with respect for the vineyard and the earth) while decidedly doing another (employing state-of-the-art technology to create the vinous equivalent of supermodels, enhancing attributes and airbrushing flaws to fulfill the commercial ideal of something that will sell).

Confronted with this state of affairs, one can say without hyperbole that it represents a fall from grace. California wine is generally thought to have "come of age" when a Napa Valley chardonnay and cabernet bested a selection of Burgundies and Bordeaux at the Judgment of Paris tasting in 1976, but if maturity means losing one's innocence— that is, transcending naive idealism to confront the requirements for survival in a brutal world—then the period when California wine *truly* came of age is the time that has passed since that pivotal event. This Darwinian scenario has played out as a classic struggle: tradition versus innovation; patience versus immediate gratification; the laws of Nature versus the hand of Man.

Does that sound familiar? Indeed, the challenges facing the wine world are the same ones that characterize society at large. The question "Is this real?" now pervades our experience, with the manipulation of our senses and resources affecting everything we do and see. Whether we're talking about athletic steroids, cosmetic surgery, genetic engineering, digital photography, or special cinematic effects, technology aspires to transcend nature in pursuit of some perceived ideal.

When I first met Randall Grahm and Leo McCloskey, I had no way of knowing that the wine world was on the verge of such an upheaval. The metamorphosis would be effected by many clever individuals, most of them Baby Boomers who had seized on wine in the 1970s as an intoxicating avenue to truth, beauty, and goodness (a trio of words that, coincidentally, constituted the title of a 1923 lecture by Rudolf Steiner). They would include such emerging wine-household names as Benziger, Casella, Ducournau, Fetzer, Franzia, Jackson, Joly, Laube, Lynch, Parker, Steele, Turley, and the somewhat less recognizable Smith, each of whom had a different notion of what characterizes an ideal wine.

More than anyone else, Grahm and McCloskey would come to represent two warring worldviews in the emerging dialectic. Embellishing his characterization of McCloskey as the id ("Antichrist" was a favorite alternative), Grahm once suggested to me that he and Leo could both be classified as *luftmenschen*—a term that, literally translated from the German, means "air men," but more accurately indicates men of ideas, or perhaps closer to the point, men with their heads in the clouds. Still, despite their mutual braininess, their respective routes reflected disparate maps of the wine cosmos. McCloskey would chart a relatively straight course from the Ridge lab to Enologix, promising to deliver "wine quality in objective rather than subjective terms"—an approach firmly grounded in the realities of numbers and dollars. By contrast, Grahm, following a twisting, tortured path to commercial purgatory, increasingly extolled terroir as "a link to something we apprehend as being vast and unbounded [and] of a highly complex and organized world that abuts our own. . . . An intimation of the vibrational persistence of phenomena, even if they are not manifestly, palpably present," which "indicates the very real possibility of alchemy, the transformation of the base, humble, and mute into the noble, sublime, and articulate." While theoretically rooted in a tangible relationship with the earth, it frankly sounded so ideal that he'd be hard-pressed to prove its existence in the real world.

In other words, McCloskey's and Grahm's definitions of an ideal wine had almost nothing in common. Still, both *luftmenschen* could have been created by the same author—namely, Johann Wolfgang von Goethe. One protagonist, promising clients a deal whereby they could gain hidden knowledge and earthly success, was a modern Mephistopheles; the other, consumed by a sweeping and sometimes self-defeating desire for cosmic insight, was a present-day Faust. In that light, it seemed to me, examining their parallel paths—along with some of their significant contemporaries and signs of their times—would illuminate not only the changes in the wine industry and the world it reflects but also something about the modern soul.

WHEN I FIRST reencountered Leo McCloskey after a fifteen year hiatus, it was in a mini–business park in the city of Sonoma. For the sake of proximity to potential customers, McCloskey moved from Santa Cruz to the wine country proper in 1994, and in the years that had passed since we'd met, his appearance had, not unpredictably, changed. Now in his fifties, his spiky hair had turned gray, and his jeans and boots had been jettisoned for the casual wine-country elegance earlier described. But despite the physical and material shifts, Leo still had the same piercing blue eyes and animated-activist style of communication: part well-spoken academic intellectual and part loosey-goosey California surfer, both of which he certifiably is, courtesy of UC Santa Cruz, where he got his PhD.

What was new was a near-evangelical, Silicon Valley–style business rap. Almost before I sat down, McCloskey had launched a diatribe about quality-management systems and customer-relationship software, conservative laggards and early adopters, books like *The Structure of Scientific Revolutions* by Thomas Kuhn and *The Innovator's Dilemma* by Clayton Christensen. "When you come along with new ideas, you're like Karl Marx," he told me. "You're considered disruptive, but you don't want to perceive the resistance as negative, because it tells you you're there." Comparing the creator of communism to the goal of enabling companies to boost profits and beat out competitors was, it seemed, about on par with equating Ralph Nader and Robert

Parker. But as I got to know Leo better, I learned that his mind is large—especially if, as Emerson maintained, consistency is the hobgoblin of small ones.

I soon found out that the Enologix database contains records of 70,000 wines—the largest file of its kind in the world, including information about soil, climate, prices, equipment, and viticulture and vinification practices, along with archived sensory analysis and critical scores, all of which can be cross-referenced by computer so that (in McCloskey's words) "I can tell you which cabernet clone Jim Laube likes best when it's grown on the Napa Valley floor." The company also predicts aging potential and evaluates wines in barrel, creating digital models of simulated blends complete with virtual quality metrics, going so far as to recommend price points via its storehouse of economic data.

To analyze an individual wine, Enologix employees run a sample of it through a high-performance liquid chromatograph (HPLC) and a mass spectrometer that, aided by round-the-clock robots, separate and measure chemical compounds. From among the thousands that exist in wine, McCloskey says he's identified about a hundred capable of effecting a human response; an Enologix chemical report groups these into half a dozen categories, which for red wines include phenols (associated with flavor), tannins (texture), and anthocyanins (color), and for white wines esters, terpenes, and essential oils (aroma). The ratios, not just the amounts, of these compounds are then compared via computer with those of bottled wines previously judged and scored by groups of professionals—more than two hundred vintners, growers, owners, and writers who, presented with an even-numbered group of wines, are asked to give half the entries a plus and the other half a minus. A wine's resulting "quality index" is an average number between -1.0 and +1.0, with +0.5 representing a 90-point rating on the "GV500" scale (as published in McCloskey's magazine, *Global Vintage Quarterly*). A separate "National Critics' Score" represents an average rating compiled from five publications: the *Wine Spectator, Wine Advocate, Wine Enthusiast,* Stephen Tanzer's *International Wine Cellar,* and the *Connoisseurs' Guide to California Wine.* Enologix classifies all wines under one of four "style" headings: For reds, Style One is pale in color and low in tannin, like pinot noir; Style Two is also pale but higher in tannin, similar to sangiovese or nebbiolo; Style Three is dark and tannic, like a lot of cabernet sauvignon and syrah; Style Four is similarly dark but only moderately tannic, like—McCloskey says—"the vast majority of successful, flagship mainstream wines, the most elegant and popular wines in the world."

McCloskey is fond of saying that the science is simply "functionary"—that equal value resides in his company's "domain knowledge" or wine-making experience. The Enologix staff includes wine-making and grape-growing consultants who advise customers about how to affect results—for example, picking grapes late or "draining down sweet" (separating fermenting juice from grape skins before all the sugar has been converted to alcohol, so as to make wine taste less tannic). McCloskey says that, on average, his customers realize a five-point rise in their scores for red wines, six for whites. His emphasis is on the former, specifically the luxury cabernet market, where wineries can afford Enologix's average yearly service fee of $20,000. The company's annual revenues (which vary between one and two million dollars) have, over the past fifteen years, flowed from such prestigious names as Beaulieu, Benziger, Chappellet, Diamond Creek, Far Niente, Groth, Merry Edwards, Niebaum-Coppola, Peter Michael, Joseph Phelps, Ridge, Robert Mondavi, Sterling, and Sebastiani.

Founded in 1967, Chappellet was the second post-Prohibition winery built in Napa Valley, after Robert Mondavi's. During the 1970s and 1980s, its owners, Donn and Molly Chappellet, employed a parade of energetic young vintners—Tony Soter, Cathy Corison, Helen Turley, David Graves—who would go on to play prominent roles in the rise of Napa. The winery was acclaimed early on for its mountain-grown cabernet sauvignon and dry chenin blanc (then the predominant white grape in the valley, along with French colombard), but as wineries proliferated and critical and consumer tastes shifted toward softer textures and sappier fruit, Chappellet fell so far behind the curve that it acquired the aura of a has-been. In an effort to turn things around in the 1990s, the owners hired a young winemaker named Phil Titus; he began working with Enologix in 1997, and in 2004 Chappellet's flagship cabernet was chosen Wine of the Year by the *Connoisseurs' Guide to California Wine.*

The winery is hidden in a grove of oaks, backed by open slopes of grapevines climbing Pritchard Hill. After McCloskey parks his car, we walk past stacks of empty grape bins, descending an aluminum stairway alongside the winery's concrete crush pad. Going through a wooden door, we enter the winery's cavernous interior, filled with racks of oak barrels and rows of stainless steel fermenters. McCloskey is greeted there by Titus, a lean, tall, dark-haired guy dressed in California-winemaker Basic: blue jeans, polo shirt, black fleece vest.

Titus immediately tells McCloskey how high the sugars have been this year: 28, 29, 31 degrees Brix. If must (aka crushed grape juice) that ripe is left to ferment without intervention, the resulting alcohol will kill the yeast before all the sugar is converted, resulting in a sweet-tasting wine; the traditional method of dealing with this— legalized only recently in California after decades of unofficial "tank washing"—is to dilute the must with water, lowering the percentage of sugar. Hence, in light of this vintage's skyrocketing Brix readings, Chappellet's vineyard manager, Dave Pirio, says, "I'm surprised Lake Hennessey is still full."

"The consumer value chain isn't responding to alcohol," McCloskey says. "It's responding to color, flavor, and fragrance. In growing-degree days, this vintage is a lot like '96, which was a great year."

"People weren't waiting for sugars in '96," says Pirio.

"Phelps was," McCloskey says, referring to one of his longtime clients. "Companies that did wait were winning."

"People in Sonoma pick a lot earlier than people in Napa," Titus observes.

"And they make lower-quality wine," McCloskey says. "They haven't figured that out yet. Napa still has it over Sonoma simply because of decision making. According to the *Spectator,* the average score for Sonoma County merlot is 81 to 82."

Merlot is what McCloskey is here to analyze. Titus escorts him to one of the tanks, from which he draws a foaming crimson sample that he squirts into Leo's glass.

"When wine is young, it's difficult to taste," McCloskey remarks.

"It's sort of a gruel—no winemaker can taste it and predict the consumer score." Nevertheless, upon sipping the merlot, Leo says, "This is a low Four."

"820 tannin," Titus reports, reciting figures from the Enologix WineFAX. "128 complex anthocyanin." These are McCloskey's two most crucial quality indexes, representing what he calls "the meat and fat" tastes of the wine. "120 is the Mendoza line," he notes—a reference to Mario Mendoza, the onetime major league infielder whose name has become synonymous with a dreaded .200 batting average. In other words, a 120 parts-per-million concentration of complex anthocyanin represents "the tipping point [below which] the consumer won't pay a high price" for a Bordeaux variety such as merlot.

"This isn't a big wine, but it's in balance," McCloskey says. "It's beautiful, briary—great blending material for your flagship cabernet."

The two move on to another tank that Titus refers to as "rocket fuel." McCloskey studies the WineFAX: 1200 tannin, 185 complex. "You're making merlot as big as the best cabernet sauvignon," he says approvingly.

"I could make a less tannic, more mainstream wine for the vintage, but I'd be leaving money on the table," says Titus. "This will be blended with other things that aren't as well endowed, so I want everything from it that I can get."

After tasting and spitting a few more wines into a drainage grate in the floor, the two take a break. "This is a language we can speak together," Titus says as they walk toward the winery's kitchen. "In my tasting group, they can't. Most winemakers tend to talk about things like 'soft' tannins, 'hard' tannins, bitterness, and acidity; you don't talk about complex anthocyanins unless you're an Enologix client. It's sort of like how you can't tell somebody about rock and roll." I'm not sure I get the analogy, but it's an interesting reflection of the cultish appeal of Enologix.

We arrive at a counter piled with cold cuts, corn chips, condiments, and bread. Evaluating the different options, McCloskey warms two flour tortillas in a toaster and folds them around a blend of brie, roast beef, and hot dog relish. The result is rich and succulent—undeniably and irresistibly tasty.

Soon we're joined by Sam Spencer and Wendy Roloson, partners in a start-up winery making five thousand cases of wine at Chappellet. The sharp-featured, fortyish Roloson has a T-shirt under her cardigan and her hair pulled back in a bun; Spencer is as tall as Titus but with a more substantial girth, which is covered by a blue-and-white shirt and brand-new boot-cut Levi's.

Spencer is brimming with anxiety and ambition. Having grown up in New York City, he came to California after college to visit a couple of family friends: Pam and Jay Heminway, who started the nearby Green & Red winery in 1972. After a sojourn in New Zealand, a partnership in a San Francisco wine bar, and an aborted winery start-up with a Sonoma chef, he and Roloson—a University of Chicago MBA who previously worked for Quaker Oats and Continental Bank—each invested a quarter of a million inherited dollars in the Spencer Roloson brand, purchasing grapes while planting syrah vines in Conn Valley, an eastern offshoot of Napa. They also raise zinfandel, petite sirah, and tempranillo—the Spanish grape that goes into Rioja—in Lake County to the north, where Spencer says, "Someone of my age and means can get their feet on the ground, as opposed to chasing your tail in Napa Valley." He says he signed up with Enologix two years ago because he "got scared. Parker gave us mixed reviews on our wines, and said some of them were below rating. Now our scores have gone up."

"Parker and Laube are very sensitive tasters," McCloskey observes. "When quality goes up, they notice."

"I'm not saying I want to make wine to please Parker," Spencer is quick to add. "But if we succeed with our natural style, it *will* please Parker. I want to manage my score the way I manage the rest of my business."

After lunch, McCloskey addresses the Spencer Roloson wines, some of which are just beginning to ferment. As yeast converts sugar into alcohol and grape juice into wine, the liquid obtains color and other qualities (tannin, texture, et al.) from the skins; according to McCloskey, "conventional wisdom" dictates pressing the wine off the skins after fermentation is finished—that is, after all the sugar has turned into alcohol. Spencer did this with the first grapes he picked this year, "but when we looked at the results," says McCloskey, "quality was low because tannin was high."

"I wasn't able to drain down into a Style Four," Spencer confirms.

"Your grapes are growing at Style Three," McCloskey explains. "That's the pitch your terroir is throwing you. But Parker, Laube, and the consumer are at Style Four, so you need to ask yourself: How can I get my wine stylistically in the right ballpark? How can you be thrown a curveball, Style Three, or a slow ball, Style One, or a straight ball, Style Four, and still hit a home run?"

His answer is that Spencer must err in the opposite direction with his remaining grapes. "You need to be so low in tannin—800, maybe 700—that you're going to feel really uncomfortable. Fire up the fermenters, get them ripping, and drain down at 16—you have to think completely outside the box."

"I think we have a chance of everything else being Fours," Spencer says hopefully.

"You need that," says McCloskey. "I'd be remiss if I didn't remind you. You don't want to end up with rustic wines. Parker and Laube are looking for elegance—a rough log milled down to a fine beam."

In the winery lab, Wendy pours a few barrel samples: La Herradura syrah from Conn Valley and Madder Lake zinfandel and tempranillo from Lake County. For purposes of experimental comparison, the wines have been aged in different types of oak.

"I'm glad to taste the wines," McCloskey says, "but I also want to win. The performance metric has to do with intensity, not attributes like oak or aromatics." With that proviso, he makes his way enthusiastically through the samples, all of which are rich and succulent—undeniably and irresistibly tasty.

"Wow!" Leo says when he comes to the tempranillo. "I really like that. These are really interesting, spicy wines—you need a venue with Parker for him to champion these wines."

"That's the plan," Spencer reveals. "In February our L.A. broker is going to taste these wines with Parker. I also want to get a bunch of Enologix wineries together and present their wines as a group to Laube and Tanzer and other prominent critics. Maybe we can create some collective bargaining."

Later Spencer tells me that at first he didn't think his budget had $15,000 worth of room for Enologix. "It seemed like a luxury," he remembers. "Enologix wasn't exactly forthcoming about how the system works—you have to sign a nondisclosure agreement to see how the metrics add up, and I wasn't convinced. But now I think it's a tool that every carpenter ought to have—an incredibly important technology for the wine industry. I'm able to categorize and organize my wines in a way that's more systematic. Winemaking isn't magic; there are a lot of calculated decisions, and without Enologix, at the very least you're making some of them based on intuition. But if you're wrong, Enologix lets you know before you make a mistake. It's like having a crystal ball—it may confirm your fears or confirm your confidence, but at least you're starting off the fight in a position of strength."

Most Enologix customers insist on not being identified, apparently owing to the implication that they've sold out and are chasing the score. "I don't like the idea that we're controlled by the press, but we are," one such highly esteemed—and highly experienced—Enologix client told me. "Can people be successful without that? Yeah, but endorsement from one of the major publications certainly helps. The problem is that consumers and critics have this romantic view of success—the public perception of expensive wines is that they just sort of happen."

Like the less experienced Spencer, this veteran vintner described himself as "hooked" on Enologix's chemical analysis. "When I first saw the tool, I fell in love with it," he said. "Enologix has helped me make much bigger, richer pinots—I've won over many people who thought they only liked cabernet. The most helpful part is knowing what your starting data is. The composition of the grape sample represents the potential of the wine; it tells you whether you can fully extract it or not, so if you get halfway through fermentation but the chemical numbers aren't halfway there, you know you have to do something. One year I agreed to buy grapes from a grower based on a bulk sample from a previous vintage that came in with high numbers; then the grower overloaded the vines—but because of Enologix, I could show him numbers demonstrating that the quality of the grapes had declined."

When it comes to winemaking, though, he was underwhelmed. "Leo is such an egotist that he makes it hard to publicize the service as much it deserves. In his idea of a perfect world, you would do all your blends on the basis of his numbers alone, without even smelling or tasting the wine. I'm afraid it just doesn't work that way—the aroma component is critical. If you have a problem during harvest, his solutions are often academic—and if you tell him something doesn't work, he won't listen. He'll just say, 'Try this,' as if it's some kind of research project. Hey, grapes cost four thousand dollars a ton. I can't afford casual research projects—it's got to be a pretty sure thing that isn't going to backfire. A few years ago, Leo's data showed that I should target my wine to one publication because of a writer's palate; it worked, but three years later that writer's palate has totally shifted, and Leo's database hasn't.

"I think Leo is especially influential with younger winemakers," he concluded. "I just tell them to take it all with a grain of salt—don't go overboard and think that Leo has all the answers."

"The younger group are natural-born managers," McCloskey tells me as we depart Chappellet. "The first year I worked with Sam and Wendy, he said he'd work with our data and make all the decisions himself. But then they didn't get what they wanted, so he started to think more about it. He's a smart guy. The thing that really impresses me about him is that he changes—he's able to adopt new ideas, which makes him a dangerous competitor."

As we emerge from the forest onto an open slope with a panoramic view of Lake Hennessey and Napa Valley beyond, I disclose that I found the Spencer Roloson wines to taste rather alike: Redolent with ripe, sweet fruit, new oak, and a soft, supple mouthfeel, the zinfandel tasted much like the syrah, which tasted a lot like the tempranillo.

"That's the high complex anthocyanin," Leo tells me proudly. "That's our signature. It's my company's trademark." In other words, when it comes to the task of impressing critics, they're ideal wines.

AFTER LEAVING THE pinot noir vineyard, Randall Grahm continues up Empire Grade into the clouds. The pinot site was sunny and warm, but the higher we go, the wetter it gets, with fog misting heavily onto the Citroën's windshield. "They get a lot of rain up here," Grahm says. "The soil is very weathered and leached because of the high [winter] rainfall. The paradox of California is that soils that are rich in nutrients tend to be too low in rainfall. In Europe you're looking at more variable weather, but it's interesting if it rains or doesn't rain, if it's hot or not so hot. In California there aren't as many wild changes. We have a different set of problems."

Along the way, Grahm points out various properties he has coveted as potential vineyard sites, starting with a Christmas tree farm on the east side of the road. "It would be totally killer, but it has an important ontological distinction: It isn't for sale. I also looked at another property that *was* for sale west of here, but you had to cut down a lot of trees—plus they wanted too much money."

These two problems are not uncommon in Santa Cruz County, which, besides serving as a bedroom community for Silicon Valley, has environmental restrictions that Grahm considers draconian. As he once wrote me in an e-mail:

> The problem in Santa Cruz, as in so many other places, is that because of their historical failure to address environmentally appropriate development, there is now a kind of overreaction leading to capricious and arbitrary enforcement of environmental

restrictions. (Anything concave is a wetland, etc.) Alas, if you plan to do anything in a cool area of coastal California with reasonable levels of rainfall, it is likely that you will run into serious environmental restrictions. . . . What makes Bonny Doon interesting in many ways for dry-farmed grapes—its prodigious rainfall, for one thing—also makes it a biotically sensitive area. If one truly takes care to heed all of the environmental restrictions about staying a hundred feet away from all ephemeral drainages—rills, freshets, swales, etc.—one ends up leaving a substantial percentage of one's acres unplanted, and your [purchase] price per [planted] acre goes through the roof. Not that I am a big monoculture guy—rather the contrary—but the level of intrusiveness of Santa Cruz County is just staggering.

For this and other reasons—e.g., "political, karmic, zoning and access issues, hostile neighbors, or crazy price"—Grahm has already looked at some two dozen sites without finding any that he deemed tenable. The closest he has come—and only to lease, not to buy—is a site at the far end of Empire Grade, at the crest of the mountains below a pair of granite landmarks called Eagle Rock and Camel Rock.

As it happens, I stumbled across this place myself a couple of years ago. In the midst of a magazine assignment, I'd driven up at dusk to take a picture of the full moon rising over the mountains to the east, and after spending some time at a defunct fire lookout atop Eagle Rock (which has a 360-degree view extending to the ocean), I noticed that the valley below, substantially cleared at some point in the past, consisted largely of rolling hills, presumably graced by efficient drainage, ample rainfall, and breezes from the nearby coast. More than anything, the spot exuded a remote tranquility—a "pacific" calm, you might say.

Apparently others had noticed the same things. As I later found out, not only was this once the site of the old Sunrise Winery (built in the nineteenth century and abandoned in the 1960s), but Grahm himself had recently arranged to lease it from the owners, a family whose local winegrowing roots extended to the nineteenth century. "I intend to plant on a mountaintop in the Santa Cruz mountain range," he declared in 2006 in *The World of Fine Wine*. "There is an extraordinary stillness to the air and a magical peacefulness to this mountaintop, despite the fact that it shares a fence-line with a very hush-hush missile guidance system testing facility. . . . There is a slight whiff of danger in the air, but whenever I have visited, apart from in the dead of winter, there are Monarch butterflies flitting everywhere. It is a thoroughly enchanting place."

I don't see any butterflies, though I do sight a scurrying covey of quail as we reenter the rolling valley. The yellow hills are scattered with oaks, buckeyes, and conifers with patches of tall green bunch-grass in the hollows as they rise toward distant forested ridges. Black-berry hedges line the road, west of which a group of red buildings (LOCATELLI RANCH) is surrounded by yellow alders; to the east, the silhouettes of solitary trees punctuate ridgelines leading to the enormous rocks. "I'm not the only person who believes that certain kinds of rocks are transducers of energy," Grahm says. "'Menhirs,' if you will: stone columns that take energy and reflect it. At the risk of sounding New Agey, this is an extraordinarily energetic spot—it's got real mojo. Empire Grade is a long, long road, and this is the very end of it. When you're here, you're way, way out there."

Getting out of the car in the thickening mist, Grahm surveys the surrounding terrain, which is increasingly shrouded in gray. "It's significant that this is a historical vineyard," he says. "A hundred years ago people had a good sense of what would work, and the Locatellis have been around forever. Somebody once told me how late the grapes were to ripen up here; we put out temperature gauges, and there was quite a bit of variation even in this little area. The side near Eagle Rock is drier and has less topsoil, but in some places there's *too* much moisture—there were biotic issues wherever you see those sedgy plants. There were something like fifty plantable acres. We were going to do whites on one side and reds on the other."

During the lease negotiations, Grahm received "the whole Locatelli tribe" at his winery. "They wanted to make sure they weren't selling to a heathen," he says. "One of them was actually a priest. In real estate you learn about all kinds of family dynamics; on one property I looked at, the parents had died and the children were debating whether to sell—the guy needed the money, but one of his sisters didn't; another sister hated the brother, who was an alcoholic. It was pretty crazy."

Eventually Grahm agreed to a thirty-five-year lease with the Locatellis. Before signing, however, he commissioned a study that found what he calls "significant levels of lead" in the soil. As it turned out, the area below Eagle Rock had once been "a friggin' firing range," a fact that Grahm had known but hadn't "put together." As he subsequently explained in a public mea culpa:

> The cost of remediating that soil would likely run to an excess of $250,000. In fact, the only thing that prevents the property from being designated as a hazardous waste site (one doesn't even wish to imagine what *that* costs to remediate) is the National Rifle Association, the powerful American gun lobby, [which] has sought and won an environmental exemption for gun clubs and gun ranges. (Can't be too well prepared against those who would threaten our liberties. . . .)

"We would have had to scrape the topsoil off, strain it with a sieve, and sequester it," Grahm explains. "You can also inoculate it with morel mushrooms—which concentrate the lead—and burn them, but the sum total of effort and expense tipped it the other way."

For followers of Bonny Doon, this turnaround called to mind an even louder false alarm from the previous decade. In 1996, Grahm announced with considerable fanfare that he had purchased the historic Ruby Hill winery in the Livermore Valley east of San Francisco Bay, hoping "to restore this wonderful building to its former splendour . . . and begin the replanting of the potentially wondrous adjacent vineyard, beginning in 1998." Over the next year, he met with a series of architects including Frank Gehry—creator of, among other things, Bilbao's Guggenheim Museum and the Walt Disney Concert Hall in Los Angeles. When Grahm learned that Gehry was taking antibiotics for a cold, he admonished the renowned designer to switch to Chinese herbs, and Gehry subsequently demurred that his high-powered firm would constitute "overkill" for the project. Grahm ultimately brought in a feng shui master from Los Angeles, and when "Dr. Wu" (that's right, but with only one Wu) gave it a thumbs-down, Grahm pulled out of the deal altogether.

In light of episodes like this, Grahm is fond of acknowledging his role as "the boy who cried everything"—one of the factors that led to his put-up-or-shut-up business overhaul in 2006. Still, even after avowedly committing himself to the path of terroir, the task of identifying a suitable vineyard site remains fraught with uncertainty. "One day you think something is important, and another day you think another thing is important," he admits. "Then you realize you know nothing." Or, as he nakedly agonized about the Locatellis' lead-poison problem in *The World of Fine Wine:* "If I am apparently incapable of discerning the rather obvious, side-of-the-barn-sized 'issues' of a given property, how then might I have the wit to make a very refined, sophisticated and highly intuitive determination of the putative brilliance and uniqueness of this or indeed any other property?"

As a Francophile who believes that there is basically no contest between the quality of Old and New World Wines ("When I taste my own wines and compare them to their Old World counterparts, I become slightly nauseous"), Grahm is tortured by the fact that he lives in California, which, besides being rainless half the year, has only about a hundred years of winegrowing experience behind it. "Great wines are absolutely predicated on great vineyards, which is something that happens only by chance," he says. "A great site solves problems that its neighbors don't—it drains better, ripens better, retains acidity, gets more sunlight, doesn't frost as frequently. . . . It has to do with solving environmental challenges elegantly, which leads to a vineyard's distinctiveness relative to its neighbors. I think the monks were originally drawn to the great sites in Europe partly by chance, but also by acute powers of observation—and perhaps by divine instruction, which is not something we can really count on." What's more, he believes that the soils in European vineyards, having been cultivated for so long, have established a synergetic—even collaborative—relationship with vines. As he wrote in an essay titled "In Search of a Great Growth in the New World":

In the Old World, there has evolved a sort of homeostasis, a "learning" between vine and soil under the watchful eye of a human being. Vines have in some sense "taught" soils—through the mediation of their symbiotic microbial demiurges, mycorrhizae, and the like—what their specific needs are. . . . Over many generations a sort of stately, rhythmic dance has emerged. The most interesting wines that arise from this dance are the ones that have captured this distinctive rhythm or waveform, this unmistakable signature that we call terroir.

"Our problem in the New World is that we don't have the benefit of centuries of iteration and experimentation," Grahm says. "We're essentially trying to create a great wine *de novo* in one generation, which represents a serious disconnect. I mean, how did the Chinese work out acupuncture? One person can't do that in a single generation; you need hundreds of years of study, experimenting on thousands of people, until you've accumulated this mass of knowledge about how energy systems and pressure points work on human beings. By the same token, how could one person work out a Grand Cru vineyard— what to plant there and how to plant it—in one lifetime? It just seems impossible; nevertheless, I think it's extremely worthwhile."

As Grahm has put it in various essays, one titled "Terroir and Going Home":

For me, the vineyard represents my spiritual path, perhaps the only shot I have at bringing balance into my life and achieving something like contentment. . . . I am looking to create a wine contained within itself, one that seeks nothing further. . . . This mystical connection is something I personally aspire to but, owing to my own limitations, perhaps will never find. . . . I can't quite put words to why I am profoundly comforted by the fact that a wine can also be a place, that mere fermented grapes can coalesce into a product of such rare beauty and meaning. There is something deeply primal about the whole notion of a place or "home"—the idea that everything has a place, that everything (and everyone) has a home. . . . Without a home, a touchstone, there is no place for us to rest, to repose.

At the end of Empire Grade, an imposing iron gate bars entry to a space-research facility run by Lockheed Martin, extremely off-limits to the general public. Grahm considers the place to represent "radical evil"—a circumstance that, even if lead poisoning hadn't turned out to be a problem, might seem to put a kink in the area's karma. Grahm says it puts him in mind of Thomas Pynchon, who, in the novels *V.* and *The Crying of Lot 49*, portrayed an aerospace company called Yoyodyne, which had a manufacturing plant in the fictional town of San Narciso, California.

"It's all about control," Grahm says, dissecting Pynchon's paranoia. Then, segueing back to the *narciso* mode: "This, of course, is my bête noire. Part of me wants to control things so they will come out well—especially if there's a lot of money involved. But if you want something to turn out *interesting*, you have to cede a lot of that control. Admittedly, agriculture isn't natural—we use trellises; we pick ripe bunches and not unripe bunches. But if you can somehow capture that natural quality, you produce a far more complex product. It's a bit of a paradox—an artifice of naturality, or using artifice to somehow render a sense of place. It's a question of trust versus distrust: Is the universe benign or not? Unfortunately, the way viticulture is practiced in the New World, we want to control everything to the nth degree without allowing any possibility of originality to express itself. The way we plant our vineyards and grow our grapes virtually assures that a vineyard can never be great."

The mist is now so dense and murky that it can be classified as drizzle. For the moment, Grahm surrenders—to the weather and the conundrum of finding a great site.

"My expectations are shrinking daily," he says, getting back into his Citroën. "At first I wanted it all. Now I just want *something*."

ALTHOUGH RANDALL GRAHM was born and raised in Los Angeles, and Bonny Doon's former general manager Patrice Boyle reports that Randall "missed the music gene—big-time," his mother and father, Ruthie and Alan, both have musical roots on the East Coast. As a teenager growing up in Brooklyn, Alan played sax and clarinet in a swing band that performed in the Catskills; he was reportedly offered a scholarship to Juilliard but was so eager to escape his (Jewish) family that instead he went to Lynchburg College, a Christian school in Virginia. Ruthie's father, Lou Herscher, was a trailblazing Tin Pan Alley songwriter—one of the first members of ASCAP (the American Society of Composers, Authors and Publishers) and composer of "Dream Daddy," sometimes cited as the first recording to gain popularity through the medium of radio. In 1934 Herscher also wrote the first tune ever performed on the floor of the U.S. Congress: "Song of the N.R.A.," extolling not the National Rifle Association but FDR's National Recovery Act (lyrics by Rep. William Sirovich, D-NYC).

"Randall takes after my father," says his mother. "He didn't fit the mold either—he was very creative, always into new things and different perspectives. He was a pacifist and a vegetarian long before it was fashionable, and as a songwriter he would never sell out. During the Depression he had an offer to write military music, but he said, 'No soldier is going to his death singing my songs'—just like Randall won't make chardonnay because he doesn't believe in it." (Her son describes his grandfather as a "pacifist-aggressivist," which, judging from the testimony of those close to him, earmarks Randall as a projectionist.)

During the Depression, Ruthie remembers that "People wanted bread, not songs." Hoping to write music for the movies, in 1935 Herscher moved his family to Los Angeles via Greyhound bus. He went on to release an album with *Guys and Dolls* composer Frank Loesser and to contribute tunes to some twenty films, including *Sarong Girl, Campus Rhythm, Bowery Bombshell, South of the Rio Grande,* and *Sweetheart of Sigma Chi.* Upon arriving in Hollywood, Ruthie was tapped by a talent agent looking for redheaded kids, and she subsequently appeared as an extra and bit player in some two hundred films. She has also written songs recorded by Patsy Montana ("Mama Never Said a Word About Love") and Louis Prima and Gia Prima ("Baby, I'm the Greatest," inspired by Muhammad Ali).

Ruthie met Alan in Southern California, where he settled when discharged from the navy after World War II. He studied psychology and theater arts on the GI Bill and, after getting a master's degree from University of Southern California, supplemented a teaching income by selling vacuum cleaners. Finding that he preferred the latter to the former, he proceeded to build an import-export business that dealt in everything from tools to housewares to perfumes to appliances to handbags. ("My father didn't want any business opportunity to pass him by," says Randall.) Ruthie describes Alan as "a salesman's salesman—a real go-getter, very driven. Nobody could keep up with him." He was also "a stern taskmaster" who "didn't take a lot of time with the kids. They used to ask me if the stock market had gone up or down that day; if it went down, they stayed in their rooms."

Randall, the oldest of three children, was born in 1953. He was a hyperliterate toddler, prone to pointing out letters of the alphabet on cereal boxes in the supermarket. His IQ was later calculated to be 151, a level of brainpower that manifested itself mainly in the sciences. One time, when he forgot to take his lunch to school, Ruthie delivered it herself, only to encounter the principal in the hallway, also looking for Randy Grahm. Ruthie couldn't believe that her son was in trouble ("He didn't do bad things")—and sure enough, the principal just wanted to meet the boy who, for a science project, had built a plywood city in the shape of an atom with a carbon-dioxide-powered monorail.

The Grahms kept a kosher household. They ate dinner together every night, and as Ruthie remembers it, whenever Randy was called to the table, he emerged from his room with a book. (Today he claims that his "primary former of sensibility" was *Mad* magazine: "That ironic, sardonic, skeptical tone activated my smart-ass gene.") When he was a teenager, the family moved from West L.A. to a one-story corner stucco house in Beverly Hills, and in the transition Randy skipped half of tenth grade at Beverly Hills High School, alma mater of (among others) Jack Abramoff, Albert Brooks, Nicolas Cage, Richard Chamberlain, Jackie Cooper, Jamie Lee Curtis, Richard Dreyfuss, Nora Ephron, Carrie Fisher, Rhonda Fleming, Gina Gershon, Joel Grey, H. R. Haldeman, Angelina Jolie, Lenny Kravitz, Monica Lewinsky, Lyle and Erik Menendez, André Previn, Rob Reiner, Alicia Silverstone, David Schwimmer, and Daniel Yergin. His brother's best friend was Corbin Bernsen, who would gain fame as Arnie Becker, the divorce attorney on *L.A. Law*. More than its movieland glamour, Randall says, "What was interesting about Beverly Hills was the school." He could, for example, take classes in film, and a literature teacher encouraged his interest in writing. Ruthie calls Randy's friends "the superintellectuals—they would come home from school and do their homework together." When not studying, however, her son also created a radical leftist newspaper called the *Daily Sun*, whose agenda is described by his brother as "kill all the lawyers."

Randall's parents aspired for him to attend an Ivy League college and—stop me if you've heard this one—become a doctor. Ruthie had urged him to write to Harvard when he was only twelve, but *Mad* magazine had already taken a psychic toll—when it came time to actually apply, his first choices were Hampshire and Antioch, alternative schools in Massachusetts and Ohio. As it turned out, Hampshire turned him down, and upon actually visiting Antioch, Randall decided that he wasn't ready for "complete anarchy." He thus ended up on the newest—and coolest—campus of the University of California: Santa Cruz.

· · ·

Today it's hard to picture the atmosphere at Santa Cruz in 1971. The campus had existed only since 1965, when it was added to the UC system as part of the university's master plan; holding that higher education should be available to all, this scheme declared that any graduating high school senior could go to one of California's community colleges, with the top third guaranteed admission to a state university (San Francisco State, Long Beach State, Chico State, etc.) and the top eighth to a University of California campus (UC Berkeley, UC Riverside, UCLA). It also authorized the expansion of two of the latter campuses—Santa Barbara and Davis (near Sacramento)—and the creation of three new ones, at San Diego, Irvine (in Orange County), and Santa Cruz (on the coast south of San Francisco). Separated from the city by redwood-clad mountains, situated on a series of rolling hills above a sleepy surfing town that seemed to exist in a world of its own, UC Santa Cruz had a progressive and semiexperimental mandate: no letter grades, emphasis on independent and interdisciplinary study, and housing in "residential colleges" that provided a more intimate social environment than a typical state school. Relatively small in its own right with a total of 4,000 students, situated in a pacific setting where forests and mountains met the sea within easy tripping distance (i.e., a stoner's throw) of UC Berkeley and San Francisco's Haight-Ashbury district—twin epicenters of the youth revolution of the 1960s, which was then morphing into the "ecology" movement—Santa Cruz soon became the hardest UC campus to get into. In the words of David Graves, a member of Grahm's college class who would later cofound the Saintsbury winery near Napa, it was Zeitgeist U: "Berkeley had history and urban reality, but at Santa Cruz you could read Thoreau and feel connected to it. There was a sense of getting back to the garden."

This spirit was embodied in Alan Chadwick, an Englishman who taught gardening at the college. Born in 1909 into the English upper class, Chadwick was a violinist, landscape painter, skier, skater, Shakespearean actor, and student of Rudolf Steiner, who reportedly tutored him as a boy. After two decades on the stage, Chadwick had turned his attention to the garden, which he considered "the mother of all true culture"; he combined Steiner's biodynamic principles with the methods of French intensive gardening, which, by sowing seeds close together in raised beds and nurturing the plants with organic compost, was capable of conferring several crops a year.

In 1967, having restored the twenty-six-acre admiralty garden in Cape Town, South Africa (where he'd immigrated after serving as a naval officer in World War II), Chadwick was invited to UC Santa Cruz to create a student garden and apprentice-training program. Tall, handsome, dramatic, passionate, articulate, and energetic—in other words, a charismatic figure—he found fertile ground there for his message, which held that organic gardening could save the world by nourishing beauty, creativity, and humanism through reverence for nature. Also a devout Roman Catholic, he preached that the garden was "man's introduction to the whole of Creation"; one of his apprentices compared him to "an Old Testament prophet, railing against people's falling from the Way into sin and decadence." Chadwick's lectures were theatrical performances, attracting crowds that overflowed the confines of campus lecture halls. In time his program, which bore the earmarks of a cult, was also found to include many students who weren't enrolled at the university. His tempestuous personality combined with his lack of formal academic credentials resulted in his departure from Santa Cruz after only four years, though he went on to found other important gardens at Green Gulch Farm Zen Center near San Francisco and the Institute for the Study of Man and Nature in Round Valley, near the town of Covelo in Mendocino County. His legacy at UC Santa Cruz, the Farm and Garden School of Agroecology, has sent scores of socially responsible growers to all corners of the globe, and by some accounts Chadwick—who died at Green Gulch in 1980—is more responsible than any other individual for today's sustainable-agriculture and fresh-food movements.

Randall Grahm arrived at UCSC just before Alan Chadwick departed. As per his parents' wishes, Randall was officially premed as a freshman, though he found himself more interested in philosophy and literature. "UCSC offered extraordinary opportunities for learning and growth," he explains. Among the resident professors were literary critic C. L. "Joe" Barber (author of *Shakespeare's Festive Comedy*), philosopher Albert Hofstadter (*Truth and Art*), anthropologist/

linguist/semiotician/cyberneticist Gregory Bateson (*Steps to an Ecology of Mind, Mind and Nature*), and Freudian-Marxist-Dionysian-mystical classicist Norman O. Brown (*Love's Body, Life Against Death*), who taught in the History of Consciousness department. "You really got to spend time with these guys," Grahm recounts. "You could take a walk with Norman O. Brown and ask him questions, and he would respond in Greek, or Latin, or haiku. Not that I was a brilliant or diligent student; I was more interested in getting a girlfriend, and I kept changing my major. That was the curse of Santa Cruz—no one could ever make up their minds." Randall was assigned to College V ("Five"), whose academic orientation he describes as "flakiness." The dorm consisted of two floors, one devoted to alcohol, the other (home of the "Space Cadets") to LSD. "For what it's worth, the Space Cadets beat the other floor soundly in softball," notes Grahm, who admits affiliation with neither side.

In a last-ditch attempt to fulfill his parents' premed plan, in his junior year Grahm transferred to MIT, where he studied chemistry and physics. He soon discovered a problem with the proposed career, however. "You actually had to work. More to the point, I didn't want to be a doctor. The only reason I was there was to further my chances of getting into med school, but I didn't like the idea of cutting up bodies." Ultimately he returned to Santa Cruz and decided to major in philosophy, declaring his intention of writing a senior thesis on the Heideggerian concept of *Dasein*—a view of being that conceives of an individual as an "activity" rather than as a "subjectivity." By graduation time, however, he hadn't gotten around to it, so he finished college without a degree.

Part of the problem, Grahm concluded, was that he didn't know German. Hence, in the summer of 1974, he moved to Bavaria and lived with a family in the town of Kochel am See while studying at the Goethe Institute. "There were a lot of Spaniards and Italians there," he says, "so in German I developed a Spanish inflection." On this, his first trip outside North America, he began to perceive "the enormous political divide between the U.S. and the rest of the world. It was different, being the ugly American in Europe. Watching the Nixon impeachment proceedings on German TV was surreal." He made at least one side trip to Italy but, oddly, can't recall if he visited France; more memorable was a Danish woman who made wine in her bathtub. Perhaps most significant of all was the fact that 1971 German wines—by consensus the greatest riesling vintage of the twentieth century—were available on local shelves for three dollars a bottle. Grahm proceeded to "slurp up" semisweet spätlese and auslese every night of the week.

He was and wasn't prepared for this by the fact that his previous experience of German wine—like that of most Americans—consisted solely of Blue Nun, the mass-market import ubiquitous in the United States. "One of my girlfriends' mothers drank it, so it seemed like the height of sophistication," Randall remembers. "My parents drank Mateus, so that could not possibly be acceptable." (Ruthie Grahm confirms that "wine was *so* not a part of our family. Only on occasion did we have cold duck, Lancers, or Manischewitz." Her son would later recall "a single bottle of Manischewitz Elderberry, produced during the Johnson administration, that lasted us at least until the ouster of Tricky Dick.") In Santa Cruz, Randall had begun to branch out at a downtown place called the Cooper House, which staged tastings every Wednesday at five. "If truth be told, I was not, strictly speaking, of age. It was just a tiny introduction—they would pour something like four chenin blancs, or sauvignon blancs, or zinfandels. Now it seems silly, but then it seemed encyclopedic."

Back in Beverly Hills that fall, Randall tried to face his thesis but inexplicably got "bogged down." Thinking to take a "break" for a few weeks, he scanned about for a diversion and, a mere two blocks from his parents' house, discovered a shop called the Beverly Hills Wine Merchant. Still at a nascent stage of "intrigue" about wine, he applied for—and obtained—a job sweeping floors and stocking shelves, which struck him as potentially "better than selling shoes." As it turned out, it would set the course for the rest of his life.

At that time, Southern California, like most of the rest of the country, was a wilderness as far as fine wine was concerned. The number of good shops in the L.A. area could be quantified on the digits of a single grasping appendage; as another Beverly Hills Wine Merchant employee, Jason Brandt Lewis, recalls, "This was when people still drank

Scotch throughout the meal." Lewis was in a position to know, as his uncle Stan Weller owned Stan's Wine & Spirits in Redondo Beach and Hermosa Beach. A bomber pilot in World War II, Weller had been stationed in London, where he developed a taste for wine; one Thanksgiving with the family in the early 1960s, he opened several bottles of rare trockenbeerenauslese (TBA) Riesling, which are made only in select vintages from grapes that have shriveled into raisins. Weller allowed his ten-year-old nephew to taste examples dating back to 1937, alerting Jason to the existence of "wines that were a lot better than Manischewitz." On his thirteenth birthday, he received a copy of Alexis Lichine's just-published *Encyclopedia of Wines and Spirits;* by the time he was sixteen, he was working in one of Weller's stores.

At the time, Napa Valley had just launched the renaissance that would soon make it a household name. In the early 1970s, when Lewis was still a teenager, he started making buying trips to Northern California, proffering a letter of introduction from his uncle. "It was very confusing for people like Joe Heitz and Louis Martini and Bob Travers [of Mayacamas Vineyards]. I wasn't going to buy any wine without tasting it, but I wasn't old enough to taste it, so we'd go into a back room and they'd pull some samples when no one was looking."

In 1974 Lewis went to work at the Beverly Hills Wine Merchant, founded three years earlier by former Sotheby's employee Dennis Overstreet "to create excitement about wine when this town was still about spirits." In Overstreet's conception, the store was designed to merge the atmospheres of England's oldest wineshop, Berry Bros. & Rudd, with the upscale Paris grocery Hédiard. Fresh flower arrangements graced the counters, with wood paneling on the walls and red carpets on the floors. In the middle of the store, near a chilled case of caviar, was a display box containing a jeroboam of '29 Château Mouton Rothschild. Since Baron Philippe de Rothschild himself was a periodic visitor, the clerks wore ties and burgundy-colored blazers with embroidered patches that bore a striking resemblance to the Mouton insignia.

Not unpredictably, the Beverly Hills Wine Merchant had an illustrious clientele. Two of Overstreet's founding partners were *Laugh-In* TV stars Dan Rowan and Dick Martin. According to Lewis, "Martin was always complaining that he owned all these expensive wines but couldn't show them off because they had to be kept in a temperature-controlled cellar." Finally Rowan gave his partner a bottle of '37 Blue Nun to put on his mantel. Despite the haute-cuisine/couture ambience, the shop had a certain fraternity-house spirit, reflecting the cultural transition Overstreet aimed to effect. The customer who most perfectly portrayed this (unsurprisingly in light of his performance in the movie *Arthur*) was Dudley Moore, who enjoyed staggering around the store waving a bottle of La Tâche or covering himself with a sheet when he'd had too much champagne. When the Doors' lead singer, Jim Morrison, came in looking for Jack Daniel's, the owner informed him that only wine was allowed within the walls of the Wine Merchant. One of Overstreet's biggest challenges was represented by the Rat Pack contingent of Frank Sinatra, Dean Martin, and Sammy Davis Jr. Sinatra once ordered an unspecified case of Overstreet's "most expensive white," which the owner obligingly fulfilled, delivering a wooden box of the world's most coveted dessert wine, Château d'Yquem. Later he received a call via satellite phone from Sinatra's yacht, announcing that the contents of the case had been dumped overboard because the wine was sweet.

Some stars were more enologically advanced. Rowan, a Bordeaux connoisseur, was a devotee of Château Latour; Orson Welles preferred Lafite. When Yul Brynner was on tour, he had Overstreet ship him a St.-Julien, Gruaud-Larose (although, when Brynner drank white wine, he placed an ice cube in the glass to dilute the acidity). Pouilly-Fuissé went down well with comics—it was a favorite of both Lucille Ball and Jerry Lewis—but other wines made for surprising bedfellows: Piesporter Goldtröpfchen, a German riesling, was admired by both Bob Newhart and Joe Namath, while Dom Pérignon was a favorite of Jane Fonda and Ronald Reagan. The most counterintuitive political pairing played out between John F. Kennedy and Richard M. Nixon: The reputedly crude latter was enamored of Château Margaux, while the supposedly suave former loved emerald riesling, an undistinguished hybrid developed for high production in the fine-wine-challenged San Joaquin Valley. A regular customer with whom Lewis had a "nice business relationship" (aka "huge crush") was Candice Bergen, who took advantage of the Wine Merchant's lavish gift wrapping—enclosing a toothless comb, for example, with a bottle of champagne for her bald father, Edgar. In her then-recent film, *The Wind and the Lion*, Bergen was kidnapped by Sean Connery after she ordered a bottle of Château Margaux—prompting Lewis to observe that it was a shame she'd never gotten to drink it. When Bergen replied that, as a matter of fact, she never *had* tasted Margaux, Lewis grabbed a bottle off the shelf and gave it to her as a present.

This was not out of keeping with Overstreet's MO, which involved uncorking expensive bottles on a regular basis. His motivating philosophy, custom tailored to the clientele, was that wine is a privilege the elite deserve. Even though he didn't have a license for open containers of alcohol on the premises, he often invited wealthy clients in for exclusive tastings—a horizontal of '67 St.-Julien, say, or a vertical of Cheval Blanc. "At one point Dennis figured out how many bottles of first-growth Bordeaux and Grand Cru Burgundy he was opening," Lewis says. "He told me to return some bottles to the supplier (for credit, claiming spoilage), but you couldn't return empty bottles of Château Pétrus and Cheval Blanc." Overstreet claims that his biggest importer required that bottles be returned *without* liquid—but in any case, he says, "With the amount of product we were moving, if you say pick it up, they pick it up."

"Dennis would take someone upstairs to his office, and they'd end up buying five cases of this or that," says Lewis. "He always assumed you wanted five cases, because the wine was 'going to age out beautifully.' Dennis would tell people, 'You need to have this in your cellar! What? You don't have a cellar? Well I have some space downstairs you can rent.'"

Not all of the Wine Merchant's customers were actors, producers, and directors. Most were doctors, lawyers, or agents who bought wine not just for personal enjoyment but also for professional purposes. "Anybody with money came to that store," Lewis says. "There was this amazing aura that we had *everything*. In the midseventies, it was easy to find '70 or '71 Bordeaux, but you could walk into the Wine Merchant and also find the '66 and '45 and '29 Bordeaux sitting on the rack. Some came in legally, others from sources that were slightly questionable. At the time, it was illegal for a store to buy from a private individual, but I have no doubt that some of the wine came out of personal cellars."

At the time, California wine commerce was governed by fair-trade statutes (later repealed by the courts for restraining trade) that regulated the minimum retail prices of all alcoholic beverages, as dictated by producers and wholesalers. Thus prevented from discounting, stores made money by buying in volume—they could get 5 percent off on a five-case order, 10 percent off on a ten-case order, and so on. "Other than that, nobody had any incentive [to offer customers] except service—free delivery, better selection, more knowledgeable salespeople," says Lewis. "Dennis did all of that, but he saw that it wasn't going to be enough—somehow he had to get the stuff in cheaper."

A loophole that Overstreet succeeded in exploiting was the fact that wholesalers in different regions could post different prices on imports. Châteaux in Bordeaux, for example, sold wine on futures through local *négociants*, who struck different deals with different importers. Thus, "Dennis would buy Château Lafite-Rothschild from a wholesaler in San Francisco and have them put a little sticker on the bottle that said, 'An Ezra Webb Selection,'" says Lewis. "Then he could say, '*This* '66 Château Lafite-Rothschild is different from *that* '66 Château Lafite-Rothschild' and get it posted at a different price. It might be $60.50 retail [in L.A.], but we'd bring in cases and cases and cases of the Ezra Webb stuff by common carrier from San Francisco, posted with the state of California for $33. Then we could legally advertise it much cheaper than anybody else. Basically, [the Wine Merchant] was a discount store when discounts were illegal."

At the time—a year before the '76 Judgment of Paris—French wine still wasn't an easy sell in the beer-and-soda-pop-crazy U.S. A favorable (for Americans) dollar-to-franc ratio in the mid-1970s made their situation that much more desperate. As a result, a flood of Bordeaux and Burgundy was available for a song—and, in a reverse scenario from that of today, the farther west French wine traveled, the cheaper it got. A fifth-growth like Lynch-Bages, which sells now for over $100, sold then for $6.95; a top-flight name like Château Pétrus, now worth thousands on release, could be had for $24.50. Taking advantage of this imbalance, Overstreet and his new apprentice, Randall Grahm, composed full-page ads for the *Los Angeles Times* declaring that "The Franc Has Fallen" and "Let Them Eat Cake." The next morning, customers lined up outside the shop before it even opened. "We went through two or three hundred cases of Comte de Vogüé Burgundy, which was unheard of at that time," says Lewis.

In the evenings, after the store closed, the staff would repair to the owner's office, where Overstreet would open some extraordinary bottle or other. When he first started work at the Wine Merchant, Grahm says, he was clueless about such customs. "On my birthday, Dennis wanted to have chocolate cake with Château d'Yquem," he remembers. "My reaction was 'Before dinner?'" As he grew more accustomed to Overstreet's way of doing things, however, he began tasting the great wines of the world on a regular basis. Chief among them in his memory is the '64 Cheval Blanc, a Bordeaux blend of cabernet franc and merlot so thick and rich that Overstreet declared it suitable for serving on French toast. "It was of a different order from anything else I'd experienced," Grahm says. "I began to apprehend the possibility of wines that are so eloquent—so coherent and intended—that they say something and *mean* something."

The attending discussions were equally deep. Lewis departed when the conversation got "too esoteric," but Overstreet and his Heidegger-quoting employee would parse profundities into the wee hours. Overstreet recalls at least one conversation touching upon the revelations of Nostradamus; another time, he alleges, Randall disrobed so as to "get closer" to a TBA Riesling. "Wine was my LSD," Grahm explains. "It was like discovering sex—it created all sorts of possibilities that weren't there before, and added a richness to life that was all new to me."

In light of such born-again zeal, it wasn't long before Grahm was promoted to the sales floor. Building on his own recent experience, he decided that riesling was "God's gift to the planet," and in no time, Lewis says, "Randall knew more about German wine than anybody." As Overstreet essayed to educate him on the array of parameters that govern the international enological landscape, it was a window onto Grahm's vision that, confronted with such a dizzying kaleidoscope, he found himself excited by the "sense that there was a *finite* [italics mine] body of knowledge—that you could pretty much learn everything there was to know. The universe of wine felt much more bounded and finite then than it does now. You could identify all the classified growths of Bordeaux; you could know which were the first, which were the fourth, which were the fifth. And wines still had terroir, so Margaux tasted like Margaux." To ease their identification, Overstreet provided a set of clues: Margaux tasted like strawberry jam; Pauillac like pencil lead; St.-Julien like mint. "Randy believed every word I said," Overstreet remembers. "He had a very strict observance of ritual."

Lewis agrees that "Randall had an intensity of passion I've seldom seen in anybody. He wanted to absorb everything, big and small—not only to learn the most minute details, but to understand why they made a difference. It didn't necessarily matter to customers, but he would explain why the grower used this sort of pruning technique, or grew the grapes in this kind of soil, or what they did in the winery that made the wine so great. He seduced people with the romance and mythology—he would tell them how the grapes had been picked by virgins caressing each grape between five and seven in the morning, but he could also be very technical, explaining *Botrytis cinerea* rot and saying, 'When you taste it, you'll see what I mean.' His passion was infectious, though he was still way too brilliant and esoteric for some people. My approach was to make wine accessible, whereas Dennis was the other way around—he'd capitalize on customers' innate intimidation." ("I'm an expert," Overstreet says, by way of describing his MO. "Don't fuck with me.")

On the anniversary of the store's opening, Overstreet threw a party for employees and a few favored customers. In no particular order, he uncorked a '62 Dom Pérignon, a '71 Cristal, a '29 Latour, a '47 Cheval Blanc, and a bevy of old Burgundies including a '59 Comte de Vogüé, a '61 La Tâche, and a '62 Romanée-Conti. Before the anniversary bash, Lewis had been a Bordeaux devotee, but after that night, he says, "I was in love with Burgundy." This same infatuation soon overtook Grahm. After he'd worked at the Wine Merchant for a while, he signed up with Sotheby's to explore buying old wines at auction ("something you could still do back then"). Sometime after that, he managed to enter a successful bid for a mixed case of village Burgundies that were marred by low neck fills and smudged labels, but from good vintages, dating back to 1928. It took a year and a half for the wines to arrive, during which Randall began to experience buyer's remorse; hence, he asked a few collector-customers if they wanted to go in on the case with him. Applying the merciful point of view that he was "just a kid," they took him up on the offer and, assuming that only one or two of the bottles might be drinkable, opened all of them one night at a house on Laurel Canyon. As it turned out, Grahm says, "Every single bottle was out of sight—vibrant, alive, extraordinarily great . . . *beyond* great. The takeaway lesson for me was that Burgundy ages better than Bordeaux—but since we'd opened all of them, we had to drink them that night."

Lewis had similar experiences with customers. "Sometimes we'd open up bottles and party in the store, then get invited to join the party as it rolled on somewhere else. One year Heublein did its big annual tasting in Las Vegas, so Dennis flew up there while Randall and I drove. Everybody decided we had to play keno, and although at first Dennis didn't want to play, he ended up winning something like seventeen thousand dollars. So he was really happy and high at the tasting, and he didn't like waiting, so when Heublein opened a case of '53 Pétrus for a roomful of a thousand people, Dennis grabbed one of the bottles and poured me a full glass, saying, 'This is your birth year—you deserve it.' Michael Broadbent, the Heublein auctioneer, proceeded to get on the PA system and announce that, eager though the public might be to taste the wine, people should please wait for it to be poured."

"Dennis has theatrical flair," Randall explains, "though it isn't exactly Shakespearean quality. He's the Hollywood wine merchant—he enjoys being unpredictable, and he's given to extravagant pronouncements, some of them shockingly outré. He's a little bit of a court jester, or a naughty puppy dog—you have to love him." Sensing the applicability of those same observations to himself, he acknowledges: "In retrospect, maybe I took that quality on—the ethic that, if people like you and laugh at you, maybe they'll buy your wine."

· · ·

To experience the Beverly Hills Wine Merchant in person, I stopped by the store on the day after Thanksgiving in 2008—in other words, in the midst of the nationwide economic collapse known as the Great Recession. The shop is now on Cañon Drive in Beverly Hills, across the street from the plaza gardens of the Montague Hotel. I was greeted by a display case of Sauternes as I entered the shop, but most of the front room was devoted to California wine, with imports ensconced in the rear. I found Overstreet—a tanned, slender, sixtyish man in a blue grocer's jacket with a broad grin and thin graying hair—in this inner sanctum, sitting at a table with a slight, soft-spoken Englishman whom Overstreet introduced as Albert Hammond, composer of "To All the Girls I've Loved Before" and "It Never Rains in Southern California." Remembering a poignant personal moment when the latter song had been playing on my car radio, I piped up: "That brought tears to my eyes in 1972!" This inspired Overstreet to leap out of his chair, laughing hysterically and slapping the smiling Hammond on the shoulder. Apparently he had just alerted the songwriter to the fact that the producer of a new Napa Valley cabernet, which got a good score from Robert Parker, had been using this song to promote the wine without permission. "I once told Albert not to let Julio Iglesias use his name on ads," Overstreet divulged.

Hammond had to leave a few minutes later, at which point Overstreet said he had another appointment with some "television people"—two dark-haired men and two blond women, all aged around thirty. One of the guys worked for a luxury-travel TV show, the other for a company that sold doors for security vaults. "A vault door is like a woman," the latter guy explained when the group arrived. "You can always get in—it's just a matter of time."

Overstreet invited me to tag along, so we went next door and took an elevator to a second-floor lounge with a view of the gardens across the street. To enter "The Suite," as it was called, Overstreet pressed his fingertip to a print-scanning pad by the door, gaining entry to a room furnished with black leather sofas, a flat-screen TV, low glass tables spread with wine books and magazines, and elevated counters with Riedel stemware, tablecloths, and stools. "This is open three hundred sixty-five days a year," Overstreet disclosed. "You can rent a private storage locker here for sixty dollars a month. The idea is that, when you're in town, you can come and take a bottle out of your locker—or, if you're in a restaurant, we'll send one over as a gift, since it's tacky to buy a thousand-dollar bottle off a list."

"It's like a country club where you provide the golf," one of the girls ventured.

"It's a place where people can meet," Overstreet explained.

"Like in *The Tipping Point*," said the girl. "You're the Connector."

The rest of us sat down on the stools, facing the mirrored wall behind Overstreet. "I think the typical wine store won't survive over the next year and a half," he said as he removed the foil from a bottle of Lynch-Bages. "Retail is about detail. It's not about being aggressive— it's about the wink and the smile." As he uncorked the wine, he divulged, "I also own the most successful bar in L.A.—Rage, in West Hollywood. I saw a need and filled it—gays never have to go home to their wives and families, and they're always looking for something new."

Eyeing the wine, the guy who sold vault doors said, "Last year the *Wine Spectator*'s wine of the year was Clos de Pape or something. You think it's good?"

"Châteauneuf-du-Pape," Overstreet corrected him. "It has thirteen different grapes in it. I like that—it's like having twelve weirdos and me." Pouring the Lynch-Bages, he asked, "Do you like French wine?"

"Napa all the way," the guy replied. "European wines are . . . I don't know. Gamey?"

"That sounds like when somebody went from one woman to another," Overstreet observed. "You like Napa the way you like rock and roll. But quality rises to the top—when you stop grinding your teeth, come talk to Daddy."

The guy took a sip of the Bordeaux. "You like French wine better?" he asked.

"Do I want to do your mother?" Overstreet responded. "Yes, I do!" Since this might have struck some as a non sequitur, he clarified, "You might think your girlfriend's cute, but if you want to find out where it's at, check out her mother."

"Some wines are too old to drink, right?" asked the TV guy.

"Not if you're into necrophilia," said Overstreet. "I liked doing Marilyn Monroe—she didn't move, but still. . . ."

When the Lynch-Bages was gone, Overstreet opened a minifridge and brought out a bottle of Louis Roederer champagne. One of the guys made an approving sound, prompting Overstreet to forewarn, "The next one's on you." Then, pouring the champagne, he said, "50 Cent came in one time and wanted to buy all my Cristal. He was double-parked, so I told him he was going to get a ticket. He said, 'I don't care about tickets.' So I told him that they'd tow the car. He said, 'I'll have a limo here so fast!'"

"Very riche," said the vault-door guy.

"We always knew there was no middle class," Overstreet said. "Fine wine is for people who raise horses."

"It's affordable art," said the TV guy.

"It's the last thing that differentiates thinking people," said Overstreet. "Jesus could have turned water into anything—he could have chosen to turn it into pineapple juice, and we would have been fighting over Hawaii for the last two thousand years. But he turned it into wine." He raised his glass. "Wine is like falling in love," he declared. Then, if his guests hadn't yet gotten the point: "This is exciting!" And finally to drive it home: "My nipples get hard!"

This inspired laughter and applause. The guests raised their glasses. "I smell a reality show here," said the vault-door guy. "A docudrama."

"Dennis is a rock star in France and Italy," said the TV guy.

"Have you ever had a bad scallop?" Overstreet inexplicably inquired. "You throw up for a week. I couldn't touch myself!" In the wake of another apparent non sequitur, he went on: "I flew to Paris and told the Four Seasons that I wanted a banana peeled in front of me. Then I had them pluck the hairs off a raspberry and put it in a glass of champagne. They'll do it too—they charge a lot of money, but Bernardo at Georges Cinq is the best sommelier in the world."

"What makes a great sommelier?" the vault guy asked. "Palate? Knowledge?"

"Personality," Overstreet declared. Then, turning to me: "Randy Grahm's personality was just captivating to me. He was an intellectual, but no one was more enthusiastic about wine. It was a burning, searing thing with him—almost a religious devotion, like having Dionysus or Bacchus in our midst. With his eyes and hair all amok, he was a Rasputin kind of character—when he stared at you, you weren't sure if he was playing with you or dead serious. There's an expression: 'Genius looks like everyone, but no one looks like a genius.' Randy could be so much like you when you were talking to him, but then you'd turn around and say, 'What the hell were we talking about?' If you didn't agree with him about a wine, he would say, 'Are you not hearing that orchestra under your nose? What are all those nostril hairs for?' With him it wasn't just a product or a sales job—it was passion and romance. He cared. Customers would walk away feeling touched by something."

None of Overstreet's visitors had heard of Grahm or Bonny Doon. "There aren't enough Randall Grahms out there today," Overstreet confirmed. "There's no more sitting down and tasting and being characters. Back then, we were buying great wines and didn't even know what was going on—even the French didn't have a clue. Now we've moved into this Internet-based business mode, with suits regurgitating Parker reviews. The wine industry became the food industry. But buying wine at Costco is like living in China. Everyone wears the same clothes—they're called Kirkwood."

I had to leave before this curious meeting ended, so I never figured out what, if any, specific purpose it served. Was Overstreet auditioning for the luxury-travel TV show? Trying to get young people interested in wine? Conducting a tutorial in entitled eccentricity? All of the above?

"We get a little carried away in this town," he acknowledged as he showed me out. "We have a cadre—the whole world follows what we do, and wants to live the way they see us living in movies and on TV. So this is how we do business—the town encourages it. Catering to youth and creative bullshit is what keeps me young. You have to use reverse psychology to make them curious—to create the argument. Here Randy saw the effect on the Gregory Pecks and Billy Wilders. It was a magical convergence: The clouds parted, and Randall Grahm walked into a wine store in Beverly Hills. If he'd been born in Texas, maybe he would have drilled for oil instead.

"At some point, he was supposed to be *moi*," Overstreet disclosed. "I was going to pass him the baton—with his quirkiness, I thought he would be great. But then I saw in him something bigger happening. He was getting ready to go out there and wave the *Star Wars* wand, and he can fight that battle better than I can. I'm Yoda."

No matter what high-grossing movie it might resemble, soon after going to work at the Beverly Hills Wine Merchant, Randall Grahm heard his siren call. "It was my intuition that the life of the winemaker would allow me to do what I do best," he says now. "I'm not a great thinker or analyzer; if I have a great talent, it's putting things together. My basic nature is to be a synthesizer—a rip-off artist who integrates disparate elements. Maybe that's just another way of saying 'engage in terminal dilettantism,' but the magic of wine and its aesthetic was somehow resonant with my own nature. It actually seemed like a way of life where eclecticism might serve me well."

In other words, when it came to capturing all sides of Grahm's complicated mind, wine was ideal.

As it turned out, Randall Grahm—a Baby Boomer who realized after finishing college that wine was an arena combining sensory pleasure, intellectual stimulation, aesthetic significance, and closeness to the earth—wasn't exactly alone. In 1970 the Viticulture and Enology department at the University of California Davis had contained ten advanced students, most from established families in the state's wine industry; in 1974 it contained nearly a hundred, most with scant previous experience of wine. Roger Boulton, an Australian who began teaching at Davis in 1976, points out that this upsurge in enrollment coincided with the end of the Vietnam War, though it seems unlikely that returning veterans swelled the ranks of incipient vintners. More to the point, a whole generation of liberal arts–educated (and drug-seasoned) college graduates, faced with the prospect of locating a livelihood in the wake of Watergate and Vietnam, were searching for some form of existence that (1) did no harm and (2) promised more enjoyment of life than the example of their parents. Although the imminent Judgment of Paris had yet to shake the earth, tremors had already been touched off by California "renaissance" wineries like Heitz, Ridge, Joseph Swan, Chalone, Mayacamas, Stag's Leap, Chateau Montelena, and Chateau Souverain; more than anyone, Robert Mondavi kindled a flame that had begun to illuminate Americans' attitudes toward wine.

Most of these born-again would-be vintners enrolled as grad students in pursuit of master's degrees in enology or viticulture (which were separate but equal in the department). Some, however, reenrolled alongside younger undergraduates, seeking second bachelor's degrees in fermentation or plant science. Despite four years of college, Grahm—having failed to finish his thesis on Heidegger—still lacked a *first* bachelor's degree, so after taking a weekend class in wine microbiology from Ralph Kunkee, a professor of enology at Davis, he wrote letters to several wineries in Northern California, offering to work for a nominal wage. Encountering a profound silence, he called the Davis V&E department and was told that, to be admitted as an undergraduate, he would first have to take chemistry, biology, and physics. He proceeded to do so at the UCLA Extension, inspiring his father to predict that he would remain a student for the rest of his life.

This sort of penance was common among liberal arts–loving would-be winemakers. David Ramey, who grew up playing Little League baseball with Apple Computer cofounder Steve Wozniak in Sunnyvale (near Leo McCloskey's home town of Cupertino), had, courtesy of the Bargetto winery in Soquel, fallen in love with the grape as an undergrad at UC Santa Cruz, which he'd attended at the same time as Grahm. (The two had once connected on a ride board for a car trip, during which they'd talked nonstop about ethics and phenomenology.) After graduating with a BA in American literature, Ramey secured a job teaching English in Colombia, but en route there by automobile, he underwent a *coup de foudre* between Hermosilla and Mexicali: "Wine makes people happy, doesn't mess up the environment, and, unlike a literature seminar, after you finish it you have something besides hot air." Ramey turned his car around, enrolled in biology, chemistry, and precalculus classes at San Jose State, and arrived at Davis in 1976. Another UCSC product, David Graves, was a grad student in ecology and evolution at the University of Chicago, where, between December 28, 1976, and February 8, 1977, the temperature set a record by remaining below freezing for forty-three days in a row. Suspecting that, as a newly minted professor, he could look forward to a contract job at some state teachers' college in the upper Midwest, the Bay Area–raised Graves noticed how much more interested he was in the curriculum of his local wineshop. His future partner at Saintsbury Vineyard, Dick Ward, had an engineering degree from Tufts but couldn't imagine working with any of his fellow students; instead he married a woman from Los Angeles, bought his first case of wine ('67 Château Trotanoy, Bordeaux) at $7.67 a bottle from the Beverly Hills Wine Merchant, got caught up in the "fascination of history, geography, and cultural diversity all brought together to make a product that's wonderful," enrolled in life sciences at Cal State L.A., and entered UC Davis in 1976. Doug Nalle, who graduated from the University of Redlands in 1969 as a history major, spent time in the Peace Corps in Kenya, pitched for a semipro baseball team, and went to work as a bank trainee after getting engaged; when the nuptials were called off, he was at a loss for what to do with his life, but as the member of his family who "always knew when the milk was about to go bad," he suddenly realized that he had a genetic predisposition for enology. He moved from Southern California to Sonoma County, worked as a cellar rat for Jordan and Chateau Souverain while studying chemistry at Santa Rosa Junior College, and enrolled at UC Davis in 1977. John Buechsenstein, who would go on to a career at Joseph Phelps, McDowell, Fife, and Sauvignon Republic, got interested in wine while majoring in music at UC Berkeley, near which the city's so-called Gourmet Ghetto (the brainchild of yet more Boomers who had been exposed to fine food and wine in Europe) was taking root off campus. A part-time printer who produced wine lists for Chez Panisse and the Potluck Restaurant (owned by chef Narsai David), Buechsenstein cultivated the acquaintanceship of a rhythm-and-blues singer named Sandy Lynch, who, in order "to be able to buy more harmonicas," sold wine twelve hours a week out of an eight-hundred-square-foot shop under his given name, Kermit. After tasting a 1955 Châteauneuf-du-Pape from *négociant* Alfred de Montigny, Buechsenstein (who had previously studied the physics of music) took a night class in chemistry and embarked for Davis in 1975.

The department upon which they all descended was the preeminent winemaking school in the United States. The University of California's enology and viticulture program was actually the oldest in the world—it had existed for almost a century, ever since Eugene Hilgard, a professor of agriculture, convinced the regents to fund wine research and education on the Berkeley campus in 1880. Twenty-six years later, the University Farm, a site for laboratory and fieldwork, was created in Davis near the state capital of Sacramento in the agricultural wonderland of the Great Central Valley. With the double whammy of World War I and Prohibition, research on alcoholic fermentation was prohibited, and all academic work on wine and wine grapes was suspended—but after repeal in 1933, the V&E department resurfaced at Davis, where its new mission was nothing less Herculean than to rebuild the California wine industry. By that time, most of the state's winemaking technology was obsolete, and much of its winemaking and grape-growing knowledge had disappeared.

The task of resuscitation fell to the first researcher the department hired in 1935: biochemist and plant physiologist Maynard Amerine. An unexpectedly urbane student who grew up on a Modesto farm and did his PhD thesis on the climatic influences in grape growing, Amerine believed that the road to success in California would consist of table wines made from European varieties grown in places with conditions appropriate to each, as opposed to the scattershot New World custom of planting everything everywhere, including all manner of regions and varieties that were poorly matched. In this enterprise, he teamed up with viticulturist Albert J. Winkler in a decades-long study of the state's winegrowing areas, dividing them into five categories based on heat, assessing the quality of wines made there from dozens of different grapes, recommending the best types for each region, and promoting the practice of labeling them according to their varietal names, a marketing approach that now dominates the industry worldwide. Amerine was a singular figure—worldly, well spoken, dignified in bearing, impeccably attired, and epicurean enough to include James Beard and M. F. K. Fisher among his dinner guests. Equally attuned to art and science, Amerine's expertise extended to all aspects of wine, from fermentation to aging to analysis to judging; in the course of a sixty-year career, he published four hundred scientific papers and sixteen books, including such classics as *The Technology of Wine Making*, *Wines: Their Sensory Evaluation* (with Edward B. Roessler), and *Wine: An Introduction for Americans* (with Vernon L. Singleton). After he retired from teaching in 1974, he kept an office on the ground floor of Wickson Hall, where he continued to confer with students and delivered annual addresses that served to inspire future vintners. As one such acolyte observed, "If Dr. Amerine spoke to the wall, the wall would be impressed."

The rest of the faculty, if not as mythic, counted several world authorities among its ranks. Amerine's assistant, Cornelius Ough, was himself an expert in wine analysis and stability; Vernon Singleton in phenolics and aging; James Cook on vine nutrition; Harold Olmo in grape breeding. James Guymon specialized in brandy distillation, which somehow fit with the fact that he was always smoking cigars. Dinsmoor ("Dinny") Webb was equally admired for his knowledge of sherry and his gentlemanly, old-fashioned manner, augmented by a mustache, bushy eyebrows, and an ever-changing series of bow ties, reportedly made every day by his wife. Ralph Kunkee, a trailblazer in wine microbiology and malolactic fermentation, was popular for his parties, where he donned funny hats and served that noted nonvinous libation Jägermeister.

All of these men were members of the department's "Old Guard," appointed around the time of World War II. When they arrived at Davis, the campus was still known as the College of Agriculture, and many of its professors came from farm-experiment stations; almost none had worked in the wine industry, nor (other than Amerine) had much acquaintanceship with European wine. Indeed, some veterans who had helped deliver France from German occupation were disinclined to revere the customs of the Old World. Amerine and Webb— respectively, a former captain in chemical warfare and an ex-chemist on the Manhattan Project—dismissed many traditional winemaking practices, insisting that the experience of the past was of interest only to maintaining the status quo. The university's task was to *improve* the quality of California wine, which effectively meant, in the wake of Prohibition, rehabilitating a run-down neighborhood by creating a corps of construction experts.

"At Davis they have one goal: to make a stable product," says Sacramento wine merchant Darrell Corti. "Every wine school has that same objective, which is very important. When you go to cooking school, first you have to learn how to scrub pots and cook vegetables; at Davis, first you have to make clean wine."

Clark Smith, who attended UC Davis from 1980 to 1982 (and from whom we will hear more), describes modern winemaking thus: "Harvest sound fruit; crush gently to minimize harsh tannins; adjust pH; convert to clean wine with temperature-controlled fermentation in clean vessels (after) inoculation with beneficial yeast and bacteria; protect the resulting wine from oxygen and microbial contamination; age and flavor in oak barrels if appropriate; maintain sulfur dioxide levels; minimize oxygen exposure; cold-stabilize and bottle sterile. Cleanliness, freshness, and varietal character are quality watchwords."

"It was looking at wine in terms of defects instead of complexity," says Mark Lyon, who has worked at Sebastiani Vineyards ever since graduating from Davis in 1978. "There was nothing about blending, or choosing barrels, or how to make fine wine from a plot of land; the classes weren't taught on that level. Instead they taught you how to set up experiments on what makes wine turn brown."

John Kongsgaard, who attended Davis between 1976 and 1979, is even more blunt. "Davis had nothing to do with winemaking," he says. "There wasn't even a winery on campus. It had more to do with chemistry and microbiology, which scared us liberal arts grads to death. We huddled together in the front row of physical chemistry, a required class that was totally unconnected with what we wanted to do—it was just there for rigor, to make sure that wine merchants couldn't get a degree in enology."

Like his classmates Michael Martini and Kathleen Heitz, Kongsgaard had grown up in Napa Valley. Easygoing, tall, and handsome, he was a kind of local aristocrat: His great-grandfather Lilburn Boggs was a former governor of Missouri who had come west with the Donner Party in 1846, but he split off from that group before it resorted to cannibalism in the Sierra Nevada winter. Boggs later became a regional California governor under General Mariano Vallejo. With his wife, Panthea (daughter of one Daniel Boone), he had a son (John's grandfather) who, with money made from a quarry-block business—his company created Treasure Island in San Francisco Bay—amassed a sprawling cattle ranch near Berryessa, east of Napa. John grew up riding horses on a hill called Stonecrest, where one of his neighbors was André Tchelistcheff, the renowned Russian émigré who had elevated the quality of California wine at Beaulieu Vineyards. John's father, Thomas, a superior court judge, was the de facto local emcee and eulogizer, and the Kongsgaard home was a social center that served B.V., Martini, and Inglenook wines to neighbors like the Mondavis and Brother Timothy of Christian Brothers. Still, when John graduated from high school in 1969, there were only eighteen wineries in the entire valley.

Kongsgaard went to Colorado State intending to major in either English or forestry. On one of his trips home from school, however, he drove up the valley to St. Helena to pick up some Stony Hill wine for his parents. The Kongsgaards rarely visited the rural, agricultural northern part of the valley; it was as rife with prunes and walnuts as it was with wine grapes, and it had no decent restaurants, so for special events the family drove to San Francisco. But when John encountered the Stony Hill proprietor, Fred McCrea—elbow propped on his fireplace mantel, holding a glass of chardonnay while listening to *Parsifal*—the younger man said to himself: "I want this guy's life." Not inconveniently, the number of local wineries was in the process of multiplying, and "suddenly there weren't enough winemakers around." After a year studying music, literature, and architecture in Vienna, Munich, and Prague, Kongsgaard spent another two and a half years catching up on science at Monterey Peninsula and Napa Valley community colleges. On Tchelistcheff's advice, he planted a zinfandel vineyard on his parents' hill and entered UC Davis in 1976.

Having grown up around wine, Kongsgaard was different from most people at Davis. "Everybody was a hick to me," he discloses. "I already had a wine worldview, so I was there on the take, for whatever I could get out of the science. I was engaged with the other students, but detached from the institution—I was only forty-five minutes from home, and I was the only son and heir apparent in my family. I didn't need success at Davis to succeed in the wine business." Thus shrugging off any academic urgency, Kongsgaard focused his attention on the off-campus "curriculum." Since Davis didn't permit alcohol on campus, and students couldn't look to teachers for much education about wine itself ("Professors don't make enough money to have nice cellars," says

Ralph Kunkee), they cohered into private tasting groups conducted on their own time and tab. "On Tuesday nights we took over Collette's, a restaurant specializing in omelets," says John Buechsenstein. "Or we'd meet at somebody's house to taste port or sauternes, and everybody would bring a bottle. What was so cool was that we had these diverse backgrounds, but were all studying what we loved."

Coming to Davis from South Africa, which was then being boycotted for its apartheid policies, Hildegarde Heymann hadn't been exposed to much international wine variety. However, her Australian housemate Pam Dunsford's scholarship stipulated that she direct some of the moneys toward tasting. "She had an endless supply of interesting wine," Heymann recalls. "French, German, Californian . . . Australian semillon, muscat, and shiraz . . . verticals of Heitz cabernet. . . . We tasted from ten p.m. to midnight on Monday, Tuesday, Wednesday, and Thursday; later we started going to other people's houses—Rollin Soles's, Rich Cushman's, Janet Myers's, Kathy Joseph's." The in crowd consisted of graduate students like Kongsgaard, Buechsenstein, Ward, Nalle, John Williams, Cathy Corison, Paul Hobbs, Nick Martin, Dan Lee, Tom Peterson, Jack Stuart, and their crony David Graves, who didn't actually matriculate but took a full course load through UC Davis Extension. Ward, who had a wife and baby, also worked part-time in Corti's Sacramento wineshop, enabling him to contribute a complement of Italian bottlings, supplemented by sundry northern-European benchmarks. He and Kongsgaard were the most frequent hosts, though the custom stipulated that everyone bring a dinner course and a wine to go with it.

"The idea was to bring the most bizarre, cool wine you could think of," Kongsgaard remembers. "One time I brought a dry white '45 Carbonnieux Bordeaux, with a turban of sole stuffed with spinach and salmon mousse. Ramey's specialty was zabaglione with dessert wine; Dick hung pheasants in his cellar for three weeks. We got lots of good Bordeaux together and tasted them in flights of six—one wine for each commune, Left Bank, Right Bank—and identified them blind. Ward was learning about port at Corti's, so one time we had an all-Fonseca tasting, with the best vintages of each decade going back to the 1920s.

Normally, to do that kind of thing you had to be a rich connoisseur nut, but we were just eager beaver grad students. We all had to chip in, and it took a year to get them all together. Everybody had their port awakening that day, when we all ended up ranking them exactly the same—according to age."

Before some tastings, samples of wines would be extracted from bottles with hypodermic needles for laboratory analysis. "It was a huge familiarization with questions like, What's the proper acid balance? Should chardonnay be malolactic? What are the effects of different barrels?" says Ramey. "We helped each other pick out faults like *Brett-anomyces* and volatile acidity—if you weren't trained to identify them, they might not bother you as much. One wine that I ranked really high somebody told me had hydrogen sulfide—I had found it an element of 'complexity,' but after I learned to pick it out, I stopped appreciating it. We'd get wines from Napa and Sonoma and mix and match them with their European models, trying to figure out what wine was and what it should be. We had no interest in anything else like law, medicine, or business; we were completely absorbed and fixated on wine. There was so much to learn—we couldn't do it fast enough. We shared our lab reports and helped each other out, in school and after. It was all really collegial. There were no secrets."

A couple of times a year, Kongsgaard's group reassembled the best wines for a party at his parents' hilltop house in Napa, augmented by classical music and a view that stretched from Stag's Leap to Mount Saint Helena. "It was a gala event, with just the great wines," Kongsgaard says. "I would con my rich friends into bringing something like a '45 Latour or TBA Riesling. My Carmel boarding-school roommate, Dade Thieriot, provided us with old Bordeaux and Burgundy from Connoisseur Wine Imports—startling wines that helped us become connoisseurs."

Kongsgaard was also an acquaintance of Nathan Fay, the Napa grape grower whose fruit would eventually find its way into Stag's Leap cabernet. At the time, Fay was selling it to Heitz and Mondavi, but in 1977 he agreed to sell three tons to Kongsgaard and his friends, each of whom produced a sixty-gallon barrel—the first wine most of them had ever made. Kongsgaard thus defined a role that culminated in actually making wine on campus. Despite Davis's lack of a production facility, the department did own four barrels, which Kongsgaard managed to commandeer for research on barrel fermentation. Thinking perhaps of his pal Ramey, "the boy wonder of the liberal arts class," who wrote his master's thesis on *Volatile Ester Hydrolysis or Formation During Storage of Model Solutions and Wines,* Kongsgaard says, "All these people were doing arcane studies, but as the practical Napa guy, I just wanted to figure out where the yeast was in the barrel."

Kongsgaard also revived the practice (begun, over the objections of some faculty members, by Jed Steele, who would alter the course of California wine at Kendall-Jackson) of inviting professional winemakers to speak to the students, attempting to bridge the gap between the department and the industry. Since it was possible to get a degree in enology without taking all the viticulture courses—or any at all in business—André Tchelistcheff informed his listeners that they needed more of both. To illustrate the importance of marketing, an ad executive from McCann-Erickson described the development of Italian Swiss Colony's TV commercials featuring "that little old winemaker, me." John Franzia of Bronco, future copurveyor of Two Buck Chuck, maintained that his company made only two wines: red and white ("We used to make rosé, but decided to simplify"), and that the term "premium" should be restricted to crackers. A representative of Franzia's uncles' company, E. & J. Gallo, explained how hundreds of thousands of cases of their Hearty Burgundy were made in monthly batches, each identical to the next. At the opposite end of the quality spectrum, Joe Heitz, a member of the UC Davis class of 1951, advised against rinsing glasses with water when switching from one wine to another, seeing as how "all wines have more in common with each other than any of them have with water."

The students themselves didn't lack for eccentricity. As someone who had actually grown up in a winemaking family, Mike Martini commanded a degree of fascination among his peers; it didn't hurt that he also played guitar in a rock band and got around by motorcycle. Rollin Soles's Texas accent was impressive in a different way, as were the softball abilities Doug Nalle displayed on the department's intramural team, the "Haut Sauternes." Gil Nickel, a rich kid (and future proprietor of Nickel & Nickel) who was auditing classes, was known for following the V&E bus into the vineyard in his gold Mercedes. Mark Lyon, an undergraduate from Arizona, attracted attention with his orange jumpsuits, which he now says he wore as "a disguise, and to show I was different, instead of telling people I'd spent the weekend at a wild party in San Francisco dancing and having sex all night." At the height of the Harvey Milk era, this complied with the customary east-of-San-Francisco "don't ask, don't tell" policy, which Lyon navigated in the usual ways—privately registering, for example, Ralph Kunkee's avowal of affection for disco heels. "If I heard a derogatory comment about Amerine making a pass at some guy, I knew that [the speaker] wasn't somebody I could be open with," says Lyon.

Ramey remembers Lyon as one of two students who "always asked the weirdest, most exasperating questions in class." The other was someone whom Kongsgaard recalls as "an odd duck from L.A."—a "straight arrow" in John Buechsenstein's estimation, a person whom David Graves "could have picked out of a lineup by his well-laundered pink shirts." Indeed, where everyone else went around in T-shirts, flip-flops, and shorts, even on vineyard trips this weirdo wore a coat and tie, just as he'd learned to do at the Beverly Hills Wine Merchant.

"I was a jerk," Randall Grahm acknowledges. "I was freaked out at Davis. I felt completely different from the other students—on the outside looking in. Being socially inept, I didn't talk to anyone very much; I was a snob, but my air of superiority was masking my insecurity. After all, I'd been at Santa Cruz and MIT and the Beverly Hills Wine Merchant, by comparison to which Davis seemed flat and dull. I'd drunk French wine and hobnobbed with insiders, so I thought I knew wine. But sitting next to people named Martini and Heitz was more impressive to me than movie stars. They actually knew how to do stuff—they could drive a tractor, and knew which end of the pruning shears to use. I couldn't tell one weed from another! I felt I was more intense than most of them, but it turned out these guys *really worked hard.* I was shocked—I'd always been commitmentphobic, and suddenly I looked at myself and said: *Dude, do you realize you've just committed to a career by accident?* I definitely wasn't in the groove, and my first quarter I didn't get good grades. I had to recalibrate: *Dude, you're gonna have to work hard for the first time in your life.*"

Like Mark Lyon, Grahm's study partner Janet Pagano had gotten interested in wine as a teenager. Growing up in San Francisco, she was a self-described nerd who "fell in love with the aesthetics and sophistication" of wine through classes at UCSF Extension (a trick she pulled off by looking "older than my age"). Like Grahm, she had embarked for college with the idea of becoming a doctor but thought that in the meantime "viticulture and enology classes seemed like an incredibly sexy way to get premed credits."

On her first day at Davis, Pagano attended Vernon Singleton's introductory course, which included off-the-cuff advice on food-and-wine pairing. "He recommended something like muscatel with shrimp," Pagano remembers. "It was startling how much the Central Valley influenced the curriculum—it had very little to do with the kinds of wines I was interested in. When the class ended, I bumped into Randall on the steps, both of us reeling from this information which was so completely different from what we'd expected. It turned out we had a common interest in European wines, and a lot of overlapping classes—as fermentation-science majors, we had to take a whole slew of other crazy classes like food mycology and plant sanitation. It seemed wacky—we wanted to be winemakers, but we were spending all this time studying food science. I'm sure that enhanced Randall's sense of disconnect."

As a defense against their mutual befuddlement, Grahm and Pagano formed an alliance that Randall refers to as "Nerd Central." Neither they nor Lyon ever became part of any tasting cliques. "Randall was truly different from the rest of the students," says Pagano. "He was intellectually engaged in a way that I didn't see with the others. He was really driven by a desire to make profound wine, and he was already thinking in a very big aesthetic context—asking very big questions. I was only nineteen at the time, so it was very stimulating for me to be around him. And yes, Randall was the only person I knew whose shirts had visible creases from laundering."

Though it doesn't compute for anyone who has spent time around him recently, Grahm even wore a coat and tie to Jim Cook's pruning class—at least until he started sweating. Perhaps as a result of removing it, he underwent an epiphany. "Pruning was cosmic—a lovely, soothing, meditative experience," he says. "It felt so natural and great—especially with head-trained vines, you could visualize the shape and make a sculptured thing. I adored pruning in a way that I certainly didn't love science classes."

This is partly why Grahm ended up majoring not in fermentation but in plant science (which also happened to get him out of taking physical chemistry, the course that Kongsgaard identified as preventing "wine merchants" from obtaining enology degrees). It was in Cook's class, however, that Grahm had one of his most contentious—and notorious—educational encounters. A quintessential "ag" professor, the fair-skinned, blue-eyed, white-haired, potbellied, Georgia-reared Cook was known on campus as a redneck (with a nose to match: when classes went on field trips to the Martini winery, the staff would always have several cases ready for him). It was said that Cook chafed in the shadow of Winkler in the same way that Ough did behind Amerine—albeit more pugnaciously, resulting in a personality that was alternately humorous and irascible. "You didn't want to talk to Cook before eleven a.m. when he got up to speed," John Buechsenstein says. "He could be nasty."

One morning well before eleven, Grahm put a characteristically irritating question to Cook. "Since pinot noir is known by Francophiles"—of whom Cook was not, it's safe to say, one—"to reach its highest expression in the limestone soils of Burgundy," Grahm asked, "might it not make sense in California to dig holes under pinot noir vines and there deposit calcium carbonate?"

A dark look clouded Cook's ruddy face as he considered the question. "Why not just bury cash instead?" he barked at the overthinking Angeleno. "It would be a lot less trouble and have the same effect."

Grahm's questions about pinot noir soon became a joke in the department. "He would ask about pinot noir no matter what the topic was," says Hildegarde Heymann. "Even if a professor was talking about the western, highly salinated slopes of the San Joaquin Valley, Randall would want to know how to grow pinot noir there." Raised on the Old World academic model, where "professors were gods"

(Christian Mouiex, a Davis transfer student and scion of the famous Bordeaux family that owns Château Pétrus, caught his belt on the back of his chair when jumping up as a teacher entered a classroom), Heymann was incredulous at Grahm's impertinence. "Randall and I had Roger Boulton's wine-processing class together," she remembers. "It was in Hutchinson Hall, which had a front entrance with doors on either side of the podium. Randall would show up ten or fifteen minutes late every time, carrying his bike up the steps. With his hair going everywhere, he reminded me of the lead actor on a British TV show called *Doctor Who*. I was in a state of shock that anybody could get away with this."

Another notable transgression occurred in a class taught by Ann Noble. A flavor chemist and expert on tomatoes who "didn't know anything about wine when I came here," Noble (like Boulton) was a recent arrival at Davis, having been hired from Massachusetts in 1974 to teach the sensory-evaluation course inaugurated by Amerine. In the food industry, sensory evaluation is a hard-core science incorporating such notably nonsubjective disciplines as inferential statistics, multivariant analysis, and threshold testing. As taught by Noble, the class also reflected the thinking behind her famous "Aroma Wheel," which catalogs common wine fragrances by comparing them to smells from the animal, vegetable, mineral, and chemical kingdoms. Class members studied four wines per week, learning to identify them by characteristic flavors "the same way you can identify a Doric, Ionic, or Corinthian column." Thus students who anticipated a fun class on "wine tasting" were as rudely awakened as those who had come to Davis expecting to study "winemaking."

"We learned from Ann how to look at results and figure out if they were real or random," Kongsgaard says. "In a clinical situation, you'd be given a wine spiked with varying levels of tannin, volatile acidity, or *Brettanomyces*. You learned that sugar masks tannin, and acid masks sugar, and all kinds of other things. In strict sensory science, you have to discipline yourself not to say that a wine is 'sexy' or 'suave' or 'superficial.' Even if you want to be a poetic taster, it's good to know *why* a wine seems sexy or superficial."

Noble also conducted research on bitterness and astringency, which perhaps influenced her personal style. An infamously abrasive character whose "mind is light-years ahead of her mouth" (Buechsenstein), Noble was known for brusque dismissals, frequently issued in four-letter form, of people who tried her patience. When Cook advised her that she'd never get tenure if she didn't stop cursing, Noble said, "'Fuck you!' He cursed all the time." If a student's lab report wasn't up to snuff, she employed a pair of rubber ink stamps—one showing a picture of a chicken, the other simply saying SHIT. Calling upon these same tools, she flunked Kongsgaard's first lab report because she thought he was having "too much fun." (Kongsgaard, who calls Noble "a dear soul with a gruff exterior," gave her a book of Kenneth Patchen's poetry.)

Heymann, who did her PhD work with Noble and later succeeded her in teaching sensory evaluation at Davis, says that her mentor "can be difficult or very generous. If you drop a tray of glasses you'll be annihilated, but if you drop a gas cylinder that could be a bomb, she's very calm." Heymann relates the story of how, after getting her PhD and going to the University of Missouri to teach sensory science, she was diagnosed with lymphoma via a telephone message on a Friday night. "Ann happened to call me on Saturday morning, and she could tell that something was wrong," Heymann says. "After I told her the news, she said to do this and this and this and hung up. I just went back to bed, but at six p.m. my doorbell rang and it was Ann. She'd hardly even had time to get there—the time difference with California is two hours, and the flying time is more than three. But she got me out of bed and made me go for a walk, and I came back and slept for the first time in three days." Today Heymann is cancer-free.

As another poetic soul admittedly inclined toward "airy-fairy" wine descriptions, Grahm was not naturally disposed toward sensory science, which he describes as "far too rigorous for someone as ADD-afflicted as myself." Hence, one day when the topic of discussion was—er—pinot noir, Randall found himself objecting to something that Noble said in class. Although today there's disagreement on exactly what it was—Noble, now retired, thinks she was "pooh-poohing his pinot fetish," while Grahm believes that Noble was "talking about how interesting a grape was pinot noir, and I saw a hanging curveball and went for it"—both confirm that, as he sat in the class-room and Noble stood at the lectern, Randall accused the caustic prof of "pinot envy."

"The whole class looked at me to see how I would react," Noble remembers, "but I couldn't say anything, because I was doubled over laughing." Today Noble unequivocally calls Grahm a "genius" who was "always thinking outside the box."

Ralph Kunkee remembers Grahm as "kind of quiet" and "not a standout," but recalls with fondness a pinot experiment that Randall proposed. "He bought a lot of expensive Burgundy and wanted to filter out the bacteria to use for malolactic fermentation in California," says Kunkee. "To check it, we put the bacteria into a nutrient base, and it all turned out to be dead. I wasn't surprised, but I was sad; I thought it was a good idea."

An idea not unlike importing limestone into your vineyard. "I thought I could make European wines in California," Grahm says now. "I was so naive—I had this clunky mechanical view that if you get the right clones, and limestone soil, and find out what barrels those Frenchmen are using, and pick the grapes at the same [sugar level] as them, you could make the same wine. In other words, what are the *things* that you need? I didn't apprehend that you have to find a site that has rhythm, or intelligence."

Needless to say, rhythm and intelligence were not conditions that the faculty was inclined to study, much less endorse. "The viticulture department was still very much in the thrall of Winkler, who was sort of an American-California jingoist," Grahm observes. "What could a French person possibly understand about grape growing? We are bathed in light; they are mired in darkness. We are science; they are superstition. Davis was like the Alfred Kinsey of the wine world: If you're obsessed with studying, understanding, and controlling, you miss out on the most interesting aspects."

"Academics are more comfortable with objective standards, even though subjectivity is what makes wine interesting," agrees Mark Lyon. "Roger [Boulton] might say there's no chemical difference be-tween filtered and unfiltered wines. But what about taste?"

Kongsgaard, who did his master's thesis under Boulton's supervision, agrees. "Boulton was a chemical engineer who could tell you everything going on in wine, but not what it should taste like," says Kongsgaard. "He's not interested in the culture of wine—only in the chemistry. He wanted us to understand that wine is more stable and fresher at a lower pH, which encouraged people to pick earlier. He's also antimalolactic for white wine—he thought it was all about freshness, where we thought it was about complexity."

Today Boulton, who emigrated from Australia to teach at Davis the same year (1976) that Kongsgaard, Ramey, and Ward arrived as students, is, more than any other individual, the professor who represents the V&E department to the outside world. Renowned for his influential work on things like filtration technology and color extraction, but (as Kongsgaard's comments show) disparaged for contributions to trends like the much-maligned move toward high-acid "food wines" that characterized California in the early 1980s, Boulton is a quintessential scientist. "Roger simply showed up at Davis with something no one had ever employed before—a chemical engineer's organized inquiry into wine's nature and the best ways to tackle its production," says Clark Smith. "He built in his head an amazing model of winemaking, and then taught it to us." Unfortunately for the liberal arts crowd, this required "a working grasp of equilibrium dynamics, crystallization kinetics, fluid flow behavior, and interactions between such disparate concepts as pH, temperature, speeds of competing reactions, enzymatic effects, plant metabolism, [and] properties of metals."

"In my first class I couldn't understand him," says (the South African) Heymann of Boulton. "But others told me, 'Don't worry. We can't understand him either—he's Australian.'" Somewhat surprisingly, today Heymann also calls Boulton "the most passionate man I've ever met." Daniel Press, who within a few years would be working for Randall Grahm, remembers Boulton's eyes welling up in class when the professor was going through a divorce. "One day I came to his office to explore the idea of interning in Australia," Press recalls. "He started telling me about Gallipoli and the toll World War I had on his country, and he sobbed there in front of me. I was very moved—and a little flustered."

In my experience, the personable, mustachioed, soft-spoken but fast-talking Boulton is remarkable for his patience and willingness to explain complex topics to all comers—students, professionals, and unscientific laymen alike. Like most of his colleagues in the V&E department, he seems committed above all else to rationality, data, and proof. When I visited Boulton in his office (Wickson Hall has been recently supplanted by the spanking-new three-building Robert Mondavi Institute for Wine and Food Science), he told me that the goal of the Davis education is "understanding, not knowledge. We're here to give students a toolbox, not our personal opinions about what to make, drink, or grow." Ann Noble had made a similar remark: "If I *tell* you something, your expectation will affect your perception," she said. "That's not how to teach about wine."

After Boulton quietly regaled me about the talents of V&E students ("Their combination of brilliance and passion really is unusual"), the department's international reach ("UC Davis has two degrees of separation worldwide"), the baby winemaker boom ("The seventies generation had a special time and opportunity"), and the effect of corporatization on quality ("You don't even have to have a friggin' winemaker"), I relayed David Ramey's—and, by inference, Randall Grahm's—desire that Davis spend more time studying the science behind traditional Old World practices. For example, allowing grapes to ferment on natural yeasts from the vineyard, rather than inoculating them with selected commercial strains.

Framing the proposal in light of the department's teaching philosophy, Boulton said: "We would give our view of [such practices] and the reason they're not consistent if something works half the time. Let's say you've got ten tanks of chardonnay, all inoculated with native flora. Five of them begin fermenting in the first day or two, and the others take a week or more. What can you conclude about natural flora? That it's variable. And if you look at the population that dominates at the end, it turns out to be the same strains that are typically [used in commercial winemaking]—so then you get back to variability, and which tanks to hold up as an example. You have to look at the very best and very worst and ask: Do we want this every year? Do we want to wait a week or more? In the world of science, we argue that the only way you can talk about the benefits of native yeast is to have blind tastings with some designation of how much percentage of the yeast is native. Of your ten chardonnays, which vineyard they come from and what levels of phenolics and nutrition they had in the vineyard has more to do with how they're going to ferment than whether you used natural flora or not. We don't demonize wild yeast; we just don't think it's a very effective way to get a fermentation done reliably."

I noted that he did mention the importance of tasting—which, I guess, is where "sensory science" comes in. "Most of the [traditional] knowledge in Europe was empirical," Boulton continued. "The problem with empiricism is that the answers are very local, and very much from the individual. Most things that are empirical are right some of the time and wrong some of the time; their beauty is that they've been shuttled to and fro, and juggled a bit, and maybe there's a [valid] part that's come forward, but you don't know if a false part has also come forward. So if they say, 'We run around the vine three times because that's what we do here,' in the science world we say, 'What happens if you only run twice? Or you run around this vine but not this one? Or if you don't run?'"

In other words: We are science, and they are superstition?

"If you go to a place like [Burgundy] and ask people why they do things and they answer that they do them because that's the way they do them, it doesn't get you anywhere," Boulton said. "That was quite apparent, even in the seventies. Amerine's and Winkler's understanding of climate didn't come from Bordeaux or Burgundy. If you like pinot noir, you can try and find a place *like* Burgundy, but it's not Burgundy, so when you realize you never can make Burgundy here, what are you going to do? How do you make use of the empiricism known there and translate it to a place that isn't the same? The role of the department has been to encourage people to go to the next level and do those things."

And so they would, for better or worse.

LTHOUGH HE NEVER benefited from the UC system, Leo McCloskey—like Randall Grahm and so many other Davis students—grew up in California. Leo spent his early childhood in San Francisco during the 1950s—a period that, preceding as it did the "Manhattanization" of the city's skyline, has been called its golden age. Leo remembers riding the bus around town by himself for a nickel, seeing numerous poets and artists wearing "little black hats," and (somewhat later) hearing Jimi Hendrix at the Fillmore. Leo's father had a manufacturing business called Tropicraft, making Asian-style window shades supported by bamboo slats, on Howard Street south of Market; one job took him to "Heart o' the Mountain," Alfred Hitchcock's retreat in the Santa Cruz Mountains, and in 1958, when Leo was in the third grade, the family moved forty-five miles south to the foot of those same hills, settling in the newly incorporated city of Cupertino in the Santa Clara Valley. There the McCloskeys lived on a street bordered by prune and cherry orchards, although—attended by an explosion of industrial parks and shopping centers and start-up companies like Hewlett-Packard and Fairchild Semiconductor—the so-called Valley of Heart's Delight was already beginning its metamorphosis into Silicon Valley.

As a boy, Leo—the oldest of seven children—was as much into painting and drawing as he was into science, inclined toward creating moody self-portraits and "Alice-in-Wonderland-style" fantasy landscapes. Not that he was so dreamy as to neglect the bottom line: Starting with a push mower but quickly upgrading to fossil fuel, he was a local lawn-maintenance magnate, going door to door to gain customers and even employing other kids. The proceeds supported his surfing and audio-engineering hobbies: When not crossing the mountains on Highway 17 to catch the waves at Shark's Cove and Pleasure Point, Leo taught himself Morse code, built his own amplifiers and stereos, and turned the roof of his family's house into a formidable ham-radio installation (ultimately condemned by Pacific Gas and Electric when the jungle of antennae extended higher than the neighborhood's telephone and electricity lines). Passing the FCC novice test at age eleven, the young communicator soon found himself engaged in intimate conversations with considerably older insomniacs. "One guy told me all about his marriage problems at one o'clock in the morning," McCloskey remembers. "I would try to make my voice deep, but after a while he asked: 'How old are you?' When I said, 'Twelve,' he hung up."

As a freshman at San Jose State, McCloskey planned to major in art, but when his mother got wind of the idea ("She came from a farming background and wanted me to be a professional"), he transferred to Oregon State and majored in general science. Alongside standard-issue courses in chemistry and biology, the subject that gripped McCloskey's imagination hardest was the *philosophy* of science—particularly the work of Thomas Kuhn, whose 1962 book *The Structure of Scientific Revolutions* maintains that science progresses by revolutionary transformations or "paradigm shifts" rather than through the gradual, orderly accumulation of knowledge.

"The average scientist is so conservative," McCloskey comments. "Change is usually rejected because it would empower younger people. The wine academy, for example, rejects anything not developed at the academy because it would mean they're the last to know. Mavericks are the ones who make changes." Upon graduating in 1971, he planned to pursue a PhD in the philosophy of science ("I didn't want to be a cog in the wheels of industry; ever since I was in high school, I wanted to be a professor or an artist"), but he failed to win a fellowship, and his "parents weren't interested in funding a PhD program. They were more of the Horatio Alger persuasion." As a result, he came back to Cupertino and got a job at Syntex Pharmaceutical, doing research on the drug naproxen; unfortunately, upon his arrival, "they had a dog cut open in the operating room, and it was still alive. I couldn't take it—I was gonna barf."

At the time, McCloskey had an acquaintance who, in exchange for serving as caretaker at Ridge Vineyards, happened to occupy the oldest cabin on Monte Bello Ridge, two thousand feet above Cupertino. Winegrowing in the Santa Cruz Mountains had a hundred-year history, starting in the Vine Hill area near Scotts Valley, expanding into the Ben Lomond district around Bonny Doon (founded by a Scottish immigrant named John Burns), and extending north to the "Chaine d'Or" above Cupertino and Woodside, where Emmet Rixford raised legendary cabernet sauvignon and the Frenchman Paul Masson made sparkling wine at the turn of the twentieth century. More recently, a lawyer named Chaffee Hall and the Francophile stockbroker Martin Ray had championed varietal estate bottling, followed by postwar experimentalists like Hewlett-Packard engineer Dan Wheeler and dermatologist David Bruce.

Originally planted in 1886 by a San Francisco doctor named Osea Perrone, Ridge's Monte Bello vineyard was owned by a group of scientists who had resurrected the estate in 1959: David Bennion, Hew Crane, Charlie Rosen, and Howard Zeidler, who all worked at the Stanford Research Institute (SRI). Autumn of 1971 was the second harvest overseen by the now-iconic winemaker Paul Draper, who was just beginning to increase production and organize the place. Despite its foundations, Ridge was not a very scientific winery—it was known for pure, powerful products made by primitive Old World methods, largely on their own recognizance with no intervention by such uptight intrusions as filters or fining or monitoring of preservatives such as sulfur dioxide. Some of the wines were produced in pickle tanks, and basic microbiological processes like malolactic fermentation (which turns tart, appley malic acid into soft, buttery lactic acid) were still something of a mystery, often occurring by accident and sometimes after wines were bottled, resulting in unplanned effervescence and obnoxious aromas.

"Multiple cars of people were driving back up to Ridge with fizzy bottles of wine," McCloskey remembers. "Some of the whites were cloudy and oxidized, and some of the reds were refermenting. Some had hydrogen sulfide, which smells like rotten eggs." Although, as Draper points out, the '70 and '71 Monte Bellos were two of the best California cabernet sauvignons of the era, between the University of California at Davis—the industry's standard bearer for chemically stable, lab-certified wine—and the emerging boutique sector there was a gap you could drive a grape truck through. "Except for Amerine's *Technology of Wine Making*, a relic from the 1950s, you couldn't read a book in English on fine-wine production," McCloskey says. "The academy just said to filter and use mass-production techniques to turn it into bland wine, but the [artisan approach] was to have no quality control at all. It was silly in America, the land of science."

Upon arriving at Ridge, one of the first things McCloskey noticed was a bumper sticker that read MAKE WINE, NOT WAR. Hired to wash barrels by Bennion—the winery's sole vintner during its first decade—Leo liked the atmosphere of the place. The owners' kids were usually around, and in the heyday of the *Whole Earth Catalog*, the winery was populated by independent and innovative thinkers. McCloskey knew nothing about enology, but as a biology student he understood fermentation and yeast, and winemaking was a pursuit that merged his artistic and scientific sides. He proceeded to round out his education by reading every existing issue of the *American Journal of Enology and Viticulture*, to which Bennion subscribed. The open-minded older man took a liking to the ambitious younger one, who stuck around for the ensuing harvest, assisting with Ridge's tiny production of white wines. When one of these—a blend of chardonnay and sylvaner from the historic Vine Hill vineyard—remained cloudy after fermentation was finished, Leo (already conversant with the contents of wine-lab catalogs) suggested using a cellulose-and-gelatin compound called Sparkalloid to "fine" the wine by precipitating out its suspended solids. After getting a green light from Bennion, he applied the product in late afternoon when no one else was at the winery; as he later described the results to wine historian Charles Sullivan:

I looked down into the tank and saw something moving. I ran and got a drop light and poked it down into this pickle tank and it looked as if there were manta rays swimming in the wine. . . . It wouldn't settle. I sat down and waited on into the evening and was really getting nervous. I'd just recently been hired and things were going well and it looks as if I've screwed up this huge batch of wine. And this was my idea. Finally I called Dave later at night, maybe eight o'clock. So I told him about these huge sheets of Jell-O in the wine and he said, "Don't worry about it." . . . To him winemaking was not an emergency situation. And the next morning the wine was beautiful. It was the first fined wine made at Ridge.

The following year McCloskey continued to work at the winery while reenrolling at San Jose State to pursue a master's degree in chemistry. In spring of 1972 Bennion took him to the annual meeting of American Society for Enology and Viticulture (ASEV) in Monterey, where he got a glimpse of Maynard Amerine, the UC Davis professor credited with resurrecting the California wine industry after Prohibition. "He looked like someone from a 1940s film," Leo remembers. "Elegant and in charge—a superstar. This was the man who had developed the technology of winemaking."

Prior to McCloskey's arrival, Ridge's laboratory consisted of roughly three pieces of equipment, which were capable of testing wine for alcohol, total acidity, and volatile acidity. When the young chemist asked permission to improve on it, his scientist bosses—the only people McCloskey had ever met who liked to stay up late talking about things like spectrophotometers—said, "Sure." Thus endeavoring to fill the winery's enological gaps, by the time McCloskey was twenty-three he'd published his master's thesis on enzymatic methods for measuring alcohol and malolactic fermentation (both now standard industry procedures), and by twenty-five he had patented methods for detecting acetic acid and ethyl acetate. As he later told Sullivan, "Robert Mondavi had people out of Davis who had the basic winemaking chemistry down perfect, but people were still looking at Ridge as being out on the edge. For them it was like having an experimental winery run for you for free."

As wineries in the Santa Cruz Mountains multiplied, Ridge's phone began ringing with calls from vintners seeking advice. Hence, on his father's recommendation, McCloskey started a consulting business called Santa Cruz Agricultural Chemistry. To bolster his credentials, he bought a Peugeot 504 (matching those owned by Draper and Bennion), the better to confirm that France was the standard of style, quality, and performance. He couldn't afford to put a radio in it, but his father assured him that he could buy one as soon as he started getting clients. With this as an incentive, before long he had compiled a roster that included Calera, J. Lohr, Monterey Peninsula, and David Bruce.

In the course of his consulting, McCloskey encountered a Western Airlines pilot named John Pollard, who aspired to start a winery in the Santa Cruz Mountains. This MBA-toting aviator had already formed a partnership with a local grape grower named Jim Beauregard, whose family's roots in the region ran generations deep. Beauregard's grandfather Amos had acquired 250 acres around Bonny Doon in the 1940s, when the area—a hotbed of mining, bootlegging, and property disputes—had been nicknamed Battle Mountain; a sometime sheriff's deputy, Amos had been involved in numerous shootouts and once beat up a judge. His son Emmett (Jim's father, aka Bud) had started a well-known wine-selling grocery store called Shopper's Corner in Soquel, and the family still owned an old head-pruned vineyard in Bonny Doon that had been a local station for the climate research that Maynard Amerine and Albert Winkler were conducting for UC Davis. One day, when Bud was positioning his tractor to pull out an old chestnut tree that had been split apart in a storm, Amerine pulled up in his car and—asking for a zinc bolt, cable, and couple of steel plates—instead helped Beauregard rebuild the tree, which today still covers half the yard in which it stands.

Besides his family property, Jim had leases on the old Vine Hill and Hallcrest vineyards, both of which contained a lot of riesling vines. Pollard and Beauregard had each made red wine at home, but neither had any experience with white, which is much more fragile. Hence, after showing off his Peugeot (but not saying anything about Sparkalloid), McCloskey was soon not only their winemaker but also a one-third owner of the company. ("My father counseled me to get a little piece of the action everywhere I went," Leo says.) Pollard, the president and business manager, had been planning to produce the first vintage in a garage, but McCloskey—a consultant, after all— insisted on a more "presentable" winery. Inside of a month, Pollard had arranged to acquire the old Hallcrest facility, a venerable red-wood-and-concrete building complete with a bell tower and cellar excavated from an adjoining hillside. In disuse for decades, it was choked with cobwebs, but after refurbishing the winery and outfitting it with a state-of-the-art Demoisy crusher, Sirugue French-oak barrels, and three-hundred-gallon casks, the partners rebonded it with the name of the road on which it was located—a steep, four-mile-long connector between the sleepy town of Felton and the lofty spine of Empire Grade: Felton Empire, suggesting suitably grandiose fortunes.

Felton Empire aimed to focus attention on the Santa Cruz Mountains, specifically with grapes from vineyards that the company controlled. On the Hallcrest property, this included forty acres of cabernet sauvignon and eighty acres of riesling. McCloskey duly drove to Temecula in San Diego County to visit Karl Werner, a German immigrant who was making riesling at Callaway Vineyards—and that spring, carrying a letter of introduction from Werner, he flew to Europe and traveled the valleys of the Rhine, Mosel, and Saar, visiting illustrious names like J. J. Prüm and Serriger Vogelsang, whose dizzying vineyard was so steep that laborers were lowered into it with winches. "Serriger Vogelsang from the Saar and Wehlener Sonnenuhr from the Mosel are only an hour apart, but they smell completely different," McCloskey says. "Riesling aromatics are driven by terpenes, so its terroir expresses itself differently as you move around." Though postwar Germany had led the way into modern wine technology via sterile filtration and stainless steel, McCloskey noted that many old-line producers still used oversize oak casks and aged the wine on its lees (sediment left over from fermentation and pressing). The main thing that impressed him, though, was that fermentations typically took place in cellars that were "icy cold, so they lasted for four months instead of a week."

September in the Santa Cruz Mountains that year was unusually hot, and the Hallcrest fruit got very ripe—uncharacteristically so for the cabernet, which typically ripened only about one year in three. At the end of the month, an early-fall rainstorm blew through, exerting no effect on the cabernet (a notoriously rot-resistant grape) but turning the riesling black with mold. Beauregard—who despite a decade of grape-growing experience had never heard of *Botrytis cinerea*, the "noble rot" that, by dehydrating grapes and concentrating their sugars and acids, is responsible for the great German trockenbeerenauslese (TBA) dessert wines—thought they had a disaster on their hands, but McCloskey exulted, "This is just what we want!" Refrigerating the juice at forty degrees Fahrenheit, they fermented it on German yeast for 110 days and stopped the fermentation at 10 percent alcohol and 7 percent residual sugar—resulting not so much in a dessert wine as a semisweet spätlese style "that you could drink toward the beginning of a meal—not just floral but a little bit spicy, with a lot of acid and structure. It was smooth and clean, not cloying." Hoping to fetch three or four dollars a bottle for it, the partners decided to bottle the wine early, and by midsummer all five thousand bottles had sold out at eight dollars each. The wine later won a gold medal at the Los Angeles County Fair.

McCloskey also made wine that fall from Vine Hill, source of the sylvaner and chardonnay in which he'd released the manta rays. Ridge had since sold the vineyard to Dick Smothers of the Smothers Brothers TV comedy team—who, after seeing the results of Felton Empire's first vintage, asked McCloskey to make wine for him too. Leo describes Smothers as "a nice, even-keeled guy," though he reports that the brothers' stage roles—Dick the straight man, Tom the goofball—were misleading, as Dick was a "bon vivant" and "very funny." Nevertheless McCloskey must have found Smothers somehow handicapped in the fun-loving department, because in order "to show him how to have a good time," Leo escorted the entertainer to a meeting of the Santa Cruz Mountains Winegrowers' Association, held at David Bruce's house.

"At the time, Dick was the most famous person in the California wine industry," McCloskey remembers. "Knowing he'd be there, the place was packed. But the association was very eccentric, and people started giving him the business." To wit, this group of self-sufficient mavericks—whose ranks included wineries with names like David Bruce, Thomas Fogarty, Martin Ray, and Roudon-Smith—demanded to know why the newcomer had titled his winery after himself. In response, a deadpan Smothers launched into a story about a botched poultry birth on his ranch, explaining that duck and geese eggs are so big that they often get stuck on their way out of the bird. As a result, he maintained, he'd considered calling his winery "Impacted Egg Vineyards" but eventually elected to go with a better-known name. By the end, McCloskey says, "Everybody was in stitches."

Continuing to follow his father's advice, Leo signed on as vice president and 50 percent owner of Smothers's winery, investing his labor as sweat equity in return for stock. In 1977 he made a chardonnay, a sylvaner, and a selection of rieslings ranging in style from trocken (dry) to spätlese (slightly sweet) to auslese (sweeter yet) to beerenauslese (you get the idea) to trockenbeerenauslese, the latter bottled in 375-ml tenths. A couple of years later, seven Smothers wines won medals at the L.A. County Fair, giving rise to a certain tension among McCloskey's Felton Empire partners. Hence, fewer than two years after joining on, McCloskey sold his stock back to Smothers. "At first he only offered me the value I'd invested," McCloskey says. "But my plan all along was to make a profit, so I said, 'Pay me my price or I'll put [the stock] up for sale in the newspaper.' I had decided to be a businessman, not just a scientist-functionary at a winery."

Lurking behind McCloskey's resolve was a revelation that for him ranks with Newton's apple or the words "Mr. Watson, come here!" In 1977, Leo had stumbled across the work of one T. C. Somers, an Australian scientist who was studying the color chemistry of red wine. In a series of papers published between 1966 and 1975, Somers showed that, contrary to conventional wisdom—which assumed that the color of wine came from grape pigments called anthocyanins—the most durable color density was actually attributable to "polymeric" pigments formed when anthocyanins combined with tannins after grapes were crushed and fermented. More important to consumers and critics (whether they knew it or not), the amount of such "ionized anthocyanins" in the finished product could be shown to correspond with a wine's quality level as evaluated in the mouths of experienced judges. As McCloskey later told Charles Sullivan:

> This was the first time that flavor chemistry in wine was directly related to the ranking of wines in taste evaluations. For me personally this is the equivalent of what Pasteur did. Pasteur observed that the acetic acid content was high in wines that were ranked sensorially low in the 1850s. He introduced the first biotechnology which was applied to wine. . . . Pasteur lays down the basic law that if you measure sugar, acid, alcohol you have quality assurance for the basic primary chemistry of wine. That's what we did at Ridge in the early years. What we didn't do, and what hadn't been done at Davis, was to make another quality jump in the flavor chemistry.

McCloskey admits that, after seeing this study, he became more interested in Somers's work than he was in winemaking. "The reason it's so compelling is it shows that great wine actually exists," he said when I first met him. "It's not just that somebody *thinks* it's great." Deciding to be an early adopter and "make this idea my own in the United States," in 1979 McCloskey went back to Ridge (where he was still a consultant, then developing a method for detecting the spoilage yeast *Brettanomyces*, which makes wine smell like manure) and asked the owners to help fund research that could link the flavor chemistry of Ridge wines with their sensory and economic value. Just as they had a few years earlier when McCloskey asked to expand the lab, the Ridge scientists said, "Sure."

I N OCTOBER, I ride along with Randall Grahm in his other car—a Porsche Carrera—as he visits vineyards in Monterey County. This is the site of Ca' del Solo, the property he bought in the early 1990s, partly to supply the Big House brand. We bypass Soledad, however, on our first pass down U.S. 101, driving farther south toward Greenfield at the southern end of the Santa Lucia Highlands. Over the past fifteen years or so, this prominent north-south scarp, clearly visible from the freeway, has been thoroughly colonized by vineyardists; reminiscent of similar winegrowing areas in Italy's Veneto district (or, in a less viticultural context, the bajadas of the Mojave Desert), the appellation consists of one long alluvial slope, descending from the Santa Lucia Mountains in the west to the Salinas Valley floor in the east. Dozens of wine companies have now staked out sections of this striking geological formation, most of them growing pinot noir that tastes like it would rather be syrah.

We're bound for the Beeswax Vineyard, situated at the southern end of the scarp where it lifts off the valley floor. Since 2003, Grahm has bought grapes here, specifically roussanne and grenache blanc, for dessert wine and Le Cigare Blanc. At this point in the harvest, the fruit has already been picked for the latter, but for the former it's still hanging on the vines and lying on the ground, arrayed on paper mats.

"The objective is to concentrate the fruit sugar content," Grahm says of the latter—a goal that will be achieved as the liquid content evaporates in the sun. A traditional path to such concentration is *Botrytis cinerea* rot conferred by fall rains (à la Felton Empire's '76 riesling), but this year there hasn't been any, so Grahm resorted to misting the vines artificially, then spread the clusters on the ground to dry. "In '06 we had a crazy amount of botrytis," he says. "That year it was foggier and more humid, and the wine was outrageously good. This year we held out as long as we could, but we didn't get any rain. So this is a Hail Mary pass, because my colleagues seem to think we don't need twenty tons we can't use. We were budgeting for dessert wine, and in the new regime we don't have the luxury of missing or failing at anything."

Honeybees and yellow jackets crawl among the golden grapes, which are turning purple as they raisin. "They've been lying here for about a week," Grahm says. "I might be deluding myself, but maybe we'll get a slightly more gentle drying process now than if we'd dried them three weeks ago—the sun isn't as high in the sky." The October air temperature is still ninety degrees Fahrenheit.

Beyond the vineyard is the backdrop of the southern Salinas Valley, the etched brown slopes of the Pinnacles baking beyond the vines, whose autumn leaves are turning yellow beneath the clear blue sky. At our backs, the uncultivated hillsides are strewn with *Atriplex*—aka saltbush, a blue-gray shrub that thrives in dry, saline environments. As an agricultural corollary, black plastic water hoses run along the ground of the vineyard, dividing the space between vine rows. "I've made very small contributions to California viticulture, but one good idea I had was convincing the grower to irrigate in the center of the rows here," Grahm says. "That way the roots have to reach farther for water. But since I'm the boy who cried everything, nobody even notices when I have something real."

Leaving the vineyard, we make our way back along the straight, flat farm roads toward Ca' del Solo. In Soledad we stop off at Starbucks, the sort of establishment that wasn't present when Grahm started growing grapes here in the early 1990s. A smaller, chillier version of California's Great Central Valley, the Salinas Valley is similarly dominated by Big Ag and populated by union farmworkers, a far cry from the creature comforts to which a Beverly Hills–bred, Santa Cruz–based winemaker is accustomed. "As a general class, these are not my people," Grahm acknowledges. "It isn't a place I would have chosen to have a vineyard, but the Bonny Doon estate vineyard was in decline. I needed a backup plan, and the McFarland family sold us this property at a very favorable price. It seemed I didn't have much to lose, which was a misconception on my part.

"What could possibly go wrong?" Grahm asks. "I'll tell you: Quality was variable; acidity was off the charts; yields were lower than expected. . . . We made some very good wines, but the costs were so high that you couldn't sell the wine for enough money to cover them—it was off by a factor of two or three." In a 1999 newsletter, Grahm accused the Soledad soils of being "feloniously sandy," and moreover admitted that "we have found virtually every grape variety grown in our vineyard . . . to, um, ah, er . . . stink." Which was to say that the wines smelled like rotten eggs (an indicator of hydrogen sulfide) and, not all that surprisingly in the "Salinas" Valley, also exuded a briny quality.

When it came to farming, the salt-packed earth also turned out to be heavily compacted. "We wanted to do it organically, even back in the midnineties," Grahm says. "The McFarlands [who continued to manage the vineyard after selling the property] are good farmers, but organic was not their thing—and if you're not set up for it, it's painful. There were a lot of weeds and ground squirrels, and we were just getting our brains beat out with costs. Now we've got someone managing it every day, but for thirteen years I've been monkeying with it, toying with it, trying to fix it . . . and I still haven't figured out the best grape to grow there."

Traveling north and east out of town, we drive toward the ninety-five-acre vineyard, situated on the eastern (i.e., drier) side of the valley at the parched foot of the Pinnacles. Stopping for a moment to get out of the car, we're assaulted by rampaging air currents. "The wind here makes you crazy," says Grahm. "We planted some trees as a windbreak, but they sucked up a lot of water in what is already a low-rainfall site. I understand now why growers don't plant virused material, and why they drip irrigate to play it safe. I don't think they'll ever make great wine, but it's not my place to judge them—especially if you're operating a for-profit business, which ultimately you have to do, or at least I do. To make something great, you have to be prepared to take enormous risks, and the financial consequences are staggering."

Getting back into the car, Grahm elaborates: "There are basically two wine businesses," he says. "Industrial and artisanal. An artisanal wine is largely, if not entirely, predicated on the quality of a particular vineyard site. That's what makes it distinctive—it's the site that's special. Industrial wine can still be very good wine, but it's not predicated on the distinctiveness of the site—it's predicated on the cleverness of the winemaker as blender, so there are limits to how great that wine can possibly be. In the New World, we're basically making wines on the industrial model. All of our sites are hit and miss, because we haven't had time to determine what is a great vineyard.

"When I started out," Grahm says, "I wanted to plant a great vineyard and make artisanal wine. But I didn't appreciate the complexity of the task and, despite my efforts, the wines were fairly mediocre. In retrospect, Bonny Doon wasn't such a bad site—eventually I grafted it over to roussanne and syrah, and miraculously it made pretty good wine. But then it died from Pierce's disease, and after that I was so traumatized that, deep in my unconscious, I felt that finding a great vineyard was too hard—and even if you do find one, it's probably gonna die. It was much safer to just buy grapes, and I planted this vineyard with minimal expectations. I thought it would be a *good* vineyard, but I didn't have the courage to do something great."

As we enter the vineyard in question, we come to a block of nebbiolo grapes—the raw material of Barolo and Barbaresco, planted during Grahm's "Italianate" phase. He loves the wine he makes from the vines, but says, "I think it has problems with soil fertility—it gets one ton per acre, costs thirty dollars a bottle, and still doesn't earn enough money. Apart from that, it's brilliant." Next we intersect a block of grenache, about which he is more upbeat. Typically grown in a warmer climate—e.g. Spain, southern France, and Australia's Barossa Valley—"It turns out that, if you can get it ripe in a cool climate, it rocks. Contrary to all received wisdom, we can grow really good grenache in Soledad—which is kind of an achievement, because we're doing something the Old World can't do. This is a Samsonite* viejo clone; it gets two and a half tons an acre, which for a Burgundian is shockingly high but for a

* Brought into the United States in a suitcase.

Californian is shockingly low—at least for commercial purposes when you're looking at costs of four thousand dollars per ton."

Next is a block of dolcetto, the effusively purple variety from Piemonte. "A certain genera of wine is cursed," Grahm says. "Eventually we sell it, but we can't make very much of it. Dolcetto is a challenge for a biodynamic regime; if you can't use copper, it's a stinker." Which is to say that copper sulfate, when added to a wine that smells like rotten eggs, binds to the hydrogen sulfide and precipitates out, eliminating the odor. Its use is prohibited, however, by Demeter, the biodynamic certification agency.

Although biodynamic farming has become popular in the American wine industry in the past ten years, Grahm says he first got interested in it through winemaking friends in Europe. "I saw improvements in their wine after they made the switch," he says. "It was subtle in a certain way, but in some cases quite profound. Ostertag [in Alsace] changed quality tremendously; their wines are just a lot tighter, more coherent, and more vibrant—more *what they are.* You would have to see for yourself. I'm in the process of seeing it."

While it seems to invite classification under the heading of California kookiness, biodynamics' major impetus continues to emanate from Europe, and its tendrils have taken root as far afield as Australia and New Zealand. It's generally perceived as an extremist offshoot of organic farming but actually preceded organic as a certified method of agriculture. As legend has it, soon after the introduction of chemical fertilizers and specialized agriculture a hundred years ago, European farmers began to complain about a decline in their soil quality and the health of their crops and livestock. In response, Rudolf Steiner—a then-prominent figure in European intellectual life, who influenced not only agriculture and education but also medicine, art, architecture, economics, religion, and care for the disabled—gave a series of lectures (now collected in a book titled *Agriculture)* prescribing a system of holistic practices intended to rehabilitate land. Reportedly derived from his study of ancient and peasant agriculture (though who knows where Steiner, a reputed clairvoyant, really got it), the governing idea was the "whole farm" concept, which envisions an agricultural property as an independent organism.

Like his equally controversial contemporaries Wilhelm Reich and Nikola Tesla, today Steiner is considered a visionary by some and a charlatan by others. A student of Goethe who wrote thirty books and delivered six thousand lectures, he was educated early on in mathematics and natural science, but in the final third of his life he conceived the "spiritual science" of anthroposophy, a kind of religion of the human organism. Steiner believed that spiritual forces—a "deeper reality" obscured by materialistic modern thinking—play a direct role in life on Earth, but that by following a series of steps we can regain access to their power. Since farming is dependent on the natural world, Steiner's system is predictably attentive to such cyclical patterns as dawn and dusk and summer and winter, but consistent with the concept of an organism, he broadened those ideas to include such processes as expansion and contraction, inhalation and exhalation, gravity and levity—organic rhythms that characterize all of nature, extending downward into the earth and upward into the atmosphere. By thus attending to celestial phenomena like lunar cycles and planetary alignments (and thereby appearing to adhere to astrology), biodynamics inspires eye-rolling among many scientific onlookers, for whom the over-the-top aspect is "the preparations"—a series of earthy concoctions extracted from plants, animals, and minerals and buried in unusual containers before being applied in homeopathic concentrations to land and compost. Preparation 500, for example, consists of cow manure buried in a cow horn for six months (from the autumnal to the vernal equinox), then dug up and sprayed on soil at sunset—via a dilution of one-quarter cup per three gallons of water, distributed over an acre of ground—to stimulate root growth. Conversely, Preparation 501—quartz silica, used to promote photosynthesis by concentrating the rays of the sun—spends the opposite six months of the year underground before being applied (in an even weaker concentration: one-quarter *teaspoon* per three gallons of water per acre) to foliage at dawn. Preparation 502, which is sprayed onto compost, consists of yarrow blossoms buried in the bladder of a stag; each of the other preparations—chamomile, stinging nettle, oak bark, dandelion, valerian, and horsetail—requires a different organic vessel and is alleged to impart a unique influence or "nutritional intelligence." For example, cows—associated with gravity—"ray" (radiate) inward, while deer, which epitomize levity, ray outward.

As we circumnavigate the upper end of the vineyard, we pass a curved sculptural device that seems to be made of cement. Grahm refers to it as a biodynamic flowform. "If you were a materialist, you'd say it's to oxygenate the water," he says. "If you were an etherealist or transcendentalist, you'd say it's to dynamize the water. It has to do with laminar versus tubular flow—it's important to have good water, obviously, and here the flowform is said to ameliorate the saline qualities of the site. This is also why water is dynamized before putting the preparations in—you're wiping out the prior memory of the water. People are working on that now with electronic frequencies. I have a friend in Germany who's working with 'informed' water—preparing the preps with information, not material."

This is another hot-button topic. The homeopathic concentration of the preparations is so infinitesimal that critics question how, when an aqueous solution no longer contains detectable molecules of a substance mixed into it, the preparation can have any effect. Supporters (such as Grahm) respond that water is a mysterious substance that behaves in surprising ways. "Water has certain qualities when it passes through natural material," says Grahm. "It's capable of transmitting all kinds of information, which is another way of saying that it has intelligence."

As biophysicists will testify, molecules are prone to vibration, emitting "signature" electromagnetic frequencies. Some adventurous scientists—champions of a field known as digital biology—maintain that these signals can be recorded and replayed. When such a conceptual framework is applied to homeopathy, water indeed acquires the role of a "medium," or vehicle of information, that might serve to amplify molecular signals that impart biological effects. The most notorious work in this area was performed by Jacques Benveniste, a French immunologist who published his findings in the journal *Nature* in 1988; the scientific community reacted with such force, however, that Benveniste repeated the experiments—and failed to reproduce the results. So controversial was this "scandal"/"witch hunt" (take your pick) that an entire book—*The Memory of Water,* by Michel Schiff—was written about it.

Much of biodynamics' mental territory is in the province of that mind-bending modern field known as quantum mechanics, which—explaining how some causes and effects don't play out as predicted in the laboratory—views certain phenomena in physics as organic. As William T. Vollmann observed in the *San Francisco Chronicle* (reviewing Arthur Zajonc's book *The New Physics and Cosmology*): "Because quantum physics implies an apparently determining role for the human mind on the phenomena observed, it shatters Western notions of objective reality. The new physics and mind science both lead quickly to questions once considered the sole province of spirituality." In this light, biodynamics appears to occupy the same sort of status as acupuncture: Even if its effectiveness were attributable to a placebo effect, its influence on the attitude of the farmer brings about results.

In any event, Soledad seemed resistant in other ways to biodynamic treatment. "We tried burying horns here, and it didn't work," Grahm says. "There wasn't enough rainfall, so the soil was too hard. The manure didn't cure."

We rejoin the freeway and drive back north, passing through the city of Salinas and the venerable eucalyptus forest that lines the hills along U.S. 101 near Prunedale. Instead of turning back toward Santa Cruz, though, we go east toward San Juan Bautista, site of a potential vineyard property that Grahm has been investigating. When he told me about it some months earlier, he described its biological effect as that of a "woodland," which didn't sound all that suitable for a vineyard. When I asked him to elaborate, he clarified, "It gives me an erection."

As we approach the property, I can sort of see what he meant. Making a series of turns onto roads that grow progressively narrower, bumpier, and quieter, we enter into a long tunnel of black walnut trees, which provide shade from the surrounding yellow-brown hills. As the air temperature drops from the nineties into the mideighties, a ridge rises up from a grassy valley on our right, leading into the loftier chaparral by way of . . . well, a woodland. The area exudes the ambiance of the original heart of California—that munificent oak-dotted savanna that sustained the Ohlone Indians, greeted the Spanish explorers, and, for better or worse, gave rise to the Franciscan missions. "This was a sacred Indian site," Grahm corroborates, the result of his research in a book called *San Juan Bautista: The Town, the Mission, and the Park*. "Apparently the Mutsun tribe preferred to spend time on this hill, rather than in the mission. They claimed that a spirit appeared and talked to them here, so the Franciscans put up a cross on the site. After that the spirit no longer appeared, which pleased the padres greatly."

The property in question consists of some 450 acres, bordering on the Gabilan Range below 3,169-foot Fremont Peak, varying in topography from alluvial grassland to rolling hills to windswept ridges. The owner, who has a home on a secluded part of the site, originally intended to subdivide it for housing but put it on the market when his plans were rejected by San Benito County. He and Grahm subsequently engaged in extensive talks, with Randall going so far as to install weather gauges and conduct soil tests, but ultimately the property was sold to a group of investors from Texas. However, since the county still seems more receptive to agricultural use than intensive housing (and, moreover, is free of many of the environmental restrictions that prevent development in Santa Cruz), Grahm has stayed in touch with the Texas buyers, hoping that some sort of further subdivision might yet be possible.

"What I like is that most of the exposures are north and northeast," he says, looking up into the hills. "In California, south and southwest exposures"—the most popular orientation—"are not appropriate for grapes: They get burned. We crystallized some of the soils, and they were unlike anything we've seen—more complex and organized, very beautiful. The property has only been used as pasture for grazing horses and cattle, so there are no toxic problems. Our tests showed an abundance of minerals, and there's every kind of soil here—clay, loam, granite, and limestone.

"I could go on about the soil structure," Grahm says, "but to tell you the truth, the main thing is that to me the place has magic, or mystery." In fact, it imbues him with memories of his first year as a winemaker: 1982, when he leased space from Josh Jensen at Calera in Hollister, just east of here. As he would later write:

I drove every morning through Santa Cruz, down Highway One through the sleepy town of Watsonville, across the strawberry and lettuce fields of the Pajaro Valley, to Highway 101, then reversed course to head north for a couple of miles, passing the stately, magical eucalyptus portal that welcomed one to San Benito County, *terra mysteriosa*. Hanging a right at Highway 156, I would drive right past the turn-off for San Juan Bautista, heading out to the Cienega Valley where Calera was located. In some deep part of me, I know I was then creating a model of my as-yet-to-unfold career as a winemaker; the repetitive route was a sketch of a dreamscape. Maybe I have come back to this area because it feels so much to me as if I am just now beginning again. . . . As the Mutsun would say, "Wattinin-ka rukkatka." (I am home.)

On the other hand, Grahm says as we get back into the car, "There ain't an acupuncturist or City Lights bookstore anywhere nearby."

A S A LEGION of California-bred Baby Boomers was being loosed on the wine world by UC Davis, one of their East Coast contemporaries was entering the industry from a different direction. Mike Benziger had grown up in the liquor business in Westchester County, New York, where his father, Bruno, was one of the principals in Park, Benziger & Co., an importer-exporter that made its name with products like Harvey's Scotch, Duval Vermouth, Lanson Champagne, and Kahlúa. Mike, like Leo McCloskey the oldest of seven children, worked summers in the company's office and bottling factory, but on the day in 1973 when he graduated from Holy Cross college in Massachusetts, he embarked for the West Coast via the Trans-Canada Highway. When he and his girlfriend, Mary, ran out of money in San Francisco, Mike mined his father's connections for a job at Beltramo's, the premier purveyor of wine and spirits on the peninsula south of the city. Although he knew a lot about liquor, Mike wasn't very conversant with wine, but on his first day of work he met Joel Butler, who would later become one of the first two American masters of wine. With Butler as his Svengali, Benziger was befallen by the obsession that afflicted so many of his peers. "I became totally fanatical," he says. "I spent all my money on wine and music. I read wine books into a tape recorder and played them while I drove my car."

At the time, the number one wine at Beltramo's was Charles Krug Chenin Blanc. Number two was Wente Blanc de Blanc; number three, Weibel Green Hungarian; number four, Blue Nun. (Gallo's Hearty Burgundy led the reds, followed by Lancers and Mateus.)

During Benziger's period of employment, however, "the California wine business exploded," notably due to the nitroglycerin of the 1976 Judgment of Paris. Hence, Mike and Mary (by then his wife) spent most of the following year in France, walking vineyards with Hugh Johnson's *World Atlas of Wine* in hand and collecting rocks, which he mailed to an address in Paris. Traveling by bicycle with Harry Bird, a friend from Beltramo's, Benziger was eagerly received by the CEO of Champagne Laurent-Perrier, who gave the two "stinking, unshaven hippies" a couple of bottles each of Grand Siècle, the $100 house cuvée. Unable to carry all four bottles on their bikes, they rode a couple of miles down the road, dismounted, and drank a bottle each, waking up in a rainstorm in the middle of the night. When Benziger was ready to return home, he put his bag of rocks on the plane to New York, where—since it also contained soil, in violation of agricultural-import statutes—it was confiscated by U.S. Customs.

By this time, Mike's brothers Bob and Joe had started a fine-wine shop in Scarsdale, New York. In debt to his father after the European trip, Mike went back to work for Bruno, creating a California wine division for Park-Benziger. In the post-Vietnam era, however, the Oedipal relationship evinced a certain strain. "I couldn't stand it," Mike sums up. "My dad was an ex-Marine—a hard-driving, old-school guy. He was charismatic and people loved him, but you were either his friend or his enemy, and we argued about everything." When their disagreements turned into wrestling matches, Mike went back to California to look for work in wine production. When things calmed down, Bruno, an amateur gardener who had always dreamed of running an orchard and nursery, told his son to let him know if he found a suitable piece of property.

Mike ended up with a harvest job at Stony Ridge, a new winery in the Livermore Valley that operated on the old site of Ruby Hill, a still-standing structure built in the nineteenth century from first-growth redwood. The three-hundred-acre property boasted some venerable vines of zinfandel, carignane, semillon, and French colombard, but as a start-up "shoestring operation," Stony Ridge also bought distressed grapes from outside sources. Benziger remembers the place as "a wine emergency room" whose chief surgeon was Bruce Rector, a

Davis-trained magician whose palate was capable of performing miracles in triage.

As far as Mike was concerned, Stony Ridge was an apprenticeship for his family's future winery, location still TBD. The Benzigers couldn't afford Napa or Sonoma, so every weekend Mike and Mary drove their VW to a less precious part of the state—the Sierra foothills, Monterey County, Temecula near San Diego. They almost made a deal for a sheep ranch in Anderson Valley near Mendocino, but Bruno backed out at the last minute, allowing the property to be acquired by Champagne Louis Roederer as a North American production site. Later, acting on a tip from a Livermore neighbor, they drove to Glen Ellen in Sonoma Valley to look at a place on the northeastern flank of Sonoma Mountain.

The eighty-five-acre site was an elevated, natural bowl imbued with local history. Once the site of a Wappo settlement, it was later bequeathed by General Mariano Vallejo to the carpenter who'd built his house in Sonoma; after that, it was a haunt of Jack London, whose name graced the state park just up the road. The property was already growing ten acres of cabernet sauvignon, but as it turned out, the owner—a Dr. Patrick Flynn—told them that it wasn't for sale. "He planned to die there," Benziger says. "He had owned it for nine years, and before that the Wegener family had it for a hundred and ten. There used to be a village named Wegenerville there with a winery, distillery, hotel, and blacksmith shop. The place was incredibly beautiful, and while he was showing us around, I had sort of a premonition—something told me not to bother looking any farther. Sure enough, he invited us back later and asked if we wanted to buy it."

Benziger gleaned that Flynn wanted a million dollars for the property. Mike called his father in New York from a pay phone, and Bruno advised him to get a contract, so Mike went to a nearby stationery store and bought a one-page document, which he and Flynn both signed. Within a few days, Flynn reportedly changed his mind—he'd found a group of developers who were willing to pay him more, but brandishing the contract, Benziger retained a lawyer friend who "hardballed the deal and made it stick." In the end, Flynn agreed to finance the loan himself, but the parties signed the final agreement in separate rooms to avoid any unpleasantness. Mike and Mary moved onto the property on Halloween 1980, and a few months later, they were followed by Bruno, his wife, Helen, her mother, Katherine, and Mike's half dozen brothers and sister. "It's pretty amazing what Dad did," Benziger says. "He was a New Yorker through and through—he had good friends and a successful business there. But he gave up a great life because he saw that he had an opportunity to live his dream." The dream didn't include any more wrestling matches with his son, but the Benzigers' blend of wizened New York business savvy and youthful California energy would have remarkable results.

Bruno never got around to planting the orchard. The first order of business (after buying a refrigerator at Sears to establish local credit) was putting in vines and building a winery. Most of the banks the family approached said that "the last thing California needs [in 1981] is another winery," but Mike put together a ten-year plan that envisioned a gradual expansion to fifty thousand cases of boutique cabernet, chardonnay, zinfandel, and sauvignon blanc, plus a low-priced generic red and white. After funding was finally obtained (at a rate of 21 percent), ground for the winery was broken in July, barely a month before harvest. Mike Lee, the winemaker at Kenwood—which had previously bought Flynn's grapes, but apparently didn't resent losing them—told Mike about some chardonnay and sauvignon blanc fruit that was available from Sonoma-Cutrer, which was starting its own winery that same year. In their incipient state of development, the Benzigers' only fermenters were a couple of redwood tanks that Mike had gotten from Stony Ridge in lieu of a last paycheck.

One August evening at the London Lodge in Glen Ellen, having a beer after working on the winery construction all day, Mike met the owner of a local junkyard who mentioned that he had some used milk trucks. Hence, Benziger's first grapes from Sonoma-Cutrer—which came in at 11 p.m.—were directed into a fleet of vehicles whose sides said MILK: IT DOES A BODY GOOD. The fruit, having been picked late in the day, was delivered very warm, and fermentation approached infernal proportions, forcing Mike's mother, Helen, to drive to a bait shop in Sonoma three times a day for dry ice.

During that first harvest, Mike says, his life frequently flashed before his eyes. The fermentations were attended by "eight million fruit flies," and after the estate grapes were picked, the bottom fell out of one of the fermenters, effecting the loss of half the '81 cabernet. Somehow the remaining wines all finished their fermentations—the chardonnay turned out rich and buttery, the sauvignon blanc grassy and acidic, the cabernet dark, minty, and tannic—and, unbeknownst to Mike, were submitted to the 1982 Sonoma County Harvest Fair competition. He subsequently got a 7 p.m. call advising him to come to the fairgrounds in Santa Rosa, and when he arrived, he learned that his "Glen Ellen" chardonnay had placed second in its class in the wine competition—not too shabby for the maiden voyage of a funky start-up winery. But there was even more staggering news: The sauvignon blanc (which one critic had compared to shellac) won the white wine sweepstakes award for the entire show. It proceeded to sell out overnight, putting Benziger on the map with its first vintage. "It was a joke," Mike says in retrospect. "If people had seen our fermenters, they would have been blown away."

To Bruno, this was a coup to be exploited without any lollygagging. "Dad's credo was 'When success strikes, run as fast as you can,'" says Mike. "He was a relentless salesman, but he didn't understand wine. He wanted to bottle and sell the '82 that had just been picked—he didn't realize that first it had to be aged in barrel."

To take advantage of its publicity windfall, the family held a meeting to discuss whether to buy and bottle bulk wine they hadn't made themselves. This would be a step down from their boutique mission, which Mike thought should be preserved and protected. But seeing as how—as Bruno hammered home—opportunity might not ring repeatedly, they agreed to buy five hundred cases of ripe, nutty French colombard from Seghesio and five hundred more of soft, rich cabernet for $1.65 a gallon from Martini & Prati in Santa Rosa. To distinguish it from run-of-the-mill jug wine, the Benzigers put it in square-shouldered 750-ml bottles, topped with corks instead of screw caps, and released it for the holidays as "Proprietor's Reserve White" and "Proprietor's Reserve Red" at a retail price of $4.99. Bruno sold both out in a week, so they went back and bought more. "Dad was in heaven," says Mike. "He loved to wheel and deal, and he had friends who thought he was crazy to come out here. Now he could go back to his old-crony network of brokers and offer them an opportunity to get into the business with wine that was easy to understand and sold for less than five dollars a bottle."

That first season, the Benzigers sold 1,800 cases of wine; the following year, they sold 10,000. In California, they were assisted in the sales department by a family from the San Joaquin Valley town of Ceres. The Franzias (who were related by marriage to the Gallos, from nearby Modesto) had been in the wine business since the nineteenth century, though their company was sold in 1973 to Coca-Cola Bottling of New York, which retained the rights to the family name on its mass-market boxed wines. This decision hadn't gone down well with three of the younger Franzias—two brothers and a cousin, named Joe, Fred, and John, who subsequently formed their own business: Bronco, which (depending on which story you believe; both are accurate, and neither negates the other) is a contraction of Brothers 'n' Cousin or the school mascot of Fred's alma mater, the University of Santa Clara. The trio started out as *négociants*, buying and selling grapes and bulk wine for "super value" JFJ Bronco and CC Vineyards bottlings; they also formed what was then an anomaly—a statewide distribution company called Classic Wines of California, which soon included Robert Mondavi and Glen Ellen among its clients.

"Joe Franzia was the person who built up Glen Ellen into a huge brand," Randall Grahm's old Beverly Hills Wine Merchant cohort Jason Lewis reports. Like Dennis Overstreet, Lewis says, Joe could also "sell snow to Eskimos—but only by breaking the Eskimo's arm. You had to get up and walk away from him, but then he'd follow you, because he could not take no for an answer. Finally you gave in just to get rid of him." Franzia pioneered what would become—for small wineries and boutique retailers—the bane of the wholesale wine industry: the sale of wine by the truckload. Traditionally, regional distributors liked to offer graduated discounts for multiple-case orders: 5 percent off five cases, 10 percent off ten cases, etc. With statewide distribution, says Lewis, "Joe figured out that if he didn't have to deliver x number of cases to x number of stores himself, it would save him a fortune. So he would say to Safeway, 'If you buy a full truck, or 1,188 cases, you'll get the maximum discount of 15 percent *and* a five-dollar-per-case pickup allowance.' In that way, Safeway could save— do the math—six thousand dollars. It was nothing for them to load up a semi and truck the wine to their central distribution warehouses, from which it could be sent out all over the state." In time this practice would evolve into two-truck orders, three-truck orders, and—with the advent of Walmart and Costco—eighteen-truck orders.

Despite Glen Ellen's success with cheap generic wine, by the early 1980s the premium market had embraced varietal labeling: The era of California "burgundy" and "chablis" was waning fast, and to connote even minimal acceptability, a label had to bear the name of a grape—even Gallo was now selling a vintage-dated "reserve" cabernet. By Proprietor's Reserve or any other name, Glen Ellen's "red" and "white" were excluded from such cachet—a fact that came up for discussion in 1984, when Bruno was meeting in New York with Mike Shaw of Paramount Distributors. Inspired by Shaw's advice and his own favorite negotiating beverage—Harvey's Scotch—Bruno called Mike in California, where the younger Benziger was meeting with Bruce Rector, the Stony Ridge blending wizard who had joined the staff at Glen Ellen. Bruno asked if they could add enough chardonnay to Proprietor's Reserve white to meet the 75 percent varietal rule enabling the wine to be labeled "chardonnay." As it happened, he and Mike had just located several hundred thousand gallons of bulk chardonnay that, combined with the colombard that had previously dominated Glen Ellen white, could indeed amount to three-quarters of the total. That year they sold more than 100,000 cases of Proprietor's Reserve, and doubled it the year after that.

Clearly, this was something that the world had been waiting for. As Lewis puts it, "By the 1980s, varietal wines were getting pricey, but you still had a whole bunch of people who were drinking jug wines—retirees or college kids just getting into wine—who wanted something better and didn't want to spend twelve dollars. Glen Ellen's timing was perfect." In other words, for that stage of America's enological awakening, it was an ideal wine: Conferring varietal prestige at a jug price, Glen Ellen became ubiquitous at potlucks, openings, and—in 187-ml screw-cap bottles—commercial airplane flights. To meet the overwhelming demand, the company veritably drained the bulk market: Whereas, a couple of years earlier, Rector had rejected 90 percent of the wines he sampled, to meet his production quotas in 1985 he was accepting about half, with the inevitable prospect of diminishing quality.

The upshot was that, instead of simply buying wines to blend, the Benzigers had to buy more grapes and make the wine themselves. As a result, Mike says, "Bruce organized a team to fan out all over the state. It was a very lean and mean operation—we signed most of the growers between Bakersfield [in Kern County in the southern San Joaquin Valley] and Ukiah [in Mendocino County in the redwoods of the north] to multiyear contracts, so it wasn't until '87 or '88 that Sutter Home, Beringer, Fetzer, and Sebastiani even got into the marketplace." Crushing and winemaking took place near the grape sources—at Delicato in the Central Valley, Cypress Ridge in Monterey County, Martini & Prati in Santa Rosa, McDowell Valley in Mendocino County. The fermented wines were transported to Glen Ellen for blending and bottling, but in 1988 a facility was built south of Sonoma, where thirty thousand cases could be turned out every day. Not all the wines were ready for bottling at the same time, so blend compositions changed throughout the year; but, Mike says, "I would challenge you to tell the difference." Though Benziger had never abandoned its boutique aspirations (its estate sauvignon blanc won the Sonoma County Harvest Fair sweepstakes again in 1984), Mike says, "Glen Ellen customers were way more picky than Benziger customers—there was a taste profile we had to hit. The whole goal was to make a ten-thousand-gallon tank taste like a sixty-gallon barrel by blending."

Throughout this heady trajectory, Mike and Bruno continued to clash, enlisting professional mediators when "Mom got tired of being the referee." By 1989 Bruno's health began to falter; he came down with pneumonia and died of heart failure that summer at age sixty-four. By that time, Glen Ellen was selling more than a million cases per year and, in the short time that had passed since its founding, had created an entirely new wine category. For decades, cheap wines made to secure market share had been called "fighting wines"; now, reflecting both the changing market and the marine who led the charge, the most hotly contested sector of the market was "fighting varietals."

T EN DAYS AFTER my visit with McCloskey to Chappellet, Sam Spencer visits the Enologix office with samples of wine that he drained a day later. Studying the numbers—189 complex anthocyanin and 922 tannin—McCloskey says, "That's a home run."

"I literally babysat the fermenter," says Spencer. "I pressed at 14."

"You couldn't do this without the system," McCloskey reminds him.

"Why wouldn't I want to use data to be a better winemaker and get my wine into the market where people can enjoy it?" Spencer asks. "I want to use every tool at my disposal. I think this is a logical end to agricultural endeavor."

With that, McCloskey and I drive across town to Sebastiani Vineyards, the venerable Sonoma winery that recently celebrated its centennial. Once associated mainly with jug wine, the company recently sold its eight-million-case "consumer" division to Constellation Brands in order to focus on the premium market.* One ensuing result is that its winemaker—Grahm's old classmate Mark Lyon, who has worked at Sebastiani since graduating from Davis—was chosen 2003 Winemaker of the Year by *Restaurant Wine* and was also one of a half dozen California vintners spotlighted by the *San Francisco Chronicle* in 2004. "Mark has the theories nailed cold," McCloskey says. "He was my first client to accept the idea that Sonoma should abandon Style Three and try to make Style Four. Now he's won more 90-point scores

---

* Since this writing, the rest of Sebastiani has been sold to the Foley Wine Group.

than all other Sonoma County producers combined. He's making wine that the consumer likes."

"I'm making wine that isn't screeching in tannin," Lyon—a bald, slightly built fifty-year-old with a calm and candid manner—confirms when we arrive. "To a certain degree it tastes like the grape and reflects the region, but the reality is that people are popping the cork and drinking my cab right now, so I *am* going for a deliciousness factor. I'm looking at questions like: Is the oak there? Is there really nice fruit? More than: What is Sonoma County Cab supposed to *be*?"

McCloskey is here partly to talk about Sebastiani's Cherryblock vineyard, located across the street from the winery. Planted in the 1960s by August Sebastiani, son of the winery's founder, it produces the company's flagship cabernet. After ushering us into an office alongside the parking lot, Lyon takes out an Enologix WineFAX that shows various unpicked blocks testing out as Style Three, with unimpressive quality indexes of .19 and .25. Block eighteen is falling in quality the longer the grapes hang on the vines.

"It might be bad sampling," McCloskey suggests. "Pickers go for grocery store fruit, but the good stuff is the shriveled stuff. The fruit that looks velvety is where the action is."

"Should we go ahead and pick block eighteen?" Lyon asks.

"Next week is the window," says Leo. "We're in a poker game, and we're not holding the cards yet. I would do another sample, but if the vintage deals you only a 170 [in complex anthocyanin], that's not necessarily a bad thing unless it's too tannic. With 1000 tannin, I think you can still turn that into a Style Four. Do a cold soak."[*] Lyon agrees to try and "get all the goodies up front."

Leaving the office, we enter Sebastiani's high-tech tasting room, distinguished by built-in stainless steel spittoons and permanently numbered place settings for glasses. Lyon has just staged a tasting here, trying to divine what inspired James Laube and the *Wine Spectator* to "beat up on the St. Francis merlot" with a score of 75 points.

---

[*] The technique of holding picked grapes in a tank at low temperatures prior to fermentation so as to extract phenolic compounds in the absence of alcohol, in the hope of increasing color and intensifying flavor.

Conclusion: The wine was too "vegetal," exhibiting the kind of green pepper/cigar-box character once considered characteristic of Bordeaux varieties but lately earmarked as anathema by critics.

"In Sonoma Valley we have to get away from vegetal terroirs and high tannin," Lyon says. "That's been the problem here [with cabernet]—it's too tannic and isn't blended early enough with merlot. In the Médoc it would be crazy to say, 'Our terroir is from gravelly knolls, so we're going 100 percent for that style because that's the essence of Médoc cabernet.' They don't do that; instead they blend in merlot and petit verdot to make something a little more aromatic and drinkable. Leo has helped me get merlot and malbec and softening agents into the wine early in the game—otherwise cabernet goes off in this hard-edged direction. If you try and blend at the last minute before bottling, you've already missed the boat—it's already dried out. I think the art was already there in Bordeaux, but Leo has proven it now through his matrix."

"I bring my AAA knowledge of Château Lafite to anyone I work with," says McCloskey.

"Chateau St. Jean is the only company in Sonoma Valley that's doing really well on Bordeaux varietals without using Leo's services," says Lyon. "The *Spectator* gave their merlot 90 points, and now it's selling like hotcakes. It's a claret-style; they didn't go for power and overripeness the way Parker does."

"Parker represents the public," says McCloskey.

"Parker and Laube are necessary," Lyon acknowledges. "We're following their style to some degree, but you have to have accountability. Lots of Napa Valley wineries are victims of their own success; I don't want to use the word *greed*, but when they calculate that they can make more money at ten thousand cases than at five thousand, there's a lot of pressure to overproduce. Now Parker and the *Spectator* are punishing some of them for it."

"The fundamental problem of most California wineries is scaling quality and volume," says McCloskey. "Maintaining quality as they grow. Château Lafite makes forty thousand cases, so one French company equals about twenty American producers. Which is the better value? The French, because the more widely available a wine is, the more fun it is to talk about and the more comparisons can be made by people who drink wine. No American wine company has ever made forty thousand cases of one wine that sold in the seventy-fifth percentile of Lafite's price—and gotten 90- to 100-point scores—for more than three years in a row. Just look what happened with Mondavi."

The Robert Mondavi Winery, once the poster label for Napa Valley in particular and California wine in general, was—after increasing production and subsequently coming under stylistic criticism from both Parker and Laube—recently sold (for a billion dollars) to Constellation Brands.

"Laube will pick on certain wineries, like he's doing now with St. Francis," says Lyon. "He's deliberately dethroning them as the premier merlot winery in Sonoma County. He did the same thing before with Matanzas Creek, and now they're passé. It's nice to be on his good side."

Lyon leads us inside his own winery, which contains two dozen three-thousand-gallon fermenters. Ascending an elevated catwalk, he opens a hatch on one of the tanks. "This wine had the same quality that the *Spectator* dinged the St. Francis merlot for," he says, "so I held it out longer and used oak chips to reduce the veggie-herbal tones."

"The vineyard delivered a certain level of quality in the market," McCloskey explains. "Now Mark's adding value. Only with my data can he do this—you can't do it by taste."

Despite his embrace of laboratory and digital technology, McCloskey's avowed winemaking model is the old-fashioned, low-tech "French wine farm." He says he's against such modern technologies as reverse osmosis, spinning cone, and micro-oxygenation, which allow vintners to alter the alcohol content, concentration, and mouthfeel of wine. "Those technologies just make it harder for me to figure out what's going on," he says. "I can't help people if they use a machine to increase the chemistry. Concentrating a wine doesn't necessarily make it better; you might be concentrating the bad with the good. I'm not focused on defects, only positives."

In Lyon's case, however (as well as many of his other clients', whether or not McCloskey knows it or they admit it), he makes an exception. "I use micro-ox technology to do barrel aging without barrels," Lyon admits. "I'll use reverse osmosis to get rid of volatile acidity. Things like de-alcoholization have really bailed me out. I was alarmed at the high Brix readings coming in this year; I'm trying to make concentrated wine, not thin and diluted, so I don't want to add tons of water. So I took some of the wine to Clark Smith at Vinovation and drove the alcohol down to 4 percent, then added it back. I think that's going to be standard operating procedure after this year—it's working very well."

"You can look at it as a form of *élevage*," says Leo. "In November, December, and January, the wine-farm people in France have a ninety-day period after harvest when the wine is being 'brought up' or 'educated.' It's like breeding dogs and cats—it goes from a wild, rustic cur to an obedient, tasteable critter."

"I wouldn't use micro-ox on Cherryblock or my core grade-A wines," Lyon demurs, "but to get a good ten- to fourteen-dollar bottle of wine without using tons of new barrels, I have to use tricks to get the cost down. On a twenty-five-to-fifty-dollar bottle, I can do the right thing and use new or one-year-old French or Hungarian oak barrels, but with the county lots, I've discovered that in most cases I'm better off doing micro-ox. It's a great tool, because it allows you to add air to the wine [as barrels do]."

"Maybe ten years from now, winemakers will be sophisticated enough to say this is a form of *élevage*," says McCloskey, "but right now they want to distance themselves from [admitting that they use] it."

"Yeah, 'cause it's too anti-terroir or something," says Lyon. "Some systems have clickers that let you give wine a dose of oxygen in barrels—when Parker comes around, you give it a little shot of air, which makes the wine seem rounder and more developed. If it's been oxygen deprived, it can get lean and structurey."

This proposed scenario—"When Parker Comes Around"—is a popular parlor game. "Since Parker has decided that filtered wines are bad, you'll make sure your filter is nowhere in sight when he comes to visit," another of McCloskey's clients told me. "Reverse osmosis and spinning cone are not discussed, because people want to think wine is made the old-fashioned way. But if they knew what the old way was, they wouldn't want to drink it."

McCloskey likes to call this "The Cover-up": winemakers' refusal to acknowledge the use of modern technologies that conflict with romantic marketing images. "No winemaker would be caught dead admitting they have a problem," he says. On the other hand, he has been accused of engaging in his own brand of obfuscation. Since he doesn't reveal the identities of the individual chemicals he tracks, for example, his method has been disparaged as a "black box," aloof from scientific scrutiny.

"The Enologix method isn't available to anyone else in the world to be able to verify whether [it would be valid] for somebody else if they did the same thing," says Davis's Roger Boulton. "There's no publication of results to allow people to see how reliable or verifiable they are. If Leo is so sure about these things, why are they hidden? If you're not going to reveal your methodology, you're probably not going to be very convincing to people who actually know what you're talking about. But for people who don't understand science, these things can be very convincing."

Indeed, the popular notion of the Enologix Score doesn't conform to what the company really tracks. Although McCloskey is widely perceived—thanks in large part to his own propaganda—to be chemically profiling the taste of wine critics, his GV500 score actually reflects the preferences of regional California winemakers, assembled via tastings that McCloskey convenes. Since critics' tastes are now assumed to have "gotten inside the wineries," he insists that these two metrics are closely linked; on the other hand, he maintains that regional winemakers are inclined toward "Mom's home cooking—they aren't judging themselves harshly, so we show them how to become cosmopolitan."

Also, for all his pronouncements that "the consumer is king," sales performance isn't a factor in the Enologix index. McCloskey merely presumes—as per the, er, conventional wisdom—that buyers obey the critics, another deduction that rankles Boulton. "Show me some data proving that consumers have any correlation with scores," Boulton demands. "Many people who employ [Enologix] don't want to actually go and find out what [consumers] want by surveying people about what made them purchase a wine, then follow up on whether they liked it or not. If a group of people tastes a wine that scores 92 [from a critic], you'll get a range of scores [from the group]—the results will be all over the map. Which part of that range or spectrum matters to you or me? What I like in wine, or beer, or whiskey, or tequila should not impact your assessment at all."

This is the usual objection to wine scores. The way in which anyone responds to a wine depends on myriad variables: stylistic preference, mood, and the accompanying food, not to mention the prejudices and expectations that attend a wine's reputation and price. For the same reason that a thundering symphony or screaming guitar solo may not make the best dinner music, wines that do poorly in competitive tastings sometimes fare better with meals than those attention-grabbing ones that impress judges in isolation. Hence, by keying his chemical evaluation system to critical scores, McCloskey makes the (not uncommon) assumption that intensity is tantamount to quality, when it's often equivalent only to extravagance.

"A single number can't capture a multidimensional component," Boulton says. "Would you read a review to find out whether you might be interested in buying a book? Of course. Would you buy a book based on whether it got an 89 or a 92 from a critic? I hope not. A score is saying, 'You couldn't possibly know about wine, so you have to buy my newsletter to find out.' It's so un-American that I'm amazed it's so accepted."

The charge of unpatriotism runs counter to McCloskey's propaganda, which holds that the Score is a democratic approach to evaluation. As McCloskey himself asked me, how else can consumers figure out what to buy in today's dizzying, international wine world?

"They can get into tasting groups and try ten wines at a time to determine what they like," Boulton says. "People do that all over the world. The Score goes back to who the judges are. Most wine writers are moving targets—if you give them six wines in a jumbled order, can they reproduce the same results? Even if you believe that critics can give scores reliably, wines change every day, so presumably the scores should change [too]. When did Parker taste the wine? What if he analyzed it six months or a year from now? When you understand bottle-to-bottle variation due to things like shipping and closure [e.g. corks], you begin to see that even six bottles of the same wine off a shelf will get different scores. So what if Parker gave this one a 95? It may have been shipped differently from the one that Leo got. Is it even close to the one that I got?

"All these things contribute to the fact that the score is not particularly useful," Boulton says. "But even if it were, there's no evidence that Enologix is capable of predicting it. I've never seen predictions of a judge's score before he scored; there's been no evidence of confidence intervals, or how well you can do it. Could [Enologix chemistry] distinguish between cabernet sauvignon and merlot? Probably not. Does it reflect how well a wine was made? It probably doesn't."

I mentioned McCloskey's claim that the Enologix index accurately predicts critical scores 81.18 percent of the time. "The average guy on the street gets 50 percent," Boulton said. "Most [statisticians] require 95 percent to say it's significant. If somebody says the Dow Jones will go up this afternoon and it does, is that a fact [of predictive ability]? No; it's an interesting observation, or a coincidence. If you spray bullets all over the place and a few get to the center of the target, do you talk about only those, or also about the ones that went everywhere? As a scientist, you have to look at all of them."

When I conveyed these criticisms to McCloskey, he responded with his customary charge that academics are unreceptive to innovations from outside their wheelhouse. "It's not that I'm keeping things secret, with leprechauns running around locking doors," he said. "It's that I'm not in the tenure-track business. I followed the academic rules and published papers for a while; I found that it was insanely slow. If you walked up to Steve Jobs and asked him to reveal everything, he'd say, 'Get out of my face.'"

I N THE SPRING of 1975—when Leo McCloskey was preparing to help found Felton Empire, Mike Benziger was touring Europe, and Randall Grahm was working at the Beverly Hills Wine Merchant—Larry Turley bought a 125-year-old farmhouse in Napa Valley. Turley was employed as an emergency room doctor in Santa Rosa, about ten miles from Calistoga over the Mayacamas Mountains; he commuted back and forth by motorcycle, his primary form of transportation since his student days in Georgia. Turley had been born in 1945 on a de facto organic farm in Tennessee, where his family raised cotton, tobacco, and dairy cattle, but after the herd came down with brucellosis and had to be exterminated, his father was offered a job in Augusta with the Swift meatpacking company. One condition of his employment was that he play volleyball for the company team—the elder Turley was six foot six, as was his son; Larry's older sisters, Mary Anne and Helen, were both six foot one. "Helen and I both played basketball," Larry confirms. "We were the tallest kids in the state."

In Georgia the Turleys had a few acres with some cows and rabbits. The family was Baptist, and alcohol was off-limits—a circumstance that got Larry kicked out of Sunday school. When he gave the wrong answer to the question "Would you rather dig ditches for thirty dollars a week or drive a beer truck for forty?" he was banished from class and, sent outside to wait in the car, expressed his frustration by melting the end of the vehicle's gearshift knob with the cigarette lighter. Surveying the damage, Turley's father, instead of further disciplining his son, excused his kids from ever attending Sunday school again.

"Later they converted to Episcopalianism so they could drink some," Larry says, "then became full-bore Catholics, which totally took the onus off."

At Barnard College in New York City, Mary Anne became a sculptor and subsequently lived for a few years in France. On one visit home, she brought a couple of bottles of Bordeaux that "opened the eyes" of her brother and sister. Their mother put out a white tablecloth for the occasion, and Larry found himself overcome with visions of King Arthur and the Knights of the Round Table draining hearty draughts from brimming goblets. Helen, for her part, went to St. John's College, a small liberal arts school in Annapolis, Maryland, whose curriculum consists of the classics of Western civilization, as well as four years of French and Greek, four of mathematics, and one of music. Larry at first studied aerospace engineering at Georgia Tech, but in his junior year he decided he wanted an "education" instead of the kind of specialized "training" that graduate school was for. He transferred to St. John's' other campus in Santa Fe, New Mexico, and in the summer traveled to Europe, where a friend introduced him to Hans Marberger—the urologist who performed a "transitional" operation for Erik Schinegger, an Austrian skier who had previously won the 1966 Olympic women's downhill race as "Erika," possessing, as she unknowingly did, internal male sex organs. "Marberger drove all over Europe doing lectures," says Turley. "Wherever he went, bearded guys would show up saying they were female. I was fresh off the farm, and thought this was all a little strange—but Marberger was very caring. He had grown up dirt poor, and he was a real people's doctor. People paid him in chickens, eggs, and wine."

Inspired by Marberger's example, Turley decided to be a doctor too. At the Medical College of Georgia in 1969, however, he didn't exactly fit in. For example, he was the only student who wore an *Easy Rider* Stars and Stripes motorcycle helmet. "I was probably just as conservative as the rest of them," he demurs, "but my value system didn't include racism." Which is to say that, one day when he saw a drunken black man getting beaten up by a campus security guard with a tree limb, Turley intervened and drove the victim to the hospital. He subsequently found himself at the door of the college's president, Harry

O'Rear, whose office was filled with art. Larry asked if he should remove his shoes before entering, to which O'Rear responded without looking up, "I'm surprised you're wearing any." Turley subsequently gave O'Rear a ride on his motorcycle, and the president recommended his transfer to the medical school of the University of New Mexico. (At first the UNM admissions officer assumed O'Rear's letter was a joke, as he'd signed it only with his colorful name and no accompanying title.) Once enrolled there, Turley paid visits to small-town doctors in the Rocky Mountains, choosing the youngest ones he could find who weren't members of the American Medical Association. Learning that many of these doctors had alcohol problems, inadequate incomes, and "zero family lives," he decided to pursue his internship in San Francisco, where he discovered that "the ER was where the action was—especially when heroin was king."

Turley did his residency at Santa Rosa Memorial Hospital, in Sonoma County. Before long, he'd bought the old Bale house between St. Helena and Calistoga. Arriving there after the night shift one morning, he found a tent pitched on the property; when he inserted the front wheel of his revving BMW inside its front flap, a fresh-faced young guy with shaggy hair jumped out. "What are you doing here?" the six-foot-six physician demanded, to which the five-foot-ten John Williams responded: "I thought I might have a glass of wine," and proceeded to uncork a '68 Sutter Home zinfandel from the Deaver ranch in Amador County.

Williams had just arrived from upstate New York, where, like Turley, he'd grown up on a dairy farm. Having worked for Welch's during high school, he'd majored in food science at Cornell's college of agriculture, where he'd studied dairy fermentation and cheese making. When he found out he could obtain academic credit for working in the wine industry, he got a job with the Taylor company in the Finger Lakes region—at which point, having never drunk a glass of wine in his life, he "knew in about ten minutes that I wanted to be in the wine business. I suddenly saw that I didn't have to divorce myself from agriculture to be part of this other thing."

Wine-appreciation courses were taught at Cornell's school of hotel administration, where Williams met Larry's sister Helen. After graduating from St. John's, she and her husband, John Wetlaufer, had moved to New York City, where he edited a physics journal while studying philosophy at the New School for Social Research and Helen developed a consuming interest in food and wine. She subsequently got a sales job at the Sherry-Lehmann wineshop, and ultimately enrolled in grad school at Cornell. She was torn between winegrowing and oceanography, but since flavor science had a "design your own" program that enabled her (like Randall Grahm and his fellow plant-science majors at Davis) to get a BS without taking organic chemistry, the sea of wine won out.

When Williams was nearing graduation from Cornell, he applied to the UC Davis graduate school of viticulture and enology. Helen mentioned that her brother had just bought some land in Napa Valley, and prior to the subsequent camping confrontation, John had ridden a Greyhound bus across the country to visit Davis and Larry. After verifying Williams's identity, the ER doctor let his sister's friend stay at his house in exchange for fixing it up. In the course of becoming a physician, Turley had also become a gourmet chef, so at night he and Williams and "a passel" of other people cooked and ate and drank. Turley loaned Williams his truck to make trips to Davis and also introduced him to another St. John's alumnus named Warren Winiarski—an ex-professor who, on Turley's recommendation (backed up by a promise to repay Williams's salary if he didn't perform up to snuff), hired the young New Yorker to work at his five-year-old winery, Stag's Leap Wine Cellars.

Williams didn't have a car, so he got to work by hitchhiking. On Williams's second day of employment, Winiarski loaned him his Datsun sedan to run an errand on the Oakville Cross Road, where another driver crossed the center lane and ran into Williams. Winiarski, a notoriously intolerant boss, summarily terminated him, but upon learning the cause of the accident from a cop, he called Williams and told him he was late for work. After harvest began in September, Williams and Turley made five gallons of wine from Winiarski's handful of chardonnay vines, cooling the fermentation in Larry's frog-filled creek. Eventually Williams bought his own motorcycle to get back and forth between Stag's Leap, Davis, and the Robert Mondavi Winery, where he was permitted to run centrifuge experiments for his thesis between 1 a.m. and 5 a.m. ("Basically," Williams divulges, "I slept in class.") One of his first tasks at Stag's Leap was bottling the 1973 estate cabernet, a chore for which his perfectionist employer wanted to pay him in bottles—an offer that Williams, who held out for cash, would later regret declining: In 1976, the '73 Stag's Leap cabernet won the red tasting at the Judgment of Paris.

"Warren had no idea what had happened to him," Williams recalls. "He told me we'd probably be getting more retail sales, but pretty soon so many cars came that I couldn't get my work done. I was the only one working in the cellar, and now I had to take care of that, too." When Williams protested that he couldn't handle all the traffic, Winiarski told him to take care of only the most expensive-looking cars.

After Williams got his master's degree in 1977, he returned to New York State, which had just passed a law encouraging small-farm wineries to get started. He had an offer to be the head vintner at a start-up winery called Glenora—"a collection of four farmers that I knew from my Taylor days to be good growers, with access to some of the best grapes." Even though Williams had no supervisory experience, the owners turned everything—"tanks, presses, style decisions, setting the whole winery up"—over to him and paid him better than he could ever have hoped for as an assistant in Napa. He subsequently became the first person to make commercial wine from the cayuga and ravat grapes, and he also befriended Lyman Smith, a New York State supreme court justice who happened to be a Bordeaux collector. "He was always reading this newsletter by a guy named Robert Parker," Williams recalls. "I remember thinking it was pretty cool that one guy was tasting all these wines."

In 1980, Williams came back to California to become the winemaker at Spring Mountain Vineyard, another winery that had taken part in the Judgment of Paris. After only three years away, he hardly recognized Napa Valley. "In 1975, downtown St. Helena had been practically derelict—half the buildings were empty, and about the only things happening were a diner, a hardware store, an old dive bar, and Mel's Clothing, which sold workman's clothes and straw hats. Even in

'77 we were saying, 'These wines are pretty good, huh?' *We* believed it, but there were still a lot of questions and experimenting; everyone was taking it on faith that it would become a world-class region. The only person actually saying so was Mondavi, and we were glad to let him say it, because I don't think we had the confidence to say it.

"When I came back," Williams says, "the world believed it. There was a swagger in people's step—elegance was coming into the cellars, money was being spent on tasting rooms, and Mondavi was coming into full flourish with its concerts and Great Chefs program." '81 was the first year of the Napa Valley Wine Auction, and also the first year of *Falcon Crest*, the TV series whose location was none other than Spring Mountain Vineyard. As a result, one year after returning to the place he remembered as a backwater, Williams found himself hosting a winery tour for Joe DiMaggio.

Spring Mountain's owner, Mike Robbins, was a flamboyant personality with an odd confluence of character traits: He seemed both starstruck and superior. He didn't think customers should be able to taste his wine before buying it any more than a diner in a restaurant is allowed to taste a dish before ordering it. On the other hand, *he* paid the producers of *Falcon Crest* to use the show's name on a second label, selling off old wine that Williams thought should be bulked out. Eventually Spring Mountain would go into foreclosure, but before that happened, Williams and Turley, in the face of Napa's new self-seriousness, decided to launch their own project. "When I came back in 1980, Larry said, 'Let's do some more homemade wine,'" Williams says. "I thought we'd make a few jugs or a barrel, but he hired a whole crew to go out and pick three tons of second-crop cabernet from Spottswoode. We borrowed a friend's hot tub to ferment it, and we had a blast."

Turley also had some sauvignon blanc vines on his property, so the next year he and Williams decided to bond their own winery. In light of Williams's work history, Napa Valley's swelling cachet, and the amphibious infestation on Turley's property, they put their tongues in their cheeks and called the brand Frog's Leap. Flipping a coin to determine who would be president and who would be chairman, they went so far as to hire a business manager, but John's wife, Julie Johnson (a hospice nurse), kept the sales and mailing records. After buying equipment and paying the requisite fees, they had three hundred dollars left over for a label design—a job they offered to Chuck House, a graphic artist in Santa Rosa. "We told him, 'Just don't make it green and amphibious,'" Turley says. "John was going to pay him the whole three hundred dollars, but I said, 'Let's pay him a hundred and have a party.' [Napa] was still a really friendly atmosphere—if someone had a party, everybody in the valley showed up."

House came up with a choice of four images. Julie, Larry, and his wife, Jeanine, outvoted John to pick one that was both graceful and whimsical*—an "amphibian Nureyev," augmented by corks marked RIBBIT and a warning on the base of the bottle that read OPEN OTHER END. They released their first vintage—seven hundred cases of '81 sauvignon blanc—in the spring of 1982, and on July 4, after glimpsing a bottle on a visit to Spring Mountain, Terry Robards published a story titled "Frog's Leap: A Prince of a Wine" in the *New York Times*. Syndicated in three hundred newspapers around the United States, "it helped us establish distribution literally overnight," says Williams. "People said some good things about the wine, but more about the approach." One person in Texas wanted to buy all of their seven hundred cases, but Turley says Williams "wanted to have a broad base." Turley also claims that he had a perfect sales record on the road. "We had a rule that if we sold wine to a restaurant, we had to eat there first," says Williams, "but we had to give up on that program pretty quickly. Larry would go into a place with his mom and dad and sister and her husband, drop off a case, and then drink seven bottles of it. We would send Larry's mom into a store to ask, 'Have you got that Frog's Leap?' Then she'd buy six bottles, and we'd pay her back."

Trying to meet nationwide demand afforded by the *Times*, Frog's Leap exceeded its five-year production plan in its second harvest, expanding the inventory to include chardonnay, cabernet, and Turley's favorite grape, zinfandel. Williams made the first few vintages at Spring Mountain, but in '84 they borrowed more money and moved

---

* To the extent that it would win that year's American Institute of Graphic Designers' Design of Excellence Award.

to Turley's property on Highway 29. Their cabernet from that vintage was chosen as a "Spectator Selection," and despite the fact that "the *Wine Spectator* was just a trashy-looking little paper," says Williams, "all of a sudden the dynamic changed from a couple of guys fooling around with a frog on their label to 'Oh my God, this is a 95-point wine.'

"Frog's Leap had been partly a joke, partly an attempt to recapture the atmosphere we'd known in 1975—that feeling of, 'It's just wine. Let's have fun with it,'" says Williams. "We didn't know we were going to get caught up in this whole other thing."

A FTER THE HARVEST is over, I taste a few wines from barrel with Grahm and his winemaker Jillian Johnson, a good-humored woman in her early thirties on her third tour of duty at Bonny Doon. A native of Menlo Park on the San Francisco peninsula, Johnson first worked for Grahm as a cellar hand in 2001 after graduating from UC Davis; she'd then moved to Australia, but when she returned the following year, Grahm recruited her to run the night shift, upping her previous pay. After a year she departed again, this time for South Africa, where she learned about biodynamics—and where she would have remained if not for the objections of her mother, who preferred that she come home. Upon doing so in September '04, she heard that Grahm still needed an assistant winemaker.

"I wasn't that excited about Bonny Doon," Johnson admits. "It was such a big company. But Randall told me he was changing direction—he said he was getting into biodynamics and back to focusing on the vineyards. In '05 I worked twelve- and fourteen-hour days—the harvest started in July with sixty-eight tons of raspberries, which came in supercold in fifty-five-gallon stainless steel drums. You add sugar and dump them into a pump, fortified with high-proof grape spirits; then you mix them up for three weeks, tasting every day. When it's reached a level of consistency and saturation, you press it and separate it from the skins and seeds, using a cheesecloth drain sock, like a sausage. It's a sticky, messy, horrible job.

"Next came Cardinal Zin, which took three weeks to process four hundred tons from Contra Costa County. After that, it was a nonstop stream of grapes all the way through November, and after we'd caught up and pressed everything, we took the muscat out of the freezer and started pressing it to make ice wine. We fermented into January, and then it was bottling season—first malvasia, then vin gris, then Big House Pink, then Big House White, then the '04 reds, and so many other smaller lots. It took a couple of years off my life, but by '06 I felt we were in a good relationship—we had some new systems, and better communication with the marketing people. I was involved in all the blending, and even Big House was fun to make in a different way. But I still prefer hands-on, so I was going to move on to a smaller place until Randall announced the downsizing. Now I feel our quality is improving—the wines are getting more ageable due to biodynamics, screw caps, and more natural winemaking; we're not using tannin additions or watering back or acidifying, all of which we did a lot before."

Like many un-state-of-the-art wineries, the Bonny Doon compound on Ingalls Street—located on the west side of Santa Cruz, a few blocks off Highway 1 before it leaves the city limits and heads up the coast—is a Byzantine complex of tanks, ovals, puncheons, and barrels, arranged according to a labyrinthine logic known only to intimate users. Johnson says there are fifty-two tanks, each of which she tastes three times a day during harvest; Grahm tastes them once a day when he's on-site. "At the sorting table, Randall can focus," Johnson says. "Also when he's pruning vines. This year he was at his happiest when he came back from working on that pinot noir vineyard up on Empire Grade."

When Grahm joins us, he says he was involved in another task heralding the new regime. "I'm trying to get rid of my Porsche. It's really expensive every time you have to repair it—like four to six thousand dollars. And unfortunately I'm a bad driver, in the sense that I tend to bump into things."

Alongside a door leading to the winery office—blocked by vertical, meat-locker-style strips of thermal plastic—is a single, small, horizontal barrel that Grahm refers to as "a modest R and D exercise. It's a roussanne and grenache blanc blend, on which we're experimenting with flor yeast, which is used with sherry and vin jaune in the Jura.

It grows on the surface after the wine is dry, and gets oxidized but doesn't acetify."

The first wine we taste is the aforementioned Empire Grade pinot noir. Johnson extracts the wine with a glass pipette, distributing pale red liquid into our glasses; the fragrance is beguiling, exuding the classic cherry-rhubarb character of pinot noir, but it isn't matched in the mouth, where it tastes rather harsh. "It came in at 22.5 Brix," Grahm says. "It had a high pH, and we had to acidulate it." This is counterintuitive: By contemporary California standards, 22.5 is considered underripe, indicating high acidity and thus a *low* pH. "If we'd picked it riper, the pH would have been even higher," Grahm says. "The fact is, the vineyard is out of balance. It should have ripened sooner, but it has too much vegetative growth—it gets a lot of rainfall, so there's not enough stress on the vines early to get them to slow down. It's a good example of a dry-farmed vineyard that's not in balance with itself. It needs more vines per acre, and more cover crop. Or a different cover crop."

We cross the wet cement floor, moving farther into the cool, warehouselike space. "In the next incarnation, we'll have floors that slope and floors that drain," Grahm says in passing. Stopping to taste from a barrel of syrah from Bien Nacido—a highly esteemed vineyard near Santa Maria on the Central Coast—Grahm says, "This should have been picked a week earlier."

"Randall says that about everything," Johnson remarks.

Nearby is an upright oval that served as another Bonny Doon experiment. Impressed by wines he'd tasted from concrete fermenters in France, Grahm decided to line some of his wood tanks with cement. Unfortunately, the wine stored in them turned out to taste rather . . . hard, exuding decidedly chalky notes of lime and clay. "Not such a bad thing at homeopathic doses," Grahm says, "but we also allowed the cement to dry out, provoking some infiltration of wine into its interstices—a microbiological nightmare. Some of these things are a lot clearer in retrospect."

From Bien Nacido we move south in the cellar but north in appellation, to the Ca' del Solo vineyard. First we taste the wine that Grahm described as "kind of an achievement, because we're doing something the Old World can't do"—that is, making good grenache from a cool climate. True to its billing, the wine is vibrant, underscoring its delicious fruit with a surprisingly bracing backbone. "It's a little salty," Grahm now demurs, harking back to the "salinas" character, "a little brut, a little simple. It needs more flesh to hit on other parts of your palate. It's a perplex. This is why Ca' del Solo is an interesting site, but not a genius site. Except for nebbiolo—that's perfect."

Actually I find Bonny Doon's nebbiolo to be a perplex. As expressed in its native habitat, Barolo and Barbaresco, nebbiolo is powerful wine, not necessarily in color or alcohol but in structure—specifically tannin and acid, requiring long aging to reveal its trademark amalgam of tar, tobacco, truffles, and roses. California nebbiolo has never approached the complexity of the Piemontese model, and while Bonny Doon's is better than some, it tastes light and fruity by comparison with its Old World (and even its California) counterparts. I once took a bottle of the '05 to a blind tasting with some wine professionals, one of whom said he thought it was good—if it was grenache.

"It might be house palate," Johnson acknowledges, referring to winemakers' tendency to develop ingrown standards applying only to their own products. She says the '05 nebbiolo had been vinified in two ways: Half the fruit was put on raisin trays to dry and concentrate, and the other half was picked a week later. "The dried batch was fabulous but high in alcohol," she said. "We kept the two tanks separate and swapped the juice—like cofermenting.* The blend was fantastic."

"This is a big wine," Grahm says, tasting the '08. "You know what we need to do with this? Leave it in puncheons for a relatively short time; then put it into a big tank for three or four years. Nebbiolo doesn't like oxygen. That would be a slower maceration."

"First we have to bottle the '07," says Johnson.

Speaking of which, next is the 2007 Le Cigare Volant. This was the wine that made Grahm famous, helping establish his early reputation; since its unveiling in 1984, however, it's gone through all manner of

---

* Putting different grape varieties in the same tank and fermenting them together as one wine.

permutations as Bonny Doon's flagship wine reflecting various experimental approaches and mirroring the vicissitudes of Grahm's career. The current MO is to age two lots of the same blend separately—one in puncheons (which, being larger than barrels, impart less contact between wine and wood), the other in an upright tank (which, being larger yet, imparts even less). Ultimately the two will be blended, but some of each will be bottled separately for members of Bonny Doon's DEWN (Distinctive Esoteric Wine Network) club.

"The blend won't be released until 2011," says Johnson, "but we'd like some feedback earlier. We might invite local DEWN members in and ask them their opinion."

This idea, smacking as it does of focus-group research, seems to rankle the head vintner. "Forgive me," Grahm says, "but fuck 'em. They're not the winemaker. Ultimately we have to make the wine we believe in."

"Why involve them then?" asks Johnson.

"For the sake of education," says Grahm. "To get them intellectually involved in the process. They get to be included in the discussion, but this isn't *American Idol*."

Johnson draws out a sample from one of the uprights. Upon tasting it, Grahm raises his arms above his head—one still holding the wineglass—shrugs his shoulders, narrows his eyes, and shakes his head, all with the wine still in his mouth. I've often seen him issue this response, which seems to ask: "How can there be any argument about this? The truth is self-evident." Until the wine leaves his mouth, though, it's hard to tell if the expression is positive or negative—it can apply either to a wine Grahm thinks is great or one he considers gross.

In this case it's the former. "Delicious!" he proclaims. "It reminds me of the '85. The first three Cigares were all in uprights. The '85 tasted like a raspberry milk shake." The wine is indeed attractive—rich but balanced, fruity but not effusively so, viscous but not in the unctuous way of so many recent high-end reds. Grahm attributes the wine's savoriness to lees—the leftover sediment, pulp, and yeast cells that settle out of a wine after it's been pressed. In the squeaky clean UC Davis paradigm, this is the devil's playground, a breeding ground for microbial activity of the seamy-underbelly sort. Lees consumes oxygen, for example, contributing to the chemical phenomenon known as reduction—the tendency of a compound to gain electrons, which in wine can give rise to foul-smelling things like mercaptans and hydrogen sulfide. The usual way to avoid such unpleasantness is by emptying the vessel, aerating the wine, discarding the lees, and putting the wine back in the vessel—a labor-intensive, time-honored process known as racking, which is conducted regularly and repeatedly until bottling. Sometimes, however, lees is left in contact with wine to enhance richness, complexity, and texture. This technique—identified on the label as *sur lie*—is employed mainly on whites (classically chardonnay and melon, the grapes of white Burgundy and Muscadet), which, containing fewer phenolic compounds than reds, are more susceptible to adverse effects from exposure to air. The oxidation that might thus endanger them—enabling the growth of acetic bacteria, which can turn wine into vinegar—is soaked up by lees, which is sometimes stirred intentionally, a technique known as *bâtonage*.

Pinot noir can also be made this way, but even then it typically takes place for no more than a year in barrels. On other reds, *sur lie* aging is rare. But one of the Santa Cruz Mountains' pioneering postwar winemakers, Dan Wheeler, caught Grahm's fancy by (1) aging various red wines on their lees (2) for years (3) in airtight glass carboys, using (according to Grahm) "a very precise ratio of lees to volume based on the reductive capacity of the wine." It seemed to exert a positive effect on the wines' longevity, leading Grahm on to Emidio Pepe, an Italian winemaker who employs a similar technique. Upon tasting Pepe's 1975 Montepulciano d'Abruzzo—a wine not usually associated with cellaring potential, but which in this case was still "youthful, vibrant, and strong" at more than fifteen years of age— Grahm had become transfixed by the power of lees. Equating it with the immortality of a soul—or, in mineral terms, the indestructibility of gold—he had dispatched assistants to research glass water-heater tanks for storage purposes, at the same time developing the parallel concept of "lees hotels": stainless steel shelves providing a sort of sediment roost inside tanks.

"We're not like a lot of wineries," Johnson says. "All our wines are aged on the lees, and we don't really rack much. We don't stop stirring the previous vintage until the next harvest." Given the stinkiness that arises from lees during a wine's *élevage*—a wine's period of cellaring and maturation between fermentation and bottling—this regime requires faith on the part of the producer.

"We never used to have reduction issues," Grahm acknowledges. "Now we do. I don't know whether to be happy or sad, but I think happy."

"We also use screw caps," Johnson points out. Similar to *sur lie* aging, screw-capped wines—sealed off from even the minimal oxygen that enters a bottle through a natural cork—are reductive.

"Screw caps are like *The Picture of Dorian Gray*," Grahm says. "The wine tastes delicious; then you put it in screw caps, and all these issues emerge. Wines that have vitality or minerality tend to smell like shit for a while—they go through a dark phase, but wines that are all sweetness and light throughout their *élevage* are like vapid waitresses in Aspen, Colorado. Reduction is like a guy with a lot of testosterone—it may unnerve some women, but it's really just a management issue. At the end of the day, it's better for the life force and longevity. The '05 Cigare just came out of its funk and is delicious; it has a savoriness that's right on the edge of acceptability—an umami quality, which is literally MSG. There's a lot of glutamate in lees and yeast."

Johnson pours a sample of the other '07 Cigare lot—the one aging in puncheons. It's similar to the sample from uprights but more rounded, with slightly more sweetness from the extra oak. "I like this too!" Grahm says with surprise. He hadn't expected to like the puncheon wine as much as the upright; still, in spite of his satisfaction with both outcomes, he tells Johnson, "We can't keep making Cigare the way we did."

Why not?

"Because Randall likes to change," Johnson says.

"We should put it in glass carboys," Grahm suggests. "Something magical happens to wine in a large-format glass vessel. It rocks."

Johnson divulges that, not long before this, a syrah stored in a glass carboy accidentally got hidden on a shelf in the winery, preventing it from being racked or otherwise exposed to air. "It was awesome," she reports. "Glass allows the grapes to express themselves without any other influences." As a result, Bonny Doon is about to purchase 250 five-gallon glass carboys. "We'll have to build a special shelf for them," Johnson says. "We'll stir the lees every two weeks, and if it's successful—and I think it will be—we'll have to find a way to do it in volume."

Following the Pepe-Wheeler model to the fullest extent, this would be the most reductive approach possible, totally starving the wine of oxygen, without the influence—either oxidative or gustatory—of any wood whatsoever. "I'm a big fan of oak alternatives," Johnson says. "Not necessarily chips, but . . ."

"But . . . chips," says Grahm.

"Untoasted oak chips help stabilize color," Johnson explains. "You can get them in all kinds of configurations now."

"We need to get decahedral polygons," Grahm says. "We should also consider other woods—there's a whole forest of possibilities out there. Birch would be great for a wintergreen element."

Somehow this doesn't sound exactly like "allowing the grapes to express themselves without any other influences." Since Grahm sold his big brands and got biodynamic religion, Bonny Doon has reportedly sworn off artificial flavor enhancements. "I still have all these catalogs of wine additives," Johnson tells me with some nostalgia, in the manner of an ex-drunk who maintains a bottle collection from her old intemperate days. "It's incredible what something like MegaPurple* can do—it fills in the midpalate and can give the wine a backbone. But it's really just sugar and color. It's something like 60 Brix—like steroids for wine. Additives are like a drug addiction. '06 was the first year I didn't use enzymes to get the wines to settle and come clear—they break down the pectins, which takes about a day. Without enzymes it was taking so long that I freaked out, but Randall said, 'Just go ahead and rack it.' It turned out that a lot of the solids *had* settled, and everything turned out wonderful—the flavors are more complex, because you're leaving more in the wine."

After Grahm goes back to selling his Porsche, I ask Johnson what it's like to work for someone with such a constantly shifting methodology.

---

* A superconcentrated grape product used to enhance color, flavor, and texture in wines.

"It's hard to keep people with Randall's IQ focused," she acknowledges. "His brain is going a hundred miles an hour, and sometimes he doesn't think of the practical side. He loves to throw out ideas and come up with new products, but he forgets that it confuses people. At one point we had eighteen grape varieties in the Ca' del Solo vineyard, with five different trellis systems in one block. There were some short vines close to the ground, some on a pergola system, some syrah with three-foot spacing. . . . It made it very difficult to figure out the crop load. You could never just say, 'Block One is ready,' and I'm not sure if the trellis experiments were even tracked. This year we decided that '08 would be the last dolcetto; we pulled it out and grafted over to grenache, and then it got a gold award in the [San Francisco] *Chronicle* wine competition. In '06, Randall wanted to make a sparkling riesling from Ca' del Solo; now it's aging and it's fantastic, killer. But since riesling wasn't in line with the new Bonny Doon brands, we ripped the vines out, and now we can never make it again. He didn't wait to see the result before making the decision. When I first came here it was exciting to have so many experiments going on, but I would end up doing ten experiments that were mediocre instead of following two all the way through. Now I'm saying we have to follow them through.

"I think Randall truly believes in the wines we're making now," Johnson says. "I've heard him say, 'I actually drink our wines again!' I've learned so much from him about that reductive, leesy, complex style—you don't have to pick at high Brix, water back, and add acid to make fantastic wines. He has a much more European palate, so he's never given in to that trend. I think we've developed a good working relationship now—we have good rapport, so I can tell him exactly how I feel, and we argue and joke about it. He injects the creative side, but I'm more practical, so I'm able to help him realize his dreams. The problem is that he wants everything right now, and it's hard for him to be satisfied with one thing. I look at him and say, 'Randall, just be happy with what you have!' But that's not what he's about."

THE PLACE WHERE our tasting occurred wasn't the original winery occupied by Bonny Doon. When Randall Grahm graduated from UC Davis, he'd managed to find his way back to the Santa Cruz Mountains in short order; clearly fate played a role not just in returning him to the scene of his philosophy studies, but also in the fact that Grahm, having held only one previous job—at the Beverly Hills Wine Merchant with its behind-the-scenes connections to *Rowan & Martin's Laugh-In*—obtained his second (and only other) paid position at a winery owned by Dick Smothers, cohost of the other iconic 1960s TV comedy-variety show. In light of the Smothers brothers' history of bucking network censors to air topical material on television, Randall was "expecting tirades about the oppression of the masses," but was surprised to find Dick rather apolitical. "He was a party animal," Randall divulges—presumably not the Democratic kind.

As providence would further decree, Grahm arrived at Smothers the year after Leo McCloskey left. He thus felt the Leo Effect only via the recriminations of Smothers's head winemaker, who seemed to Randall to have been "traumatized" by the experience. "Maybe every little winery is inefficient," Randall posits. "I had nothing else to gauge it against, but we spent a lot of time working late into the night making messes and then cleaning them up." If Grahm harbored any doubts that he would prefer to be his own boss, the Smothers job dispelled them; his mother, Ruthie, recalls before very much time had passed, "Randall called us up and said, 'I really, really wish we could start our own winery.' He presented Alan with a very efficient plan; Randall doesn't necessarily have the best business head in the world, but he was very diligent." Presented with a proposal for a winery and vineyard, Grahm's father figured the worst-case scenario was that he'd end up owning some real estate. Hence, he told his son to look for property and keep him posted.

Randall subsequently scoured the West Coast from San Diego to Washington State. Armed with maps and data from the U.S. Geological Survey and National Oceanographic and Atmospheric Administration, he was, not unpredictably, searching for suitable conditions for pinot noir—a mission that led him briefly to Oregon's Willamette Valley, whose wine industry was just getting off the ground. "In one weekend I visited nine of the twelve Oregon wineries," he remembers. "David Lett [Eyrie Vineyards' pioneer of Oregon pinot] was very discouraging, though probably he was trying to minimize competition. It was just a snap judgment, but I came away thinking that you couldn't grow good grapes there. How were the vines going to suffer? The soils were too deep and rich. And, of course, you need limestone."*

Around this time, Grahm tasted an "inspiring" pinot made by Ken Burnap from the Vine Hill area in the Santa Cruz Mountains, not far from Smothers. Still, he homed in on Bonny Doon because of a misconception. "In the old Davis textbooks, the weather data said Bonny Doon was one of the coolest places in California. It turned out that that data was collected right at the fog line, and there are many different microclimates depending on where you are." Not coincidentally, Jim Beauregard—McCloskey's Felton Empire partner, who was then spearheading a drive to create a Ben Lomond Mountain appellation that would include Bonny Doon—began receiving calls from Grahm. "I had studied geology, oceanography, and plant morphology in school," Beauregard explains. "For a new appellation, you have to outline what makes it specific, so Randall was asking me what the best places were in the Santa Cruz Mountains. I told him everything

* Later, in the Bonny Doon newsletter, Grahm would acknowledge another impediment: "There is something terminally goyish about the state of Oregon. Maybe it is the ubiquitous presence of double-wide trailers or perhaps it is the woolen shirts."

I thought, and all of a sudden he popped up and outbid me for one of the best vineyard sites, the old Bertolli ranch—I had terms, and his parents had cash. Later it turned out that the neighborhood was not in favor of his putting a winery on it, so he split it into two parcels, sold one to a logging company, and the other got split again into ten-acre parcels."

The Grahms also bought two other properties in Bonny Doon. One housed a local bar called the Lost Weekend; the other was a fifty-acre parcel upon which Randall planted thirty acres of chardonnay, pinot noir, and—departing from his Burgundian mission—a combination of Bordeaux varieties including cabernet sauvignon, cabernet franc, merlot, and malbec. Against the advice of Professor Cook ("If he told me not to do something, it's a fair bet I would do precisely that"), prior to planting he spread three hundred tons of limestone in the vineyard to simulate soil conditions in Burgundy. But newly planted grapevines require roughly three years to begin producing fruit, so to start making wine immediately, in '81 Grahm purchased some Sonoma County pinot noir grapes that he rendered into a rosé and a red (which he would later remember as "most inauspicious and best forgotten") at the Devlin winery in Soquel.

The next year, already running out of room, Grahm called Josh Jensen, who was then in his fifth year making Calera pinot noir and chardonnay near Hollister to the east. Jensen agreed to rent Randall some space, an experience he later described in the Calera newsletter:

> Our protégé was a guy from Santa Cruz with long scraggly hair and clothes from a 1960s rock concert. He'd tasted a zillion wines and had a very good palate, but always talked cryptically, in riddles. If you asked him how much wine he made last year, he'd answer, "less than you might imagine," or "It's hard to say." If you asked him how much vineyard he was going to plant, he'd answer, "just a few vines," or "We may not proceed down that avenue." But he was very eager [and] he also had a seemingly endless procession of beautiful coeds from Santa Cruz who would come over and help him punch down, clean the tanks, load the presses, shovel stems and the like—all for free. He, of course, was making the

usual number of rookie mistakes, in fact, he really seemed to make *a lot* of them. So we, the grizzled veterans, would give him *that look* whenever he'd pull a bonehead stunt or make an incongruous statement. The long-legged coeds, however, were giving him entirely different looks: they thought he really had his act together. Worse, they thought *we* were out to lunch. . . .

Stories about this guy started to proliferate. One of our cellar workers once found him with his hand over an inch and a half fitting on a full wine tank. He'd taken off a cap . . . but dropped the clamp. It was a classic finger-in-the-dike situation: if he took his hand off the fitting—the fitting is like a hole in the side of the tank—he'd lose a lot of wine while he bent down to the floor to get the clamp. Our guy picked up the clamp, and together they got the cap and clamp back on without losing too much wine. But they both got drenched. . . .

Within a month of his arrival at our winery, the unanimous verdict was in: this guy could not possibly make it in the wine business . . . [he] simply wasn't on the same channel as the rest of us. We were watching NBC, or ESPN, and he was tuned into the Science Fiction Channel, or Discovery. He was trying a bunch of off-the-wall grape varieties, and when none of them seemed too great on their own, he mixed them all together, also adding some cabernet sauvignon he'd made, and called the resultant combination "claret." He eventually bottled this and priced it real low, like $3.50 a bottle. None of this made any sense at all to us at Calera.

In fact, Bonny Doon's "Mendocino Claret" was a classic Bordeaux blend. More auspiciously, thanks to David Bruce, Grahm "lucked into finding some brilliant old vines" producing grenache near Hecker Pass south of Santa Cruz. Although this marked his first intersection with grapes used in the Rhône valley, he ignored Old World tradition and, "assuming that the wine-buying public greatly appreciated laconic understatement," combined it with cabernet and merlot in a "California Vin Rouge." Sales failed to confirm his assumption, but the wine won a gold medal at the Los Angeles County Fair.

Although Bonny Doon Vineyard was bonded in 1983, it wasn't

a slam dunk proposition to establish a winery in the town of Bonny Doon. Nestled in the redwoods 1,200 feet above the Pacific, the place defined the dual concept of sleepy hamlet and countercultural enclave. Its residents (who, at the time, included the science-fiction writer Robert A. Heinlein) put a premium on privacy and peace and quiet, and however much they might value wine in their personal lifestyles, the introduction of a new commercial-industrial operation didn't fit the picture. Partly owing to his quick-profit turnaround of the old Bertolli ranch, Grahm had already acquired a reputation as an interloper from L.A.—an image he did nothing to improve by shutting down the Lost Weekend Saloon, converting it from a biker bar into a tasting room: clear evidence of yuppie gentrification, whether or not there had previously been (as his future manager Patrice Boyle put it) "a motorcycle crashing into the mailbox every weekend." At a house he acquired as part of the sale and subsequently rented out, he further invoked the community's ire by ordering the tenant to destroy a pot farm that had previously supplied scores of Santa Cruz customers. Randall himself took up residence in an A-frame alongside his new vineyard, where he lived with a dog named Bonny Doon and a pair of cats named Franny and Zooey.

The Santa Cruz County board of supervisors restricted the new winery to twenty thousand gallons, or about eight thousand cases. The winemaking facility was a former equipment-rental shed, situated next door to a chicken farm downhill from a one-room auto-repair shop. Retrofitted (without benefit of an architect) to accommodate tanks, presses, pumps, barrels, and puncheons, it remained "dysfunctional from a production standpoint—we worked until one a.m., instead of three a.m. like we did at Smothers." Still waiting for his estate vineyard to come on line, in '83 he augmented his nascent Rhône "portfolio" with syrah from the Estrella River vineyard in Paso Robles, as well as La Reina chardonnay from Monterey County and—retooling his earlier snap judgment—Willamette Valley pinot noir from Oregon's Bethel Heights.

When the latter grapes were crushed, Grahm later recounted, "both the bees and the crew went into a frenzy over the intense, honeyed fragrance." The resulting wine (which received favorable notice from the *Wine Spectator*) effortlessly outdid the California pinots he was making, including the '84 from his own estate. "The pinot from Oregon was so much better, I thought, 'Why bother?'" Grahm says. "If I can buy better grapes than I grow, what's the point of growing them?" By contrast, the syrah he made from the central California coast—spicy and smoky, with the trademark white-pepper-and-anise nuances associated with syrah from the Rhône—succeeded in channeling some of the character of the authentic article.

For Grahm to refocus his attention from northern to southern France was an aesthetic decision akin to the New Orleans–reared Marsalis brothers' shifting from their classical music training to jazz. As he began to gravitate toward Rhône grapes, Randall developed the habit of haunting Kermit Lynch, who by then had expanded his harmonica-procuring hobby to become a pioneering importer of obscure French wines. "Randall would come into my shop and go right to the Rhône wines," Lynch remembers. "He wanted to find out everything about them. He had this huge head of hair—we called it a 'natural'—and this searching vibe; he was very curious, always looking for information. Mainly he'd ask me questions about practical stuff, like what kind of cooperage they used in Côte-Rôtie. And he wanted to know about grape varieties, which was unusual then."

"Kermit was probably the most significant person in my wine consciousness," Grahm says today. "I mean: Côtes du Rhône? Hello? He had me try a million Crozes-Hermitages, Cornases, and Gigondases. I couldn't make heads or tails of them. Some were like science experiments gone terribly wrong. In those days, nobody knew anything—for example, that grenache needs a moderate climate, that syrah needs a cool climate and granitic soil, and that mourvedre needs a long, warm season but not too much water stress. Kermit knew more than anyone else."

Like Grahm, Lynch had little use for most New World wine but felt that Rhône varieties were a better fit for California than were grapes from northern France. "Pinot noir would ripen in Châteauneuf-du-Pape," Lynch acknowledges, drawing an analogy between that region and the Golden State. "You'd be harvesting black pinot noir every year in the third week of August. It would be even bigger than California pinot, but [the French] weren't looking for that. In Burgundy, pinot noir barely ripens at all. Same with mourvedre in Bandol. One of the big differences between France and the U.S. is the decisions about what to plant where—here it's about fad and fashion, but in France the decisions were made long ago, first by monks and then by the aristocracy. Many old vines in California were planted by people from Europe who knew where they *should* be planted—they knew what to look for, like the Romans who always picked the right place to build a little town. It may be that Rhône grapes in California show more terroir just because of those old plantings."

To augment the old-vine grenache from Gilroy, Grahm began searching the state for other plantings of Rhône varieties—a tough assignment. At the time, California's syrah vineyards could be counted on one hand; its producers consisted of Estrella River, McDowell Valley Vineyards in Mendocino County, and Napa Valley's Joseph Phelps, where John Buechsenstein had gone to work (for head winemaker Walter Schug) after graduating from Davis. Soon enough, Grahm showed up on their doorsteps to pick their brains, as well as that of the encyclopedic Sacramento wine seller Darrell Corti, who clued him in that, on the sweltering banks of the Sacramento–San Joaquin river delta near the town of Oakley in Contra Costa County, there was a secret treasure trove of century-old mourvedre locally known as "mataro." Having survived the phylloxera epidemic because of the area's sandy soil, it had been grown since Prohibition mainly for shipping to home winemakers, who paid Oakley's Spanish and Portuguese farmers about $150 a ton. Instead Grahm paid them handsomely by the acre and directed them to drop half the fruit, the better to concentrate the juice and emulate an Old World wine that American consumers had never heard of.

Grahm later explained that, in the wake of his experience with his California Vin Rouge, it gradually dawned on him "that if I wanted people to actually buy the wines, I might think about giving them some sort of conceptual hook, or at least a stylistic referent." Hence, in the first official Bonny Doon newsletter (spring 1985), he told his customers: "If you think about it for more than a nanosecond, you will realize how eminently sensible it is to produce Rhône-style wines here in California. The climate of the Rhône is not at all dissimilar to many California microclimates." He duly went on to explain that syrah was "the authentic article that traces its lineage back to the Persian Shiraz" and "grenache grapes grown in California can produce wine every bit as perfumed, heady and intense as in Châteauneuf-du-Pape." With the latter claim, he set the stage for a wine that would catapult him to rock-star status just as the market for California wine was exploding.

In 1984, in search of a "a high-concept differentiated wine," Grahm concocted a Châteauneuf-style blend of grenache, syrah, and mourvedre. Resolving—again based on the Vin Rouge debacle—to give it a "catchy name," he stumbled on a fateful concept when, leafing through John Livingstone-Learmonth's *The Wines of the Rhône* one day, he came across the fact that, in 1954, during the worldwide UFO craze that included the Roswell incident, the French village of Châteauneuf-du-Pape had passed an ordinance that prohibited flying saucers from landing. Delighted by this far-out fact (and knowing that many UFO sightings described the alleged crafts as "cigar-shaped") Grahm's *Mad* magazine/*Laugh-In*/*Smothers Brothers*–honed psyche began to conjure a label that, on the thirtieth anniversary of the actual episode, would pay homage to his own wine's roots in a way that was both serious and silly. "With Le Cigare Volant, a certain ironic distance was perfectly established," he later wrote. "The wine bears a relationship to the French product but also maintains an appropriate separation. Oh, those wacky French."

Until then, Bonny Doon labels, like Grahm's traditional appreciation of connoisseur-sanctioned wines, had hewed to a classical model of tasteful fonts and flowing script—the only picture was an image of a grapevine, over which an elegant typeface was superimposed. Now, in pursuit of an envelope-exploding image for Le Cigare Volant, he turned to Chuck House, whose sole previous wine commission had conferred instant solvency on Frog's Leap. Working from old illustrated books, House came up with a composition that juxtaposed a dignified domaine with a lurking airborne spaceship, the latter casting a lurid red light onto the pastoral village; to heighten the sinister feeling, Grahm asked him to partly conceal the saucer behind a tree. Randall explained the name on the bottle's back label and in his newsletter, ending with the decree: "I hereby proclaim that Flying Cigars are permitted to land here, by order of the Laird of Bonny Doon."

Prior to Le Cigare Volant, most California wine, for all its upstart enthusiasm, had been prey to the pompous seriousness that had kept so many mainstream Americans from embracing the product from abroad. A rare recent exception was the aforementioned Frog's Leap (founded the same year as Bonny Doon), with its titular turn on the hoity-toity Stag's Leap/Judgment of Paris cachet. Despite its whimsical marketing, though, Frog's Leap made familiar wines—cabernet sauvignon, zinfandel, sauvignon blanc—which hewed to the predominant New World paradigm of single-varietal bottling. Although Joseph Phelps was experimenting with syrah, and Bob Lindquist and Adam Tolmach (of Qupé and Ojai) were beginning to work with it near Santa Barbara, the idea of making a Rhône-style blend out of several synergistic varieties—common in nineteenth-century California—was on almost nobody's 1984 radar. "Everybody was making cabernet and chardonnay, so all we paid attention to was Bordeaux and Burgundy," Grahm's old classmate David Ramey remembers. "We didn't think about the Rhône at all."

In that sense, Le Cigare Volant was an ideal wine for establishing an original and irreverent reputation—but it had to be brought to people's attention. The southern-Rhône provenance inspired the Classic Wines company (which imported E. Guigal from France into Massachusetts) to take Bonny Doon on, winning Grahm his first out-of-state distribution. He had always sold the wine himself in Northern California, but when he "couldn't figure out how to park in San Francisco," he turned it over to Bay Area distributor Alexia Moore. In L.A., meanwhile, he gave his portfolio to someone who he knew would, although inexperienced, represent the wine with passion and conviction.

"I'm a housewife and songwriter," his mother, Ruthie, demurs. "I know less than nothing about wine. I couldn't tell a red from a white, but Randall asked me to take it around to restaurants until he could come down and find a local rep. I knew that Randall was very conscientious and diligent, and whatever he did would be terrific; so I said okay."

This proved a transformative experience not just for Ruthie but also for many of her incipient highfalutin accounts. "It was like taking an infant and dropping them into a swimming pool," she recalls, "or sending *I Love Lucy* out to sell wine. Randall mailed me some samples with blurbs, but I didn't even know what you carry the wine in. At first I put it in a Ralph's grocery-shopping bag; then I used a Gucci bag for a couple of weeks, but I'm not a Gucci type of person and the bottom fell out. Eventually a friend gave me a basket to carry the wine in. I was really inept; I tried to be dignified, but I felt so ignorant—everybody else was so knowledgeable, and I didn't even know how to properly open a bottle. I would take the wine into places like Perino's and Skandia, and they would say, 'Who made this?' and I would say, 'Randall Grahm.' They would say, 'Isn't *your* name Grahm?' But whoever tasted it went crazy for it—the reactions were spectacular. They thought the wines were so different, and they liked every single one. At first people were afraid to take it because they'd never heard of Bonny Doon, but if they didn't, I just kept calling until they did."

It seems that Ruthie's lack of polish exerted a kind of jujitsu effect. "Eventually one of the sommeliers told me, 'You know, Ruthie, when you come in, I feel very safe.' I didn't have the suede shoes, but I believed in the product, and my goal was to have it in every restaurant in the city. After a while, I made a list of the famous places that were carrying the wine and handed it out to everybody I visited. People would say they didn't care what other restaurants it was in, that they would decide for themselves, so I'd say okay; I respect that. Then, as I was bending over to get the wine out, I'd see them looking at the list out of the corner of their eye. Pretty soon distributors saw how people reacted to it, and then *they* wanted it—I started getting calls from wine stores, and I ran out of allocations. People were *begging* me for more.

"Then Randall started sending me to wine festivals. My husband was used to coming home and having a meal on the table at six, but

Randall would call me up and ask if I could go to London next week. If I was pouring at a big tasting and somebody asked me a question, I'd just turn to anyone who I thought might know the answer. It's an incredible world, the world of gourmets and epicures—so different from anything I'd done or knew about, but I had the time of my life. Maybe because I come from a showbiz background, I felt very comfortable with people in the wine business. The only rough part was carrying the wine—twelve bottles can get heavy."

Jason Lewis agrees that show business played a part in Ruthie's success—sort of. "If there's a wine-world equivalent to the Jewish stage mother of Hollywood fable," he says, "it's Ruthie. 'My son made this—you should buy it!' She's a force of nature. She's a dear, warm, sweet person, but I'm glad she never called on me as a sales rep."

"Nobody had any sort of defense mechanism to counter the winemaker's mother," Randall agrees.

With the success of Le Cigare Volant, Grahm's creative streak got positive reinforcement, and he rode it like a big-wave surfer, diving headlong into both Rhône-wine production and off-the-wall marketing. Abandoning his original goal, he soon replaced his estate pinot noir vines with syrah and began grafting over the chardonnay and Bordeaux varieties to the white Rhône grapes marsanne and roussanne—or so he thought. Imported via his "Samsonite clone" program (i.e., brought through customs in a suitcase), the roussanne turned out to be viognier, the highly floral and difficult-to-grow grape of Condrieu. Grahm blended it with the marsanne and called it Le Sophiste, a name connoting both refinement and insincerity—labeled with a dashing (though headless) figure sporting spats, a tuxedo, and cane, the bottle was crowned by a plastic top hat. He also bottled a fruity, nouveau-style grenache called Clos du Gilroy—an insider joke on Clos du Roi, decorating the label with a picture of Proust and explaining that, though the fruit hadn't made the cut for his flag/airship wine ("Clos but no Cigare"), it was also grown "close to Gilroy." Amid a nationwide boom in white zinfandel—cheap pink sweet wine that tasted like soda pop—he marketed a dry rosé called Vin Gris de Cigare, similar to wines made in the southern Rhône, with a back label that could be read only through the liquid inside the bottle. Spoofing the Châteauneuf-du-Pape wine Vieux Télégraphe, Grahm made a mourvedre called Old Telegram, for which House created an embossed relief label with a manual typewriter:

GRAPE OF COTE DE PROVENCE AND SOUTHERN RHONE E G BANDOL STOP IN AMERICAS AND ESPANA ALSO CALLED MATARO STOP SPICY PEPPERY MEATY WILDLY AROMATIC CHARACTER STOP WELL SUITED TO FLAVORFUL FOODS STOP WHEN SEE ON SHELF OR WINELIST STOP THIS CORRESPONDENT WOULD WRITE MORE STRAIGHTFORWARD LABEL COPY BUT SUFFERS FROM ADVANCED ETIQUETTORHEA CANT STOP

Not all of Bonny Doon's antics were derived from Rhône traditions. As an homage to German eiswein—sweet "ice wine" made from frozen grapes, whose sugar is naturally concentrated when their liquid component freezes—Grahm created a "vin de glace" dessert wine by putting muscat grapes into a commercial freezer. The U.S. Bureau of Alcohol, Tobacco and Firearms subsequently informed him that anything called "ice wine" must be made from grapes frozen on an actual grapevine—a problem that Grahm solved by renaming the product Vin de Glacière, or Wine of the Refrigerator. After pressing, the leftover low-sugar grapes were thawed, fermented on their skins, and distilled into a fragrant grappa that Grahm the Francophile called *marc*. To make off-season use of his tanks, pumps, and presses, he had the brainstorm to make "infusions" of berries—*framboise* (raspberries), *fraise* (strawberries), and *marion* (blackberries)—by fermenting and fortifying them with distilled spirits.

Since most of these things required explaining, both technical and philosophical ("Wine represents possibility, the conversion of one state to another. . . . The distillate is the essence of an essence. The spirit rises"), the role of the Bonny Doon newsletter expanded along with the winery's production, though the printed content soon transcended the task of simply selling the product. For all his passion about wine, Grahm clearly needed to express himself in ways other than enological. In college he had foreseen his future as that of a professor and fiction writer, and his newsletters of the late 1980s were a form of frustrated grad-student literature—each edition a tour de force of erudition, imagination, literary and philosophical allusion, viticultural terminology, and sophomoric punning, in which every other word was foreign, italicized, or polysyllabic. In 1987 they began to include lengthy literary parodies, the first of which—titled "How I Spent My Summer Vacation," channeling the spirit of *Ulysses*'s Molly Bloom— was told from the point of view of a ripening grape:

My old man wanted me to stay on the farm all summer long. He told me I was permanently grounded. . . . I had to just hang around the vineyard all summer, vegetating. A real stick in the mud. I was this awkward gangly creature, see, growing it seemed about three inches a day. My old man assured me that when I was a little older I would blossom into a real beauty.

The days were warm and bright, the evenings cool and breezy. I could feel the wind rustle under my canopy. As the days grew longer, my skin turned soft and rosy. I felt myself maturing, ripening, but for what?

The dark-eyed boys who hung around the vineyard were at last beginning to notice me. "Pick me, pick me!" I mutely cried out to them but they just walked on, their sharpened knives gleaming in the late summer sun.

A sweet-faced boy came upon me and said, "I have to have you" and suddenly it was done. Feeling cut off from my roots, I was en route to a mysterious end. I was quite frightened when I felt my perfect skin being bruised and crushed. That intense pressure seemed to last forever and then suddenly I felt my juices begin to flow. A feeling of warmth spread over me; a heady, almost intoxicating sensation devoured me. As I tumbled and rolled it was so complex velvety full yes rich and powerfully explosive yes such finesse and balance yes brooding depth yes mouthfeel legs yes dazzling breadth staggering length yes sublime robust virile unctuous harmonious complete yes

Subsequent efforts included "Spenser's Last Case" ("I'm a wine dick. Which is to say I make my living with my nose"), "A Wan Hunter Had Your Self Solid, Dude" by "Gabriel Marquez Garcia y Vegas y Reno y Grosset y Dunlap," "B" by "Thomas Puncheon" ("A screaming comes across this guy"), and "The Maven" ("The prospect of twelve dull Chardonnays barely drinkable / Seemed to this taster most unthinkable"). The staid wine-marketing world had never seen anything quite like this, though Grahm claimed in a footnote to "Summer Vacation" that this "shameless example of viti-porn, at least the soliloquy portion of it, was lifted almost in whole-cloth from the recent newsletters of the most august Mr. Robert Parker."

Curiously enough, Parker's newsletters had recently given a boost to Bonny Doon. The Baltimore attorney, who had begun circulating his opinions in the *Wine Advocate* in the late 1970s with a 100-point scoring system that Americans immediately embraced, had, ever since his endorsement of 1982 Bordeaux created a runaway market for that vintage, become the world's most powerful wine voice. In February 1987 he recommended Grahm's '84 syrah and '86 Clos du Gilroy, adding, "I highly urge you to experience these wines from one of this country's great talents." Over the next few years, Parker would (as he is wont to do) go totally over the top, crowing that "the Bonny Doon winery is remarkable in every sense"; that "this lanky, shaggy-haired genius has turned out a series of brilliant, complex wines that are nothing short of a winemaking tour de force"; that "working with unfashionable and heretofore unheard of grapes, [Grahm] is making wines as complex, stunning and as pleasurable as anyone in the world"; that Bonny Doon's "success with these unglamorous grape varietals is perhaps the greatest winemaking story from California this decade"; and ultimately that "Randall Grahm is one of America's national treasures." In private, Grahm referred to Parker as "The Pope," with irony but no less awe than a bona fide Catholic. "Randall called me up and told me he just got a phone call from Robert Parker," Ruthie remembers. "He said, 'He loves the wine! Parker said he never calls anybody, but he was so excited that he just had to!' The day after Parker's newsletter came out, the phone started ringing off the hook."

By the time of this anointing, at least twenty California wineries had begun working with Rhône varieties. In December 1987 they all got together at Lalime's Restaurant in Berkeley to found a formal alliance, settling on the name "Rhone Rangers" as a moniker for the group. By that time, others like Bob Lindquist and Steve Edmunds (of Edmunds St. John) were more committed to Rhône grapes than was Grahm, who, in addition to his infusions and ice wines, had begun to get interested in Italian varieties; but Randall's rising fame made him the movement's most prominent figure, a status that was confirmed a year later when the *Wine Spectator* pictured him on its cover, holding the reins of a white horse and wearing a mask and cowboy hat with a couple of bottles in a double holster on his hips. To an aspiring American wine idol, this was tantamount to the cover of *Rolling Stone*, but Grahm's swelling adulation wasn't limited to the wine world. Alan Richman subsequently published a feature in *GQ* titled "My Son the Winemaker," introducing his subject thus: "Bonny Doon's Randall Grahm is the most inventive winemaker in the world, but his mother, Ruthie, whines that he's married only to his vines." The article went on to call Grahm "perhaps the most talented, and surely the most versatile, producer of wine and spirits in California, maybe anywhere," to declare him "the Gabriel García Márquez of wine-speak, publishing the industry's most profound, amusing, and labyrinthine newsletter," and even to proclaim that "Grahm is to wine what Van Gogh was to painting, except Grahm markets his product better."

"Nobody, anywhere, has Grahm's way with grapes," Richman waxed. "Nobody makes so many different kinds of wines that are so good."

Patrice Boyle, who became Bonny Doon's general manager in 1987, still speaks wondrously of this heady ride. "With the rise of Cigare, Randall realized his ability to market wine," she confirms. "That goofy fairy tale was such a powerful presence—people were going crazy for it, and not just for Cigare but Vin Gris, Le Sophiste, Old Telegram. . . . I remember doing allocations in 1988, when I would line up all the distributors and give them percentages of wine according to what they did the year before. It was an exciting time, and a lot of fun. It had to do with a whole confluence of forces—Parker; the late adolescence of the California wine scene; the fact that people had money and were just discovering wine. It was a great time in the wine business."

Boyle had met Grahm at Davis, where her husband, Nick Martin, was also a winemaking student. The couple had since gone on to start the Martin Brothers winery in Paso Robles, but when they broke up in 1987, Grahm called and offered Boyle a job at Bonny Doon. She demurred that she was already planning to go to Italy for a few months, whereupon Grahm recommended that she go to France instead; Boyle went to Italy anyway, thank you, but agreed to relocate to Santa Cruz when she returned in the fall. Upon reporting for duty, however, she was surprised to discern the identity of the person who had hired her over the phone. Somehow, in her memories from Davis, she had gotten Grahm mixed up—not insignificantly—with Gil Nickel, the guy known for driving his Mercedes to viticulture classes.

Boyle's first task on arriving at Bonny Doon was to negotiate a number of legal proceedings that Grahm's "neurasthenic" (his word) neighbors had initiated against the winery. Objections to live music emanating from the tasting room—an activity not included in the winery's use permit—had drawn scrutiny from the county, resulting even in a public hearing. "The weird thing about Santa Cruz is that it's not just the merits of the product but what kind of attitude you have," Grahm told Richman of GQ. "It's like second grade: 'Randy has a bad attitude. He has to stay after class. . . . Randy is very sarcastic. He has to clean the erasers too.'"

"People were suing for all kinds of things, probably because Randall had parties and didn't invite them," Boyle says. "Randall is nothing if not obtuse when confronted by people who are demanding things of him, so one of my first chores was fixing things with the neighbors, which took two lawyers and two years. Randall can be kind of bumbling; basically, he needed help with everything. All the winery records were in shoe boxes, and there was only one phone—his. There wasn't even a desk. He didn't want to fill out a BATF-702 (summary of operations) form—he'd lock himself in a room, and you could hear him screaming through the door. It was funny and pathetic at the same time. I wasn't then, and am not now, a bookkeeper, but I was the one who signed all the checks, and on the first payroll after I arrived, there wasn't enough money to pay people. Randall just said, 'Call my mom.' I was mortified, but Ruthie said, 'Okay, no problem.'"

As the 1989 *Spectator* story revealed, "Most of the employees who started with Grahm in the early 1980s are gone, having found it impossible to live on the meager income they were able to earn while the winery was operating in the red." One of these was the aptly named Daniel Press—a 1984 Davis grad steeped in French wine culture, having apprenticed in Burgundy after being raised by a Moroccan mother and Jewish father. "At first I said, 'Oh boy, I'm going to be working for another Francophile Jew!'" Press (now a professor of environmental studies at UC Santa Cruz) remembers. "I thought we would have a certain tribal dynamic based on humor and irony—I mean, how many Jewish winemakers were there in 1985? Not many. So I thought we should have complicity, but in the end I couldn't overcome Randall's managerial style."

Replacing Rick Flowerday, Grahm's original winemaking assistant, Press "walked into the winery when it was evolving out of the elegant Burgundian thing. Randall was just getting the idea for the Cigare Volant label, and the first Old Telegram we made in fall of '86 was a revelation to me—it smelled like raw meat in the fermenter. From the start, Randall said, 'We're expanding out and up.'" To augment the former equipment-rental facility, Grahm built an addition modeled on a French château; winery operations still had to take place while construction was in progress, however, and that summer a group of "militant women" came to help bottle on a day so hot that the carpenters were working without shirts. Demanding equal privileges, the women took off their shirts too. In winter, on the other hand, the building was too cold, and whenever sulfur additions were made indoors, everyone got gassed.

"The place was a motley mix of junk cobbled together to make wine," Press says. "It looked like spaghetti, with all these PVC pipes running everywhere. There were a lot of logistical hassles in a not very user-friendly winery. The Vin de Glacière was a bitch to ferment, freezing muscat grapes in Watsonville and pressing them in January at 40 degrees Brix. We used a foot-operated corker that jammed constantly; the bottling equipment was always breaking or blowing up, but in Santa Cruz you're not near any of the Napa repair shops, so eventually we learned to order extra parts. I spent a lot of time trying to refurbish old ovals—Randall thought big cooperage was very nice, but big brand-new cooperage is also very expensive. So he bought some old cooperage, but it turned out to be shit. It came from a sacramental wine producer—the ovals had had a religious version of Thunderbird in them, and were full of holes made by insect borers. Randall wanted us to use a belt sander to shave the insides and epoxy to plug the holes, but they had these little teeny doors that you could get only one shoulder through at a time. In the end, we never used them. Then he bought a thousand-gallon tank for chardonnay, soaked it up with water, and all the wine leaked out overnight.[*] Randall bought new uprights for grenache and syrah—beautiful Burgundian barrels and puncheons—but on a Sunday there must have been a short in the utility room, because a fire broke out and burned its way into the new room, where we had sixty barrels of syrah. Some burned and some didn't, but when we tasted the wine, Randall thought it smelled like burned plastic. He was afraid we'd be pilloried for it, so he didn't want to release it—which was a shame, because it was a lovely syrah. We bought some white on the bulk market, put it in our barrels and sold it in the tasting room. Randall asked brokers for red wine, which was usually expensive and bad. So finally I made a representative sample from the sixty barrels of burned syrah, put it in two bottles with unbranded corks, placed them in a shipping package, and told Randall it was bulk wine that had just come in—I said it was 70 percent petite sirah and 30 percent gamay. He swirled and smelled and said, 'That's the ticket!' I said, 'Yeah, and it's really inexpensive because it's sitting in your front room.' We bottled and sold it that season as 'Grahm Cru' red, and nobody ever complained." A photo of the winery crew graced the label, with all members wearing storm gear and terrified

[*] Mel Knox, the barrel broker who sold Grahm the tank, says that the Bonny Doon crew didn't insert the wax closure correctly. "Their insurance guy told me he'd already been there three times that year," Knox recalls, "and it was only April."

expressions while Grahm towered over them sporting a sextant and commodore's cap.

Eventually the strain of serving as Grahm's first mate took its toll on Press. "Randall was a hard man to work for," he says. "He was just becoming famous, and he very much liked getting photographed and featured, smiling all the while. He worked hard, but he was on the road a lot, which left it to the crew to implement his ideas. We were constantly moving things around—we'd have to de-plumb a row of tanks and move them again after we'd just done it; we'd hardly figured out how to make one wine when we were off making a different wine, or using other techniques. Maybe that's how things should go, but you also need to concentrate on things that work. Lurching from one wine to another resulted in some not very good wines, and eventually I developed a sense of futility—I felt like Sisyphus. I might have liked it better if I'd felt more appreciated; on the one hand, Randall wanted everybody to share in the great enterprise with enthusiasm, but you also got the sense that he didn't trust his employees very much. I actually had to read him the California Administrative Code to get him to pay me overtime. I admit that I wasn't being very visionary; I could have been more involved in the big picture if I hadn't been so grumpy about moving tanks around—I could have traveled with him, for example. But I was too serious—too focused on minding the store."

Store-minding ultimately fell to Boyle, who proved to be the right person for the job. "There were huge challenges, but it was fun because I could do anything I wanted," she says. "My goal was for the winery to be solvent, and for Randall rather than his parents to be the owner." And although Ruthie and Alan never expected anything back from their investment, Boyle reports that, when she was managing Bonny Doon, money did start flowing back in the direction of Beverly Hills.

A FTER RANDALL GRAHM departed UC Davis in 1979, the lingering vacuum in the department of viticulture and enology had been partly filled by another ex–MIT student who was reborn while working in a wineshop. Clark Smith, a self-described "egghead" good at math and science (in other words, another *luftmensch*) had originally matriculated at MIT in the footsteps of his father—an engineer who, among the achievements that ultimately earned him a presidential commission from Ronald Reagan, had helped build the engines for the *Apollo* spacecraft. As an undergraduate, the holistically inclined Clark set about trying to "tear down the wall between the arts and sciences and the rest of the world," but after dabbling in math, biology, psychology, chemistry, linguistics, and cinematography, he found himself—not surprisingly—unable to declare a major, other than in a self-designed field titled "The Nature of Things," which the MIT faculty rejected. Thus embarking on an academic hiatus, Smith drifted across the country to Berkeley and, having worked as a cook and busboy while growing up, he got a job as a bartender at Chez Panisse when Alice Waters opened the restaurant in 1972.

"I worked the day shift, mostly wrapping prosciutto around melon slices and serving spritzers to frumpy housewives," he says. "I was never really sure what went wrong, but I was just a snot-nosed kid from Jersey, and I don't think I projected the kind of class [Waters] was looking for. The first time she fired me, I sat on the curb and cried for hours until she gave me another try. That lasted a week, until she took me aside again and said, 'No, it just won't work.'"

During this brief attendance at the birth of California cuisine, Smith obtained an "inkling" that something was going on in the local wine world. "By 1970 the three-martini lunch had gone out of fashion. The commercially viable wines were pretty light, but there were the beginnings of serious collectible wines. The benchmarks for cabernet were B.V. Private Reserve, Martini, Inglenook Cask—largely from Chuck Wagner's fruit [at Caymus Vineyards] and Charles Krug, with Wente dominating the classic whites, Stony Hill exploring great whites, plus a few hard-to-get legends like Martin Ray and Joseph Swan playing with pinot noir. A lot of historically groundbreaking wineries emerged in that era—Ridge, Heitz, Mondavi, Souverain, Schramsberg, and the Sutter Home zins from the Deaver Vineyard."

Deciding to investigate employment in wine sales, Smith was able to get a job at an Oakland liquor store known as a "bomber." At the time, California fair-trade laws still mandated uniform retail pricing, but the Three Barons gave under-the-table discounts to locals who could prove that they didn't work for the Alcohol Beverage Control board. "We had about seven thousand customers, including our share of sheriffs, judges, and Treasury agents," says Smith. "In the fifties, only 5 percent of California wine had been table wine; the rest was port and sherry, and even in 1970 it was still mostly 'chablis,' 'rhine wine,' 'sauterne,' 'burgundy,' and rosé. One day a customer brought a bottle of Paul Masson Emerald Dry Riesling up to the counter and asked me if it was any good; I said I had no idea. I didn't like being a dumb ass, so I took a bottle home, and pretty soon I'd tasted everything in the store and was giving out a lot of advice.

"As a retailer," Smith remembers, "you needed to create a brand-new language with every customer, unique to their experience, several times a day. Consumers mostly don't know how to talk about wine; hell, neither do most of the people who write about it. In the U.S., there's not enough agreement about language to be able to communicate about wine, the way there is in France and Italy. So you start from scratch: You ask people to describe what they like or don't like, triangulate by suggesting some things for them to try, and see what they think of it. I found the most useful approach was to use holistic descriptors like 'macho,' 'generous,' or 'aloof'—anybody can relate to human personality terms, so they apply them to wine more easily than reductionist terms like 'strawberry' or 'tobacco' or 'tar,' which are mostly just confusing."

Ultimately the ABC shut down the Three Barons, at which point Smith moved on to Jackson's Wine & Spirits—an East Bay chain he describes as "the Library of Congress for California wines." Its nine stores carried all the eighty-odd labels then produced in the state—"about a thousand wines, as well as the same number of imports, including most of the interesting Bordeaux, Burgundies, Champagnes, German Rheingaus and Mosels, and the few Rhône wines that were available." A store tasting was conducted every Wednesday, and one of the older employees periodically opened his cellar of Beaulieu, Martini, Dom Pérignon, and Perrier Jouet. "I found that California cabernets, as we made them then, got very sweet as they aged. They tasted like Turkish coffee—unlike Bordeaux, which tended to dry out. We sold the '52 Montrose for two dollars a half bottle—I used to drink it at lunch with a pastrami sandwich and a Cadbury bar."

Smith compares the California wine scene of the 1970s to "being a German physics student in the 1920s—a time of unbridled growth and development. In those days everybody was talking to each other and trying to figure out together how it all worked—there were new wineries, and even new styles, being invented all the time." As examples, he singles out Wente's '72 Arroyo Seco Johannesburg Riesling Spätlese ("the first successful botrytised wine—a real eye opener") and Walter Schug's '75 TBA riesling from Joseph Phelps, which, preceding Felton Empire's version by a year, "proved we could make these wines as good as the best of the Germans. Cary Gott's '74 Montevina sauvignon blanc opened up the door for me on that varietal—at 16.3 percent alcohol it was perfectly balanced anyway, which showed that we can't get European aromatics unless we have more ripeness. From '76 to '80, Mount Veeder made the best California dry chenins I've ever seen—and they'd planted the grape by mistake because the nursery mismarked it as cabernet sauvignon. The '73 Ridge chardonnay, and '75 Freemark Abbey, Spring Mountain, and Mayacamas, set the bar for really exquisite wines we'd never seen before—not as big as today's, but very rich, with depth and complexity that, at least by my memory, is hard to find today."

In the cabernet department, Stag's Leap and Chateau Montelena—which within a few years would win the red and white tastings at the Judgment of Paris—set a new pricing standard at six dollars a bottle. "By comparison, Château Latour and Lafite cost $14.50," Smith says. "Then the '72 Caymus and '72 Mount Veeder came in at $7.50 and blew everybody away with their intensity. The '72 Stonegate, '73 Fetzer, '73 Liberty School, and '70 Louis Martini ushered in the new era for *affordable* cab—they all came out at about the same time, at around $3.50. At that price, the Souverain of Rutherford '72 petite sirah was maybe the best red wine value I ever sold."

Even confronted with such a spectrum, Smith says, "If you worked at it, you could taste everything and meet everyone involved and be right in the center of it." Almost every weekend he visited some wine region or other, and in 1976, driving away from the Tualatin winery in Oregon, he told his wife that he wanted to make wine himself. ("She said, 'I've been wondering how long it would take you to figure that out.'") He started by fermenting grapes at home and in 1977 got a cellar-rat job at Veedercrest, an East Bay winery that vinified premium fruit from Napa and Sonoma. "It was owned by Al Baxter, a larger-than-life personality in the mold of Warren Winiarski and Mike Robbins. In those days, since nobody knew what to do, we needed domineering, driven, passionate leaders who would work from instinct and just drive the bus, come what may—so different from the winning strategy today. Al used to keep a bronze sculpture of a snail on his desk, rearing his poised, alert head and projecting his beautiful little antennae despite the huge shell he was lugging on his back. It was called *Grace Under Pressure*."

Baxter processed his frustrations with the wine business by composing revenge limericks that targeted grape growers. To Rene di Rosa, owner of the celebrated Winery Lake vineyard:

In the sullen sixth circle of hell
May the Carneros grape picker dwell

For the leaves in his bins
Were as red as his sins
And they clogged up my must pump as well.

Or, on being required to buy merlot and pinot noir at $1,000 per ton for the privilege of also purchasing chardonnay:

The vintner's directive
In place of invective
Delivered in livery on a satin cushion:
"You may drive your Mercedes
To the black gates of Hades
Before I'll buy pinot at a thousand per ton."

Smith performed various jobs at Veedercrest, including sales rep, "trying to sell the equivalent, in today's dollars, of forty-dollar rieslings and rosés." But they were "stunning," barrel-fermented dry rosés, made from pinot noir and cabernet with the help of a "gravity dejuicer" that Smith devised to separate the pink liquid from the red grape skins. This innovation—essentially a colander inside a fifty-five-gallon drum—earned him a mention in *Practical Winery & Vineyard Journal*. "Ridiculously simple," Smith demurs, "but back then, everybody was inventing stuff all the time and sharing the information."

In the course of all this, the MIT dropout decided that, as far as "the nature of things" was concerned, wine was that rare pursuit—music being the other—that was capable of merging life's two central questions: "What is the nature of physical reality?" and "What does it mean to be a human being?"

"Science at its purest looks at the world as it 'really is,'" he explains. "The notion is that objects exist and interact physically, whether you know it or not. The solar system didn't come into being when Copernicus described it; it was there the whole time, and just needed to be discovered. Ditto for the atom, the periodic table, and the physical laws themselves. This is the inquiry into the nature of physical reality. But when you look at the world from an *artistic* perspective, the only interesting part is how physical manifestations affect us as humans.

Art is reflexive—a mirror for the soul. Its essence is an inquiry into what it is to be human."

Smith says his problem with declaring a major in college stemmed from the fact that he didn't believe in separating art and science. "If you're looking for a place to study these two phenomena together," he says, "I find it compelling to pick a very pure medium—something abstract, which has as few static physical attributes as possible. Music is great, because it's invisible, has no aroma, and no taste—it's sound which moves us emotionally and can carry us through phrases of tension and resolution and reproduce moods. Noise, on the other hand, is sound that we don't commune with in that way. Wine is like music, in that it has no innate shape or sound but carries emotional modalities, and the sense of what works and doesn't work is strongly shared."

Smith likes to describe wine as "liquid music." He says he believes that the goal of a vintner is to put "an opera in a bottle," and he's fond of describing wine as a "mysterious, soulful, visceral" experience that exposes the essential "fraudulence" of science. "Science doesn't know anything," he declares. "In winemaking, it's the caboose." Still, "the pursuit of this inquiry—the laboratory for merging art and science—was what drew me to winemaking."

As we've seen, the various laboratories in the department of Viticulture and Enology didn't include one for fusing art and science. Nevertheless, Smith eventually went back to school at UC Davis, where he quickly made an impression among his fellow classmates. Bill Dyer, who would go on to become the winemaker at Sterling Vineyards in Napa Valley (before starting his own winery with his wife, Dawnine, of Domaine Chandon), remembers Smith as an "exuberant, enthusiastic" student who was "really good at understanding concepts delivered in class and taking them to a practical level—he'd hear things that were theoretically possible mentioned in lectures; then he'd go there." Another classmate, Rick Jones, received his first exposure to Smith in an undergraduate biochemistry course: "There were about two hundred and fifty students in this big lecture hall, and the teacher was talking over a microphone about the shapes of molecules and stereochemistry of glucose. All the people in the class were pretty smart, but this one poor schmuck stuck his hand up and said he didn't understand. The teacher went over it again, but the guy still said, 'I'm confused.' At that point the teacher got kind of snitty and said, 'Maybe somebody else in the class would like to explain it.' Clark practically came out of his seat, waving his hand like a kid saying, 'Me, me, me!' He bounded down the stairs, grabbed the microphone, and explained it in front of the whole class. I kind of knew he was a winemaking student, and I remember feeling a mixture of envy and embarrassment—he was so guileless, but he had such balls. A lot of people have that mixture of emotions about Clark they admire him, but there's a part of him that makes people very uncomfortable. He'd probably say it's because they're afraid of him."

Which is to say that Smith wasn't exactly accepting of the kind of education he received. "I dearly love Davis, and it breaks my heart to see the tragic disconnect that exists between its students and the wine industry," he says. Among the institutional problems he cites—over-subscribed classes, inexperienced professors, emphasis on research rather than on teaching—his main beef is the curriculum's inapplicability to the actual world of winemaking. "You need to know a lot about what motivates consumers, and even more about how wine works and the techniques that can shape it. You can't expect to get any of that at Davis. Even though the department was created by the state legislature to teach 'the art and science of winemaking,' the arts are entirely left out. Ray Kroc's* claim that you can't manage what you can't measure has become pretty much the department's credo, which limits them in ways they simply don't comprehend."

In spite of this, Smith obtained not just a bachelor's degree from Davis but also a master's, winning As in every course but one: Ann Noble's class on sensory evaluation, where he got a B. "We didn't agree on anything. In the MIT tradition, I gave her the right answers instead of the correct ones, which were bullshit. For example, she didn't believe

* Founder of McDonald's.

that air could improve a wine, and she thought holistic descriptors were unprofessional. After that, I just told them what they wanted to hear so I could get scholarships. I came to look at getting straight As as something I did for a living, and I had to sort of steal the education I wanted on the side."

A decade after leaving Davis, Smith touched off an academic brouhaha with an article titled "Does UC Davis Have a Theory of Deliciousness?" Its premise was that, in its analytic-reductionist ethos—analogous, Smith believes, to the practice of Western medicine—his alma mater was missing wine's main point. His graphic way of illustrating this was a 360-degree "Musical Tone Wheel" that parodied Noble's famed Aroma Wheel, breaking a symphony orchestra down into forty-six different sounds—"blast," "tweet," "chime," "toot," "thud," "oompah," etc. "A conductor doesn't make the good instruments play loud and bad ones play soft," he says. "Everybody plays together in a single, unified voice. For an audience member, that's when you say, 'Oh boy, I'm glad I spent a hundred dollars to sit here for a couple of hours.' Profundity isn't based on complexity; it's based on simplicity. The greater the wine, the less people have to say about it, because language is inadequate to describe it."

Upon leaving Davis, Smith was hired as the founding winemaker at R.H. Phillips, an operation in the Dunnigan Hills to the north. The place was owned by the Giguieres, a family of wheat farmers who, in the wake of the Iran hostage crisis (which raised the price of oil) and the Russian invasion of Afghanistan (which inspired an embargo on wheat sales to the Soviet Union) decided to get into grape growing. "It was a chance to apply the modern winemaking principles I'd learned at Davis to a new viticulture area with the taint of the hot Central Valley," Smith says. "It had a lot of natural advantages, starting with cheap land. The Giguieres were smart, talented growers who taught me about agriculture, which is a really complex form of gambling. They'd thought about planting chardonnay and cabernet, but because it was Region Four, the geniuses at Davis recommended French colombard and chenin blanc. Davis didn't believe that soil composition was important—they thought Winkler (the heat-based classification framework) is a grading system, which is an example of linear thinking doing a face plant. In the Dunnigan Hills we had heavy clay, which has a lot of water in it—so, when the sun goes down, the vine recovers really well."

Under Smith's guidance, R.H. Phillips pioneered the practice of harvesting at night to ensure cool temperatures in the fermenting grapes. "We set up a North Coast–style winery, grew really good sauvignon blanc and Rhône varieties, and made money on wine that cost $3.99 a bottle," he says. Between 1983 and 1990, he presided over a production increase from 3,000 to 300,000 cases per year, constituting a crash course in winery construction and equipment. "We invented everything—the brand, the wine style, the physical plant, the market. I worked out a system for researching quality through vineyard experiments and figuring out what would work for specific sites and climates—I did seven years of studies on vineyard variable effects on wine quality, applying sensory-evaluation methods to hundreds of replicate trials on maturity, yield, trellis, and so forth, and on winemaking variables like harvest temperature, skin contact, fermentation temperature, and yeast strains. I was given absolute power, and I was completely isolated—I became a very good white wine–maker, but it became clear that I didn't know jack about red. I had texture problems, reduction problems, oak-integration problems. . . . I was coming from a twenty-year background with red wines that were soulful, moving, and profound, but whenever I tasted a great one, I still couldn't figure out how it happened."

In fact, owing to the practices promoted at Davis, Smith felt that great contemporary red wines from California were few and far between. "Whenever I went to Napa Valley and saw the Robert Louis Stevenson sign saying THE WINES ARE BOTTLED POETRY, I said, 'Horseshit.' Certainly there were exceptions, but whenever I tasted a wine that had texture and soul, neither my university training nor my cellar experience offered any clues as to how it was done. Some wines handled *Brett* or oak a lot better than others, so the 'solution theory' of wine seemed incomplete. I started getting the feeling that we'd lost track of something—sort of like when you go visit Yosemite and you think, 'Christ, why am I not here all the time?' I had no clue then, but my background had perfectly prepared me for later revelations I would get from France—a whole new way of thinking about and working with wine."

O N A N O V E R C A S T winter day, Randall Grahm meets with Bonny Doon's new national sales manager, Bradley Martin, in the company's new tasting room on Ingalls Street in Santa Cruz. The room is an architectural adjunct of the Cellar Door, the café that Grahm opened behind the winery after selling Big House and Cardinal Zin. The design of the dual-purpose facility is inspired: The space is divided into two airy, high-ceilinged rooms—one for tasting, the other for dining—but allows passage back and forth by way of a cutout tank once used for wine storage. This transitional oval chamber is crowned by a stack of light columns that resemble a chandelier, but flash on and off in bright primary colors, calling to mind the spaceship landing in *Close Encounters of the Third Kind*. Most of the restaurant seating is family-style, with tables for fourteen, eight, four, and two; a fanciful wood-and-metal sculpture of a Jules Verne–style spaceship hangs from the ceiling, augmenting the lights above the tasting bar, each bulb shaded by an upside-down bottle. Extending this glass-vessel motif, the room's north-facing window is filled with empty green bottles, illuminated from outdoors and arranged horizontally, as if stacked in a wine cellar. Along one wall is a flowform with water coming out of a cow horn; few straight lines are evident anywhere. You might say the place has positive feng shui—so much so that, after visiting, Leo McCloskey declared it "the best tasting room south of San Francisco."

In addition to its stand-up bar, the tasting room contains several booths—also built from old oak ovals—in the wall that separates it from the café. Grahm sits down in one of these alcoves with Martin, a tall, dark-haired, square-jawed guy who has come to Bonny Doon after ten years at Morgan (a Monterey County winery run by Grahm's old Davis classmate Dan Lee), preceded by stints at Southern Wine & Spirits and Seagram Chateau and Estate Wines in Florida. Still learning the ropes at Bonny Doon, he's meeting with Grahm to discuss sales strategy for upcoming out-of-town trips; the first one will be to Boston, where a big distributor is receiving lots of account representatives on the same day. "They're only giving us fifteen minutes," Martin says.

"Okay," says Grahm. "We'll do it as a Zen koan—read a poem and present a flower and we're out of there. What about New York?"

"I can't do New York," says Martin. "They won't see me—I'm just a sales guy. They'll only see rock-star winemakers."

"It's a tribal thing," Grahm explains. "They don't like salespeople except for the ones they like—if you're part of the tribe, you're in. I don't know why we're underperforming there; when I go, the wine sells. That's true anywhere, but in New York it's not one case—it's nine or ten."

Martin mentions a distributor outside of the New York area. "They like deals," Grahm advises. "Cut them a deal on something that's going away. I see sangiovese in their future." Regarding another distributor in the South, Grahm says, "They were chagrined by Big House; then they were chagrined when we sold Big House. They're just generally chagrined. But it's a good company—we want to stay with them. We need to show them the love. We need to go there. But not too much."

"Every other year?" Martin suggests.

"Um, maybe every third year."

Georgia, Michigan, New Mexico, Ohio, Tennessee, and Virginia are all mentioned as more examples of underperforming areas—in Grahm's estimation, "states that are broken" as far as Bonny Doon sales are concerned. As Martin points out, however, they're also "franchise states," in which the law protects wholesalers from being terminated by suppliers without "good cause," proof of which must often be presented in court. "So we can't just switch distributors," Martin points out.

Texas and Florida are underperforming too. "My take is that the distribution there is well intended, but they're growth oriented and acquiring too many brands," says Grahm. "They're telling me we're their key brand, but maybe they say that to all their brands because they get no sell-through and no repeat orders. They say we need better Parker scores or *Spectator* scores. Texas is all about status—it wants to be L.A. Who are you sleeping with? How big is your car? It might be amusing to put together an ironic brag sheet for them: '*We* don't care about scores, but if *you* want to know . . .' In Texas that would work; they wouldn't even know it's ironic. Texas is an irony-free zone."

"Any ideas for these other places?"

"I thought of one that would be fun and tie it all together. There's still a perception in the market that Bonny Doon is that wacky, goofy winery, which creates cognitive dissonance: 'They're supposed to be wacky, but now they're serious?' I think we should make a training video about some of the wines, but make it funny. I was thinking about having my daughter in it—maybe dress her up in an alien costume and give her a ray gun. It's in our ability to do, and it's not expensive. Every salesperson would get a CD that they can then put in their computer. Twelve people could sit around watching it."

"I like that," Martin said. "People are inundated with words these days."

"We'll start with Cigare," says Grahm. "Things where we have a lot of dollars on the table and have to sell the wine."

"Who'll write it?"

"I'll do it."

"I'm all for having fun," says Martin. "You can say, 'This wine has enough acid for a Grateful Dead concert.' If people don't get it, that's okay."

They begin to brainstorm about consumer giveaways at wine festivals. "What can we give people that they'd want to keep around for a while?" asks Martin. "There's so much clutter nowadays."

"At the Wine Experience, we brought some sensitive crystallizations," says Grahm. "People seemed to take an interest in it."

"That's good," says Martin. "There's so much paper at these things."

"It's hard to be heard," Grahm agrees. "I hate oversimplying things, but people have no bandwidth or tolerance for ambiguity and complexity. What I really want to get across is that we're trying to make wines of soul and distinction—the take-home message is that Bonny Doon is on a learning curve, thinking about things in a way that's different. We're looking at soil and other things, but if there's one single message that encapsulates what we're trying to accomplish, unfortunately we *can't* say that we're trying to capture the terroir. After all, we're drip irrigating in a sandy desert that gets six inches of rainfall a year."

"Terroir is dirt," Martin says. "Right?"

"Not at all," says Grahm. "It's all kinds of things. Human culture is part of it too."

"So it's going to be a difficult thing to circle the wagons around."

"I hate to reduce things to a sound bite," says Grahm. "But: innovation, experimentation, natural . . . our story now is that we're attempting to produce wines with more life force."

"I get the impression there are skeptics about biodynamics out there," says Martin.

"Ya think?" says Grahm. "Stay with the life force: Which wine lives and which one doesn't? I think it's demonstrable that biodynamic wines have the capacity to withstand oxygen—or, I should say, tolerate oxygen. They'll stay good and not degrade for five, six, or seven days after they're opened, and wines that have that ability have more integrity. Check it out—open a bottle of Burgundy, and it will live for a week. Open a California pinot noir and it might live for a couple of hours."

"I had one recently that was good for a week," says Martin.

"That's a miracle," Grahm says. "There was something special about that pinot noir."

"It might be the wind," says Martin. "It was a Morgan wine from the Salinas Valley."

"Wind is a mixed gig," says Grahm. "It's good for vine health, but it's problematic from a photosynthetic perspective. I think life force is more correlated to terroir or minerality. Biodynamics isn't the only route to that end, but I think it's the most straightforward and efficient route. It certainly speaks to the issues involved in *cultivating* minerality, which is essentially about the biological activity in the soil. To put it simply, if your soils are alive, you get minerals from them."

After his meeting with Martin ends, Grahm continues to wrestle with the task of translating his spiritual aspirations into a salable product. "All the greatest religious thinkers have realized that the masses need a metaphor to understand the sacred," he muses. "Terroir is a metaphor—it allows a person to explain to another person why they should be interested in this product. The Parker Score is a metaphor too. So is a spaceship, though I wouldn't necessarily choose a spaceship if I had it to do all over again. Still, I'd prefer not to lose the customers I already have."

Grahm says he has to make some phone calls (which may mean that he needs a Twitter fix), so I take the opportunity to go next door and visit Philippe Coderey, his biodynamic adviser. A tall, severe-looking but gentle-natured Frenchman in his late forties, Coderey came to Santa Cruz after working for Michel Chapoutier, the controversial Rhône Valley vintner who, among other things, pioneered the labeling of wine bottles in braille. Coderey grew up in Provence, where he says his family has been in the wine business forever. "In the past, people didn't make wine to get drunk," he tells me. "Monks made wine—it was the blood of Christ."

In the 1980s, Coderey extended his family tradition by going to work in Switzerland for a company that marketed chemical pesticides to winegrowers—a job, he later concluded, that literally poisoned him. "I got bruises on my skin, and my liver was affected. A doctor told me to stop drinking, but I never drank wine daily—my skin was absorbing the chemicals I worked with. I thought, 'If this is happening to my body, what's happening to the land?'"

This prompted an overhaul of Coderey's life. "I was done with chemicals. I had to find another job, but I couldn't do anything else. I had some friends who had a biodynamic garden, and they said, 'Why don't you go to America? There's a school in Pennsylvania.'" This was Camphill Village in the town of Kimberton—inspired by Rudolf

Steiner, it's a farm community where people with (and without) developmental disabilities live and work. After studying farming there for several years, Coderey went back to France to take care of his family vineyards and later worked on a biodynamic farm in Corsica; he managed vineyards for Chapoutier from 1999 to 2004, at which point—after "praying every day of my life from age twelve to forty-two to come to California"—a corporate headhunter connected him with Bonny Doon.

In Coderey's office are a number of wooden boxes containing petri dishes—platforms for the "sensitive crystallizations" that Grahm mentioned in his talk with Martin. This is a biodynamically inspired process that involves treating a wine sample with copper chloride, then studying the visual pattern that emerges as the solution evaporates. In a talk titled "The Phenomenology of Terroir" at UC Davis in 2006, Grahm inspired some amusement in the audience by claiming that the resulting mandalalike images demonstrate a wine's "degree of connectedness to the soil, to its organizing and growth forces . . . the degree of organization of a wine and its life force, speaking directly to its overall harmony and ability to mature and improve."

To demonstrate, Coderey shows me a crystallization he did from an irrigated block of riesling (since pulled out) in the Ca' del Solo vineyard in Soledad. Suspended on a black background, the circular image suggests a photograph of a distant planet, bordered by a series of rings on its circumference. The interior is characterized by fibrous shoots, bunched so densely at their apparent source—a couple of hollow-looking recesses that Coderey refers to as vacuoles—as to resemble X-rays of tendons or ligaments.

"Divide the picture into its center and periphery," Coderey instructs me. "Fruit is [indicated] in the center—these huge vacuoles represent the aromatic potential. Minerals are indicated on the periphery, but you can see that the needles become chaotic near the edge because the roots have no connection to the earth. This wine is a fruit bomb—it lasts for five seconds in your mouth, and then you forget about it."

For comparison he chooses another crystallization from an old, abandoned vineyard in "the French part of Catalonia, about five miles north of the Spanish border, right on the Mediterranean Sea. Look at the organization and complexity—it's extremely fine and well defined. That's the power of wisdom versus the power of youth." Compared with the tension exuded by the preceding image, this one seems relaxed—it looks like a lush, verdant network of tendrils, which themselves resemble a root system radiating from four tiny black dots. "The vacuoles are very small," Coderey says of the dots, "but the periphery is very organized. That's because the vines have very deep roots and are extracting lots of minerals. They were growing on a rocky hillside, and they've been on their own for decades without any care, so they've had to adapt to the environment to survive. The quality of this wine was astounding—the most mineral wine you could ever taste, like sucking on a piece of rock. It sticks to your palate and your tongue, and the mineral content makes it last longer in your mouth."

Last, Coderey shows me another crystallization from Ca' del Solo—this one from a block of pigato in its first year of conversion to biodynamics. The picture portrays an array of explosive patterns, the needlelike fibers shooting out, sunburstlike, from several loci, but it's less tensile than the riesling image. "This one shows a lot of power from the biodynamic method, but it's chaotic because of the lack of chemicals the vines were used to receiving," says Coderey. "It's still in detox, but you can see there's something happening."

Coderey tries to make me see the fruitful vacuoles and mineral-poor periphery, but to my untrained eye, interpreting these images is akin to reading entrails. Moreover, he doesn't explain *why* the patterns indicate or result from the things he says they do ("We don't have the imagination to see why things are the way they are with us, the earth and the cosmos"), so in lieu of scientific evidence supporting the assertions, they simply have to be taken—like so much about biodynamics—on faith. In this sense, even though it's essentially spiritual rather than mercantile, biodynamics—like Enologix—might be said to constitute a black box.

Coderey says his tutor on sensitive crystallizations is one of the leading authorities on the subject: Christian Marcel, a person who, after Coderey sought him out for training, turned out to be an old schoolmate of his from Provence. When he gets free of his iPhone, Grahm describes Marcel to me as "someone who looked at thousands of wines and crystallizations and compiled a database. He's not infallible; he's sometimes wrong, but he's made some observations that are quite impressive. Knowing the wines that he analyzed, he was spot-on." As an experiment, Grahm once gave several of his Bonny Doon staff members vials of the same wine to carry around for a day, then turned the samples over to Marcel coded not by names but numbers. "The results were all very different, but when he made observations about people's personalities based on the crystallizations—this person has this issue, and so forth—they were right, right, and right.

"It's a different kind of gestalt," Grahm admits of reading the crystallization patterns. "Your eyes have to be trained to look at it in a different way, with a different kind of eyesight. There are certain gross things I can see, and subtle things where I can't see shit. But there *are* certain consistencies I've observed, and over time you can actually identify characteristics in wine from them. A striking terroir wine will have a very coherent image, for example. One thing that is clearly evident is the difference between wines from a single place and wines that are blended.

"What really would be super interesting and useful," Grahm goes on, "is if there were a language to talk about these things—organization and beauty and life force—other than the compendium of descriptors like 'fruity,' 'jammy,' and 'hedonistic.' As it is, all you can really say about wines that have this quality is that they don't oxidize easily—so if you really believe in the specialness and beauty of terroir, it's nice to have some kind of other support for it. For me, the image of the crystallization is extremely to the point as another translation of the aesthetic of wine. Something I think would be *really* cool is to put them on a wine list alongside prices and appellations—you could look at the crystallization and say, 'Wow, that wine looks really beautiful and interesting' or 'Shit, that wine is really chaotic—I'm gonna pass.'"

As in his brainstorming session with Martin, Grahm's problem seems to boil down to translating obscure, enigmatic forces into tangible sales—another job that seems to require training in occult divination. "All I can say is that there *are* people who make a living reading tea leaves who are pretty good at it," Grahm concludes. He isn't talking about Leo McCloskey, but he could almost be an Enologix client when he says: "The take-home for me is, if you're gonna have somebody read entrails, make sure you get a good one. Find somebody who really knows their entrails."

ACCORDING TO PAUL DRAPER, Ridge owner Charlie Rosen (head of the robotics division at SRI) considered Leo McCloskey a genius. Rosen and Hew Crane duly introduced him to Ridge investor Carl Djerassi, whom McCloskey considered "the most commercially successful scientist in the country." A Stanford professor of chemistry, president of Syntex, and one of the inventors of the birth control pill, Djerassi suggested that McCloskey, who impressed him as curious and open-minded, consider getting a PhD. Leo says that Maynard Amerine (with whom he served on an industry panel after glimpsing him at the ASEV conference in 1971), had invited him to get a doctorate at Davis with the aim of joining the faculty, and McCloskey had gone so far as to interview there with Vernon Singleton and Dinsmoor Webb; instead of encouraging him to pursue enology, however, Djerassi advised McCloskey to study "real" science and apply its principles to wine.

"Nobody ever won a Nobel prize for enology," Leo observes. "Nobody needs to read a winemaking book before going to medical school. There are no principles of winemaking that govern physics; it's the other way around. Enology is like a social science: Some people are into drug treatment; others are into love and art." Djerassi thought McCloskey would derive more benefit from analyzing the phenolic compounds in plants other than grapes. This was the budding purview of chemical ecology, a discipline then being spearheaded at UC Santa Cruz by a biologist named Jean Langenheim—an expert on terpenoid resins who, working with three-hundred-million-year-old fossils, had discovered the evolutionary (i.e., defensive) role of tropical amber.

This field of chemical ecology arose in the 1960s, when scientists began looking more closely at the relationships between organisms and their environments in an evolutionary context, aided by revolutionary new analytical techniques. "Because of breakthroughs in spectroscopy and magnetic resonance, a whole new group of chemists was showing that compounds had been misidentified in some products for fifty years," McCloskey says. In botany, the so-called secondary chemical compounds—not proteins or carbohydrates, but alkaloids, terpenoids, and phenolics—are produced only in some parts of a plant, furthering not its "primary" metabolic goals of growth, respiration, and photosynthesis, but "secondary" environmental functions like defense, distribution, and survival. Alkaloids such as caffeine, cocaine, and nicotine, for example, discourage animals from eating the plants that produce them (if not their less self-preservation-oriented human brethren); the terpenoids found in mint, cloves, cinnamon, and eucalyptus not only repel herbivorous insects and disease-causing microbes but can also attract pollinating insects. Phenolics intensify the color of some flowers and fruits, encouraging animals to eat them and excrete their seeds over the landscape.

"Plants are in the business of controlling the chemicals they produce," McCloskey submits. "Primary chemistry, which was discovered first, was originally thought to be essential to the life of the plant, and secondary chemistry wasn't. But in 1949, breakthroughs in chromatography allowed biologists like E. C. Bate-Smith to show that phenolic chemistry was tightly controlled within each plant family. Today we know that secondary chemistry is essential to evolution." Owing to such survival "skills," secondary chemical compounds provide a veritable cornucopia of potential drugs—analgesics, anesthetics, anti-inflammatories, decongestants, narcotics, and stimulants—not to mention applications for products like mustard, nail polish, and perfume.

Providing an important perk to UC Santa Cruz, the Ridge owners agreed to furnish a high-performance liquid chromatograph while McCloskey pursued his PhD there. Still, when McCloskey appeared in the biology department, Langenheim put him on notice that, in her opinion, wine people lacked scientific discipline. "She said, 'I'm going to break you,'" McCloskey later told Charles Sullivan. "'I'm going to be your football coach.'" Following Djerassi's lead away from grape chemistry, Langenheim ("the Knute Rockne of terpenoids") directed

McCloskey to analyze phenolics in the resin-producing tropical trees that she was researching in Latin America.

This was how Leo came to find himself in the town of Puerto Marquez on the west coast of Mexico south of Acapulco, where another of Langenheim's grad students was studying leaf resins on the legume *Hymenaea*. As it happened, Swedish-born Susan Arrhenius's lineage included two Nobel chemistry laureates. Her great-grandfather Svante Arrhenius won the 1903 prize for his theory of ionization, in addition to postulating the greenhouse effect and developing the Arrhenius Equation, which correlates chemical reaction rates with increases in temperature. Her Hungarian grandfather George de Hevesy had won the 1943 Nobel for inventing radioactive tracers, as well as discovering the element hafnium. Susan's father, Gustaf, was a professor of oceanography at UC San Diego's Scripps Institute, and her ancestry also included an archaeologist, a geologist, a mineralogist, and a president of Finland (Carl Gustaf Mannerheim). When she met McCloskey, however, Arrhenius was most reminded of her great-great-grandfather Adolf Nordenskiold, who had discovered a northeast passage between Europe and Asia. ("Leo is also an explorer," she explains. "His frontier is the idea that there are objective measures to quality, which goes against the grain of what people believe.") Thrust together in a threatening—well, hot and sultry anyway—environment far from home, the two were forced to answer a biological imperative. "At first she told me she had a boyfriend," McCloskey remembers. "I said, 'Of course you do—all attractive women have boyfriends. I wouldn't be interested in any woman who *didn't* have a boyfriend.'" Bringing such logic to bear, the charismatic trailblazer wore down Arrhenius's evolutionary defenses, and the two were soon engaged.

McCloskey's PhD thesis, *Leaf Phenolic Compounds in the Tropical Tree Genera* Hymenaea *and* Copaifera, compared and contrasted the chemistry of two broad-leafed trees that occur throughout the neotropics. Besides Langenheim, his advisory committee included other eminent authorities in the field: Boston University's Tony Swain, an English protégé of E. C. Bate-Smith ("the king of plant phenolics," according to Leo) and inventor of important tests for tannin, and UCSC's Kenneth Thiemann, an internationally renowned botanist who identified the role of hormones in plant growth. McCloskey completed his doctoral work in four years, while continuing to work at Felton Empire and to consult with private winemaking clients; confronted with this maelstrom of professional ambition, some of his teachers weren't sure how his academic work measured up.

"There was no question about the value of his chemical analyses," says Langenheim. "Only the care of some of his ecological interpretations of the data. Leo was known as a salesman—he wanted to get out and get going on his wine. He was always saying how his work was 'earthshaking' and talking big about it in a way that might impress some people, but his committee was less convinced. One of the things that saved him was that he's such a creative thinker—he's full of ideas, but trying to sell his ideas on the basis of his scientific prowess was questionable. The committee finally decided that his thesis was acceptable, but that basically he just wasn't a scientist."

McCloskey didn't publish a single paper from his PhD work, which is not to say that he didn't derive any professional benefit from his studies. "Chemical ecology is the idea of terroir in scientific form," he expounds. "It says that a wine's flavor, color, and fragrance are expressions of its ecosystem. For example, red Burgundy is under the genetic control of the pinot noir grape and the environmental control of its ecosystem. In Langenheim's group, terroir would be called 'detectable ecotypic expression': To attract [pollinators and dispersants], a plant needs a minimum concentration of detectable compounds. Same with a wine that needs to attract the consumer."

In the course of his doctoral work, McCloskey read surveys on plant chemistry from around the world, from which he learned that all woody plants contain a certain "suite" of chemicals. Tannins and anthocyanins are both phenolic compounds, and McCloskey says his doctoral thesis "put phenolics into an agroecology model," based on his observation that much of the impetus for the study of chemical ecology arose from agribusiness interests in the United Kingdom. "All these British guys [at the Royal Botanical Garden] were getting samples from government-run research centers around the world and linking their natural-products chemistry to the value of crops [such as rubber and bananas]. The trees in a forest have been adapting and tuning themselves up for millions of years, but Jean Langenheim noticed that when a tree moves into a different environment, physical factors in the new site change the chemistry of the tree.

"Bingo!" McCloskey says. "That was the missing model for wine. With grapes, man is forcing the plant into an ecosystem where it didn't evolve. But winemakers were still empirically based—they were like the natural historians of the nineteenth century: observers who made deductions but didn't do experiments. California winemakers would fly to France and say, 'Since they're dry farming here, I'll go back and advocate dry farming,' ignoring the fact that France has high rainfall and California doesn't. Agriculture isn't 'natural'; it involves human intervention to make up for what nature doesn't provide. In Langenheim's group, you would do the opposite—you'd ask, 'How will this plant perform in the new location? Will it be true to its genre? What can I do differently to make it thrive? How can I make my Napa Valley agroecosystem perform as well or better than the benchmark European system?'"[*]

When it comes to that question, McCloskey says, Napa has an innate ace in the hole. "Napa Valley's advantage is that it isn't prone to defects," he says. "Even if you're a dumbbell farmer who plants a vineyard with no controls at all, you still don't have too many problems—your grapes will have high color and tannin and won't taste too herbal and vegetal. It's *safe* to make wine there, so a businessman [for example, Baron Philippe de Rothschild] can come out on a Learjet and form a cartel with Mondavi and claim they're making the equivalent of Bordeaux in America [for example, Opus One] and get away with it because they have so much money. It wasn't that they were superlative; it's not like the Santa Cruz Mountains or Sonoma County couldn't be a *better* place. The Santa Cruz Mountains could have been a really good wine region, but it's a bunch of mavericks who didn't band together, so urbanization left it with no way to develop, and today it's a backwater. It doesn't have enough land to scale up volume among

[*] Langenheim points out, however, that her research dealt with trees that had naturally adapted to different environments over thousands of years, as opposed to *Vitus viniferera* clones transferred across hemispheres by *Homo sapiens* in a single generation.

any one category of winemakers, so it was never able to provide what the future requires: a quality classification of the agroecosystem of California."

The seed (or, more accurately, the fungus) for this point of view was fostered at Felton Empire, whose production mushroomed while Mc-Closkey was getting his PhD. To finance the winery's expansion during the bull market of the mid-1980s, the partners took out a bank loan and sold stock to new investors, including a pair of corporate-nutritionist brothers named Jerry and Bob Brassfield, who now owned Alfred Hitchcock's "Heart o' the Mountain" estate nearby. Before much time had elapsed, however, the Brassfields—who pumped some $350,000 into Felton Empire—filed a lawsuit against their new partners, alleging that the winery's growth didn't adequately reflect their investment. (Jim Beauregard, who had introduced the Brassfield brothers to his other partners, alludes to "a dirty story," but will say only that there were "shenanigans" going on in the winery.) In any case, John Pollard soon departed California for Utah, leaving Mc-Closkey to become president of the company, and eventually Ridge's lawyer Mario Rosati—by then another Felton Empire investor—negotiated a settlement of the suit in return for wine.

Ironically, Felton Empire's expansion was largely attributable to the fact that, just before McCloskey went back to school, he and his partners decided—in the face of a building "neoprohibitionist" movement that led to health warnings on wine bottles as well as a fivefold increase in excise tax on alcohol—to explore the market for nonalcoholic varietal juice. "A lightbulb went off in Leo's head," remembers Phil Crews, a winemaking friend of McCloskey's and professor of chemistry at UC Santa Cruz. "He said, 'If we can make low-alcohol riesling by filtering, why can't we harvest it at 17 [Brix, insufficiently ripe for table wine] and not ferment it—just filter it, bottle it, and sell it?' It *tasted* like wine, and the high acid counterbalanced the sugar; they started selling it, and they sold a *lot* of it." In 1981, courtesy of Mothers Against Drunk Driving, this product would get McCloskey invited to a reception at the White House. "I felt like *Mr. Smith Goes to Washington*," he told Sullivan. He didn't get to meet the Reagans, however—only the Doles. "Let's just say I wasn't overly impressed with who was running the country. Inside the Beltway there's a mentality of toeing the line—everybody there was an Eagle Scout. I was more of a John McCain type."

By 1984, Felton Empire was producing fifty thousand cases a year, half of it nonalcoholic juice. Abandoning its original aim of sticking to the Santa Cruz Mountains, the company also introduced a lower-priced "Maritime Series," including pinot noir and chenin blanc, from vineyards up and down the coast, from Mendocino to Santa Barbara. In retrospect, Steve Storrs—now an independent winemaker in Santa Cruz, but then a recent Davis graduate who took over Felton Empire's red winemaking when Leo went back to school—says, "Felton Empire was trying to do a lot of different things—perhaps too many. Along with the grape juice product, we were continuing in the vein of riesling and gewürztraminer, expanding the chardonnay program, and making coastal pinot noir while working with local cabernet and zinfandel. It was a very interesting situation to learn to make wine in, but nothing was very well defined."

"We had phenomenal growth," says Brooks Painter, who oversaw the white winemaking in the early 1980s. "The most successful juice was riesling, which relies so heavily on terpenes and aromatics from the grape. It was aging beautifully, but we couldn't satisfy demand, so we started expanding into other varieties like cabernet and gewürztraminer. But the same year we increased production, we hit a saturation point in the market."

McCloskey confirms that "the market rejected riesling in the early eighties. People were turning to French wine culture, and the media decided that the new storm was chardonnay, Bordeaux varieties, and Napa Valley. You had to have deep pockets to play that game, because chardonnay required French oak barrels. It was a shock to the system—the entrepreneur in me said, 'Struggle on,' but from riesling I learned that the market decides whether you get to exist at all."

Where in the early 1960s there had been some 1,200 acres of riesling in California, but not enough chardonnay to even register on the state's Bureau of Agricultural Statistics report, by 1978 (two years after Chateau Montelena's chardonnay won the Judgment of Paris) chardonnay had flooded the state with 13,500 acres, drowning riesling in its wake. To adjust to the changing market, Felton Empire set about increasing its chardonnay production, largely via the ten-year-old Tepusquet vineyard in Santa Barbara County owned by Al Gagnon and Louis Lucas—respectively, a vice president of the consulting firm Booz Allen Hamilton and a farmer whose family grew almonds and table grapes in the San Joaquin Valley near Bakersfield. After the two became partners in Tepusquet, Gagnon had taken Lucas on a tour of blue-chip vineyards in Europe: Lafite, Mouton, Haut-Brion, and Cheval Blanc in Bordeaux to look at cabernet and merlot; Chablis, Meursault, Musigny, and Romanée-Conti in Burgundy for chardonnay and pinot noir; Hugel and Trimbach in Alsace for pinot blanc and gewürztraminer; Schloss Johannisberg and Fischer in Germany for riesling; Épernay, Moët & Chandon, and Louis Roederer for sparkling wine; Vouvray in the Loire Valley for chenin blanc; Pio Cesare in Piemonte for nebbiolo. With an advance contract in hand from Beringer and consulting advice from Albert Winkler of UC Davis, they came back and planted a thousand acres of grapes along the Santa Maria River, a few miles inland from the Pacific coast; their inventory included a diverse array of varieties, but half the total acreage—planted in 1970 and 1971—was riesling.

When Beringer canceled its contract a few years later, Tepusquet scrambled to sell its grapes to any wineries that would take them. One of their customers was a fledgling operation up north called Chateau du Lac, owned by a real estate lawyer from San Francisco. Having grown up poor during the Depression, this fifty-year-old attorney— Jess Stonestreet Jackson—had put himself through law school at UC Berkeley by working as a longshoreman and cop, and after twenty subsequent years specializing in fair compensation for private property confiscated by the government (plus representing Joseph Gallo in an unsuccessful case against his brothers Ernest and Julio for one-third ownership of the world's biggest wine company), in 1974 Jackson procured some real estate of his own. North across the mountains from Napa, he bought an old pear and walnut ranch in Lake County and planted some grapes, which he sold to Barney Fetzer, another relatively new winemaker for whom Jackson had arranged a loan through the Bank of America (where Jackson was an officer).

In 1980, Jackson contracted a winery in Napa to make a thousand cases of chardonnay and eight hundred of cabernet sauvignon. The year after that, he brought the winemaking closer to home, crushing his fruit at Konocti Cellars in nearby Lakeport. (So low-key was Chateau du Lac that its first vintage was hand-bottled by secretaries from Jackson's law firm.) In 1982, Jackson finally built a no-frills, fifty-thousand-case cinder block facility of his own near the local municipal airport, consulting with Paul Dolan of Fetzer Vineyards and hiring a young Fetzer cellar worker named Fred Nickel to oversee it. As it turned out, that year Fetzer, which had grapes coming on line from its new Sundial vineyard in Hopland, decided it no longer needed Jackson's fruit; thus, indicating the scale of his own ambitions, instead of retreating Jackson branched out. In addition to his own grapes, he bought more chardonnay fruit from Tepusquet, from Sonoma-Cutrer's new Les Pierres vineyard, and from McFarland's La Reina property in Monterey. In all, Jackson collected enough juice for some thirty-five thousand cases, much of which—further revealing his level of aspiration—he aimed to ferment not in big tanks but in small oak barrels along the lines of Burgundian *barrique.*

All of this proved overwhelming to Jackson's young cellar master. "I was an immature winemaker and manager," Nickel admits today from neighboring Mendocino County, where he still works as a commercial vintner. "The volume was daunting, and in those days we didn't require any reporting from vineyards—for example, when was the last time the grapes were sulfured?"* Among the things he wasn't conversant with in 1982, Nickel also mentions excessive temperature and insufficient nutrition—all of which might be why, as the '82 harvest wound down and the Lake County winter set in, several of Jackson's chardonnay lots quit fermenting before all the sugar was converted to

* Commonly used to suppress microbial activity in wine—thus the designation "contains sulfites"—sulfur is also employed in vineyards to control mildew on grapes; if too much of it remains on the fruit when picked and crushed, however, it can inhibit yeast from working.

alcohol, rendering them vulnerable to oxidation and volatile acidity—not exactly what the owner had in mind when he'd gone shopping for premium grapes all over the state.

Desperate to find a more experienced hand, Jackson consulted various winemakers, most of whom hewed to the single-vineyard-designate mentality that had taken hold at the high end of the market. Eventually he called Ric Forman, the highly regarded vintner who, in the early 1970s, had pioneered barrel fermentation at Sterling Vineyards in Napa Valley. Having remained with Sterling's founder, Peter Newton, after that winery was sold to Coca-Cola in 1977, Forman was now known to want out of the partnership. "Jess said, 'You don't know me, but I have a little winery up in Lake County,'" Forman recalls. "'I need help, and I hear you could use some legal advice.'" As a quid pro quo, Forman agreed to drive up and "take a look" at Jackson's troubled wines, whose fermentations the owner still hoped to get restarted. "It was so late in the game, it was difficult to get them all to go," Forman says. "So I said, 'I've got another idea. Let's try to put together a decent bulk chardonnay, and maybe we can blend it out with a subliminal amount of residual sugar.'"

This trick was far from unheard of in California, which had been slowly working its way back toward dry table wines ever since the repeal of Prohibition. "Christian Brothers knew in 1955 that people talk dry but drink sweet," says Mel Knox, a longtime Bay Area barrel broker. "They like a low pH [associated with high acidity] to zip up the flavor, but residual sugar to mask the acidity." As Randall Grahm's old Wine Merchant cohort Jason Lewis explains: "Residual sugar in a low dose won't seem sweet—put 0.5 percent sugar in water and you don't taste it, but it will seem rounder, richer, more expressive, fuller-bodied, and softer on the palate." Still, despite the seductiveness of this style, it was repellant to the refined Forman, as was Lake County itself. Trying to think of someone more amenable to non-Napa conditions, Fetzer's Dolan recommended Jed Steele.

Steele was another native San Franciscan who, while "waiting out the draft" after graduating from Gonzaga University on a basketball scholarship in the late 1960s, had gotten a cellar-rat job at the same place that provided an epiphany for John Kongsgaard: the Stony Hill winery in Napa Valley. Steele also worked part-time as a railroad brakeman, in which capacity early one morning he forgot to throw an important switch, causing two locomotives to derail and shutting down the Southern Pacific line between Oakland and Sacramento. Suspended from his duties without pay ("Eventually the union got my job back, but they said, 'They'll stick it to you now if you show up for work a minute late'"), he decided to enter the restaurant trade and began migrating between New England and Florida as a waiter and bartender in 1969. Noticing that "something was going on"—something called Heitz, Mondavi, and Ridge—in the industry where he had briefly worked, Steele took the obligatory year of science classes, enrolled at UC Davis, and with Ralph Kunkee as his adviser, got a master's in food science with a specialization in enology. In 1974 he began making wine for Deron Edmeades, whom he'd met steelhead fishing in Mendocino County's Anderson Valley, and stayed on for nine vintages, during which he didn't even know how much it cost to produce a bottle of wine. "I was a hippie," Steele says. "That's why I was in Mendocino County."

After parting ways with Edmeades in 1982, Steele was planning to take some time off, but Dolan told him about "a guy in Lake County who was really in a jam." Arriving in Lakeport to investigate, Steele found Jess Jackson "very discouraged. His first wife [Jane Kendall] was not enamored of the wine business, and he was just trying to salvage what he could and get out." From his contacts in the industry, however—and from his personal penchant for submitting other wineries' products to laboratory analysis—Steele knew of at least two popular chardonnays that contained residual sugar. In Ukiah near Anderson Valley, Parducci's version varied from 3 to 6 grams of sugar per liter, and in Sonoma, the commercially *and* critically successful example of Chateau St. Jean (where Steele's assistant at Edmeades, Milla Handley, had previously worked) contained 5. Steele set about blending Jackson's lots in different percentages and permutations. Including a little chenin and gamay blanc in the mix, he eventually came up with a lip-smacking, well-balanced blend that melded the tropical-fruit character of Tepusquet, the pear and citrus flavors of chardonnay from farther north, the refreshing acidity associated with cool coastal growing regions, the vanillin taste of oak, the softness that came from malolactic fermentation (which some of the wines had undergone spontaneously), *and* 7.5 grams per liter of residual sugar. To Steele's palate, the end product was a "very rich wine that had more affinity with high-end than low-end" chardonnay. Jackson okayed the labeling of three thousand cases as "Kendall-Jackson Vintner's Reserve," bottling another fourteen thousand as "shiners" without labels or branded corks.

At the time, "luxury" chardonnays like Chateau St. Jean's (or Chateau Montelena's, Chalone's, Acacia's, Mondavi's, Mount Eden's, or Stony Hill's) sold for about $15 a bottle, below which there was mainly jug fare for $2. Noticing "a hole in the market you could drive a truck through"—a chasm that Glen Ellen had just begun to mine—Jackson priced his Vintner's Reserve chardonnay at $5 and helped sell it himself, flying to New York City to pour samples at restaurants and wineshops. Marketed as "attainable luxury," the first three thousand cases of Kendall-Jackson Vintner's Reserve chardonnay sold out right away, and the other fourteen thousand, quickly labeled and rushed onto the market, were gone in six months. Jackson convinced Steele to stay on, and the following year they increased production—but since, as Steele says, "Confidence had been so low from the '82 that we didn't have a lot of grapes lined up for '83," they added wine bought on the bulk market to those from fruit they vinified themselves. This time the residual sugar came from botrytised Anderson Valley riesling, which Dolan declined to accept for Fetzer but which, bottled by itself, won the Prince Metternich Award for the best late-harvest riesling at the International Wine Competition in London.

Based on a couple of decades' experience selling wine in the United States, Tom Halby—a veteran marketer with whom Jackson soon entered into a partnership—thought that K-J's Vintner's Reserve was an ideal wine for the American palate. He spent two straight months on the road introducing the wine to distributors around the country—a challenge that (considering the price) he likened to using a firearm on flounder *en barrique*. K-J sold 50,000 cases of the '83 edition, and the following year—with a coherent production plan now in place—100,000 cases of the '84. By 1992 it would be the bestselling chardonnay in the United States, having commercially established what is still considered the characteristic style of California chardonnay: soft, buttery, fruity, oaky, and—perceptibly or imperceptibly, depending on the taster's palate—sweet.

As K-J's comet ascended in the 1980s, its allocation of Tepusquet chardonnay soared proportionately, from twenty tons (for which Lucas and Gagnon had had to resort to market enforcement to get paid) to hundreds. In the meantime, Tepusquet was also "supporting" Felton Empire. "We provided Felton Empire with grapes, even though in some cases they didn't pay us," recalls Lucas, now the seventy-year-old proprietor of the Lucas & Lewellen winery in Santa Barbara County. "They were innovative guys, and this is a tough industry—to increase your production by ten thousand cases, you need to invest a million dollars." In lieu of payment for fruit, Lucas and Gagnon worked out an equation to assume ownership of a fourth of Felton Empire.[*] Unfortunately, the real owner was Wells Fargo Bank, whose feet began to refrigerate during the recession and savings-and-loan crisis of the 1980s. In addition to funding Tepusquet, the bank was also financing the Lucases' farming business in the San Joaquin Valley, which in 1983 was inundated by an El Niño downpour, as well as being saturated with internal family problems. Eventually these various pressures took their toll on Gagnon.

"Al got disillusioned with the wine business," Lucas says. "He was in his seventies, and he was disappointed that we never really made money. We broke even a lot, and Tepusquet was holding its own; Al marched all over California selling grapes, but still we had a couple of years where we couldn't get rid of our fruit—everybody wanted chardonnay, and we had four hundred acres of riesling. We tried everything: I converted all the riesling and gewürztraminer and cabernet to chardonnay; we had a seventy-two-thousand-case label, and we made bulk wine. But finally Al decided he'd had enough."

---

[*] According to McCloskey, Gagnon (who died in 1991) also invested a quarter of a million dollars in cash. He was bullish of Felton Empire's nonalcoholic juice, envisioning it as an eventual 100,000-case product.

When Wells Fargo began to hold Tepusquet accountable for the Lucases' other business problems, Gagnon cut a deal with the bank that allowed him to escape with his own equity intact. At the same time, Wells Fargo acquired Felton Empire's primary lender, Crocker Bank—and, soon thereafter, demanded payment of Tepusquet's Felton Empire shares in cash. "We were in shock," McCloskey told Sullivan. "We could see that profits were dropping in the wine business for the small to medium producer. Cost of goods produced was going up steadily. Everything was going up."

As a result, he concluded, "Al and I sat down and did some thinking and decided to sell the winery." McCloskey consulted Gomberg, Fredrikson & Associates, a wine-industry analyst based in nearby Woodside, which told him that selling the winery wasn't going to be easy. "Jon Fredrikson told me, 'The Santa Cruz Mountains is considered pretty ticky-tacky by wealthy people from Virginia,'" McCloskey told Sullivan. "They had a hundred wineries in the Napa area that people were willing to sell." Indeed, unable to interest buyers in "a company making riesling in Santa Cruz," the owners ultimately decided to hold a liquidation event. On one day (admittedly a long one— the summer solstice) of June 1987, they sold their winery building, product inventory, winemaking equipment, and commercial brand to different buyers, generating a total of two million dollars—half of which went to paying off debts, with the remainder divided among the owner-investors. As McCloskey told Sullivan, "We escaped by the skin of our teeth, but it was a hell of a lot of work."

"Felton Empire was disappointing," admits Jim Beauregard, whose family had contributed most of the money to buy the Hallcrest building and start the winery, but who says he "never got a dime" from the sell-off of assets. "It didn't turn out how I expected. I thought it would perk along and develop the Santa Cruz Mountains appellation, but it got too complicated." Today the soft-spoken Beauregard, who has a small, eponymous brand with his son Ryan as winemaker, says that he doesn't have partners in anything except his sailboat.

Louis Lucas still hoped to hang on to the vineyard he'd planted at Tepusquet. As part of the foreclosure proceedings, he thus negotiated a right to match any offer Wells Fargo received for the property, and went looking for potential new partners. Eventually he called Jess Jackson, telling him that he was in danger of losing the Tepusquet fruit.

"I knew the quality of the grapes," Jackson later told Joshua Greene of *Wine & Spirits,* explaining why he was motivated to make a deal with Lucas. "I wanted the vineyard, and if Wells Fargo sold it, I'd be able to acquire it." Sure enough, the bank soon got a cash offer of $11.9 million from Tepusquet's original customer, Beringer. Still in the early stages of K-J Vintner's Reserve, Jackson didn't have that kind of money on hand, so the seasoned real estate litigator joined forces with one Robert Mondavi and—exercising a right of first refusal acquired from Lucas—succeeded in snatching Tepusquet from the grasp of Beringer. Jackson named his share of the property Cambria, and the rest became part of Byron Vineyards, Mondavi's flagship foray into the Central Coast.*

"It's too bad Al never got a chance to see what that vineyard did with chardonnay and a price," Lucas says today. "The sad part is that the best three years of Tepusquet were the ones after Jess Jackson got it. I ran it for him for the first couple of years; I was supposed to run it for the rest of my life, but then he jumped in bed with Mondavi and they started fighting." Though Lucas's price for the right of purchase included a stipulation that he stay on as vineyard manager (and he says he never received all the money he was promised for the rest), within a few years he was informed that his services were no longer required—a message underscored by a Santa Barbara County sheriff's deputy, who escorted him from the property.

All of which prompted Leo McCloskey to observe, as Felton Empire faded into the Santa Cruz Mountains sunset, "The wine business was changing from an entrepreneurial enterprise onto a more businesslike footing."

---

* Twenty years later, after Mondavi was acquired by Constellation, Jackson bought Byron too.

IN FEBRUARY I accompany Grahm on a visit to Rhys Vineyards, a relatively new winery near Woodside on the peninsula south of San Francisco. Its owner is Kevin Harvey, a software entrepreneur–cum–venture capitalist who has funneled some of his earnings into high-end winemaking. In this, Harvey is no different from any number of other wine-loving tycoons, but he's departed from the usual formula in some significant ways. For one, instead of transporting his dreams to Napa, he planted them on the edge of Silicon Valley, in the northernmost part of the Santa Cruz Mountains. Starting literally in Harvey's own backyard with thirty-five vines, Rhys (a family name, pronounced "Reese") has since expanded to five vineyards with varying soils and elevations, all farmed biodynamically, within hang gliding distance of the Pacific Ocean. Moreover, the wine lode Harvey is mining is not in the overripe cabernet vein, but rather traditional, Burgundian-style pinot noir—"far more about finesse and complexity than extroverted fruit" (Stephen Tanzer's *International Wine Cellar*), "balanced and harmonious . . . unencumbered by excessive alcohol" (PrinceofPinot.com), "a beacon for those who value grace, balance, structure and distinctiveness in wine" (Eric Asimov, *New York Times*). It's only natural, then, for Grahm to be curious.

The winery location doesn't exactly reflect the Old World associations of the wines: It's in an industrial park in San Carlos, close by the stream of commercial traffic on U.S. 101.* The person who receives

---

* Rhys has since completed a thirty-thousand-square-foot underground facility on its Skyline vineyard property at the crest of the Santa Cruz Mountains.

us is not Harvey but his general manager and winegrower Jason Jardine, a bright, thirtysomething MBA who previously worked for Tony Soter, Ken Wright, and Domaine Serene in Oregon. As we enter the nondescript-looking warehouse, Jardine explains that he came to Rhys because he and Harvey—a mentor who encouraged him to commute to Southern Methodist University in Dallas to supplement his grape-growing background with a business degree—share the same notion of an ideal wine: Something that's "structurally and aromatically interesting" and "shows soil and earth." (Specifically Domaine de la Romanée-Conti.)

"Kevin has one of the most extensive Burgundy collections anywhere," Jardine divulges. "Part of our goal with pinot noir is wine that will age a long time, so a lot of people will think our young wines are too hard. But we want to allow people to have a love-hate relationship with them. Since we allow the vineyards to show themselves, it's natural that people should like some and dislike others."

Inside the building is a lineup of small stainless-steel tanks, each capable of fermenting a single ton of grapes—the amount that Jardine says Rhys can harvest from a half acre of vines "in a good year." In other words, they're farmed to produce a minimal crop, with only one cluster of grapes per shoot. "It's been a long time since I've seen this scale," Grahm comments. "It's a lovely scale."

"Last year we didn't irrigate two of the vineyards at all," Jardine says. "One we watered twice, with two gallons per vine." The latter vineyard, he explains, is a newer planting, with a spacing pattern of only three feet by two feet between vines. This results in 7,200 plants per acre, which is sort of like crowding 7,200 people into a room and directing them to make it through the upcoming summer on two gallons of water per person.

The goal of such claustrophobic planting is to intensify grape flavors by forcing the vines to compete for nutrients. As someone who wants desperately to dry farm but is still unsure of its efficacy in California, Grahm is impressed. "Are these breatharian grapes?" he asks.

"It depends on how the vines are treated from day one," says Jardine. "At first we treat them like a garden plant. We put them in a bed of compost to create humus and microbial activity, and we irrigate to half the rooting depth the first two years to encourage the roots to grow downward, which allows better water uptake and less drought stress. If they're happy the first year, they develop a natural immune system and can function on their own. After all, they're vines—it's a wild species. They're gonna find a way to survive."

"One viticultural consultant told me that in order to dry farm, you have to be ten-by-ten or ten-by-twelve," says Grahm. "I'm sure it depends on the water-holding capacity of the soil, but that just doesn't make sense to me."

"In the quarter-mile distance between our Alpine and Horseshoe vineyards, there's a ten- to fifteen-million-year difference in soil age," says Jardine. "Since they're so different, we try to determine what's best for each site. We try for a balance between root growth and vegetative growth, and before planting, we dug up the ground to see where the roots were on the native cover crop."

So animated is Grahm by the discussion that he punctuates Jardine's statements with multiple "yeahs"—uttered not just one at a time, but in duplicate and triplicate ("yeah, yeah" . . . "yeah, yeah, yeah").

"We're also really aggressive with biodynamic compost," says Jardine. "We use thirty tons of it per acre."

"That's huge!"

"It sounds like a lot, but it's only a few inches deep. The base is sludge from organic dairies—we have to transport it, so it's not cheap, but it's worth it. It doesn't add much to the bottle cost."

"The other thing I anguish over—I'm an anguished guy—is canopy density," says Grahm. "We have so much sun in California, I doubt the wisdom of VSP*—I think maybe we're better off with head training.† I was thinking about using conical tomato trellises."

"We use VSP, but we don't pull leaves," says Jardine. "Farmers hate

---

* Vertical shoot positioning, the currently fashionable trellis system designed to expose more grapes to the sun and develop more flavor by increasing anthocyanin content in the fruit.

† The traditional Old World method of raising vines as independent bushes without any trellises to support the arms.

that, because pulling them allows better spray coverage and you get less mildew. But counter to what most people think, with pinot noir we've found *less* anthocyanins with more sun exposure. If the ambient air temperature is 80, it might be as high as 130 in the [grape] cluster—and pinot skins are so thin that the sun bleaches out the stable pigments. You have to get them riper and more concentrated from dehydration to back that up, but with less sun exposure we're getting stronger, riper fruit flavors early on. I've found the same thing picking blackberries with my kids—the berries in direct sun have jammier, more pielike flavors, but if you can find some in the shade that are ripe, the flavors are cleaner, more concentrated—less cooked."

Soon we're joined by a stocky young guy about the same age as Jardine—Rhys's winemaker Jeff Brinkman, whom Jardine recruited from Husch Vineyards in Anderson Valley, where Brinkman—having previously abandoned a career in molecular biology and cancer research—worked after starting at R.H. Phillips in the Sacramento Valley. The conversation naturally turns toward vinification, which Jardine says is done with whole grape clusters crushed by foot; the juice is fermented with natural yeast and native malolactic bacteria, meaning that the latter fermentation takes place very slowly.

"Most wineries have their MLs completed, and the wines sulfured and put to bed, before Christmas," says Jardine. "Ours sometimes don't finish until August." (Until malolactic fermentation is complete, wine can't be racked, since ML bacteria reside in the lees. But as long as fermentation continues, it produces carbon dioxide, which protects the wine against excessive oxidation and its deadly accomplice, acetic bacteria.)

"I love extended ML," Grahm affirms.

"Burgundians say that long MLs are a sign of a good vintage," says Brinkman. "What I like is that it forces you to leave the wine alone. Wines can stay very, very healthy for a year with no sulfur; I actually see more bacterial problems with commercial ML strains—some of those can go really sour."

"With biodynamics, we don't have to use [yeast] nutrients," Jardine adds.

"Yeah, yeah," says Grahm, "because of the enhanced microbial life in the soil."

"We can also pick at lower sugars. Nothing in the winery is over 13.5 percent alcohol."

Moving farther into the warehouse, where rows of sixty-gallon barrels are stacked, Jardine says that oak has been the hardest program for them to figure out. "For us, the Santa Cruz Mountains has a big tannin structure. So we want a certain amount of oak, but we don't want the wine to be oaky." Since new wood helps "ameliorate tannin" better than used wood does, Brinkman says they decided to use air-dried oak from the François Frères cooperage, aged for four years rather than the typical three.

"I usually don't like François Frères," says Grahm. "It tastes like ashtrays."

"The extra year of drying makes it more subdued," says Brinkman. "You can use 50 or 60 or 70 percent new wood, and you'd never know it from tasting the wine."

"Aging reduces a lot of the lactones and natural sugars," says Jardine. "DRC [Domaine de la Romanée-Conti] just started using the same program. We have to pay a little more for it; with an extra year of aging, some of the wood splits, so you can only get nine barrels from a meter of wood, instead of ten."

"It's important to have a face-to-face relationship with the barrel builder," Brinkman adds.

"I've always been aesthetically opposed to oak chips," Grahm alleges, "but I wonder if you can use them in glass vessels. It's a question of how much reduction you want—especially with pinot noir."

"At R.H. Phillips we did experiments: neutral barrels, tanks with chips, and tanks with chips and micro-ox," says Brinkman. "After six to eight months, chips and micro-ox was vastly preferred."

R.H. Phillips is the winery where, twenty years earlier, Clark Smith was the founding winemaker. When I mention this, Brinkman refers to Smith as a "practical solution finder."

"Clark is an Aristotelian, not a Platonist," he says. Then, pointing first at the ground and then at the air over his head, he elaborates, "He thinks the truth is down here, not up there. He's a realist, not a head-in-the-clouds dreamer." Grahm declines to respond.

All that's left is to taste the wines, whose character might be described as uncompromising. One of the pinots is 12.3 percent alcohol, another 11.9; both have a focused, pristine quality that makes them seem almost austere, though the fruit is very dense. By comparison, a syrah that Brinkman pours is more sensually satisfying. "This rocks!" says the Rhone Ranger of the latter wine.

"It was de-stemmed," Jardine reveals. "The syrah is a style we want to drink well earlier—meaty but approachable."

"These wines are so old-fashioned," Grahm comments. "I think they might come into their own in ten or fifteen years."

"It's hard to know, because we have no history in the area," says Jardine. "Around the third year, they really start to sing—they're round and plush with huge aromatics. We want our pinot noir to age alongside the best wines of Burgundy."

"The New World has a different challenge from Burgundy," Grahm cautions. "To get complexity and completeness here, you have to do something really strange. I think these reds want a little something for softening; it's a quibble, but I think pinot noir should have some baby fat. I like it to be gentle, and these are very lean. So I have a really, really radical suggestion: Add 10 percent chardonnay to your pinot noir. Dare I say it? I think they could use more alcohol—and while it's utter sacrilege to suggest as much, I think maybe they might benefit from fewer stems."

Since Rhys has received a good deal more acclamation than Bonny Doon of late, it's interesting that Grahm sees fit to offer this unsolicited (and, one must observe, eminently Aristotelian) feedback. Despite his speed-date critique, however, he says he finds the wines very worthy. He must be at least a little envious of Kevin Harvey, who can obviously afford to go to extremes to create the kind of wine he idealizes.

"This is very serious," Randall says in the parking lot as we depart, gesturing in the direction of the winery. "The wines are all quite impressive, but I wonder if they'll ever become charming. They have almost preternatural concentration, which in Parker's world is a good thing, but for tasting enjoyment it may actually work against them."

I say I'd been under the impression that "Parker's world" is more about high alcohol and short-term tasting enjoyment than low alcohol and long-term aging. Perhaps referring more to his own inner anguish than to the vicissitudes of critical evaluation—or even the wines we just tasted—Grahm responds: "With pinot, all bets are off."

A FTER FELTON EMPIRE folded in the late 1980s, Leo Mc-Closkey returned to Ridge as a part-time consultant. In the decade since he'd discovered the work of T. C. Somers and gone back to school, a number of things had changed; the number of California wineries had doubled to more than 800, and U.S. table wine consumption had risen commensurately, from 262 million gallons in 1977 to 481 million in 1986. On the other hand, the stock market rise of the mid-Reagan years had been followed by the correction that helped sink Felton Empire. Amid this ever more crowded, increasingly nervous market, critics were acquiring a more prominent role on behalf of consumers. The rise of Robert M. Parker Jr. and the *Wine Advocate* was paralleled by that of the *Wine Spectator*, a former San Diego newsprint tabloid that, after being purchased by investment banker Marvin Shanken in 1979, became a glossy luxury-lifestyle magazine promoting not only wine but also dining and travel. As part of this transformation, the *Spectator* implemented tasting-evaluation panels, beginning with UC Davis's 20-point system, but adopting the 100-point scale by the mid-1980s.

In other words, McCloskey says, "Critics were starting to control the value chain" that went from the winery to the distributor to the retailer and restaurateur to the consumer. "In the old British evaluation system, wine writers were closely linked to the industry," he points out. "They promoted the idea that everything about wine was a mystery—it was salesmanship. Even Amerine's book on sensory analysis said that quality isn't real; it's about defect testing, and it promotes the use of words like *character* or *texture* to describe attributes. Quality ratings and scores and classifications were anathema to modern sensory analysis; in the seventies, if a winemaker screwed up and made an average or below-average wine, he just said, 'Too bad—deal with it. I'm Picasso.' So by 1990 everybody was discrediting the score, but I saw that the critics were going to win because Americans wanted to reduce their risk of purchase and winemakers weren't filling the information void." Harking back to the "detectable ecotypic expression" he'd studied in chemical ecology, McCloskey concluded that "Parker and the *Spectator* are like scouts for the tribe—they go out and tell the others whether it's safe to eat the stuff."

At Ridge Leo helped, among other things, to get the winery's pesky *Brettanomyces* problem under control by filtering rather than following the low-tech regimen with which the place identified itself. It's safe to say that, after fifteen years of association, McCloskey and winemaker Paul Draper maintained a testy relationship, as McCloskey constantly challenged Draper's Old World philosophy with his upstart activist ideas. In retrospect, Draper credits McCloskey mainly for presenting an alternative viewpoint to his own—for suggesting, for example, when Ridge separated cabernet grapes from their skins at harvest, that it analyze tannin in progressively tighter pressings of the fruit, rather than combining all of it in one big lot. This resulted in a more finely blended product and, ultimately, more individualistic treatment of each vintage.

"In the seventies and eighties," McCloskey later told Charles Sullivan, "we had a lot of tannic wines. There were a lot of wines that were not very sophisticated; I don't want to say crude." Indeed, high tannin was often considered a positive, owing to its sensation of substance and association with aging potential. Critics, however, were starting to reject the harsh quality it exuded in comparative tastings; in addition, the newly stigmatized "vegetal" character* of some Ridge wines was turning people off. ("It turned out that Americans would rather drink

---

* In time, Hildegarde Heymann of UC Davis would find that this quality—attributable to a group of chemical compounds called pyrazines—was ameliorated by exposure to sunlight, with the result that intensive leaf-thinning is now common in cabernet sauvignon vineyards.

wines that are raisiny than herbal," McCloskey says.) In the midst of this upheaval, Ridge brought in a consultant from UC Davis to analyze the winery's fining trials and "found out that what we thought we could taste we couldn't." In at least one blind comparison, Ridge staffers rated a Napa Valley cabernet higher than their own Monte Bello; when McCloskey analyzed the two wines' chemistry, he found that the Napa wine contained less tannin.

Until then, McCloskey had consulted for his clients in conventional ways, advising them about primary chemistry (sugar, alcohol, acidity, pH) and basic procedures like fermentation, pressing, filtering, and blending. Armed with the knowledge he'd acquired from Somers and his own PhD work, he now extracted permission from customers to analyze their wines' secondary chemistry: alkaloids, terpenoids, and phenolics (which include tannins and anthocyanins). While working at Ridge, he was able to increase the speed of the assaying process that Somers had used, and by the time I met him in 1987, he was embroiled in a frenzy of data compilation—collecting hundreds of wine samples, running them through a high-performance liquid chromatograph and gas spectrometer, isolating and identifying their chemical components, and amassing a digital archive on different varieties. Quantifying the chemical concentrations in terms of parts per million and milligrams per liter, he found that a relatively small number of compounds have a sufficiently conspicuous presence to affect the perceptible character of a wine.

"Wine scientists always thought grapes were more complicated than any other plant system," he says. "They had this Carl Sagan attitude that there were billions and billions of chemical compounds out there. But from an evolutionary point of view, wine is a really simple beverage—there are less than four hundred compounds in it that are detectable by people, and only thirty or forty that are responsible for the distinguishing characteristics in different 'genres' like cabernet and pinot noir." In his 1975 paper "In Search of Quality for Red Wines," even T. C. Somers had written, "Diversities of wine styles, personal, and regional biases will always allow room for argument, the only certainty being that wine quality just cannot be defined by mere analysis of components." McCloskey, however, seemed to be moving toward a belief that quality could be determined in a lab without even tasting the wine. In this departure from traditional mores, he again found himself at odds with Draper, who held fast to the belief that tasting is absolute.

In 1988 McCloskey left Ridge and, with his wife, Susan, founded McCloskey, Arrhenius & Co., a wine R & D company headquartered in Santa Cruz. Given Susan's academic background in terpenoids (which play a prominent role in aroma), she concentrated on white wines, while Leo, whose PhD work was on phenolics (which affect flavor and texture), focused on reds. Eventually they identified eighty-four compounds above the wine-tasting threshold of human beings—thirty-two in red, fifty-two in white—and determined that Somers's "polymeric red pigment" actually represented a complex of anthocyanins. Employing new computer software capable of processing thousands of variables for each wine, they set about correlating the chemical concentrations with tasting results and critical scores, simplifying the results into a single figure called a "quality index." When they felt they had enough data to demonstrate a coherent model, Leo went to see Dick Graff.

Graff was the founder of Chalone Vineyards, located in the Gavilan Mountains in Monterey County. A former Harvard music major, U.S. naval officer, Zen student, and airplane pilot, Graff and his partner Phil Woodward had helped pioneer Burgundian-style winemaking in California during the 1960s, fermenting chardonnay in French oak barrels and growing pinot noir in limestone ten years before Randall Grahm got (but failed to follow through on) the same idea. After Chalone's chardonnay placed third in the '76 Judgment of Paris, Graff and Woodward also acquired the Acacia and Carmenet wineries in Napa and Sonoma, and in 1984 Chalone went public, morphing into the Chalone Wine Group. McCloskey met Graff in the late seventies through one of his own consulting clients, Josh Jensen, who, before renting space to Grahm at Calera, had undergone a similar cohabitation/apprenticeship at Chalone. In the early eighties, Graff, Jensen, and McCloskey teamed up with other artisan vintners to form the Small Winery Technical Society, dedicated to the organized implementation of intensive, hands-on techniques.

Knowing Graff to be (1) ambitious, (2) entrepreneurial, (3) methodical, (4) cosmopolitan, and (5) well connected (his acquaintances ranged from the Dalai Lama to the actor Danny Kaye), McCloskey made an appointment to see Graff in the latter's office on Spear Street in downtown San Francisco, not far from the neighborhood where Leo's father had a store in the 1950s. As a matter of fact, he got his dad to drop him off for the meeting, warning him that "this guy is probably going to kick me out of his office in five minutes." Armed with his arsenal of data, the fast-talking McCloskey told Graff, "Winemakers are always surprised when their products don't work out, but I think we can predict the winners two years into the future." Instead of showing him the door, Graff flew McCloskey around the state in his Cessna, surveying Chalone Group wines of the 1980s with all the company's winemakers. Leo assembled the results and then went home and analyzed the wines' chemistry; a few months later, all the winemakers and their assistants were invited to a tasting in San Francisco, where, presented with a blind selection of the surveyed wines, each participant was asked to rank the six best and six worst. At Susan's suggestion, McCloskey produced a sealed envelope that contained his chemically derived predictions before the votes were tallied. As it turned out, he'd correctly guessed the group's top three and bottom three choices, in the correct order.

With that, Graff introduced McCloskey to one of Chalone's major shareholders—Château Lafite-Rothschild, one of the five top growths of Bordeaux. "Graff thought that, unless we based it on Europe, nobody would accept my system in the U.S. He knew it would only matter if we could make it economically important, and he believed that the French 1855 classification was true because it was based on economics and bottle prices. The French were oriented toward rating, not tasting, so if you could link [chemistry] to wine quality in America, it would be even easier in France. He got a hold of Lafite, and they agreed to hire us to assay their wines."

Indeed, the venerable Bordeaux estate soon began sending wine to Santa Cruz—bottled releases from the past ten years right up through barrel samples of the 1990 vintage. "In effect, I got a live feed from France," is how McCloskey describes the experience. "In essence, Lafite provided me a ruler with winners and losers on it. I got to see how French wines were different, from first growths to second growths to fifth growths, and from region to region. Lo and behold, the chemistry was high in good years and low in bad years, and higher for first growths than for second growths, which were higher than fifth growths." In other words, McCloskey's chemical findings mirrored the economic performance of the bottled wines. What was more, he correctly predicted all but one lot of grapes that would go into the '90 Lafite "Grand Vin."

While all of this was going on, Leo noticed that Seattle-based Microsoft had just passed $1 billion in sales, and just over the Santa Cruz Mountains in Silicon Valley (where his brother Michael was an executive), Apple founder Steve Jobs had been named Entrepreneur of the Decade by *Inc.* magazine. McCloskey's earlier patents for analytical methods had never made him any money, despite the fact that they were now used throughout the industry. "Wineries considered scientists purely functionary," he says. "They got no respect at all. My clients would just share the methods with their friends—somebody would show me something stamped DO NOT DISTRIBUTE, and it would be a copy of my work. The demographic I wanted to sell to was giving away my stuff! But what was I gonna do—sue the people I was consulting for?" Predicting that the same thing would happen with his chemical-quality analysis ("You can sue a large company for damages, but small companies will just declare bankruptcy"), McCloskey's own patent attorney advised him to maintain his new method as a proprietary trade secret. The challenge was how to report data to customers without giving it away.

Taking note of a University of Georgia study finding that the average person can remember eight figures simultaneously, Leo opted for an even friendlier figure, condensing the chemical compounds of wine into a half dozen relevant groups, but not revealing the identities of the individual chemicals. For red, the six key categories were total phenolics (which winemakers customarily connected with quality), tannins (associated with structure and astringency), monomers (bitterness), total anthocyanin (color), free anthocyanin (age), and perhaps most crucially, complex anthocyanin (the "polymeric red pigments" that Somers had found but failed to identify). For white wines, in which aroma is assigned higher importance, the six categories are total phenolics, complex yellow pigments, total oils, essential oils, higher esters, and terpenes. To make the package as accessible as a phone number, he added a seventh figure: a "quality index" between -1 and +1, arrived at by correlating the chemistry with tasting results and critical scores. A branding expert in Silicon Valley told McCloskey that the name of a technical business should have an x in it, so Leo experimentally applied that rule to every word he deemed pertinent to his mission, which was to apply logic to enology.

In 1993, McCloskey trademarked the name Enologix—and, taking note of the new power wielded by Parker and the *Wine Spectator*, enlisted UC Santa Cruz mathematician Marshall Sylvan (who had helped him create the quality index) to translate the -1/+1 equation onto a 100-point scale. Finally, in 1994, recalling Jon Fredrikson's admonition that Santa Cruz was the equivalent of Podunk when it came to wine cachet, he moved his office to "the walled city of wine": Napa.

Actually, he moved to Sonoma—the rent was cheaper.

I N 1990, JOHN LOCKE—not the towering seventeenth-century English political philosopher, but a slight, strawberry blond energy-systems analyst—was living in Washington, D.C., "crunching numbers" for a commercial law firm that dealt in interstate natural-gas pipeline regulation. Locke was a twenty-seven-year-old graduate of Michigan's Kalamazoo College, which is known for sending its students overseas—the school requires undergraduates to spend at least a term abroad, and Locke had used his to live for seven months in France, staying with a family in Normandy while attending the University of Caen. In this way, the young economics major became immersed in life in the French countryside: growing vegetables in the yard, buying milk and butter from the people who lived next door, foraging for morels in the woods and mussels on the coast, filling empty wine bottles from barrels of Beaujolais and Côtes du Rhône proffered by passing *négociants*. After graduation, Locke furthered his familiarity with wine in the same metropolitan milieu that had previously nurtured Robert M. Parker Jr. Washington, D.C., liquor stores staged free tastings every Saturday, and amid the flood of chardonnay and cabernet, Locke found himself especially enamored of an offbeat winery that Parker himself had championed.

"Bonny Doon wines were clearly different," Locke remembers. "I got the feeling that Randall, the Flying Karamazov Brothers, and Penn and Teller were different incarnations of the same gremlin. You had a sense of someone somewhere sitting around trying to bring sophomoric/postgraduate-level delight and cleverness to the enterprise—that it was never enough just to make the wine, but attaching a narrative to the process somehow made it a participatory relationship."

That fall Locke determined to participate directly. Realizing that he'd been working himself to death "without possibility of parole," he decided to quit his job, move to California, and go to work for a winery. He had four companies in mind: Bonny Doon; Bonny Doon; Bonny Doon; and if those didn't work out, Ridge.

Locke rented a U-Haul truck and, towing his Honda Civic behind it, crossed the Colorado Rockies in a snowstorm, an ordeal that he believes left him with permanent gastritis. When he presented himself at Bonny Doon, Patrice Boyle turned him down for a job but says that "John looked so cute that the people in the tasting room begged me to hire him." Locke had no experience with winemaking, but after he continued to "harass" her with applications two and three—sweetened, not insignificantly, with an offer to work for free—Boyle broke down and let him hand-label some Bonny Doon grappa, waxing the individual capsules and wrapping the bottles in tissue paper. Continuing to insinuate himself, Locke next helped make the Vin de Glacière, which meant pressing forty-pound FYBs ["Fucking yellow boxes"] full of frozen grapes. "The grapes were like marbles," he remembers. "It took three people all day to do two and a half tons, for not a lot of juice. It should have given me a clue about the Bonny Doon cost structure: Imagine the rate-of-return factor going in reverse."

As it turned out, Locke and Grahm experienced something akin to intellectual love at first sight. So completely did Locke identify with his hero that, before long, he became Bonny Doon's creative director. "Randall was my mentor, but there's a saying that the teacher needs the student as much as the student needs the teacher," Locke says. "He and I can both spend hours or days thinking about things like roomfuls of glass carboys full of lees. I would drive around with him looking at vineyard sites, or helping him make kooky wines; I would stay at his house and feed the cats or dogs when he was out of town. Randall was traveling all over the world and getting exposed to all kinds of things, but instead of just buying a case of something and drinking it—or even trying to duplicate it—he would try and put a different twist on it."

After a decade of operation, Bonny Doon had expanded to thirty thousand cases. Besides the Rhône blends, grappa, eau-de-vie, and ice wine, a slew of new products was always under development, and clearly Grahm's estate vineyard would be able to satisfy only a minimal amount of the demand (whether commercial or cognitive). Moreover, the combativeness of his neighbors made it questionable whether he would be able to remain in Bonny Doon at all—so, to augment his semifunctional winery in the mountains, in 1990 Grahm leased a former brussels-sprouts-and-granola processing plant on the west side of Santa Cruz. He also maintained contact with a diverse lot of grape growers including the McFarland family, which owned the La Reina vineyard where Bonny Doon (like Kendall-Jackson) sourced chardonnay in Monterey County.

As it turned out, the McFarlands, who were looking to shed some real estate holdings, offered Grahm a deal he couldn't refuse on vineyard property near the town of Soledad. Situated in the heart of the Salinas Valley—Steinbeck country—the town was mainly known for a maximum-security state prison, but with an open gateway to the Pacific Ocean courtesy of the Salinas River, it had a surprisingly cool climate of the kind that Randall appreciated. "It seemed like a good idea at the time," he remembers. "I was a bit of a populist, and I loved the idea of making a big, hearty, soulful red wine for the masses."

That wine would be Big House, named for the aforementioned correctional facility, but alluding to an inclusive approach—in Grahm's promotional words, "an absolute rejection of societal expectations to drink this or that status-enhancing label and act instead upon one's primal instinct for vinous jouissance." Since other wines would also be made from this new vineyard, they would all need a collective brand name; harking back to her time in Italy (and her relationship with her current employer), Patrice Boyle had a brainstorm that invoked the apt moniker of a village she remembered from Emilia-Romagna: *Ca' del Solo,* or House of the Solitary Man (i.e. bachelor).

This just happened to coincide with what Grahm still calls his Italianate Period. "I recently had the wonderful fortune to travel in Italy," he wrote in his newsletter in 1990. "Wily serpents abide in the underbrush. . . . They tantalize me with tannat, pique my fancy with pigato,

vamp with verduzzo and oh so sibilantly seduce me with sagrantino."
In step with his resulting *passion du jour*, Ca' del Solo would also go
on to produce barbera, dolcetto, nebbiolo, charbono, refosco, freisa,
and sangiovese. In other words, presented with a blank slate free of
Santa Cruz's social, political, and environmental obstacles, Randall
seemed to relate to his new property as a sandbox (which, geologically speaking, it was). At what amounted to a bell signaling recess,
he planted not just *Vitis vinifera* grapes but also American hybrids
like clinton, ives, noah, and isabella, subjecting all of the above to different systems of spacing, trellising, and irrigation. Nearby he also
planted an "experimental" orchard to provide raw material for Bonny
Doon's various distillates. In short order, Big House would explode the
confines of Ca' del Solo, becoming a catchall repository for "clos but
no Cigare"–quality fruit from all over the place. The '92 version contained carignane, petite sirah, mourvedre, and barbera; the '93 had
mourvedre, grenache, syrah, cinsault, pinot meunier, barbera, sangiovese, nebbiolo, and charbono. The Ca' del Solo label also peddled such
non-Ca'-del-Solo-grown wines as Malvasia Bianca and Il Pescatore,
the latter a purportedly fish-friendly blend of white grapes, including
chardonnay, sauvignon blanc, riesling, and roussanne.

Within the walls of the wineries in Bonny Doon and Santa Cruz,
experimentation proceeded apace. Around the time he acquired the
Soledad property, Grahm came across a pair of pressure tanks that
had been used for Charmat-process sparkling wine—so, as he subsequently announced, "Having tasted the fabulous Moscato d'Asti in
Piedmont, I am sorely tempted to use the tanks for low-alcohol friz-
zante wines." (The resulting product still had a French name: "La
Canard Froid," aka "Quackling Pinot Meunier" or "cherry soda with
an attitude," created to answer the question "What would cold duck
have tasted like had it been any good?") Another unusual offering, "La
Garrigue," consisted of French colombard chaptalized* with twenty-
five kinds of honey, whereas Garnacha ("The Strong Pink Wine") was

---

* The French custom of adding sugar to underripe juice during fermentation to
  beef up a wine's body and soften its mouthfeel.

grenache wine fortified with brandy so as to emulate absinthe ("the only *boisson* that Ernest and Gertrude would even consider sipping tableside at Les Deux Maggots"). Recioto of Barbera was made from grapes that, after being picked, were placed in a fruit dryer and fermented in the manner of Valpolicella and Amarone; Freisa con Freisa combined the Piemontese grape of that name with strawberries, which also happen to be called *freisa* in Italian. "We made a dry table wine containing both," Boyle explains. "It was almost more conceptual than real. You couldn't really call it wine—more of a specialty alcoholic beverage. If Jim Beam did it, you'd hate them for it." Later it occurred to Grahm that "instead of oak as the structurizing and antioxidative element in wine, why not simply use rocks?" On the theory that "the heady, rarified, spirituous quality of wine demands a solid, dense element for balance, a solid yang for the rarified, evanescent yin," he proceeded to submerge various kinds of stones in various wines. "There is a definite Faustus-like quality to this work," he acknowledged.

All of these products were adorned with Bonny Doon's trademark crazy-ass labels, most of which had little or nothing to do with wine. The Ca' del Solo line featured scratchboard cartoons of various individuals acting alone; Big House displayed a fortresslike building surrounded by barbed wire, illuminated by a searchlight that recalled the one projected by Le Cigare Volant. Similar to the Vin Gris, both Il Pescatore and Pacific Rim Riesling had back labels that corresponded with the aqueous contents on offer—in riesling's case, the inner picture consisted of sushi that, viewed through the liquid in the bottle, seemed to be swimming. When Grahm made the audacious move of quitting the chardonnay market, that wine's last label ("Cuvée Fin de Linea") featured a hook extending from behind a curtain to pull the product offstage.

Observing such outside-the-box exploits, other winemakers didn't know whether to roll their eyes, give Grahm a high five, or both. "I remember sitting around with friends saying, 'Wouldn't it be great if we could do that?'" says Steve Tylicki, a Mendocino County grape grower who would later work for Grahm. "One of the attractions of Bonny Doon was that Randall did everything we *wanted* to do, and was fearless about it. With his own winery and his parents' deep pockets, his mystique alone could sell five hundred or a thousand cases of anything; meanwhile, we could watch and see how it was done."

Barrel broker Mel Knox agrees that Grahm gave life to many winemakers' fantasies. "If you're known for chardonnay, and somebody offers you some nebbiolo, or moscato, or tempranillo, your first instinct is to say, 'Great!'" Knox says. "The natural tendency of winemakers is to experiment, but the natural tendency of the marketing guy is to stick with what you're famous for." Grahm, of course, was his own marketing guy (i.e., purveyor of mystique), and his consequent ability to write his own ticket was exemplified by DEWN: the Distinctive Esoteric Wine Network, which Bonny Doon launched in 1993 to sell "ultra-small lots of wine produced on an experimental basis" to members. ("Could you bear not knowing what linden-flower infused fortified Teroldego of the Icebox might taste like?" he inquired of customers.) The task of creating labels for the program fell to John Locke, who cultivated a nationwide stable of artists to come up with thematically goofy, visually cutting-edge illustrations. The first—illustrating the acronymically parallel "Distant Early Warning Network"—was, in Locke's words, "a Homer Simpsonesque *functionnaire* sitting in front of a radar screen drinking coffee and munching doughnuts while the aliens basically took over the joint." Each DEWN label was used only once, when a new product came and then went.

All of this rampant creativity came with a price. "If Randall was deciding between a crappy two-color box and a nice four-color box, the four-color box always won," says Locke. "He loved the idea of packaging Cigare in a cigar box, which no one could resist displaying on a bar; it was beautiful, but it was very expensive." Before marketing even entered into it, Patrice Boyle says, "Bonny Doon was a really complicated winery. Ten tons of grapes would go into eight different products. If it was mourvedre, first it would be divided into two different lots—one for red and one for *saignée*.* The *saignée* would go into a rosé blend,

---

* The traditional practice of bleeding off juice to reduce the amount of liquid remaining in contact with grape skins.

which would be fermented in two experimental ways; then some of the blend would go back into the first lot, some would go into Big House Red, and some would get distilled. Quite a few times we had to bottle during harvest [to free up tank space]. I remember making Randall promise that he wouldn't change the blend percentage of any wine within two weeks of bottling."

Tylicki, who began managing Bonny Doon's vineyards in 1992, says, "It seemed like Randall thrilled at the Chinese fire drill. He'd call me in the vineyard and say, 'We need five hundred picking boxes cleared by five p.m.'; then he'd call back at 4:35 and say, 'Never mind.' Then he'd come in every six weeks and give a list of twenty new things he wanted done. The Bonny Doon vineyard was a series of snapshots of whatever was the new vineyard technology of the day, regardless of suitability for the variety or the site—basically, Randall couldn't leave well enough alone. For all the things he is, temperamentally he's not a farmer; farming is doing the same thing day in and day out, year in and year out."

"At one point our accountant asked Randall if he understood the concept of compound interest—paying interest [on a loan] and a vineyard manager without anything coming back," says Boyle. "But that's not how Randall thinks—he would just say, 'Let's try this,' without including in the equation the fact that you have to pay for it. I asked him once where we were going with Pacific Rim, and he said, 'I want to sell forty thousand cases of riesling.' I asked why, and he said: 'I don't know.' He felt challenged, somehow—he thought riesling was populist and he was doing everyone a favor. I couldn't see it, but if Randall doesn't get the answers he wants, he stirs up shit and ends up just trying to get through instead of excel. Except for micro-ox, he never reflected on how to improve—only on how to heighten the entertainment factor. I didn't even know why he had a winery for a while—it was just a vehicle for his fame. He was having fun and getting acclaim and attention, and he liked being the naughty boy who was also known as inventive and creative. That provided a lot of drive, but after a while the marketing didn't reflect back into attention to wine production. I don't think he was even trying to make money, because it was a very cost-ineffective way of running a winery. If he was really cynical, he would have said, 'How can we make a lot of dough?' That was never part of the discussion—he just wanted to have fun and do what he wanted to do. He was taking people on a tour."

Grahm was not unaware of his faults, nor unwilling to examine them in print. In one of his newsletters, he acknowledged his "tragically compulsive Don Giovese Complex"—that is, insatiable "lust for new and freshly different grape skin (the inevitable vinous progeny arriving invariably about nine months later). Ferment 'em and leave 'em is what I have always said. . . . When in doubt, go for everything, perhaps best typifies our attitude here at Bonny Doon." On the danger of becoming distracted, he said, "We often find ourselves on the slippery slope that is the thrilling, high-pressure, compulsive, typical life of the restaurateur or Flying Winemaker. . . . We rush to our highly compensated ag consultant or we rush to our publicist. We must do yet another Meet the Winemaker Dinner, yet another Meals on Wheels charity benefit. Your PR person whispers in your ear that you must have greater national exposure. . . . This is part of the Faustian bargain, the infernal merry-go-round that is progressively more difficult to quit."

Amid the frenzy, however, Grahm's long-suffering employees had to admit that, compared with the mainstream wine industry, their burden was a diverting one. "We would look at other wineries and say, 'Sure, you could go work there—and do the same thing over and over and over,'" says Boyle. "If you like new things and learning, Bonny Doon was ideal."

"It was frustrating for me at the time, but that dims in retrospect," Tylicki agrees. "I still think of Bonny Doon as the most interesting job I've ever had."

R ANDALL GRAHM'S SANDBOX orgy of the 1990s coincided with a confluence of social and economic factors that created a heady new market for wine in the United States. In 1991, 60 *Minutes* aired its notorious "French Paradox" segment reporting that the citizens of France, despite a diet rich in saturated fat, had a low incidence of heart disease—a phenomenon attributed to a regular intake of red wine. This news met with an attentive audience in American Baby Boomers, who happened to be entering their years of heightened coronary concern *and* peak earning power. It also overlapped with the economic "boom" of the Clinton years, which saw a spectacular rise in the stock market: As one company after another went public, the percentage of Americans owning shares rose by 50 percent, a state of affairs epitomized in California by the infamous dot-com bubble, which made instant millionaires of all manner of high-tech entrepreneurs who had so far succeeded at selling little other than ideas. As a class, these new titans of industry were younger (read: less mature) than any such economic generation in history, and, based as so many were in Northern California—also ground zero for the food revolution that was transforming American taste—it was only natural that, in looking for ways to demonstrate their wealth and status, they would embrace the grape and its aura of cosmopolitan sophistication.

The only problem was that they didn't know anything about it. That, however, could presumably be remedied by Robert M. Parker Jr. and the *Wine Spectator*, whose image of the good life was accompanied by propaganda on the world's most precious fermented liquids.

Instant prestige could thus be obtained by following their easy-to-use (read: 100-point) instructions, with the result that any wine scoring in the 90-point range during the nineties experienced an economic effect not unlike that of an IPO. Amid this explosion, Napa Valley became synonymous with the cachet of California wine to the point that, in the public mind, it was the *only* place that produced good wine in the United States—an idea advanced most ostentatiously when its foremost champion, Robert Mondavi, partnered with Baron Philippe de Rothschild of Bordeaux to form the Opus One winery in Oakville, signaling that Napa merited equal footing with the world's most prestigious—and expensive—wine region.

None of this was lost on Leo McCloskey. Although he established his new office in Sonoma ("The Internet comes across the bay in Carneros, so I had a fantasy that Sonoma would have the fastest connections"), Leo found Sonoma winemakers to be "orchardists and hippies—lots of self-proclaimed experts with beards and mustaches. It was very rustic." Napa, by contrast, "was a company town, and the players were playing hardball. The Santa Cruz Mountains had philosophers like Paul Draper and Randall Grahm and myself, but Napa had business guys with deep pockets. That's where the money went—not the Santa Cruz Mountains, not Sonoma—so Napa was starting to cohere and bring together the things of a wine brand. The fact that it was specializing in cabernet was huge, because cabernet is the most standardized wine in the world. What is the 1855 classification, after all, but a rating system?"

Nevertheless it seemed to McCloskey that Napa winemakers "had a chip on their shoulder. The culture of the winemaker was still 'I'm an artist, not a businessman.' It was an ethos out of the sixties, but after ratings appeared, you got the sense that the owners were pivoting and winemakers were being called upon to make better products. The Old Guard became antimedia, but I was telling people to embrace the consumer by embracing scores, because now they were in a race."

One place where McCloskey assembled his impressions was at the Joseph Phelps winery, where he "planted a spear in the ground" in January 1992, before he'd even moved his office north from Santa Cruz. Founded twenty years earlier, Phelps had become a Napa standard-bearer during its first decade; as mentioned earlier, it made successful German-style wines, pioneered the production of California-grown syrah, and was the first winery in the state to make a proprietary Bordeaux-style blend (Insignia), combining cabernet sauvignon with merlot and cabernet franc. But while Parker had rated the wine highly in the early to mid-1980s, "the Pope" termed himself disappointed by it since 1987—prompting, in McCloskey's recollection, "an ultimatum from on high to turn product quality around."

Just as he'd done at Ridge—whose staffers he had revealed in blind tastings to prefer a prestigious Napa Valley cabernet to their own Monte Bello—McCloskey demonstrated to the Phelps people that they preferred another Napa competitor to their own Insignia. Lo and behold, when subjected to Enologix chemistry, the other wine turned out to have the highest levels of complex anthocyanin in Napa. Duly applying the same analysis to Phelps's just-vinified '91 wines, McCloskey convinced winemaker Craig Williams (as he'd done with Paul Draper) to compose the winery's flagship blend during the winter immediately after harvest, rather than waiting a year for the lots to mature separately. "Conventional sensory evaluation doesn't work right after harvest," he says. "Before malolactic [secondary fermentation] is finished, the wines are too raw and cloudy." By assaying the young wines' chemistry, however, "you could identify the big ones that were candidates and prospects, then weed them out according to aromatics." Hence—again like Monte Bello, which jumped from a Parker 75 in '89 to a 90 in '90—Insignia got a 92 from Parker in '91, 95 in '92 and '93, 96 in '94, 97 in '95, 92 in '96, and 96 in '97, restoring it to the front rank of the $150-per-bottle Napa Valley class.

There was soon a new breed of producer on the scene, however, who would make that price seem like chicken feed. Propelled by the bullish economy, wine nuts who'd made money elsewhere were now arriving in Napa and hiring consultants to plant grapes and make wines that targeted Parker from the get-go. "They replaced the Old Guard who were still telling the Horatio Alger story," McCloskey says. Amid this new commercial landscape, the aim was to make "impact" wines—not necessarily ones that would complement food so much as make a visceral impression on a taster. The so-called cult wineries—Bryant Family, Colgin Cellars, Dalla Valle, Harlan Estate, Pahlmeyer, Screaming Eagle, et al., many of which indeed succeeded in getting 100-point scores from Parker (especially for the superripe '97 vintage)—were made in minuscule quantities and, owing to the holy trinity of supply, demand, and hype, sold for astronomical prices. Upon being acquired by those who could afford them, they were frequently cellared as investments—not for future drinking but for eventual resale.

The apotheosis of all these trends occurred at the 2000 Napa Valley Wine Auction, the annual celebrity-studded extravaganza that, since its founding in that seminal year of 1981, had come to reflect the appellation's status—not only in the enological but economic sector. Scant months before the dot-com bubble burst and the stock market tanked, the auction raised a record $9.5 million (twice the amount of the previous year), including $500,000 for one six-liter bottle of Screaming Eagle and $700,000 for a ten-vintage vertical selection of magnums from Harlan Estate. Both were purchased by the same buyer: Chase Bailey, a former Cisco Systems employee who spent a total of $1.7 million at the event.

McCloskey says that, at Enologix, he preferred to "divorce my name from the service," maintaining a background role so that his clients could collect all the credit. The stars of the new cult show, however, were other independent consultants like Heidi Peterson Barrett and the traveling Frenchman Michel Rolland, who, although they worked for several wineries at the same time, billed their services on the basis of their own big-name cachet. As it turned out, the consultant who became most closely associated with this emerging paradigm was Larry Turley's sister.

Throughout the late 1980s and early 1990s, as Napa Valley was ascending into the firmament, Frog's Leap had continued growing by hops and jumps. Although its wines never received much notice from Parker—winemaker John Williams hewed to an old-school, food-friendly ethos of low intensity and moderate alcohol—it still had a loyal following for thirty-thousand-plus cases of cabernet, chardonnay, sauvignon blanc, zinfandel, and merlot. Williams aspired to produce more, but his partner, Larry Turley, wanted to make less—still working full-time as a doctor, Turley was now raising a family on the same property as the winery, which had multiple employees, daily tours, and a constant stream of cars. Even then, the cramped acreage couldn't contain all the winery operations—storage and bottling took place elsewhere, so staffers had to drive around the valley to conduct day-to-day business. Each autumn, Turley took a month off from work to help with the harvest; he also went on occasional sales trips, but as he approached fifty, he wanted to decrease his time at the hospital and get more involved with winemaking. Moreover, Williams's preferred style wasn't Turley's cup of claret. "Larry's favorite wine is Amarone,"* Williams reveals. "If you go out to dinner with him and he sees it on the wine list, he'll always order it." Such a mutual-dining scenario was less and less likely, however, seeing as how there was also friction between the men's spouses (both of whom have since been divorced from their respective husbands).

The inevitable upshot was to go their separate ways. Turley proposed to buy Williams out, but as the latter observes, "no one in the marketplace knew who Larry was"—and besides, "he didn't really have any money." Eventually their accountant suggested a fifty-fifty corporate split, which would enable both parties to avoid capital gains taxes if two new independent businesses were created. Hence, in 1993, half the assets of Frog's Leap were transferred to Turley Wine Cellars, after which Williams procured new partners to buy back the inventory and move the winery into a historic barn in the middle of the valley. In the bargain, Turley got his own property back, acquired the parcel next door, started his own smaller-scale (though notably bigger-styled) winery, and—consistent with the name of the new enterprise—hired his sister to make the wine.

Since leaving Cornell, Helen Turley had followed Larry to Napa, where she'd first gotten a job in the lab at the Mondavi winery. Like so many others who would go on to notoriety elsewhere, she also worked for Tony Soter at Chappellet, but she grew frustrated by the glass ceiling that existed for women winemakers. Although people like Zelma

---

* Powerful, raisiny, high-alcohol red wine from northeastern Italy.

Long, Mary Ann Graf, Merry Edwards, and Cathy Corison succeeded in fighting their way into wine production, "It took real persistence and fortitude to get a foothold in the cellar," says Randall Grahm's old study partner Janet Pagano, who herself went on to powerful positions with Cordorniu and Kendall-Jackson. "The lab was like the kitchen of the winery." Not unlike her old classmate Williams, who migrated east after UC Davis to take a job as a head winemaker in New York, in 1980 Turley moved to Paris (Kentucky), where for a year she made wine from hybrid grapes. Eventually she returned to Napa for an assistant job at Stonegate, finally getting her break in 1984, when she was hired as head winemaker for B.R. Cohn in Sonoma.

After her '85 cabernet got a 94 from the *Wine Spectator*, Turley resigned her position at B.R. Cohn (and, establishing a pattern that would be repeated in coming years, sued successfully for back wages) to work for a better-funded start-up. From his estate in Knights Valley on the western slopes of Mount Saint Helena, on the border between Napa and Sonoma counties, Peter Michael, a radio and television entrepreneur from England, gave Turley carte blanche to carve out a name for him in California—developing a steep hillside vineyard from scratch, securing other top-flight grapes from Howell Mountain to Alexander Valley, and designing not one but two wineries: a cooled and humidity-controlled one for whites, as well as a facility for reds that limited the size of fermenters to six feet by six feet (smaller than she or her brother could fit into, but good for maximizing skin-to-juice contact). The chardonnays and cabernet-based Bordeaux blend, Les Pavots, that she made there set a standard for the emerging California luxury style, but within a few years Turley departed Peter Michael too, striking out on her own as an independent consultant and soon amassing a list of clients that included Bryant, Colgin, La Jota, Landmark, Martinelli, Pahlmeyer, and—not incidentally—Turley Wine Cellars.

"I liked her wines a lot," Larry says. "Her '93 Bryant cabernet was phenomenal while it was still in the tank—it wasn't flashy or sweet, but it was so savory and approachable and appealing. It wasn't a wine that you had to work to understand." As it happens, that description epitomizes the grape Larry planned to feature at his new winery: zinfandel, which he and Helen subsequently elevated to an unprecedented plane of intensity. "Helen opened the door in '93," Larry says. "She saw that we needed to treat zinfandel like pinot noir in the vineyard. Zinfandel is known for uneven ripening, so she said to drop all the pink fruit at *véraison* and it would ripen evenly. Guess what: She was right."

I still have vivid memories of the 1995 zinfandel tasting staged by ZAP (Zinfandel Advocates & Producers) at Fort Mason in San Francisco. At that annual, uproarious lovefest for devotees of California's heritage grape, all the buzz was about the new wines from Turley and Martinelli. Made from old dry-farmed vineyards and poured from decanters, they were blockbuster creations—dark, powerful, concentrated, loaded with flavor, and weighing in at 16 or 17 percent alcohol. Late-harvest zinfandel was hardly unprecedented; it had come and gone in the 1960s and 1970s, as many of the showcase examples aged into pruny, tannic caricatures. But Turley's style was something else—soft, rich, dense, and mouth filling, without the harshness that had kayoed the handiwork of earlier generations.

This wasn't accidental. As Helen Turley established herself in California, and California located its place in the wine world, she'd seen that even a rising status quo wouldn't be sufficient to prevail on the global stage. "To succeed today, you have to go beyond the pleasant, one-note wine," she told Richard Paul Hinkle in 1994. "The challenge in the world market for superpremium wines is to make wines that retain the richness and depth of fruit flavor that have come to be associated with California wines, while incorporating the suppleness, length, harmony, and finesse that the sophisticated consumer has always sought in fine French wines." Toward that end, Turley employed such time- and labor-intensive techniques as precrush grape sorting (to dispose of subpar fruit), whole-cluster pressing (a gentler treatment of grapes, resulting in less harshness), prefermentation cold soaking (to increase and stabilize color), native yeasts (for greater complexity), barrel fermentation (to integrate the flavors of fruit and oak), long macerations (to increase skin-juice contact and extraction), close spacing of vines (to reduce their vigor and concentrate fruit character), minimal yields (ditto), and most notoriously, lengthy hang time (late picking of grapes to achieve maximum flavor). Though nobody suggests that she planned it this way—it was probably more like symbiotic coevolution—this amounted to a veritable checklist for impressing Robert M. Parker Jr., who was soon seen soiling himself with excitement over Turley's products. He compared her chardonnays to Batard-Montrachet ("loaded with exceptional honeyed, smoky, buttery, tangerine-like fruitiness in its nose and flavors . . . a winemaking tour de force") and declared her cabernets "as complete and potentially complex as any first-growth Bordeaux" ("unbelievable richness, explosive thickness, unctuosity, purity, and flavor intensity . . . enormously opulent texture, viscous richness, and huge quantities of sweet, pure fruit . . . powerfully authoritative flavors that ooze glycerin and fruit extraction . . . freakishly high levels of intensity . . . hits the palate with phenomenal concentration . . . massive yet elegant . . . no hard edges . . . plenty of velvety tannin . . . a knock-out nose . . . stacked and packed . . . awesomely endowed . . . has me drooling"). In his most infamous indiscretion, Parker flat out declared Turley a goddess.

By most accounts, this feedback went not only into Turley's pocketbook but to her head. Always known as something of a recluse (her husband, John Wetlaufer, is the more voluble of the two), she soon embellished her swelling fame with a reputation as a diva. "Clients are a means to an end," she explained to the *Wine Spectator.* "I don't have the capacity of compromise." As the *Spectator* went on to note, "Most of [her professional] affiliations ended up on the rocks, with Turley either quitting or getting fired. She even broke up with Larry; after two vintages, [Helen] quit, saying, as she often has, that her client lacked a commitment to quality control. They no longer talk."[*] As her wines commanded accolades and prices to match, Turley began to demand jaw-dropping terms from clients. Made public by a couple of lawsuits, these agreements included—in addition to total authority over winemaking and grape growing—a starting fee of $150,000 per year, increasing to $550,000 by year seven, at which time she and Wetlaufer were also entitled to 20 percent of a client's profits; they

[*] Varying theories exist about the Turleys' split. One holds that Helen refused to ameliorate a stuck fermentation; another that, as a Francophile, she wanted to distance herself from zinfandel. Ever since she departed Turley Cellars, its winemaker has been Ehren Jordan, whom Helen recruited in 1994 to help out there part-time and at her and Wetlaufer's own label, Marcassin.

required at least one customer (Roy Estate, which later sued them for breach of contract) to build a new winery according to Turley's specifications. In return for such concessions, her clients were promised not only her winemaking prowess but also access to her mailing list, media following, and critical clout, allegedly guaranteeing entry into the commercial stratosphere.

Leaving aside personal judgments about ego, ambition, and/or avarice—which of us, after all, *wouldn't* want sovereign control over our work, supplemented by a suitably royal income?—this state of affairs served to illustrate (1) how much profiteering the luxury wine market of the 1990s could bear, and (2) the extent to which the cult of the winemaker had come to dominate the industry. In light of its success and influence, the "Turley style" duly took over the high end of the market: In search of ever-richer, more intense, but softer-textured flavors, winemakers everywhere were letting their fruit hang later into harvest; no longer content to rely on a refractometer (a device that measures the sugar content of fruit) for gauging ripeness, people were now examining grapes on the vine, waiting for seeds to turn from green to brown, searching for the plush, plummy flavors that Leo McCloskey identified as the markers of critically successful wine. Conventional wisdom now held that, in sunny California, grapes' phenolic maturity (flavor development) lags behind their physiological maturity (sugar development), which—aided by new commercial yeasts that were more efficient at converting sugar to alcohol, not to mention modern trellising techniques that were more effective at exposing grapes to the sunlight—led to skyrocketing alcohol levels and bacteriological problems associated with low-acid, high-pH wines. Conveniently, however, those problems could now be ameliorated through such modern technologies as reverse osmosis and spinning cone.

The latter device is a vertical steel column that contains an alternating series of inverted cones—one attached to the column's interior wall, the other to a central spinning shaft. When liquid is poured in at the top of the column and steam pumped in from the bottom, the liquid descends over the fixed cones but, owing to centrifugal force, ascends the rotating ones in a thin film, which evaporates under pressure to form a vapor rich in volatile compounds. The original material, thus stripped of its "essence," is pumped out as a clear liquid, and the chemical-laden gas is condensed into a concentrate.

Spinning cone was originally developed in Nazi Germany to produce "heavy water" enriched with oxygen isotopes for the purpose of making atomic bombs. In the 1960s it was revived by an Australian scientist to isolate and capture the flavor of passion fruit, going on to gain popularity in the food industry for removing flavor compounds from things like tomatoes or tea leaves so that the resulting concentrate could be shipped to some distant manufacturer and reconstituted into tomato juice or bottled tea without having to deal with the cumbersome raw material. In the early 1990s, the technology was adapted by the wine industry to remove flavor, aroma, and alcohol, which can then be added back in any amount desired; it can even extract flavor and aromatics from discarded grape pomace (after a wine is pressed) to improve entirely different wines.

Reverse osmosis was originally advanced by the U.S. Navy for desalinating seawater. Rather than operating by vacuum evaporation, however, it's a filtration process that separates a wine's flavor and color from its water and alcohol by forcing the liquid through a membrane at high pressure. Similar to the postmilitary employment of spinning cone, this technology was also adapted for de-alcoholizing wine, in this case by a Davis grad named Barry Gnekow at Ariel, a winery that specialized in nonalcoholic wine. When the Benziger family decided to explore de-alcoholization in the early 1990s, it assigned the task to Clark Smith.

Before leaving R.H. Phillips, Smith had started an independent consulting business called WineSmith. In 1990, the Benzigers hired him to work on their "International Claret Project"—an examination of Bordeaux-style winegrowing which, among other things, created a forty-barrel cabernet blend from California, Australia, Chile, and Bordeaux. When the Benzigers subsequently asked him to look into de-alcoholization, Smith says, "They chained me to an RO filter to create formulas for nonalcoholic merlot, chardonnay, and white zinfandel. The only problem was that, when you took all the alcohol out, the wine didn't taste very good." In the absence of alcohol, he found, wine loses much of its depth, body, and texture. In the course of this research, however, Smith hit on the idea of running a batch of acetic permeate—obtained through reverse osmosis from a merlot that was high in volatile acidity because of a stuck fermentation—through a water softener, which operates on the principle of ion exchange. When the experiment was carried out, the acetic acid, similar to the contaminating minerals in "hard" water, was absorbed by the resin in the device; when the VA was thus removed from the wine, it began fermenting again.

Not long afterward, Smith's old classmate Rick Jones ran into him at a retirement dinner for Davis professors. "Clark told me he'd figured out a way to remove VA from bulk wine," Jones remembers. "He was looking for somebody to do it with. Clark makes lots of grandiose statements, not all of which are based on fact; people tend to roll their eyes, and I had that same reaction. But he said he'd run some tests, and he showed me a few samples."

Smith and Jones soon filed a patent on the "Apparatus and Method for Removing Compounds from a Solution." Still, they didn't expect VA removal to amount to much of a business. "We didn't think there were that many [acetic] wines out there," Jones recalls. "Between us Clark and I had made about twenty million gallons of wine, and each of us had had maybe one lot that could have used the process. We just thought it would be something neat to do, and that it might make a modest amount of money—fifty thousand dollars, say, for three or four months a year."

Smith and Jones formed a company called Vinovation—which, as it turned out, was backlogged from the moment it hung out a shingle. "We underestimated the size of the market by at least an order of magnitude," says Jones. "We discovered, to our astonishment, that there was a lot of this wine around—and a lot of expensive, high-quality wine too. We were very quickly working in Napa Valley."

Today Jones says that, ever since Vinovation uncovered this underground market, he's wondered "whether this wine existed all along but nobody talked about it. I think a large part is that we came along when winemaking styles were changing dramatically. People were picking riper and riper, with higher and higher sugars—and as every student of enology is taught, high sugar is an inhibitor to fermentation. It makes it harder for yeast to get started, and there are more lactobacillus and VA problems coming out of the fermenter. We were like heart surgeons who just happened to open up shop when people found out they really liked steak."

Smith has his own chemical-ecological explanation for the sudden appearance of so many such wines. "People didn't talk about it because it was considered a mark of negligence," he posits. "It wasn't until our eight-hundredth customer that we realized it was a mark of quality. The grapes that are best at attracting birds are the ones that make the most expensive Napa cabernets—those with superior color and flavor. Birds peck the berries, leaving damaged fruit, which starts to ferment on natural yeasts; that attracts fruit flies, which carry lactobacillus on their feet. With extended hang time, by the time the grapes get to the fermenter, they're carrying a whopping big bacterial inoculum. We used to think oxygen was required to turn sugar into vinegar, but now we know that these bacteria can do it anaerobically."

Not long after they began plying the de-VA trade, Smith and Jones also licensed a method for adjusting alcohol through reverse osmosis. The challenge lay in how to treat the water-and-alcohol permeate after it was separated from the flavor-and-color retentate; if the end product is nonalcoholic wine, which by law isn't wine at all, regulations allow you to reintroduce water that didn't come from the original wine. But if you're only *lowering* the alcohol, the water has to originate in the wine being treated. Hence, Smith and Jones developed the idea of distilling the permeate to remove the alcohol from the water, which can then be legally recombined with the retentate, after which alcohol is blended back in at whatever percentage the producer desires.

Though he says he doesn't endorse the "field oxidation" that occurs with extended hang time, Smith *is* a proponent of the contemporary catechism that grape sugar is unconnected with flavor: "Attention to Brix is an unnecessary distraction and is often out of our control. It's what nature gives us, so we tell our clients to ignore it and concentrate on the good stuff." A corollary conclusion is that any wine's natural alcohol level is independent of its most agreeable taste—that it is, in fact, usually too high to be harmonious in a properly picked New

World wine. The good news is that, thanks to reverse osmosis and spinning cone, a winemaker can now fine-tune alcohol content to an ideal "sweet spot," guided only by taste and market goals.

"Just about everything you can say about alcohol, the opposite is also true," Smith says. "It's really cooling, but it's also hot; it adds body, but it's also thinning; it's very sweet, but it's also drying. By itself it has no taste, but wines with too much of it are hot and bitter and have suppressed aromatics, while wines with too little taste thin and salty." On its face, "de-alking" a wine is no more egregious a practice than chaptalization. "Every great wine region has to adjust alcohol," says Smith. "[The French] just adjust it up instead of down."

In the United States, taxes on high-alcohol wine can be 50 percent higher than sub–14-percent-alcohol "table wine," so apart from any stylistic questions, de-alking can save a producer thousands of dollars. The controversy surrounding reverse osmosis and spinning cone arises, rather, from the nature of the technology—which essentially takes wine apart and puts it back together again—and from its creation of a more concentrated product than nature alone can provide. Removing alcohol, after all, means removing part of a wine's volume, which can intensify the flavor of the remaining product, not unlike the process of reducing a wine-based sauce on the kitchen stove.

It doesn't necessarily stop there, though. "The dirty little secret," says one winemaker who has used Vinovation for VA removal, "is that when you make your adjustment, quite legally, to remove alcohol, you're supposed to put the water back. But a lot of times, people don't." As Smith himself has written, "In Bordeaux, true ripeness often means hanging into the rain, and RO can squeeze this rain back out so we can obtain flavor concentration and alcohol balance." The legal way to do this, whether via RO or vacuum evaporation, is to remove water from grape juice before it starts to ferment. While this might be viewed merely as a more modern version of *saignée*, among purists Smith's innovations earned him Antichrist status as the wine world's leading enabler of invasive technological manipulation. The waiting room of his office displays a prominent "Wall of Shame," where Smith framed an assortment of articles decrying his insidious influence on the industry. As Smith himself wrote, "The central debate about . . .

high-tech wine production innovations is not any more about whether they work, it is about whether we will go to hell if we use them." For these reasons, as with Enologix, few wineries would admit that they work with Vinovation (or with California's primary purveyor of spinning cone, ConeTech), and—even though half the wineries in the state were now thought to engage in high-tech alcohol adjustment—Smith was contractually prohibited from divulging the names of most of his one thousand clients.

"We have the hardest time trying to bring about change in the most hyped places—like Napa Valley," Smith says. "Even though every last one of them uses [modern, manipulative wine technology], only the most courageous are willing to come out and talk about what they're doing. It seems that wine is supposed to be the last bastion of nonmanipulation—the one area of human endeavor unspoiled by technology."

As Rick Jones points out, at the time when he and Smith developed their methods of de-alking and VA removal, "Reverse osmosis and ion exchange had been approved for use in the wine business for fifteen or twenty years—anybody with any technological background could have figured it out, but the lightbulb didn't go off until we did it." A few years later, another techno-enological high beam got switched on in California courtesy of Randall Grahm.

On a trip to France in the early 1990s, Grahm's accomplice John Locke crossed paths with one Patrick Ducournau, who had developed a new technology known as micro-oxygenation. Ducournau made wine in Madiran, whose principal grape is tannat—a red variety that, as one may deduce from the name, is extremely tannic. The traditional means for softening tannin is time, bestowed in both barrel and bottle, where gradual oxidation—the infinitesimal exposure to air—allows simple phenolic molecules to join and form large polymers, which eventually precipitate out as sediment. In an effort to shorten the waiting time, Ducournau developed a device to control (read: calibrate and accelerate) the aeration of young wine via a valve-equipped cylinder and gas chamber that administer oxygen in timed, measured doses. Like Grahm, Ducournau also viewed lees as a potent tool—one that could be manipulated, in conjunction with oxygen, to near-miraculous effect on wine texture. In the autumn 1995 Bonny Doon newsletter, Grahm referred to the Bubble Man of Madiran as "Jacques Derrida's° enological Doppelganger," going so far as to suggest that, by inventing micro-oxygenation, Ducournau "may have made the most significant enological advancement in the last thirty-five years."

When the time came for Ducournau to distribute his technology in California, the company he chose to represent it was Vinovation. Having thus been—to judge by his own narrative—born again, Smith became a veritable micro-ox missionary, characterizing his own conversion by saying that he "went from being a service provider to a cooking instructor. Patrick figured out how to do what the Aztecs did: Turn something nasty (cocoa powder) into something you'd kill your mother for (chocolate). What the Aztecs taught the Belgians is that, by working with oxygen and fats and oils, you can transform raw phenolics into a velvety structure."

Characterizing the BD (Before Ducournau) mentality, he went on: "Davis taught us that wine is a chemical solution and oxygen is its enemy. It's only recently that we've learned wine's texture is caused by a macromolecular structure, and that its aroma, texture, and color depend on deviations from 'ideal' behavior. The good stuff is in the 'colloidal suspension': little particles of phenolics, pieces of goodge like clarified butter, or lobster bisque as opposed to consommé. In other words, wine is less like Kool-Aid or soda pop than it is like chocolate milk.

"Ducournau's real accomplishment is in elucidating the development of a structure, which he calls '*élevage,*' the French term for raising horses or children—*not* a passive, noninterventionist process, right? Young red wine can take sixty times the amount of oxygen it gets from a barrel, so instead of fining to get rid of tannin, we use it to create a rich, fine structure, incorporating oxygen with oak and lees to refine mouthfeel and integrate aromas into a single soulful voice. It's

° Leading proponent of deconstruction, the French literary philosophy holding that the meaning of any text is irreducibly complex, contradictory, and self-canceling.

like a finely crafted sauce—when béarnaise is made right, you get one harmonious single flavor instead of all the separate tastes of tarragon, onion, and mint. So what we're really talking about here is a winemaking cuisine. Its goal is the same as that of any chef: to be delicious."

In the winter following harvest, I visit Smith at his headquarters on Industrial Avenue in the town of Sebastopol, west of Santa Rosa. Its physical layout reflects its inauspicious address: Behind a chain-link fence is a low, pea green compound of cargo bays, loading docks, and dimly lit passageways connecting caverns of tanks and barrels and humming machines. Smith describes the complex as a former apple warehouse—a sign of the times, as the area's old-time orchard industry is being inexorably uprooted by grapes. "This is where Quaker Oats Peaches and Cream was invented," he tells me, "only it wasn't really peaches—it was apples. When peaches are dried, they don't retain structure the way apples do."

It's a chilly winter day, but Smith is wearing a short-sleeved shirt. When I ask if he isn't cold, he answers: "I'm a pretty fat guy." A more charitable description might be "roly-poly"—although Smith is admittedly overweight, he's also short. Boasting a full head of chestnut brown hair, he reminds me of a smaller version of the actor John Goodman.

Inside the administrative offices, situated in a double-wide trailer, we're met by Tom Meadowcroft of Magito Wines, a three-thousand-case winery housed, like a handful of other such operations, at Vinovation. The tall, lean, balding Meadowcroft tells me he worked in Washington State in the 1990s, but when he journeyed south to take courses at the UC Davis Extension, he came under Smith's sway. After subsequently working with Ric Forman and getting a job with a vineyard management company, Meadowcroft discovered that he'd grown roots in California, and in 1999 he bought a two-acre vineyard on the north side of Mount Veeder, above Napa.

On a conference room table in the office, a row of glasses has been poured with samples of a single sauvignon blanc, de-alcoholized in 0.1 percent increments from an original level of 14.6 percent. Its producer is identified only as a "high-end, middle-of-the-road" Napa Valley label that's trying to target a style successfully exploited by Mason

Cellars. "It has some density and a little oak," Smith says of his client's wine. "I like it at 12.3, but that wouldn't work in this market. It's more European—it would be better for New York."

The lineup of samples doesn't perform according to any discernible logic. Some taste sweet, some watery, some soft, and some fumey, but not according to any pattern pertaining to alcohol content. "I think 13.3 is the best wine on the table," Smith announces after whipping through the flight standing up. "13.9 has some nice qualities too, but between 13.2 and 13.3, you have a point of harmony that's finer and sweeter. The biggest transition is between 13.3 and 13.4—as often happens, the one just above the sweet spot is hot and bitter, with low fruit expression in the nose. We're going to say the best places to look are 12.3, 13.25, and 13.9. But we're not going to dictate his style."

When Smith started to perform sweet-spot tastings, he was surprised to find that they didn't describe a bell curve—that is, one clear ideal with diminishing preferences on either side. "It's more like radio stations with a lot of static in between. We find that about one in six is worth drinking. In this case, 13.9 is like a major chord and 13.3 a minor one. Both have harmony, but put them together"—13.6—"and you have dissonance. It's an example of how nonlinear wine expression is—proof that it's liquid music. Science can't explain it, but everybody gets it."

Warming to one of his favorite subjects—scientific bankruptcy— Smith explains that "sensory science studies the differences between people. For example, Ann Noble said that individuals salivate differently, so some perceive more bitterness and astringency. In other words, we can't all share one aesthetic, which isn't far from concluding that we're all unknowable, one from another. That kind of linear approach makes chefs and winemakers feel alone and helpless, so this [sweet-spot] study is good news. It shows that [taste] is a subjective experience, but it's strongly shared—just as we all have different hearing acuities but can still listen to a piece of music and perceive its emotional, visceral character. People will have differences in what they like, but once you tune the piano, you can do all kinds of things with it."

"You can play Jethro Tull or Pink Floyd," Meadowcraft offers.

"Right," Smith confirms. "But for heaven's sake, tune the guitar."

People dubious of the sweet-spot approach tend to suggest that, if a vintner finds it necessary to "adjust" a wine's alcohol, there's probably something wrong with his or her grape growing. "If the right varieties are grown in the right place with a balanced yield, you should be able to mature your flavors without excess sugar," one such critic told me. "But in the New World, people want to grow cabernet and chardonnay and pinot noir wherever you can grow grapes." This person is of the opinion that "Napa Valley should probably be all zinfandel—or something even more heat resistant."

In another conversation, Randall Grahm elaborated on this attitude. "In a culture that encourages the expression of terroir, it's logical to plant grapes in cool areas and have them struggle to ripen," he said. "That [practice] highlights those favored sites that *can* ripen their grapes, and encourages behaviors that enhance quality—crop yield regulation through careful pruning, thinning for uniformity, and excision of defect. The basic value, above all, is balance and distinctiveness. But in areas that are too warm—where grapes are overripe almost every year—you have to adjust, and you end up with wines that are pleasant and likable but not distinctive. It all depends on what's valuable to you as a culture. Right now, ripeness and texture and softness are valued, and distinctiveness is not. In Australia, I'm told, the model is taken to its ultimate conclusion: Grapes are grown in areas that are far too warm, harvested at very high tonnages, and if the color, tannin, acid, et cetera, aren't there, they can all be added from a bag."

Somewhat surprisingly for someone whose livelihood depends on de-alcoholization, Smith agrees that the "Australian model" isn't one to emulate. "Just because you can [leave grapes hanging on the vine indefinitely] doesn't mean you should," he says. "It makes for softer, user-friendly wine but deprives it of depth, energy, and longevity." Nevertheless he still insists that there's no such thing as an ideal location ("any more than there's a perfect-ten body type") and that no vineyard is always balanced. He even goes so far as to say that reverse osmosis isn't a winemaking tool at all, but rather "a grape-growing tool, which works to accentuate the distinctive terroir of a site through improved fruit quality."

"I look at every wine in this process to see if terroir's coming through," says Meadowcroft. "At this point, though, I've put terroir aside to see what's in the mother wine—what style the winemaker or grape grower is trying to drive. Usually you could [sell] that wine and be fine with it; alcohol adjustment is just putting a fine polish on wood that you've already carved."

After lunch we're joined by more visitors: Cameron Hughes, a young California *négociant* who buys finished wines from producers and resells them at a profit; Steve Yafa, who is starting a boutique Russian River winery called Segue; and Greg La Follette, the overall-clad, Volvo-driving pinot noir artisan formerly of Flowers, more recently of Tandem and DeLoach. La Follette acknowledges that, in 1996, he de-alked a pair of pinot noirs that were later declared the two best of that vintage. Later, in 2001, he de-VAed his Tandem Keefer Ranch pinot noir, which went on to win 90-point scores from almost every wine publication in the country. In La Follette's estimation, Smith is concerned with one driving question: "How do you find the controls that make a wine *zoom*?"

La Follette has brought a couple of wines he plans to include in De-Loach's California pinot noir blend, which retails for under ten dollars a bottle. One is from the Sacramento Delta, the other from the Suisun area east of Napa; both are over 14 percent alcohol, so he's planning to combine them with an 11 percent pinot that Smith has procured from Mendocino County. The latter wine originated as highly tannic, heavy-press juice from a producer of sparkling wine, but Smith has subsequently run it through an "ultrafilter," a device reportedly capable of capturing tannin without stripping out aroma and flavor. This process has yielded three products: a lot of light, low-alcohol, aromatic pinot noir that La Follette plans to buy; a little of a tannin-intensive commodity called "Xpress," which Smith will use to enhance the structure of weaker wines (or sell to wineries who need to do the same); and a precious quotient of "cofactor concentrate," a reputedly wondrous substance that, when added to other wines' fermentations in amounts as small as 1 percent, improves extraction of color and flavor by linking with colorless molecules and stabilizing pigments. "Clark says it's a wonderful thing to add to Russian River pinot noir that's a little bit weak," another of Smith's clients told me. "You can beef it up and get it to be a bigger and richer wine." Smith calls ultrafiltration "a revolutionary tool for making the most of what nature gives us"—the second time I've heard him use those last four words, which, judging from the common theme, he invokes to describe uninspiring raw material that can nevertheless be exploited to advantage.

At La Follette's request, Smith's staff has made a sample blend of the Delta, Suisun, and Mendocino wines, then doctored up a sweet-spot flight ranging from 13.0 to 14.0 percent alcohol. Just as with the sauvignon blanc, the samples careen chaotically in character from sweet to dry to full to empty to lively to dull. Everyone present agrees, however, that 13.7 to 13.8 is the place to be. La Follette refers to this exercise as the first stage of a work in progress. "There are basically two ways to blend. One is to put [different lots] together and taste and shave. Or you can take one component like alcohol, or color, and whittle from there—adding syrah [to pinot noir], say, to see what that does. With this blend, we'll aim for 13.7 or 13.8 alcohol and see how it works, looking at it from different angles and thinking about it a lot. We call it 'living the wine'—letting it guide us on its terms."

Gazing at the magenta lineup of just-tasted samples, La Follette says, "Sometimes it's the ten-dollar wines that take the most thought and time. A fifty-dollar wine like our Russian River pinot is pretty much what it is—we get balance in the vineyard. But this California pinot noir will be about ten thousand cases—it's really our most complex blend, so we'll need to do more buffing and shaving to make a delicious wine."

Eventually we're joined by Galina Seabrook, Vinovation's Bulgarian-born enologist and micro-ox consultant. Meadowcroft has brought along a sample of cabernet sauvignon from his Mount Veeder vineyard, which is planted to Bordeaux clone 337. "It's a fruit bomb on the valley floor," he says of this genetic material, "but on Mount Veeder it has thicker skins, so there's tannic structure to balance the fruit." Maybe a little too much, in fact: In the previous vintage, the wine was so tannic that Meadowcroft ended up blending it into a Sonoma County cabernet to lend the latter depth and backbone. The more recent Mount Veeder wine got the micro-ox treatment, which helped soften the tannins and unveil the fruit.

"It's very concentrated," Seabrook observes upon tasting the wine, "but it's bony. It doesn't have curves—it's very dry. But you can still add richness and *round out* the curves."

"I think you should be stirring lees at this point," Smith recommends. "We've gone as far as we can with oxygen structure."

"We don't have much left," Meadowcroft says.

"You can buy artificial lees now," La Follette advises.

Smith says, "We took the wine from cocoa powder to dark chocolate with oxygen. Now, to move it from dark chocolate to milk chocolate, it will need sweet oak and lees stirring to coat the tannins." There follows a seminar in tannin nomenclature, as Smith describes how oxygen redirects "raw," "green" tannin from "dry," "parching," "numbing" tannin toward "melted" tannin by way of "firm" and "rounded" tannin. "Oxygen is the wire whisk with which we create a tannin soufflé. Once we recognize it as useful, we start looking around for more." Suddenly the kitchen turns into a construction site: "It's like cementing bricks—if somebody drops a load of them in your yard, you can get upset and try to truck them away; but if you're a skilled mason, you use them to build an addition on your house." (Somebody, in this instance, being nature—bricks being what it gives us.)

Smith says that before Ducournau, he thought winemaking was just about "growing good grapes, fermenting with care, and waiting for the smoke to clear." Now—not unexpectedly—he feels what's most important "is to be very active in guiding the postfermentation evolution of the wine."

"Most winemakers today cling to the notion of doing the minimum, as if benign neglect is some sort of high moral ground," he says. "Leaving well enough alone is fine, but there's a world of difference between passive neglect and actively choosing to do nothing. You can't phone it in—if you look at winemaking as cooking, you have to show up in the kitchen. We would all prefer not to do anything, but I have to use micro-ox to make the kinds of wines I want to make."

Smith says he believes that any winemaker is trying to do one of three things: make you smile ("Yummy!"), make you think ("Ah!"), or blow your socks off ("Wow!"). "Almost everybody in California is trying to make power wines," he says. "I want to show that we can have other voices too." In this vein, he describes his own preferences—again contrary to expectation—as "Eurocentric." The epitome of his ambition appears to be the wines he makes under his own WineSmith Reserve label, which he offers as "proof that California can excel over European wines within their own classic styles." "Faux Chablis," for example, is a nonmalolactic Napa chardonnay de-alcoholized to 12.9 percent, while "Roman Syrah" is a high-altitude Sierra-foothill wine made without sulfur dioxide, the almost universally employed wine preservative. "Even though we take advantage of a lot of modern aids," Smith says, "I feel like we're getting back in touch with what the Romans knew, and what [enabled] them to make wine without sulfites all over Europe for a thousand years: Wine can preserve itself if the minerality of living soil is present to protect it."

The rap on unsulfited wines is that, in the absence of bacteriological suppression, they lack chemical stability. Hence, a consumer can't be sure that any bottle of a given wine will reflect his or her previous impressions of that same product. "It's a problem if you expect the same experience every time," Smith acknowledges. "Wine resonates strongly with the environment in which it's served—music, lighting, background aromas, the mood in the room—and organic wine reacts doubly so. It's so dynamic, it will react to the color of the wallpaper. A lot of apparent bottle variation isn't really there; a wine might taste really veggie in one place, but go across the street and it's gone."

In public presentations, Smith has made a popular game of showing how music can affect the flavor of wine. "I can pretty much make you hate anything," he boasts. For example, where the Beach Boys' "California Girls" makes Glen Ellen chardonnay more yummy, it causes Kendall-Jackson's Stonestreet chardonnay (a wow wine) to taste more alcoholic, while Louis Latour white Burgundy (ah!) becomes more astringent (aw!). Ella Fitzgerald is better for Stonestreet; contemporary jazz for Louis Latour. As a varietal rule, French horns are appropriate to pinot noir, while the Doors or *Carmina Burana* are killer with California cabernet.

All of this recalls Smith's belief that wine itself is "liquid music." "It's extremely interesting that something like that can move us all so uniformly," he says. "It's a great laboratory to see how connected we all are. The fact that this study is possible means that humans strongly share fine nuances of emotional modality and a finely tuned sense of harmony and dissonance. That belief is basic to winemaking, as it is to all cooking—otherwise, it's just throwing darts in the dark and hoping to strike a few targets at random. Winemakers need to be trained that quality exists, and that the compass is within them. They need to trust their own sense of what works."

This statement—quality exists, and the compass to it is within the winemaker—merges the seemingly opposite viewpoints of Leo Mc-Closkey and Randall Grahm. Although the first proposition dispenses with subjectivity in a way that McCloskey would applaud, the second contradicts Leo's dictum that the consumer is king—and, hence, inner-directed vintners (those who pursue, in Grahm's words, "a soul-ful connection" between winemaker and wine) are prima donna "Pi-cassos." As it happens, Smith himself is a musician—not a precious, ponderous practitioner of classical or jazz but rather (in the words of one of his clients) "a perfectly decent traditional singer" of Celtic folk music and Irish drinking songs. "Clark can't stand Thelonious Monk," Rick Jones discloses. "He thinks it's just noise—'How could anybody play that?' he says. He tried to get me to join a barbershop quartet, but that would put *my* teeth on edge."

If Jones's remark refutes Smith's assertion that subjective taste in wine and in music is "strongly shared," it's consistent with the cog-nitive dissonance that pervades the Clark Smith MO: a purveyor of cutting-edge technology who decries the "fraudulence" of science; an advocate of natural grape growing determined to ignore "what nature gives us"; an opponent of extended hang time who makes a living by lowering alcohol, claiming that the procedure "works to accentuate the distinctive terroir of a site." Although he would probably say that this dizzying assortment of assertions is evidence of wine's complexity, it strikes me as a distilled essence of the delusionality that character-izes so much of California winemaking. In his confounding combina-tion of claims—all of which, it must be said, Smith genuinely seems to believe, but which happen to add up in the end to a promotion of his product—he calls to mind the proprietor of Enologix. With both, as Rick Jones observed of Smith, the overall picture is "postmodern in its juxtapositions."

"Clark is a unique combination of twenty-first-century technology and nineteenth-century romantic philosophy," Jones told me. "It's like he's saying, 'I've discovered a better way to paint the *Mona Lisa*—we can do it with a machine. And while we're at it, we can take away that obnoxious smile.'"

I N JULY 1992, Mike Benziger was sitting in his office in Glen Ellen with Mel Dick, wine manager of Southern Wine & Spirits, when Dick got a phone call that Benziger describes as "one of the scariest things that has ever happened to me." When Dick hung up, he told Benziger that Fetzer Vineyards had just been sold to one of the biggest companies in the liquor business: Brown-Forman, the Louisville-based owner of such nonvinous brands as Old Forester, Southern Comfort, Jack Daniel's, and Canadian Mist. "My first thought," Benziger says of the Fetzers, "was 'What do they know that I don't?'"

By the time this occurred, Benziger says, "a lot of things were signaling a change" in the wine industry. Glen Ellen, for its part, was now engaged on the front lines of its fighting-varietal campaign by an onrushing horde of new combatants. "When we started there was no competition," Benziger says. "There was just jug wine and [high-end] 750-mls." Now the space between those extremes was clogged, not just by Glen Ellen and Fetzer, but by the likes of Kendall-Jackson, Sutter Home, Sebastiani, Beringer, and Mondavi-Woodbridge. Supposedly each company occupied a different niche of the market, subtly demarcated by price—a 750-ml bottle of Glen Ellen sold for $4.99, Fetzer for $5.99, K-J for $6.99—and some (namely Sutter Home and Beringer) trafficked primarily in white (that is, sweet pink) zinfandel rather than chardonnay, cabernet, or merlot. For several years, Glen Ellen had held its turf by virtue of long-term grape contracts, but when one of the Benzigers' main providers—the Tepusquet vineyard in the

Central Coast—was acquired by one of their main competitors, Jess Jackson, in 1986, the family lost access to the grapes. "Jess taught us a lesson in Contracts 101," says Mike. "The rights to the grapes should stay with the vineyard, not the owner. After that, we went back to all our growers and rewrote the contracts."

Fetzer, based in Mendocino County, was a family business like Benziger's. After its founding patriarch, Barney, died of a heart attack in 1981 (the same year that Benziger was bonded), the company had undergone similarly spectacular growth, from 200,000 to two million cases. But, Mike says, "The Fetzer kids didn't all love it. Some of them did, but it was their father's dream, whereas our family all wanted to stay in it." Ever since starting their winery, each of Bruno Benziger's children had drawn a monthly paycheck of $600 to $1,000 while living on the family's Sonoma Mountain property, furthering the parallel aims of personal security and company expansion. "We were making a lot of money, but we were investing it instead of banking it," says Mike. "We saw that, to be successful, we still had to invest millions more, and take on a lot of debt. We were fueling an incredible amount of growth, and sometimes it seemed like the tail was wagging the dog. But we saw how difficult it was to survive in the wine business." Apparently the Fetzers found it *too* difficult (or too tedious) at the size their enterprise had reached, which was still only half that of Glen Ellen's. To Benziger, the Fetzers' decision to sell was thus a signal that the wine world was morphing from a "cottage industry" to one run by big corporations. "It was turning into a commodity practice that was all about standardizing quality, production, distribution, and marketing—how much you could bring to the market, at what price, and how efficiently."

Of course, when it came to such tasks, Glen Ellen had put on something like a clinical demonstration. Still, Benziger says, after ten years the under-$10 category had become "fiercely competitive overnight"—a fact that was illustrated, within months of Fetzer's sale, by the case of *Jedediah T. Steele vs. Kendall-Jackson*.

By 1991, K-J was producing 700,000 cases of wine. Most of it was the Vintner's Reserve line led by its off-dry chardonnay, later augmented by other varieties like merlot, cabernet sauvignon, sauvignon blanc, and zinfandel. Distinguished by such high-end earmarks as barrel aging and malolactic fermentation, the wines ranked a notch or two above Glen Ellen's and Fetzer's, in both quality and price. "When a customer who was drinking Glen Ellen wanted to move up and spend a little bit more, they would go to K-J," says Jason Lewis. "Once they saw how much better it was, very few went back." As production grew, Jackson used his increasing revenues—and growing credit—to begin acquiring other properties. First had been Tepusquet in Santa Barbara County, followed by K-J winemaker Jed Steele's former employer, Edmeades, in Mendocino County; La Crema and Arrowood in Sonoma County; Robert Pepi in Napa Valley; Zellerbach in Alexander Valley (which Jackson rechristened Stonestreet after his father's and his own middle name); and Domaine Laurier in the Russian River Valley (renamed Hartford after Jackson's son-in-law). Though Jackson maintained that a corporate mentality didn't suit the wine industry, others discerned a clear shift. Jim Lapsley, a California wine historian who visited Lakeport when K-J was still called Chateau du Lac, noticed that the company already had several mailboxes—a fact attributed to the owner's background in real estate litigation, which had taught him the importance of maintaining different addresses for separate businesses. "I thought, 'This sounds very complex,'" Lapsley remembers. "It was a different type of business model from what we were used to. Prior to that, there were three: people coming in with wealth and producing wines of quality on their own land; artisans who started wineries by hook or by crook; and consumer-product packaging companies like Nestlé and Coca-Cola, who saw the wine boom happening and thought it was an industry that could grow—though they later found out that you could only grow 2 percent per year instead of 8 or 10. You couldn't just make more of a successful product—wine was too inconsistent, because it was tied to nature."

The Glen Ellen and K-J models largely succeeded in overcoming that obstacle. Employing an appellation no less broad than "California" on the label, wine could be sourced from all over the state and blended to maintain a consistent style from year to year—not unlike Gallo Hearty Burgundy, but sourced from better vineyards and embellished with upscale flavor enhancements. Still, it wasn't exactly what the ex-hippie Steele had had in mind when he'd gone to UC Davis. "I hadn't expected to be making that much wine," he says today. "[K-J] was getting more and more corporate, and I was clashing with the management style—I couldn't hire anyone without them going to Santa Rosa to interview with Human Resources. Then [the company] came out with a confidentiality statement that I refused to sign, and said that the people who worked for me wouldn't sign either."

In 1990, K-J's chardonnay was judged best in the world by the International Wine and Spirit Competition from among a field of 1,100 entries in thirty countries. Steele was consequently named Winemaker of the Year. Eager for him to remain in the fold, Jackson urged him to take on an executive role, going so far as to offer him a 5 percent stake in the company (which Steele declined to accept). Steele was rumored to be the best-paid vintner in California, but by 1990 he had made up his mind to start his own winery, a project in which Jackson was also eager to participate. Steele turned that offer down too but agreed to stay on as a consultant at K-J for three years, collecting $400,000 to train a successor plus $10,000 per month for consulting services. The agreement stipulated that he not go to work for K-J's competitors, specifically Chalone, Jordan, Kenwood, Raymond, Simi, and Sonoma-Cutrer.

After the first year of his agreement with Jackson had passed, Steele had received one check for $125,000. In lieu of the second installment, however, he says he "got a pink slip." Steele maintains that he tried unsuccessfully for months to find out the reason for his termination, but in the meantime he started consulting for other wineries. Ultimately he sued K-J for the remaining pay—to which Jackson did respond, countersuing him for $22 million.

In the court papers, Jackson alleged that Steele had cost the company $212,000 by failing to properly barrel-ferment 140,000 gallons of 1990 chardonnay. He also claimed that Steele had interfered in K-J's business relationships by buying grapes for his start-up winery from growers who also sold to K-J. But in the aspect of the case that would amount to a shot heard round the wine world, Jackson sought an injunction preventing Steele from divulging K-J's "trade secrets" to his other consulting clients (some of which Jackson identified as "huge multinational corporations"). The technique at issue was the so-called formula for sweetening that served as a "secret" weapon in K-J Vintner's Reserve chardonnay.

Among the workaday ranks of the wine industry, this claim was generally viewed as somewhere between questionable and laughable. After all, Steele himself had gotten the idea from other wineries (specifically Arrowood and Parducci), and to cite another prominent example, Glen Ellen's Proprietor's Reserve chardonnay was also slightly sweet. As Frank Prial wrote of the case in the *New York Times*, about 20 percent of California chardonnay—"mostly at the lower end of the price scale"—contained residual sugar. "This is a process known to virtually every winemaker, is a process used by other winemakers, is but one of several means of sweetening wine (with no difference in taste from one to another), and no effort was made to protect this 'secret' from the outside world," asserted Steele's lawyer Thomas Brigham. Jackson, however, claimed that K-J's *specific* method had been developed within the winery and was therefore proprietary.

Although the case was conducted in an obscure county courthouse, it quickly got the attention of the entire wine industry. "Mr. Steele's partisans, who include many prominent winemakers and winery owners, say a ruling for Kendall-Jackson could alter the way wine is made in California," Prial wrote. "They say much of the considerable success California wines have had in recent years can be attributed to the free flow of information and ideas. . . . Many of California's best-known winemakers graduated from the same schools of enology, have worked together in wineries and have followed one another in winemaking jobs as the industry has expanded. They call each other when technical problems arise. They lend each other equipment and even store one another's wine when space is short." Prial went on to quote Richard Peterson, who had worked as the winemaker at Beaulieu, Atlas Peak, and Monterey Vineyards, saying, "I would be amazed beyond belief if any winery could have any trade secrets whatsoever." Many onlookers held that, even if there were such secrets, preventing a vintner from employing a technique developed on a previous job was tantamount to barring a chef from keeping a signature recipe when he or she changed restaurants. "If Kendall-Jackson prevails," said Robert Mondavi (in a trade newsletter, the *Wine Industry Insider*), "a wine-maker won't know what to do. How would he practice his occupation?"

Presiding over the trial was Judge John Golden, a former civil-litigation attorney who was known as smart, conservative, indepen-dent, and protective of courtroom propriety. Steele's attorney Brigham (a solo practitioner from Ukiah) recalls that Golden "terrorized the lawyers of Lake County—he scolded them like schoolboys, trying to bring a higher standard and make them follow the rules. His blue eyes would bore right through you, so I would pick a spot on his forehead to argue to." Jackson's lawyer was Jeffrey Chanin of Keker & Van Nest, a twenty-four-attorney San Francisco firm that *California Law Busi-ness* called "arguably California's premier litigation boutique," having previously represented such clients as Clorox, General Electric, NBC, Nestlé, the filmmaker George Lucas, and the Black Panther Eldridge Cleaver. Although Chanin had recently won a case in which the Mrs. Fields company successfully protected its chocolate-chip-cookie rec-ipe as a trade secret, Brigham sensed that "Jackson was the lead coun-sel, not Chanin. He was clearly very involved in strategy—I saw him corner Chanin and instruct him, and one day he dressed him down right in front of the courthouse."

The trial lasted about three weeks. Some two dozen witnesses testified, including Steele, Jackson, Mondavi (via deposition), John Buechsenstein, Parducci winemaker Tom Monostori, K-J winemaker Tom Selfridge (formerly of Beaulieu Vineyards), ex-K-J employees who had since gone to work for Steele, and several growers who sold grapes both to Steele and Jackson (some of whom Steele had recruited to K-J when he'd come from Edmeades ten years earlier). Several vintners were questioned about their winemaking techniques and their degree of collaboration with other wineries. Brigham introduced documen-tary evidence that ideas were commonly shared, but Golden closed the courtroom to the public whenever "secret" processes were dis-cussed.

Steele testified for several days, largely answering questions about messages and memos. He insisted that, prior to the trial, no "formula" for K-J chardonnay had ever been written down. "Jed thought [the trade-secret claim] was ridiculous," says Brigham. "He didn't think it would actually impact him in any way at all, but nevertheless he got his back up and wanted to fight the damn thing. Admittedly, it would be hard to just ignore it and say, 'Okay, yeah, issue me an injunction that I'll be subject to for the rest of my life'—but fighting it was very time-consuming. In that sense, the tail was wagging the dog to the detriment of collecting the money he was owed."

In the end, Steele prevailed on two of four counts. Golden found him innocent of sabotaging the '90 vintage and also ruled that, since he had adequately trained his successor, he was contractually entitled to receive the rest of his pay. But he also found Steele's conduct "wrong-ful and blameworthy" in buying grapes from growers who also sold to K-J. Even though a provision prohibiting Steele from doing this had been removed from an earlier draft of his contract (and the total that Steele had purchased amounted to fifty-seven tons, compared with K-J's total of ten thousand), Golden said that, by taking advantage of grower information obtained in K-J's employ, he had "interfered with relatively durable relations between Kendall-Jackson and its growers, which were important and profitable"—a standard of behavior the judge found "neither fair nor ethical."

On the question of most moment to the industry—the trade-secret claim—Golden wrote: "Although there is general knowledge and practice in the winemaking industry concerning the use of a sweetening agent in the production of wines and a limited knowledge and practice involving the use of processes similar to the process for the purpose, the evidence does not demonstrate that the details of the process are generally known—if known at all—to the public or other winemakers." Moreover, he found, Steele didn't bring the process to K-J, but rather it "evolved over the period from 1984 to 1990 by a combination of accident and design." Finally, even though Steele had declined to sign a confidentiality agreement, the judge held that that did "not preclude a finding that K-J's efforts to preserve the secrecy of the process were reasonable." The company was thus "entitled to equitable relief aimed at preserving the secrecy of the process for K-J's exclusive benefit."

As a result of all of the above, Golden awarded damages to K-J that all but eliminated any back pay it owed Steele. "The judge's Solomon decision split the baby," Steele says today. "It was all a good joke because of how they define trade secrets in a courtroom—a legal exercise that had nothing to do with the real world." Brigham (who was later charged with contempt by K-J for discussing elements of the secret process with the press, although he was ultimately exonerated by the court), still calls the verdict "shocking," and chalks it up to "John [Golden] being John, and showing that he thinks for himself. He had a literal, linear, tunnel-vision approach to things—he thought that Kendall-Jackson's technique was unique because everybody [sweetens wine] differently, but is it a difference of substance? You and I both have ears, eyes, mouths, and noses, but do we look the same?"

In any case, it was the first time that a trade-secret rule had been legally applied to the wine industry. At first Steele sought to appeal the decision, but Brigham cautioned him that, were it upheld by a higher court, Jackson's competitive paranoia would stand a greater chance of actually becoming law. As a result, Steele—who had already spent $55,000 on legal fees—decided to drop the suit. "This surreal ruling now stands where it should," he announced. "As an aberrant decision of a county judge, with no weight as a formal legal precedent.

"I'm a winemaker," he added, "and the courts are a strange, costly, and dangerous place to dwell."

After the verdict was announced, Jackson issued a statement proclaiming that "all creative wineries, including hundreds of smaller, family-owned wineries in California, will be the victors, not merely KJ," as independent research and development could now be pursued free from fear of theft. Brigham, however, believes that the case actually had "no impact—it didn't actually prevent Jed from doing anything." Roger Boulton of UC Davis agrees that it "had no effect at all—it was just an example of one group having better attorneys than another group." At the time, Mike Benziger was quoted as saying that he didn't "know of any winery owners that will suddenly become protective of information that will thwart the learning process. I know this decision isn't going to stop us from working with other wineries and sharing information."

Others, however, cried bloody murder. Zelma Long of Simi

Vineyards pronounced herself "shocked, upset and disturbed" by the verdict; Ridge's Paul Draper said that it "sets a very bad precedent for the wine industry. The danger comes from an owner, let alone a judge, who doesn't understand that this is centuries-old knowledge—not a formula like the recipe for Coca-Cola." Paul Dolan, who had introduced Steele to Jackson in 1982, opined that "the only secret formula Kendall-Jackson had was Jed Steele." Darrell Corti stopped selling Kendall-Jackson wines as a result of the case, and John Buechsenstein (who refers to Jackson as "a bull in a china shop"), "didn't speak his name for a few years after that. Prior to that, we didn't have people behaving that way in the industry—but since then, there have been a lot of people with way too much money from other walks of life introducing barracuda into the koi fish pond." Randall Grahm, who characterizes the effect of the case as "a loss of innocence," agrees that "we'd never seen that kind of competitive intensity in this supposedly genteel business. It had always been live and let live—the pie was big enough to give everyone a slice. There wasn't this sense that you had to destroy your competitors."

Today Mike Benziger says that the verdict, in tandem with corporate consolidation of the industry, introduced an ethic of "success at all costs" into the wine trade. Whereas, in the 1980s, it had appeared that "everybody was in it together"—for example, Kenwood's tip to Benziger about a source of sauvignon blanc grapes, which ended up putting Benziger on the map, even though Benziger had just stopped selling cabernet to Kenwood, which was also in the sauvignon blanc market—a discernible "cloak of secrecy" now pervaded the business. Benziger felt that the fighting-varietal market was "a ruthless bloodbath"—one that he was "glad to get out of."

Which is to say that, two years after Brown-Forman bought Fetzer for $80 million, and one year after the case of *Jedediah T. Steele vs. Kendall-Jackson* was decided, Benziger sold Glen Ellen to Heublein for $140 million.

WHETHER BECAUSE OF or in spite of Bonny Doon's disorganization, Randall Grahm's star—or, more accurately, his asteroid—continued to ascend in the early 1990s. In 1992, Dr. Edward Bowell of Flagstaff, Arizona—at the time the world's third-leading discoverer of asteroids, having identified some three hundred celestial rocks orbiting the sun—named Asteroid no. 4934 the "Rhoneranger." According to the official citation, this was in honor of Randall Grahm, who "has steered away from the usual style of California winemaking and has set a trend toward Rhone-style wines that I very much enjoy." The asteroid itself was reported to be one-third the size of all the vineyard property in California. A tasting of Bonny Doon wines was duly arranged at Lowell Observatory.

In 1994, a more down-to-earth honor was conferred when, having twice been previously nominated, Grahm was chosen Wine and Spirits Professional of the Year by the James Beard Foundation. As it happened, that year also marked Grahm's initial angst-ridden, soul-searching evocation of terroir in print. In his spring 1994 newsletter, he described the idea as "a remarkable almost metaphysical concept having to do with the intrinsic qualities of a particular piece of ground . . . this very subtle essence, something so ephemeral as to be almost mute beneath the clamor of stylish and stylized winemaking." Citing a speech he'd delivered to that noted religious body, the Oregon Winegrowers Association, Grahm went so far as to assert that the idea of terroir is "decidedly Calvinist," in that "we inhabitants of the New World are still slogging through the Old Testament. . . . We await reception of the Viticultural Good News," whereas "In the Old World, winegrowing is the process of uncovering the expressiveness of the vineyard and of the varietal. . . . The bottom line though is that one's unworthy viticultural ass is already saved; just pay attention and don't screw it up." The organizing theme of the talk, which proposed to avert New World agnosticism via "Talmudic" self-examination, equated the search for terroir with the search for grace—an interesting conclusion when you consider that, this same year, Grahm's estate vineyard in Bonny Doon died, sending him on a decade-long odyssey in the eno-spiritual desert.

The vineyard in question was the one that Grahm had originally impregnated with limestone and planted to middling Bordeaux varieties and astringent pinot noir, later replacing them with Rhône grapes, which attained divinity in the same spot. "Winegrowers search for this perfection over the span of numerous generations," Grahm wrote of the syrah he made from the site in 1988. "I get the shivers thinking that I may have found this mystical complementarity on the first try." As noted, it was actually his second—but in any case, within a few years the vineyard had already begun to decline. Nodes, shoots, and grape clusters were shrinking; leaves were drying out early in the growing season; some of the vines were even dying. Although the site received ample rainfall and was also equipped for irrigation, it seemed to be suffering from severe water stress. "I diagnosed it as Pierce's disease as soon as I got there," says Steve Tylicki.

As Grahm would later explain, Pierce's disease is "a bacterial blight which ultimately undoes grapevines by colonizing the xylem tissue and blocking the movement of water and nutrients through the plant." It's spread by a leafhopper insect called the sharpshooter (either blue-green or "glassy-winged"), which transports the bacterium *Xylella fastidiosa* in its mouth parts when feeding on plants. The bacterium reproduces in wood and is thus found in forested riparian areas, where it thrives in the blackberries and poison oak of California's coastal mountains. "I think it may be in redwood trees," Tylicki posits. "The bacterium can't survive cold temperatures, but Bonny Doon only gets down to about thirty-one in winter. The biggest problems with it in the Santa Cruz Mountains are in historical grape-growing areas, and

Randall's site had been a vineyard back in the 1800s. There was also a lot of tan oak around. It was a perfect environment for it to thrive."

Pierce's would go on to terrorize the entire California wine industry, especially after it was perceived as a threat in Napa and Sonoma counties. Since then, federal, state, and local governments have spent upward of $60 million fighting it, but unfortunately for Grahm, it was yet another area where he served as a pioneer. He and Tylicki tried injecting antibiotics into the vines to no avail, and although Randall didn't want to be a "nozzle head," he eventually resorted to spraying the insecticide dimethoate—a suspected carcinogen toxic to birds and bees, further endearing Grahm to his neighbors (not). In the end, Tylicki was directed to rip out the vines and dismantle the trellises, a task that made him depressed. "As a farmer, you want to grow things," he says, "not pull them out."

If this was traumatic for the vineyard manager, it was devastating to the owner. "I planted the vineyard thinking I was going to make great pinot noir," Grahm recounts, "but it wasn't the right grape for that site—or maybe it was the right grape, but I didn't have the right clones. Or mixtures of clones. Or I didn't plant it the right way. Or I didn't grow it the right way. Or I didn't give it enough time. Any of those things are possibilities. So I concluded that other grapes would be better, and grafted over to syrah and the so-called roussanne, which really *were* good. Then it got Pierce's disease, so I spent a tremendous amount of money trying to fix it—and it died anyway. A vineyard is such a completely irrational proposition, but it's a proposition on which you have to base your whole business."

The bottom line was that Grahm needed yet more new sources of grapes. Unfortunately, he'd been so successful at stimulating interest in Rhône varieties that he now had scores of new competitors for such grapes all over the state. The old-time Oakley growers whom he'd discovered and flattered, elevating their undervalued fruit to fine-wine status, now stipulated that, if he wanted their mourvedre, he also had to take their zinfandel, a grape in which Grahm had zero interest ("oversized, loud, blustery, lacking finesse . . . the SUV of grapes . . . a wine for enthusiasts, not connoisseurs"). To solve the problem, he devised a new brand called Cardinal Zin, featuring a characteristically delirious label by Ralph Steadman of *Fear and Loathing in Las Vegas* fame, and to advertise it, he dressed up in Catholic vestments for the annual Zinfandel Advocates and Producers megatasting in San Francisco.

In the meantime, Grahm continued his campaign against the pretensions of the wine business in general and Napa Valley in particular. Over a period of several years in the late 1990s, he published the four-part "Don Quijones, the Man for Garnacha, or A Confederacy of Doonces," which recounted the saga of his alter ego, a young wine clerk who became "utterly unhinged to the point where he began to proclaim himself . . . Champion of the Grossly Misunderstood, Underesteemed and Unfairly Maligned Ugly Duckling Grape Varietals." In one chapter, Don Quijones and his sidekick, Sangio Panza, took a visitors' tour of a famous Napa Valley winery that "represented everything about corporate wine-culture he thoroughly despised and was sworn to resist and animadvert upon with every fiber of his idealistic, if addle-pated being." After the travelers were greeted by a guide named Bambi (who had transistorized implants in her neck) and introduced to a robotic reproduction of the winery's deceased founder, Roberto Moldavi, a computer glitch caused the robot to malfunction, forcing it to intone, "We are so lucky to be blessed with . . . wine is made in the . . . newest techniques . . . gracious living . . . barrel fermented in 100% . . . special and unique growing conditions . . . the abundant bounty of . . . new oak . . . this beautiful valley . . . made in the vineyard . . . the California lifestyle . . . world-class wines . . . gracious living . . . we are so lucky . . . soft, mouth-filling tannins . . . the latest technology . . . Old World tradition . . . we are so lucky . . . made in the vineyard . . . we are so blessed . . . Paris tasting . . . have come of age . . . we are so lucky. . . ."

The same year that "Man for Garnacha" appeared, Grahm made a move that seemed to cement his stubborn allegiance to ugly ducklings. "It seems," he announced with equivocal fanfare in 1996, "that we have recently purchased the historic Ruby Hill winery, located in Pleasanton, CA." This was the latter-day site of the now-departed Stony Ridge winery—the same place where Mike Benziger had apprenticed in the late 1970s.

Pleasanton is in the Livermore Valley east of Oakland—a rapidly suburbanizing area that, though it hadn't kept pace since Prohibition with California's more glamorous regions, had a winegrowing legacy as old as Napa's. America's first international gold medal at the Paris Exposition was won by a Livermore Valley wine in 1889, and Wente Vineyards—named for C. H. Wente, the German immigrant who pioneered winemaking in the area in the nineteenth century—was the oldest continuously operated family winery in the United States. Mainly known by the 1990s for low-priced, consumer-friendly white wine, Wente also custom-crushed grapes for other wineries, including Bonny Doon as it expanded in the early 1990s. "It was contract winemaking," says John Locke. "We asked them to do all sorts of things that they didn't normally do, and my job was to get our stuff done before other people got their stuff done."

Grahm, who was fond of referring to Pleasanton as "a bastion of right-wing Republicanism," nevertheless found himself intrigued by the Wentes' local development plans, which centered on the aforementioned Ruby Hill—an old, burned-out winery that occupied part of the property. "I don't know what he was thinking." Patrice Boyle shrugs. "We didn't buy grapes from there, but Wente was trying to develop small vineyard plots around houses to maintain open space, and Ruby Hill had to be refurbished as part of the deal with the county. For some reason Randall became enamored of it." Offered favorable terms by Wente ("Buy Now, Pay a Lot Later"), Grahm developed a grandiose plan to move Bonny Doon to Pleasanton lock, stock, and *barrique*. He subsequently dispatched Boyle to local homeowners' meetings, directed Locke to engage Chicago's Charlie Trotter in discussions about a possible restaurant, and met with a series of architects, even paying a visit to Frank Gehry in Los Angeles to discuss design ideas.

In other words, he had a new blank slate. "I have been traveling in France quite often lately," Grahm wrote in spring 1997, "and with each visit to a new and quirky cellar . . . my brain is invaded by an unbidden torrent of *nouvelles idées* and *fantasies*." For example, although the housing and open-space components of the Wentes' plan would impose severe restrictions on winery activity and vineyard design, Randall seized on the notion of planting vines in a spiral pattern—a concept that, as recounted in the newsletter, constituted a tough sell to potential financiers.

"Patrice was wondering how she might disappear into a conveniently proximal sinkhole as I explained that the vine-rows were not going to be laid out in straight lines exactly, more like in a helical pattern that would derive from the energetic center of the property, which we had divined by means of a dowsing rod. . . . I noticed that the bankers had suddenly become very quiet. 'Would you mind explaining again precisely why you are planting the vineyard in this seemingly grossly inefficient, to all apparent purposes, frankly crazy configuration?' the senior banker broke in. 'I hadn't actually said,' I replied, 'but since you asked, we're doing it this way to more efficiently capture the cosmic energy.'

"Fortunately for me, my interlocutor was not actually listening to my answer but had become lost in his own internal woolgathering. 'You know,' he said, drawing closer, 'I think that your property is in the direct flight path of the planes coming into SFO. This helix could really be an amazing marketing opportunity and will likely lead to your retail unit becoming a significant profit center. . . .'

"Someone is definitely watching over me," Randall concluded. "I try my best to *épater bourgeois* capitalist sensibilities and I end up being proclaimed a brilliant strategic running dog."

The reason Grahm had been "traveling in France quite often" was to ferret out more new sources of grapes—presumably ones that exhibited more minerality and terroir than could be found in California. "We have embarked upon a Great European Adventure," he wrote in spring 1997. "Beginning this fall, we will be importing a number of wines from Europe that have been produced, in large part, under our direct supervision and direction."

The program, overseen by Locke, was called Eurodoon. "Randall said, 'I'm killing myself looking for these grapes in California, but over there they're already growing and they're probably cheaper,'" Locke remembers. "We tried to find people whose wines we liked—sometimes they'd send us samples; sometimes I would go there and taste—and a lot of them came from old, old vineyards and derelict little wineries. I would negotiate with the producer, then go back at harvest time and come up with a package of 1,600 or 2,300 cases. The amount of input we offered varied according to the individual: Sometimes we'd make the wine together; sometimes we'd just say, 'Perfect!' and bottle it."

During its relatively brief life, Eurodoon spanned the Continent—mainly the southern parts, in keeping with Grahm's Mediterranean affinities. "Syrah Sirrah" (from "Domaine des Blagueurs," or House of the Jokers)—which boasted another Steadman label, this one depicting a deranged-looking jester—emanated from Minervois in the Languedoc; "Heart of Darkness," made from tannat, came from Madiran in southwestern France; "Grenache Village" came from the Navarra region of Spain. In Italy the program had an especially esoteric bent: Based on the terroir-derived wisdom that any place is most truly represented by grapes native to the region, Italian Eurodoon focused exclusively on indigenous varieties. "Randall would send me to Vinitaly [an annual showcase of Italian wines] and say, 'Find some interesting wines to bottle,'" Locke says. "'Think about falanghina from Campania, or verduzzo from Friuli.' Ruche grew only in Piemonte; Uva di Troia was only in Puglia. I would come back with erbaluce from Piemonte north of Torino, and Randall would say, 'Great!'" The wines were adorned with labels by the New York artist Bascove, who had designed the covers of books by Robertson Davies; as one example, Uva di Troia ("Grape of the Streetwalker") portrayed a tattooed lady of the night. All of the autochthonous wines were marketed under the "Il Circo" brand, "emblematic of the circus that Bonny Doon had become."

This point of view seemed to be shared by Robert Parker, who stopped reviewing Bonny Doon wines in the late 1990s. "Some of the wine world's most innovative packaging is created by this estate," Parker wrote, "but . . . the quality in the bottle has declined from Bonny Doon's glory years (in the mideighties) when Grahm was both a pioneer and a committed Rhone Ranger revolutionary. It now appears to be all about image and high production. . . . It's a shame one of the wine world's most talented, innovative as well as funny people has become a poster boy for massive quantities of industrial-styled, innocuous offerings."

Inwardly despondent about this development, the *Mad*-reared auteur apparently felt that the best defense was an aggressive offense. ("It is an absolutely sacred tenet that I share with Penn and Teller that one should be staunchly prepared to risk death and dismemberment if the punch line is funny enough," Grahm would later declare.) Hence, in the wake of the bestselling romantic novel *The Bridges of Madison County* (with its hero, Robert Kincaid), in fall 1997 the Bonny Doon newsletter included a story called "The pHs of Romanee County," which told the tale of one Robert Parcade, "a stocky, well-fed figure of the North American male variety," who gets lost in front of the "modest eighteen-room 15th century stone farmhouse" of Madame Lulu Allbiz—a figure strikingly reminiscent of the real-life Lalou Bize-Leroy, comanager of the iconic Burgundy estate Domaine de la Romanée-Conti. There follows a sultry, double entendre–laden encounter ("I am in favor of extended skin contact"; "Do you punch down or pump over?") in which Lulu, "who had been brought up to consider wines by the old-fashioned and outdated criteria of finesse, balance, and typicity of terroir," succumbs to a passionate liaison with "the brute, magisterial power of the numeric universe and its prodigiously formidable master." In the end, however, the American interloper finds himself "beyond all critical thought, beyond synthetic or analytic reasoning, beyond any systemization, assaying, grading, rating or ranking."

Assuming a somewhat more self-reflective posture in that same issue of the newsletter, Grahm confided to his reader-customers: "I imagine a winery which can produce wines that are interesting and unique enough to continue to challenge the winemaker and his or her clientele, absent the Good Winemaking Seal of Approval of, say, Mr. Parker." A bit more candidly, he went on, "I imagine a winemaker (myself) who will not instantly open the *Wine Spectator* the picosecond it arrives to see how they have rated his wines. If they continue to misunderstand the *Cigare,* so be it. That will simply be one of life's mysteries. I love a mystery."

In fact, Parker and the *Spectator* had never been as bullish about Le Cigare Volant as they were about the all-mourvedre Old Telegram, scoring the latter in the low 90s and the former in the high 80s. As the

California Rhone wine category grew more crowded, Cigare reflected a conundrum that stymied Grahm more and more. Originally based on old-vine grenache, later on old-vine mourvedre, Bonny Doon's flagship blend was forced to change composition as competition for grapes increased. In some cases—for example, the grenache-ridden Hecker Pass area near Gilroy—new owners of old vineyards replanted their properties with more fashionable varieties and contemporary techniques. In others—for example, the mourvedre-laden San Joaquin–Sacramento delta area near Oakley—growers began to sell grapes to other wineries, or decided to vinify the fruit themselves. The primary Rhône variety now being planted in California was syrah, so by process of elimination of alternatives, young-vine syrah became the predominant component in Cigare. Meanwhile, as all manner of ambitious vintners began to focus on Rhône grapes, a flood of new wines drew critical attention away from the original Rhone Ranger, whose pioneering efforts appeared to pale by comparison. "Our mid-1990s wines were erratic, but I don't think they were worse," Grahm says now. "They were just not better, so it *appeared* that they were getting worse." This was especially true after the 1997 harvest, when warm weather resulted in a watershed vintage of rich, dark, deeply concentrated, highly alcoholic California wines that had critics turning cartwheels and Randall pining ever more plaintively for the Old World.

"In the middle of my life, I have found myself suddenly in a dark and unfamiliar wood," Grahm wrote, echoing Dante, in 1998. "I have fair convinced myself that making soft, luscious, drinkable, albeit terroir-free wines which typically reek of primary fruit aromas is wrong, all terribly wrong, being the enological equivalent of Stephen King or John Grisham and that what I need to be doing is making wines of an order of magnitude more seriousness." The newsletter in which this lament appeared represented a high-water mark in Grahm's confessional oeuvre, spurred by a piece of news that he now had no choice but to release. Regarding the much-ballyhooed Pleasanton project, he divulged, "The plan for the new winery, once a bright and shiny idea of great eidetic clarity, has become shrouded in a vague, recondite mist." The fuzziness had to do with such discernible factors as property easements and water rights, but even more significantly,

Grahm told an interviewer, "There were ghosts at the old Ruby Hill winery, and that of course required a lot of adaptation of our plans."

The presence of said spooks was confirmed by Dr. Baolin Wu, a product of the White Cloud Monastery of Beijing. After summoning the eminent feng shui master to Ruby Hill, Grahm wrote, "The first question I posed to him through his interpreter was what Dr. Wu thought of the property as a potential vineyard and winery site. It is an ineluctable rule that when you ask the cosmos for an answer, you must be prepared to take the answer to heart."

Dr. Wu's verdict: "Very good for graveyard."

"He thought there were a lot of unhappy spirits," John Locke explains. "We were at the ruin one time, and this mammoth owl flew right through the building in the middle of the day. It seemed an ill omen. It wasn't that the property was unsuitable—just that the spirits had to be accommodated. Dr. Wu recommended an altar."

Considering the other corporeal problems, however, Grahm decided, after much gnashing of teeth, to back out of the deal. "And I was doing such a good job in learning how to talk to Republicans!" he lamented.

"I think he didn't really want to pull the trigger," Locke conjectures. "He thought something better would come along as soon as he signed on the dotted line." Grahm himself acknowledged that he "may have been done in by my eternal archnemesis—that old commitment thing." Comparing the Pleasanton episode—not insignificantly in light of his personal life—to a long-awaited wedding, he wrote: "To everyone's chagrin, the groom is nowhere to be found and the bride is visibly distraught. There is nothing to do but eat the catered food, dance and drink up the booze."

In light of his now dashed hopes that this bride would erase the memory of his sharpshot Santa Cruz Mountains sweetheart, the vinous widower frankly found himself at sea. "So, whither Bonny Doon?" Grahm asked in fall 1998, anticipating his customers' inevitable question. His answer would hold true for the next several years: "I can't really say that I know."

I N NOVEMBER 1998, in his weekly column, "Wine Talk," Frank Prial of the *New York Times* published an article under the headline "Even a Visionary Needs Time Off." Accompanied by a photo of its subject (referred to as "the Peter Pan and Ariel of wine") perched on an oversize rubber ball that doubled as an office chair, the story announced the unveiling of "a new Randall Grahm."

"Gone, for the moment, at least, is the insouciance, the lightness of being," Prial wrote. "What now seems evident about him is not self-doubt, but a great deal of introspection and perhaps a slight sulfurous whiff, not of the vinous type but of burnout." The article recapped Grahm's career from the giddily literate newsletters to the Rhone Rangers revolution to "one hundred years of Soledad," and after enumerating his travails of the past few years, went on to relate how Randall, as "an almost fanatical exponent of the European principle of terroir," found himself increasingly discomfited by the showy but shallow character of American wine. As a result, Prial revealed, Grahm was considering "a sabbatical of sorts, possibly at the feet of Nicolas Joly at Savennières in the Loire Valley."

Joly was the international leader of the biodynamic farming movement—a charismatic sixty-year-old Frenchman, whose Coulée de Serrant property, in the Loire Valley, was a fully functioning biodynamic farm, complete with cattle and workhorses providing homegrown manure. The wines Joly and his daughter Virginie produce there—Becherelle, La Roche aux Moines, Clos de la Bergerie, and Clos de la Coulée de Serrant (each made from chenin blanc, the principal white grape of the Loire)—marked by steely, pristine flavors of flowers and minerals, rich and honeyed to the nose, velvety in the mouth, are recognized among the most distinctive in the world: Under France's Appellation d'Origine Contrôlée (AOC) system—established in the 1930s to ensure the traditional authenticity of wines from respected regions—Joly's estate in Savennières is that rare property (Domaine de la Romanée-Conti is another) that has been awarded its own appellation.

This recognition of uniqueness served as a sort of certification of the biodynamic ethic—a development that, for Joly, was predictable. Convinced that modern winemaking practices obliterate the underpinnings of the appellation concept, he considers biodynamics a means of recovering its significance. "An appellation is a place where a plant can fully express its qualities," he says. "It's like when a musician finds the acoustics of a place to be good for singing. But terroir is true only if the soil is alive—if the soil is destroyed, the microclimate isn't caught by the vines, and then you need technology to get good flavor. I think the consumer has a right to know the process that was used to make a wine—like when the label on a bottle of orange juice says 'from concentrate.' If a wine is made by reverse osmosis, its label should say 'concentrated wine.'"

Today some organic farmers are moving toward biodynamics because they feel that, with increasing incursions by corporate agriculture, the "organic" label is being diluted and is declining in significance. Most prominent among California practitioners is Benziger, which, after selling its Glen Ellen brand in the 1990s, began growing grapes according to the ideas of Rudolf Steiner. Today the family's estate on Sonoma Mountain is a gorgeous natural environment incorporating wetlands, forest, and flower gardens—one of several ecological symphonies orchestrated by Alan York, perhaps America's leading expert on biodynamic grape growing. "Some aspects of biodynamics require a path of self-development more than science," York once told me. "It's a training in seeing life activities." While he acknowledges that it exhibits earmarks of magic, York retorts that "if you deny magic, you're denying the true spirit of human beings."

Serving in a sense as Joly's representative in the United States, York is a whimsical down-home foil to the Frenchman's missionary zeal. Quoting him fails to convey the uniquely deliberate character of his speech, which sounds like a southern Mister Rogers. York grew up in Louisiana, where he passed most of his boyhood in swamps, wearing waders and watching animals; fatherless since the age of three, he spent summers at his grandparents' East Texas farm, a self-sufficient operation with cows, chickens, a vegetable garden, peach orchard, three acres of blackberries, and "worms as big as your little finger." In the 1960s, when he was a teenager, some kids from California moved in next door, and pretty soon he was smoking dope and battling his stepfather, who responded by sending him to an all-boys school. Alan promptly ran away and hitchhiked to the West Coast, where he had an uncle who—after conferring by long-distance with Alan's mother—let him move into his house in Santa Barbara.

During his high school years there, Alan labored as a gardener. "The most appealing part of it was the hard physical work," he remembers. "Gardening relaxed me. It was the only thing I'd ever done, other than drugs or roaming the swamps, that made me feel good. And until I met Alan Chadwick, I'd never known an older person I wanted to emulate."

York came under the spell of UC Santa Cruz's deposed gardening guru when the latter made an appearance at the Santa Barbara Botanical Garden. By that time Chadwick had established a farm at Round Valley, near Covelo in Mendocino County; he was invited to speak in Santa Barbara by the local Community Environmental Council, which was sponsoring a series of talks on alternatives to the so-called Green Revolution—the ironically named course of chemical treatments that postwar industry had succeeded in selling to farmers. The talk was billed "Master Gardener Alan Chadwick on the Secrets of Nature."

"It was pretty hilarious," York remembers. "Chadwick was a really striking person—lean, tall, and muscular, with this thick, flowing white hair—and he was wearing a double-breasted suit and Converse All Star sneakers. He got up and started talking about the drama of nature—the dynamic interaction of the seasons, the earth breathing in and breathing out, the story of rosemary and lavender being two fallen stars, Prima Mobili and Segunda Mobili. It was like going to a show.

Artists capture your imagination, and Alan could describe something so vividly that you actually experienced it. He was mesmerizing, but right in the middle of his performance, the director of the Botanical Garden brought it to a stop—it was just too outside for him. But something in my imagination had been captured—I said, 'This is what I want to do.'"

Within a couple of months, York had transplanted himself five hundred miles north to Round Valley. Chadwick's operation had a rule that aspiring apprentices undergo a two-week trial period before being accepted, but York simply rented a house in Covelo and reported for duty. "No way they were gonna turn me down. They needed all the help they could get, and I could work like a demon. Chadwick respected that—he knew I wasn't gonna punk out after a fifteen-hour day."

Chadwick's skin was so weathered that the local Indians called him Leather Legs. His personal trademark was a logo with flames firing out of a sparkplug, under the words A.C. MEANS ACTION. Sure enough, York eventually became his chief assistant, helping him manage the gardens, orchard, greenhouse, and nursery. Hoeing, weeding, planting, cultivating, composting, and double-digging 2,500 square feet of crops bordered by herbs, flowers, and fruit trees—all by hand, without machines—Chadwick's charges had no other life; most approached it as monastic indenture, consistent with their master's medieval vision.

"It was fun if you like being a slave," York says. "The highest level of technology we had was seven wheelbarrows. Here were all these young kids who had been totally undisciplined but eventually realized that you had to do *something*—that you couldn't just be stoned, listen to rock and roll, and have sex all the time. We worked from light until dark, double-digging for fifteen hours a day, seven days a week. You couldn't be normal and go through that; it was insanity. It was like being in the army—not relaxing in any way whatsoever. Chadwick was not emotionally stable—he was a tyrant, and you never knew what was going to set him off. He was pretty tortured, actually; he thought humanity was de-evolving and society was antagonistic toward everything he held holy and precious. He kept a distance from almost everybody; he and I didn't have a whole lot in common, except that we were both wound up like a top."

After five years in Covelo, Chadwick moved on to Virginia, where he founded another gardening project in the Shenandoah Valley. "Chadwick never stayed anywhere," York says. "He was good at starting things, but he didn't go past that stage—once it got to the operational part, he was pretty much gone." Eventually York himself relocated to Michigan—where he began the formal study of anthroposophy while instructing Waldorf teachers in gardening—and Missouri, where he converted the lessons of Chadwick and Steiner to commercial farming, resorting to the use of machines in place of picks and shovels. Ultimately he returned to Anderson Valley in Mendocino County, where he began raising biodynamic apples on espalier trellises. In 1995, one of the eleven Fetzer heirs—Jim, the fourth oldest, who had his own ranch near Hopland—hired York to convert his vineyard at McNab Ranch to biodynamic practices, which brought him to the attention of Mike Benziger in 1996.

After selling Glen Ellen in 1993, Benziger had spent a couple of years reassessing his company's mission. Having begun with high-end aspirations, it had continued making superpremium wine, but even after quitting the fighting-varietal fray, it was still producing 350,000 cases a year, only a fraction of which came from the family estate. "I knew I had a unique, incredible piece of property," he says, "but I was searching for an identity for it. We got good scores—93 in the *Wine Spectator*—but we were producing wines without distinguishing flavors or textures, and the property seemed to be running down. We were always fighting disease, and the vines weren't uniform. Some were overly vigorous, some were sick. . . . There was no consistency. Every year the best wine would come from a different block. It made me realize how hard we'd been on everything around us, and how much we'd damaged the property through chemicals and pesticides."

Benziger paid a visit to a Lake County grape grower named Ron Bartolucci—who had stopped using chemicals in the 1980s when Fetzer Vineyards converted to organic practices—and Bartolucci told him what Jim Fetzer and Alan York had done at McNab Ranch. Back in the 1970s, somebody had given Benziger a copy of Herbert Koepf's book *The Biodynamic Farm*; he hadn't opened it, but after visiting

Fetzer and McNab, he fished it out and "the whole thing made sense to me within a minute." He hired York, and for the first year, all they did was study the property on Sonoma Mountain—measuring temperatures, digging pits, analyzing soil structure and chemistry. The site had already been replanted because of phylloxera, and after York arrived, it was replanted again—some of it twice.

I first visited Benziger in 2003 when I was writing an article about biodynamic winegrowing. Before meeting him, I had already encountered York at McNab Ranch, which Jim Fetzer sold in 2001 to his family's former company (which based its Bonterra wine brand on the site). Formerly a denuded, eroded sheep ranch, McNab was now a showplace of diversity—ribboned by reed-filled riparian areas, fringed by flowering shrubs that act as "insectaries," guarded by birdhouses and raptor roosts from which hawks and owls patrolled for gophers and ground squirrels. York had rehabilitated the valley's natural drainages into wildlife habitats—corridors that act as "arteries" at right angles to the "veins" of vine rows. The vineyard blocks, he said, represented the property's internal organs. "As human beings, we're made up of regulatory, circulatory, and sense-nerve systems," he told me. "No one of them is any more important than any other. In the same way, biodynamics has four governing principles: A property is an independent ecosystem; it's self-regulating; its life processes are improved by the preparations; and none of those three things is optional. In other words, no one principle is any more important than any other—the system is holistic, meaning you don't get to pick and choose."

The feature of biodynamics that has gotten the most media attention is the preparations—burying manure in cow horns, etc. "The *easy* part of biodynamics is the preparations," York declared. "The part that's difficult is the farming practices and organizational structure. I'm not interested at all in working with people who think it's only about the preps, which at most are 25 percent of the system. Using preps in a monoculture is *Napa* biodynamics." Still, he said, winegrowing was a natural fit because "grapes are more attuned to the cycles of the sun than any other fruit crop. Most fruits flower around the spring equinox, but grapes don't flower until the sun is at its highest phase [the summer solstice]. Also, their roots grow in late autumn to early winter; with other fruits, the roots grow in spring." Most important, "Grape growing already has the estate concept. Steiner said to maintain as much authenticity as possible on your site, which is 100 percent consistent with the concept of terroir."

When I met him in Glen Ellen, Benziger took up the refrain. "When I started to understand what biodynamics is about, I realized that its goal is authenticity," he told me. "We're not looking to make perfect wine from this property—we want to make a wine that's *true* and *genuine* to this property. It might have a wart, but it's our wart."

With his baggy shorts, shaggy hair, bushy mustache, and lower-lip soul patch, Benziger seemed to epitomize the hang-loose Left Coast winemaker—visually less card-carrying Baby Boomer than ganja-peddling New Age hipster. But his East Coast accent and insistent message conveyed a different character: a serious, industrious, tightly wound guy who—having survived a stormy relationship with a combative father, mastered the national wine trade in an increasingly competitive marketplace, and served for three decades as the eldest son, general manager, and chief executive officer of a sizable family enterprise—seemed to be all-business even when discussing the cycles of nature and the philosophy of Rudolf Steiner. No other enterprise in America had assumed as public a biodynamic profile as Benziger; its Sonoma Mountain estate had been transformed into a virtual theme park—a popular tourist destination replete with tram rides and a "Biodynamic Discovery Trail" with kiosks and signboards explaining the winery's ecological mission.

Benziger gave me a personal tour in his Prius, starting with a pair of ponds at the bottom of the bowl that comprises the property. The company reportedly recycles three million gallons of wastewater per year; one pond was green, the other red, both attributable to ferns that grew on the water's surface, which was cruised by ducks and herons. The perimeters were lined by lilies, irises, willows, buckeyes, olives, and palms, all encircled by vine-covered slopes that ascended toward the bordering forest, which was rife with the sound of birdsong. "We're surrounded by trees here, so you'd think we'd be decimated by birds," Benziger said, "but we don't lose a single grape. The strategy is to tighten niches—by not leaving room for an inroad, you can prevent mealybugs and glassy-winged sharpshooters."

Running along the northern edge of the property was Graham Creek, a year-round stream that was once a salmon spawning corridor. "We maintain a high overstory in the riparian areas to prevent the water from heating up," Benziger said. "A cooler environment keeps out brushy plants like blackberries and periwinkle, which are a habitat for sharpshooters. We also have habitat for wasps, which eat sharpshooter larvae." Nearby I noticed a colony of beehives within a wooden corral; clover and grasses grew between the grapevines, with a multichromatic floral insectary situated in every tenth row. Benziger said these were "all Mediterranean plants that grew up with grapes, like lavender," as well as vetch, yucca, stipa, verbena, needlegrass, Japanese maidenhair, Mexican sage, and herbs—yarrow, valerian, chamomile, stinging nettle—from which to make the preparations.

The surrounding forest was a native matrix of oak, bay laurel, madrone, and conifer. "If you look around," Benziger said, "the healthiest environment is probably the forest. [By clearing trees and planting vineyards] we created a monocrop, and we fought insects with chemicals for ten years. When you take chemicals out of the equation, other populations can start to build. Then we started developing cover crops, which are like a gas pedal: If you want less vigor from the vines, you grow grass; if you want more vigor, grow legumes. If you want to be on cruise control, grow clover.

"Biodyamics doesn't fix your farming practices," Benziger said as we turned back toward the winery. "It isn't a panacea; you already have to be doing some basic things right. A plant expresses itself by mirroring its environment, and Demeter [the biodynamic certification agency] certifies the entire property, not just the vineyard. Grapes are the lead actor, but the other areas are supporting characters—they make the lead look good, but they're just as important. So over time, we've spent less on the plants and more on the environment. We're only just starting to see the effects, which at this point are mostly subjective. The first thing I've noticed is uniformity—stunted vines have come back, vigorous ones have slowed down, and all the grapes within a block get ripe at the same time. There's less erosion now, because the soil textures are healthier. The vineyard is just healthier-looking in general—cell growth in the fruit and leaves is denser. The leaves have a leather jacket on, so the vines are more resistant to disease."

Benziger said that since converting to biodynamics, his fermentations have also gotten healthier. "They're more vigorous, less get stuck. We've built up a very strong population of native yeasts now, so the fermentations are less stressful. You have to get intimate with the wine to get a feel for the fermentation, so we have custom-made tanks—one for every vineyard block. We've been seeing a steady increase in the quality of the wines—the tannins and textures are better, with a more consistent aroma profile."

As we approached his stainless steel tanks, Benziger mentioned the so-called Charter of Quality that Nicolas Joly had recommended to ensure wine's "Return to Terroir"—not a biodynamic program per se, but one consisting of "actions which permit an appellation to express itself." It was divided into three tiers of compliance:

One Star

No weed killers
No chemical fertilizers
No synthetic chemicals
No systemic treatments
No aromatic yeasts

Two Stars

No mechanical harvesting
No exogenous yeasts
No treating of the must with enzymes
No concentrators
No cryoextraction
No freezing

No de-acidifying or re-acidifying
No addition of ascorbic acid or potassium sorbate
No chaptalization
No irrigation

In other words, the system consisted entirely of things not to do. "We're moving toward being more passive in the winery, so that the process becomes one of preservation and evolution," Benziger said. "In the vineyard, it's about getting the most energy at harvest—energy and quality being somewhat exchangeable." He mentioned that, to be "totally natural," he made his flagship wine Tribute only from free-run juice,* not just for the usual reason—to avoid excess tannin—but also "because we don't want to exert our ego. You want to establish a relationship with what's going on, but we're trying to build one that's compassionate and supportive. God didn't intend wine—he intended vinegar, so we have to intervene a little bit in the process, but some methods are manipulative and others aren't. Man did create the vineyard and the insectary, but then we have to step back and let natural harmony reestablish itself."

Leading me through the cave where he aged Tribute, Benziger brushed each barrel with his hand as he walked through, in the way that football players exchange low fives with teammates when taking the field. "I touch every barrel whenever I'm here," he said, explaining that this gesture underscores the "intention" that human beings bring to the process. "Biodynamic wine is about a personal relationship. It's all about fingerprints—of the vintage, the varietal, and the people who made it. Wine is the most impressionable liquid on the face of the earth—what other liquid can hold the expression of the land, the vintage, and the data from your farm? But all of that can be obscured by things like oak, yeast, filtering, fining, overripeness, and overextraction—each of those things is like an eraser that can wipe out the fingerprints. For us, it's

---

* Juice that drains naturally from fermented grapes without hard pressing.

important to differentiate our wine—the best thing to market is quality and uniqueness. My purpose is to make sure those influences get into the bottle, because at the end of the day, if my wine tastes like everybody else's, I'm not in business."

Looking out over his family estate, which Benziger had discovered twenty-five years earlier, used as a launchpad for a commercial juggernaut, and subsequently converted into a New Age Eden, I wondered at the transformations, which seemed to sum up so much about the modern trajectory of California wine. Like most New Waves, the biodynamic movement exuded—in principle, at least—a kind of born-again fundamentalism, which, in rejecting the corruption of contemporary values, harked back to an earlier, less tainted time. "Biodynamics in large part is back to the future," Benziger agreed. "People have the idea that Man at this moment in history is the most advanced he's ever been, but a thousand years ago he was more attuned to the natural environment and more advanced in his knowledge of how to live with it. Steiner thought Man reached his apex in his understanding of those things—if he didn't plant seeds at the right time, the whole village would die out. But once he built a roof over his head, he began to lose touch with those instincts. So biodynamics has its roots in the most ancient and traditional forms of agriculture, when Man was at his fullest relationship with those systems.

"If there's anything that biodynamics does, it strengthens your connection to the land," Benziger said. "I've been growing grapes and making wine for twenty years, and this commitment has given me a rebirth. My goal is first for people to like the wine because of its quality, but biodynamics is going to help us align with people's value systems. When they come here and get it, it's really a wow experience."

It was hard to know exactly what to make of all this. A cynic might view it as an epic snow job: Was it really possible that the people who created Glen Ellen Proprietor's Reserve—a product that, by Benziger's own description, was designed to taste better than it actually was, and to taste exactly the same year in and year out—were now devoted to truth, authenticity, passivity, compassion, naturalness, warts, and fingerprints? Although Mike himself seemed to believe it (as do so many terroir-espousing, Parker-supplicating winemakers), he had also volunteered the observation that "in the U.S. we're still all talk—we haven't been able to walk the walk."

Presumably the proof would be in the pudding—that is, the wine. To my palate, Benziger's Tribute—the apparent apotheosis of everything the company was now trying to achieve—was pretty pimple-free: big, rich, ripe, intense, mouth-coating, and composed mainly of cabernet sauvignon. Though the wine didn't have the soft, glycerine mouthfeel advocated by Leo McCloskey, I happened to know that at least one member of the Benziger family worked with Enologix. In the opening scene of this book, it can now be revealed, the winemaker McCloskey was talking to on the telephone ("You know how you're looking for those ripe, plummy flavors? You're getting them by delaying") was Mike's brother Joe, the winemaker for Imagery, the Benzigers' adjunct operation on Highway 12 a few miles away. According to its Web site, Imagery was "doing some pretty unconventional stuff and not apologizing for it"—producing, for example, a "white burgundy" blend of chardonnay, pinot blanc, and pinot meunier, and a red wine called Code Blue, "an oxidant-rich adventure in winemaking" that consisted of syrah and . . . blueberries. That sounded more like early Bonny Doon than late Enologix, but in the time that had passed since I'd ridden along with McCloskey, Joe had reportedly kicked the Leo habit.

"I think Leo taught me everything I need to know," Joe said when I called to ask him about this. "How to get bright fruit and match it with the right type of oak; how to get midpalate in the wines; how to make wines that melt in your mouth and don't have green tannins, wines that are seamless from the aromas to the finish. Leo helped me a lot with that, but for me now it's about trusting my own instincts and palate and what I believe in, rather than the numbers. Sometimes numbers get in the way a little bit. You don't only get a high score because Leo shows you the numbers. There are all kinds of other things in wine that Leo's not measuring."

Things, presumably, like terroir, minerality, and life force? When I ran Benziger's rap past Randall Grahm, he concurred with much of it but demurred, "You don't simply sell a wine because it's biodynamic. Ultimately it has to be an interesting bottle of wine." Then, applying the disarming self-reflection at which he is so adept, Grahm added: "But far be it from me to criticize someone for being a master marketer."

B Y THE END of the 1990s, Bonny Doon was producing more than forty different wines, adding up to a total of 175,000 cases. In the dozen years that had passed since Patrice Boyle joined the company, the winery had grown at an average rate of 23 percent per year, "and in some of those years we had negative growth, so it was even higher in the other years," Boyle points out. "Randall handled the wine and marketing; I handled everything else, but that kind of growth is extreme in any business organization. You need more equipment, more employees, more markets, and it's more and more overwhelming. Randall's focus was on growing the brand, and he let [the rest of it] get away from him."

"Growing the brand" basically meant making more of Bonny Doon's bargain wines: Big House, Cardinal Zin, and Pacific Rim. There were many precedents for this among prestigious wineries: Robert Mondavi had the Woodbridge label, based on cork-finished jug fare from the Central Valley; Ravenswood had the Vintners Blend line, partly composed of varietal bulk wine; Kendall-Jackson still sold its supermarket standby Vintner's Reserve, as well as ultrapremium wines from single vineyards. In the Old World, respected Rhône producers like Guigal and Chapoutier turned out mass quantities of Côtes du Rhône to augment their rarified bottlings of Hermitage and Côte-Rôtie, and Bordeaux icons like Châteaux Latour and Mouton Rothschild maintained second labels like Les Forts de Latour and Le Petit Mouton de Mouton Rothschild. The aim of any such strategy is for the lower-end products, made by cheaper methods from lesser fruit, to provide rapid turnover and quick cash flow to support the more prestigious, labor- and capital-intensive wines. The commercial danger (especially in California, where track records and reputations are less well established) is that, as the "supporting" division grows, it will overshadow the higher-end products by virtue of volume and visibility, coming to associate the company primarily with cheap wine.

Since the *60 Minutes* "French Paradox" show aired in 1991, the number of bonded California wineries had redoubled to 1,500 within a decade. Meanwhile exports from the United States to other countries had quintupled. Although this stimulated the high-end market associated with Robert Parker and Napa Valley, most of the growth in consumption was among budget-minded neophytes, who had an increasing array of imports to augment the proliferating domestic market. Cutting a swath through this cost-conscious atmosphere were Australia's so-called flying winemakers—masters of modern technology who, blessed with a wine-swilling populace and favorable physical environment, had amassed a clever bag of tricks for producing enormous quantities of lip-smacking beverages from inexpensive grapes. Capitalizing on the fact that the Southern Hemisphere harvest occurs in March and April, product-hungry retailers in the UK dispatched the energetic Aussie wizards to southern France, Italy, and California in September and October to share their ingenious methods (for a fee, of course). Complementing the tools of reverse osmosis and spinning cone, these included such innovations as ion-exchange columns, which can adjust the pH of a wine to a level that makes it palatable; toasted wood chips, which impart the flavor of an oak barrel at a fraction of the cost; "designer" yeasts and enzymes, which contribute specific flavors and aromas; powdered tannin, for improving the texture of flabby wines; and concentrates like MegaRed and MegaPurple, for enhancing the color and mouthfeel of thin, pale wines. All were godsends for grapes grown at high volume in areas like California's Great Central Valley, France's Midi and Languedoc, and Australia's Riverland, which were traditionally considered too hot to maintain the color and acidity associated with fine wine.

Needless to say, none of these tools is concerned with communicating a sense of place. On the contrary, they're intended to achieve a common drinkable denominator from nondistinctive fruit—and as Bonny Doon's bargain-priced, mass-production brands grew, it called the full complement of modern winemaking tricks into service. In addition to micro-oxygenation, spinning cone, and those technologies mentioned above, Grahm availed himself of such imposing tools as "Flash-Détente" (translated from the French as "instant relaxation")—a thermocooler system that superheats grapes to 185 degrees Fahrenheit and then chills them in a vacuum, causing the skin cells to burst from the inside, thus increasing color extraction, decreasing tannin and vegetal character, and shortening fermentation time. Then there was Velcorin (aka dimethyldicarbonate, offhandedly referred to by Grahm as the "Death Star"), a microbial agent commonly used in bottled juices and energy drinks to kill bacteria, mold, and yeast without affecting flavor or aroma. Although it's categorized as "nonpersistent"—that is, it breaks down into methanol and carbon dioxide and is filtered out after use—Velcorin is a hazardous chemical, which by law may be applied only by a licensed owner-operator of the technology.

Intended to streamline the winemaking process on lower-end products, some of these industrial (as opposed to artisanal) techniques also saw use on Bonny Doon's higher-end wines. "I have surrendered to it," Grahm told me one day over lunch. "I don't like myself for doing it, but as a rational actor in a commercial enterprise, you do what you have to do. You're in the wine business because you love it, but also because it's your livelihood—you need to make money, and in my experience, unoriginal wine is a positive thing [commercially]. The fact is, things like enzymes and cultured yeasts make wines taste better. Adding tannin changes the structure in a clunky, artificial way; MegaRed and MegaPurple change it in a weird and creepy way, like *The Stepford Wives* or *Body Snatchers*. Still, you can make the case that some cosmetic corrections are justifiable. You might be against plastic surgery if you just want your boobs to be a little perkier, but if somebody is really butt-ugly or deformed at birth—if a wine is unspeakably vegetal, say—when does elective plastic surgery become obligatory plastic surgery?"

The question eventually came back to the quality of the vineyard. "If you're fortunate enough to have had the wit or the good karma to own a vineyard, or buy grapes from a vineyard, that is well suited and has a reason for being—where you're growing the right grapes in the right place in the right way—you don't have to do anything. But if your yeasts don't have enough nutrition, vitamins, and minerals from the grapes, you're going to have problems—you're going to have stuck fermentations, and your wine is going to stink. So technical winemakers analyze their musts for things like nitrogen levels and amino acids, and then they make adjustments to ensure that they have a healthy fermentation, which from a scientific standpoint is a totally rational thing to do. It's no longer a natural wine, but unless you have a perfect vineyard where the grapes have everything they need, it's crazy to talk about the virtue of a natural wine, because making a natural wine from imperfect grapes is not a rational thing to do. But once you get down a particular path, it's very hard to get off. Why does Barry Bonds take steroids? Because we live in a highly competitive society. This is the reason why the Leo McCloskeys of the world exist—they provide a leg up, a service for people who want an advantage. We're all complicit; you can blame almost everything on Parker if you want, but the whole world has brought us here. It's the effect of globalization. It's not just the wine industry—*every* industry is massively competitive."

Of course, commercial competition didn't exactly begin with the twenty-first century. For a more time-honored example, we need look no further than the soft-drink industry, where Coke and Pepsi have been duking it out for more than a hundred years, developing and defending formulas to win a worldwide haul of customers, each of whom knows exactly what to expect when buying a bottle or can of their products. In that sense, it could be considered downright quaint that, when Patrice Boyle departed Bonny Doon in 2000 after thirteen years of service as general manager, she was replaced by Quinton Jay, an executive previously employed by Coca-Cola.

I N MIDWINTER, I rendezvous with Grahm at Kermit Lynch's house in Berkeley, hoping to get a handle on what they talk about when they talk about terroir.

During the three decades since these two met, Lynch has carved out a formidable niche as the West Coast's leading importer of terroir-based wines. As chronicled in his books *Adventures on the Wine Route* and *Inspiring Thirst,* he spends half of each year in France, seeking out small, independent producers who use traditional techniques consistent with his old-fashioned palate and ethos. Steadfastly opposed to sterile filters and new oak (not to mention, god knows, spinning cone and 100-point scales), Lynch has succeeded in attracting a nationwide following for his wares, which he sells at both wholesale and retail—the latter through a pithy, persuasive newsletter and his store in Berkeley, which is located around the corner from my house. Tucked into the same L-shaped building as two other emblematic destinations of Northern California culture—the Acme Bread Company and Café Fanny, which introduced artisan baking and Parisian breakfast bars to the Bay Area—Lynch's shop has a kind of holy-pilgrimage atmosphere: Tastefully lit, decorated with photo portraits of French vignerons taken by his wife, Gail Skoff, the room is entered via descending steps that deposit the customer among stacks of cases, each topped by an open box displaying bottles horizontally. No scores, hangtags, or other advertising accompany the products, which are identified only by name and price; descriptive details are to be gleaned from the newsletter or the human staff, who stand ready, half a dozen strong, attending to paperwork or pushing hand trucks out the door. It's not uncommon here to encounter adult versions of candy-store-crazed kids, roaming the stacks and returning to the counter to add yet more bottles to those dozens they've already collected on an apparent spending spree.

Among the various arms of his business, Lynch (reputedly a tough businessman) sells enough wine to afford houses in Berkeley, Provence, and Oahu, as well as a wine estate in Gigondas: Domaine Les Pallières, which he co-owns with the Brunier family of Le Vieux Télégraphe in Châteauneuf-du-Pape. Having delegated much of the day-to-day running of the company to employees, in recent years Lynch has even resurrected his musical aspirations from the sixties: *Quicksand Blues*—an album of his original songs produced by Boz Scaggs and performed by bandmates of Bonnie Raitt and Robert Cray and Alvin Youngblood Hart—appeared in 2005 (the same year Lynch was awarded the insignia of Chevalier de la Légion d'Honneur by the government of France), and four years later Lynch himself sang lead on *Man's Temptation*, a CD he promoted with live performances in Austin, Nashville, New York, and San Francisco.

At sixty-eight, Lynch looks sort of like an aging French film director, largely because of his outsize red-framed eyeglasses. I know him from the Acme parking lot and Berkeley farmers' market, where he shows up (between October and May, when he's in California) as soon as it opens on Saturday. (An observation Lynch is fond of making is that, during the time he's been traveling to France, the quality of cuisine has reversed: It's better in California now.) During one such meeting, when I used the term "minerality" to describe a wine, I noticed him rolling his eyes; when I asked why, he said it's a buzz term that wine buffs dispense without knowing what it means. Later, while paying for my baby broccoli, I heard a voice behind me say, "Do not confuse minerality with terroir." Turning around, I told Lynch that, since Randall Grahm considers these characteristics inseparable, if not synonymous, perhaps we should get together and discuss them. Kermit graciously obliged, inviting both of us over for lunch.

Lynch's house is in north Berkeley, just uphill from a street called the Alameda—a tony neighborhood of elegant homes occupied by citizens of solid means. As it happens, I rented a room just *down*hill from here in 1976; back then, I viewed the neighborhood as boringly suburban, whereas now it strikes me as eminently pleasant and peaceful. It's situated below Indian Rock, a volcanic lookout and climbers' magnet with a sweeping view of San Francisco Bay. Not coincidentally, Lynch's kitchen window is dominated by an enormous boulder—suitable, it would seem, for a champion of terroir.

To reach the house, I ascend a winding staircase through an ornamental forest. Just as he did when I first met him twenty years ago, Randall arrives carrying half a case of red wine, his neck wrapped in a scarf overlain by his ponytail. Before Randall uncorks his cargo, Kermit—taking a break from making mushroom soup and avocado salad—proffers a selection of whites: three '09 Corsican wines made from the vermentino grape and two '08 Burgundies from one producer, distinguished only by type of soil.

"I'm totally uninterested in tasting wines blind," Kermit tells us. "I admit that it's *fun*; everybody gets drunk and starts talking. . . . It's cool, but just don't think you've really learned anything. I did blind tastings when I first got into wine, but then I started realizing that what turned out in my cellar had nothing to do with my top scores. Now I want to know as much as I can when I taste—I don't *want* to be deaf, dumb, and blind."

"One element that differentiates your experience from almost anyone else's, Kermit," Randall points out, "is that you've actually been to the places. So, when you taste the wine, you have the richness of association of being there—the memory of what it felt like, what it smelled like, the bumpy road going in . . . all these things that give the wine secondary meanings.

"There's also an affect toward the people who make it," he adds. "If you like them, the wine tastes better."

Kermit laughs. "I rarely drink Zind-Humbrecht since we broke up," he acknowledges.

"It just doesn't taste as good," Randall confirms.

The first vermentino, from Cap Corse at the northern end of Corsica, was grown in schist: flaky, shaly metamorphic rock that contains all manner of minerals—quartz, talc, mica, graphite. The other two are from Patrimonio, just to the south—an area, Kermit says, of fossilized oyster-shell chalk or "calcaire, which I think we translate as limestone."

I don't detect much in the nose of the Cap Corse wine (which was made by Domaine Gioielli), but when Randall identifies "gunflint," I have to concur. "That's from the schist," he says. "Schist has the most terroir of all"—by which I take him to mean the most perceptible influence on character. The other two vermentino wines are a fascinating contrast—not only with the Cap Corse but with each other. Both were grown in limestone rather than schist, but one—from Antoine Arena, a fashionable biodynamic producer—completed malolactic fermentation, whereas the other, from Yves Leccia, didn't. We try the latter wine first, and tasting it immediately after the Cap Corse, I would have guessed that it *had* completed ML—its flavor is altogether richer and "butterier" (as in lactic).

"When you taste a limestone wine versus a nonlimestone wine, there's a softness—a gentleness—a roundness," Randall observes. "There's a concavity, a sculpted quality to it—like the lines of a Citroën. It *curves*."

"It has finesse and depth," says Kermit.

The ML effect in the other Patrimonio makes it more complex, but also less clean tasting. The non-ML Leccia is more refreshing and pristine. Randall and I like the Leccia, but Kermit says he prefers the Arena, which he finds "deeper and more supple."

This lesson—that the same grape can taste altogether different in the same vintage, depending on the type of soil and method of winemaking—is repeated by the Burgundies: both from '08, both from Pouilly-Fuissé, both made from chardonnay by Domaine Robert–Denogent, both with completed ML. But one (La Croix, grown in schist) tastes sharp, while the other (La Reisses, grown in limestone) tastes soft. Tasting the La Croix, Kermit says, "When I stick my nose in there, that's a wine that I would have called 'stony.' Now I guess I have to call it 'minerally.' That's the hip way to say stony."

Tasting the La Reisses, Randall says, "It has a misty nimbus around it—a soft-focus gauze, like a David Hamilton photograph. Limestone is a secondary impression. It's like a cloud that surrounds the wine—a duotone that gives it multidimensionality."

"It's less stony than the schisty one," Kermit points out. "Do you think minerality has any more meaning than what we mean when we say stony?"

"I think they're the same feeble attempt to use language to describe something," Randall says, "but there's definitely something out there, a phenomenon that makes some wines more interesting for me than others. For me the word is 'minerality,' but it could be 'life force,' or 'soul,' or 'antioxidative potential,' or any number of other things."

"With my training, I would say 'terroir,'" says Kermit. "If we were tasting these same two wines from the 2006 vintage, you wouldn't think to say 'stony.' It's a real ripe vintage, and I've noticed that what most people call minerality is more evident in a vintage when you've got some acidity in the wine. If it's flat, like 2003 in France, you never talk about minerality—unless you're the winemaker and trying to sell me wine."

This seems like a good time to open a bottle I've brought—for better or worse—in a brown bag. Since both of the previous two wines were minerally chardonnays, I pour (unbeknownst to Lynch or Grahm) a chardonnay called Quartz made by Bindi, an Australian producer that Randall told me about after he'd tasted it at a trade event in Oklahoma. When a distributor offered to pour him some, Randall at first responded, "'You know what? I'm good.' I thought, I don't like chardonnay and I don't like Australia—but I was wrong, wrong, wrong. The wine was from a vineyard outside Melbourne, where they got a geologist to do a study; they found quartz, and flagged the vines that were growing in it. They kept the wine from those vines separate, and it was all minerals, all the time."

When I pour it for them now, Randall and Kermit agree that the wine has minerality up the wazoo. Randall opines that its origin is limestone—"definitely Old World, probably Burgundy from a ripe vintage." Kermit is moderately impressed; he says he would buy the wine if it was *one* of those made by a potential client, but not if *all* of a producer's wines were like it.

When I remove the Bindi from its bag, Randall expresses more gratification than embarrassment. His off-base guess about the source of minerality causes Kermit to recall a time when he was tasting with a winemaker in Corsica. "We were looking out at this mountain near Montegrosso," he says. "It's a double for El Capitan in Yosemite, so I said, 'I really taste the granite in this wine.' The winemaker said, 'It's from limestone.'"

Having reached the end of the white flight (so to speak), Kermit goes to check on his soup. As Randall begins pulling bottles out of his box, I pour another unnamed wine—this time a red that I decanted before coming. Still, it isn't terribly tantalizing when we swirl and sniff it. "It's not speaking to me," Randall says.

"I think they could have had something here, but they screwed it up," Kermit conjectures after tasting. "There's a lot that I like about it, but the flavor isn't one of them. More the tannic structure—but it has a lack of focus. It's like a question you'd use in a TV quiz show that no one will ever get: 'What variety is this?' Mourvedre? Syrah? Zinfandel?" Randall guesses that the wine is "syrah, but god knows from where."

"What if I told you it was pinot noir?" I posit.

"No way is this pinot noir," says Randall. And yet it is: the '08 Rhys Alpine Vineyard, whose lean austerity so impressed us when we visited the winery.

"That's an additional reason for me to be disappointed in it," Kermit says upon learning the variety. "When you go into a wineshop in the mood for pinot noir, that's not the experience you're going to have with this wine."

"It's overextracted," Randall decides. "Maybe my knowledge of the winery is influencing me, but I think they let it macerate too long."

As it turns out, Randall has brought several examples of actual syrah, including four bottles of Cornas—the sturdiest wine of the northern Rhône, so intense in reputation as to be called brutish. "It took twenty years for me to understand that Cornas is not supposed to taste fruity," Randall explains. "In earlier vintages it was often beset by microbiological issues, but even when the wine is totally clean, its charms are not necessarily the most evident upon first sniff. I wanted the wines to be something they weren't, but when I finally shifted the gestalt and just let them be what they were, they expressed themselves."

The first wine he pours is an '05 from one of Kermit's most prestigious producers, Auguste Clape. "Now we're talking," Kermit says of the rich, earthy, slightly stinky syrah before finding out what it is. "There's a quality of certain wines that draws you in, as if you're on a path—they take you somewhere, and you're never quite sure where they're going to take you next. The ultimate for me is wine that takes you on a trip. I shouldn't say trip," he corrects himself. "Voyage."

"I think the statute of limitations on that expired some time ago, Kermit," Randall reassures him.

"The two greatest bottles of my life, if you leave out ancient Sauternes, were the '61 Romanée-Conti and '61 Pétrus," Kermit reveals. "The Romanée-Conti was like listening to Casals play a Bach cello suite—it just weaves along and you follow it into an inner sanctum."

"Sonorous," says Randall.

"This wine has a little hint of that in it," Kermit submits. "It's a serpentine quality that I adore."

The Clape is followed by a couple of wines that don't quite measure up to it. One is "not as focused, more diffuse" (Randall), the other "a little oxidized, a little *fatigué* in the nose" (Kermit).

"We're going in descending order of quality," Kermit observes, but that trend is halted by the fourth bottle. "*This* is a pretty nice wine," says Randall. "I have to say, this is a friggin' *great* wine."

As it happens, it's another of Kermit's coveted producers: Thierry Allemand, whom Randall has occasionally nominated as the world's greatest winemaker. A native (and onetime mailman) of the village of Cornas, Allemand wasn't born into a winemaking family, but apprenticed and saved his money until he could procure a couple of old vineyards, augmented with other rocky plots that he cleared and planted. He's said to do all of his work himself—even making the metal plows for his steeply terraced vineyards—and his wines set a standard for purity. The impossible to obtain *"sans soufre"* bottling (the one we're tasting now, as Randall was somehow able to procure it) is entirely free of sulfur, which gives it an unmistakable aliveness—its flavor and aroma hit a "high" part of the palate, as opposed to the low-down, mouthfilling sensation of superrich fruit. "It's that sinuous quality again," Randall says. "It has movement."

"It crescendos," Kermit agrees. "It's a gorgeous wine because it builds up to a grand finale. It ain't a blockbuster, but it just won't let go. You know that old song 'Don't Let Go'? It's about making love, and he's about ready to . . . you know . . . and he says: *'Don't let go!'* This wine is sort of like that. It just keeps on comin'."

"I think musicality is much more interesting than minerality," Kermit comments, turning away to toast some bread.

Biologically speaking, the last wine Randall pours is the funkiest of the five. "This one is different," Kermit says. "There's a weight that hits the palate, which makes me think it might be California."

Sure enough, Randall reveals it as the '94 Bonny Doon syrah—the last wine he made from his estate vineyard before it died. Owing to phenolic intensity attributable to shrinking yields, upon release the wine had a character that Randall's '96 newsletter described as if channeling Robert Parker: "amazingly concentrated juice . . . rich, utterly hedonistic . . . oozing gobs of decadent fruit." Fifteen years on, however, Kermit finds it "a little weedy or jammy on the palate. Compared to the others, I think that California ripeness kind of tugs it down."

"It seems a little flat or heavy," Randall agrees. "It's not as charged."

"But there you go." Kermit shrugs. "It's not the vinification—it's the terroir."

Randall confides that he added half a percent of orange muscat to the wine when he made it. Why? "Just because I could."

"I don't ever ask [winemakers] the varietal," Kermit says. "It's hard to tell customers, 'I don't know' when they ask, but the same grape grown in California will taste totally different."

Indeed, despite their fearsome reputation, in the present company these Cornas wines seem bright, lively—downright diaphanous. "Tasting them without knowing what they are, I'm amazed at how light and not alcoholic they are," Kermit says, offering a tacit endorsement of blind tasting. "This blew my mind at Clape's place once. It was either the '90 or '98 vintage, both of which were very ripe. I said, 'My god, this wine is so rich—what's the alcohol on it?' He said, '12.8—we've never seen that before.' Is that unbelievable? For these wines that have the reputation of being so powerful and intense! Since then, though, with global warming it's happening all the time. Even some Chinons* are up to 14 degrees."

"I don't like California zinfandel when it's 15 degrees alcohol, but I adore Amarone," Randall reveals. "I love Barolo when it's 14.5 degrees alcohol. The bottom line is that you have to have minerality in the wine—without that, they're grotesque. Whether it's the effect of surface tension so the alcohol isn't as volatile, or simply how the wine is organized in your mouth, the wines are much more drinkable—the mineral content somehow preserves them from being caricatures. Cornas is the most mineral expression of syrah, which I didn't understand until it came into focus that that which was the 'problem' of Cornas, if you will, was the most intriguing aspect: That hard, austere, mineral quality is what actually makes Cornas interesting."

"In the northern Rhône is where you get the granite," Kermit points out, "but the terroirs of the northern Rhône are very different. Côte-Rôtie is completely different from Cornas—it's the same variety and same climate, but Cornas is granite and Côte-Rôtie has this complexity of soils. You can really see it when the wines are a few years old and the winemaker doesn't obscure the terroir. Same if you go to Meursault—vintage after vintage there's a difference, and the difference is the terroir. It's reflected in the names of the vineyards, which is why they stuck. Charmes is charming; Perrières is stones. In the old days in the northern Rhône, everybody was doing pretty much the same vinification, but there were distinct differences when you went from village to village. Until Guigal came—then the winemaker became more important than the terroir. He made so much money that people tried to copy him: 'Let's see . . . he's getting four hundred dollars a bottle, and we're getting eighty-eight. What's going on here?'"

"Those wines are so stylized," says Randall, "and honestly, in my immature tasting days I found them to be more accessible—bright, shiny, polished with four years in new oak. . . ."

"That's the problem with me and these poor people," says Kermit. "In terms of getting out of their poverty and making some real money, I'm telling them to do all the wrong things. But for me, terroir is what

* From the Loire valley.

gives wine its interest—the right grape in the right soil with the right climate and the right winemaker."

I remind him that this is what California winemakers also claim to value. "And they're full of shit," says Randall.

"Every wine has terroir," says Kermit, "unless it's been oaked up or something."

"But that's 95 percent of California wine," says Randall. "Friggin' irrigation, rootstock, and clones. . . . Terroir is a signal, but if it's so weak that you can't perceive it . . ."

"Then it's not a good terroir," says Kermit.

"Terroir is marked by *something*," says Randall.

"Terroir is the taste of the place," says Kermit. "Not just the earth. It's the emotional side of things—to the old French and Italian winemakers, wine was a symbol. For them it was sex—certain wines had masculine qualities and some had feminine qualities. I think talking about wine like human nature is more fun than all this bullshit about whether it's schist or limestone."

Of course, Leo McCloskey—and even other oenophiles who object to McCloskey's MO—would maintain that not only minerality but also music, emotion, sexuality, trips (oops—voyages), exotic cars, pictures of ballerinas, soul, signals, and surface tension all come under the category of bullshit when applied to wine. But Lynch and Grahm are both unabashed in their embrace of such subjectivity—Kermit especially seems to revel in freedom from objective standards, unapologetically following his instincts and opening himself (and his customers, of course) to the power of suggestion in the backstory of a wine. In that sense, maybe hot air should be included among the elements of terroir, since the atmospheric context of any product will affect a person's impression of it. If envisioning granite allows you to appreciate a wine wihout fruit—well, why not?

"It's just words," Randall agrees. "At some point, actions speak louder than words."

I N APRIL I go to Glen Ellen to meet with Mike Benziger and Alan York as they plan their late-spring vineyard activities. We convene in a twelve-chair conference room lined with reclaimed redwood, Benziger Family wine bottles, a sign bearing the name WEGENER (the family that previously owned the property for 110 years), and an aerial photo of the estate, which, in light of its terraces and bowl-shaped topography, reminds me rather ironically of an open-pit mine. York and Benziger are both wearing jeans and corduroy shirts—exactly the same clothes, in Alan's case, as those he was wearing the last time I saw him, a month earlier.

"I just saw an unbelievable *Nova* program called 'Dimming the Sun,'" York says. "It was amazing, man. They were talking about why global warming has not extrapolated out the way they thought it was going to. You know what they found out? Pollution is actually dimming the sun. The size of the particles that are going into the atmosphere is actually reflecting the sun away from Earth."

"So that part of it is a cooling trend," Benziger confirms. "We also need a couple of big volcanic eruptions."

"The gist was that China and India are taking care of it for the short term."

Weather continues to dominate the first part of the discussion that follows. The spring season thus far has been cool and wet, which has played havoc with the normal schedule for spraying elemental sulfur (an approved organic practice) to prevent powdery mildew on vines. Similar conditions characterized the previous May, the time when buds become differentiated for the following year. "So," Benziger says, "not only are we late, wet, and cool, but we also have the possibility of a small crop, which will put that much more pressure on vine growth, because the energy's gotta go somewhere. I'm scared now that once this heat comes on, we're gonna have to do all the work in half the time."

In referring to "this heat," Benziger is citing the predictions of Dennis Klocek, a climatologist who (according to his Web site) "interfaces daily weather data from the National Weather Service into a geometrical system" to make detailed forecasts. "It looks like it might whipsaw us around a bit between hot, cold, and medium in May," says Benziger.

"The time to keep an eye on this year is between the middle of May and the middle of June," says York. "If we get funky weather on a bad potential crop, we'll have an even lower crop."

"May is a more critical month than a lot of people have realized in the past," Benziger tells me. "Two harvests are on the table in May. Moisture conditions this year are really going to amp up the prospects for disease and pests—the vines are gonna be so vigorous, they're gonna have a lot of that rank growth that's delicate and susceptible."

"Our vines won't do that," York says, "but other people's vines will."

"Ours will be on the edge of it," says Benziger, "but we don't have a history of building up heavy fertilities in our soils—if anything, ours are underamped. We want to be able to flip the switch ourselves, through irrigation or cultivation practices."

There follows a highly technical discussion of how sunlight and rainfall conditions affect grape size—with surprising implications for wine quality. "In 2005 we had moist conditions," Benziger explains, "which gave us more cells, which gave us bigger berries and higher yields than in past years"—all factors traditionally associated with lesser quality. "But," he goes on, "it turned out to produce better integrated tannins, of higher quality—at least on this ranch—than '04 and '03, when we had extremely dry conditions, smaller berries, and more concentrated—but more bitter—tannins. In those years, we had to be very careful during fermentation, and pull the wines [off the skins] earlier. In 2005 we could go with much longer fermentations and get all the flavors we wanted out of [the grapes], instead of having to abbreviate them because we were already peaking in the tannin profiles. The '03 and '04 wines were ripe and unbalanced, meaning that the indicators—flavor development, pH, acid, and so on—were not as tightly joined as in '05."

This outcome—better flavor through bigger grapes and higher yields, owing to excess moisture—contradicts the conventional wisdom, as well as the dictum that in California "every year is a vintage year." "It's a double-edged sword, because the critics are starting to seize on that now," says Benziger. "As we get more and more wine in the wine business, and people have more choice globally, they can start stepping over vintages [from any given country in any given year]. In the U.S., we've never made price concessions on a given vintage, but other places like Bordeaux have, with futures and so forth. So now a lot of the things we used to take for granted—like stressed grapes, smaller berries, low yields, and the idea that heat lowers acid—are being questioned."

"This is not very well understood in California," says York. "It's amazing how few people really grasp the specifics of the climate we have and how it relates to wine quality."

Returning to the current season, Benziger asks: "What do we want to do about horn manure? And what do we do about silica, as we start to really wait on growth?"

"I don't think we're gonna do that until about ten days before flowering," York says. "Sunny Slope was done last week, but here, we're gonna be well into May." The Sunny Slope vineyard is located alongside Benziger's Imagery Estate property, on the east (that is, west-facing) side of Sonoma Valley. "That's a lot easier place to make cabernet than this place," Benziger says.

"You wouldn't *believe* how much warmer it is," says York. "It's normally about two weeks ahead of here."

"The soils are better drained, but this place has much more variation, so the potential for complexity here is a lot higher," says Benziger. "Over there, the potential for high quality is more consistent. Variation here can spike up to the best quality in the world, but we're on the edge of what it takes to really ripen cabernet. The biggest variable factor is heat—Patrick Campbell at Laurel Glen is even cooler than us, and he's always got a cedary, more structure-driven kind of cabernet. Then you have our property; then Jack London Vineyard [vinified by Kenwood]. Those three wines show a pretty good spectrum of the terroir."

Recently both Benziger and I attended a conference on terroir at UC Davis, where one of the presenters had been Randall Grahm speaking about "The Phenomenology of Terroir." Before a large international audience of wine professionals, Grahm had shown slides of sensitive crystallizations, saying, among other things, that they facilitate "the glimpsing of a wine's aura." During the talk, I happened to be sitting next to the Ridge winemaker Paul Draper, who found it so hilarious that I thought I might have to shush him.

"I thought Randall was trying for a shock factor," Benziger says now. "He talked about a lot of points that we always talk about, but he took it to the next level. He put a clever twist on some stuff and he made some great analogies, like the need to have the plant and the soil talk the same language.

"I'm sure Randall wakes up in the morning and tries to figure out what he likes to do better," Benziger says. "I think he likes to write better than he likes to make wine. In wine, minerality is what drives him—that's his madness. I think he's got it right if you look at it as being kind of like a radio crystal—a substance that gives wine the ability to hold information from another place."

Speaking of which, Benziger turns back to York. "I want to make this the year of information," he says, handing York a list from his briefcase. "What information do we permanently want to key into, collect throughout the year, collect prior to harvest, and collect *as* we're harvesting, so that we can templatize it, consolidate it, figure out exactly what we want and what we don't want, and do it for all our properties."

York goes down the list. "We have that," he says. "We can do that." In passing, he refers to a couple of calculations called the "heat stress index" and "temperature variability index."

"Is that the night-and-day difference?" Benziger asks.

"Yes—if it's seventy at night and a hundred during the day, it would be thirty."

"That would be good to know."

"We don't keep records of sunshine hours," says York, continuing to look over the list. "I'm not so sure that's a critical thing. Same with cloud cover—it's not really relevant to us. And we do cluster weights and berries at the beginning of September. I'd like to be able to compare growth rates on a year-to-year basis."

"It would be good if we could start stacking it and say, 'Why, oh, why are the acids in the wine like this?', then take this slice and follow it through and see how this [weather] data lays up against it. Then eventually start seeing it from the other end, and look at how this data forecasts some of the winemaking attributes in advance. Not that we want to be able to make wine by the numbers, but it would help us with bracketing so I can figure out what my oak purchasing would be, and give me an idea in advance of how I want to manage my fermentations, rather than have the first couple be guinea pigs. Sometimes you have to go through five or six fermentations to figure out where you are with that harvest. But if we can get these trends earlier on, we might be able to make our adjustments before the grapes even come in, and know in advance how long we want the fermentations to be, for heat soaking at the end, cold soaking at the beginning, and so on and so forth."

Benziger is in the process of "reshuffling" his winemaking team. The company has just hired Rodrigo Soto, a young Chilean who has worked with York on organic and biodynamic transitions at Matetic Vineyards in the Rosario Valley. It's also engaged in the task of getting all its grape suppliers—a total of about forty growers—to commit to organic, biodynamic, or sustainable agricultural practices. Cagily called "Farming for Flavors," the program awards points to participants for their level of interest and compliance, as evaluated by a self-effacing third-party agency named Stellar Certification Services, Inc.

"All of our estate properties are Demeter [i.e., biodynamically] certified," Benziger says, "but as we've rolled Tribute out over the years, people have said to me: 'Mike, do you mean to tell me that you're here talking about biodynamics when 99 percent of your portfolio is conventionally produced?' There was a schizophrenic image for the consumer that made me really uncomfortable, so we felt compelled to align everything we did with the same message. That's how we've been redesigning the company for the last two years."

"That's as big as your succession issues," says York.

"We have to have a company to hand to our kids that means something," Benziger concurs. "One that's differentiated from Diageo and Constellation. We're the only family winery of our size left in California, but to be a successful company, you have to have superprofessional people running it. There are no niceties today—you're swimming with the sharks, so I'm putting a detailed succession plan together. It includes things like 'Flaming Hoops': All of our kids have gotta graduate from college, work for another company for three years, and work a part of our business outside of California for three years to increase the profits of the business before they can come back. It's partly to protect the employees that work here, because there's no way that a good person like Rodrigo, or some of the other pros that I have, would work for me if they thought their jobs were on the line because some silver-spoon asshole was gonna be here the next day. They have to see that this is not a parking lot for kids—that the kids coming into the company are an asset, not a liability. But to do that, you also have to step back and delegate. Think of the little tree and the big tree: You have to prune some of the branches on the big tree back so the sun can come in and the little tree can grow. That's the tough part a lot of times, but otherwise the big tree rots and falls over and kills the little tree. In a lot of cases, [other family wineries] weren't as on top of trends in the business as they should have been; maybe they took a little bit of their history for granted. You don't need me to tell you who—it's been in the newspapers."

"The easiest thing is to just sell the company," says York.

"Nobody comes and asks you to sell unless they know you're for sale," says Benziger. "They can tell, and they know we're not for sale because we've already sent out vibrations. We're spurning them. I want to have a force field around me so that if they take one little lick, they die. They're our enemy, but in a way they're our friend too. They're our enemy because they fuck up the distribution system big-time and make it impossible for you to sell wine through the three-tier system because of incentive programs and clout, but they're also creating a huge opportunity for us, because people are beginning to realize there are other opportunities out there.

"Think of it this way," Benziger says. "If you're Southern Wine and Spirits, and Constellation generates, let's say, five hundred million dollars' worth of business for you in California, and Benziger generates only five hundred thousand, and Constellation calls up and says, 'Hey listen, I need all your sales-force guys to work on this for *x* number of days,' what do you do? They don't even ask—they just *tell* you what to do. So we have to be different—we have to get our message across and be a totally different tool in the toolbox. We can't be selling screwdrivers if they've already got a box full of screwdrivers; we have to have a point of difference that's noticeable, and then be able to demonstrate that there's a demand for this different wine in the marketplace, then be active as owners so that communication goes through the sales force to the gatekeepers and the consumers. It does not happen automatically—it takes energy and willpower to do it. Sure, there're a few lucky ones out there that are blessed with wines that sell no matter what they do, but those guys are rare—most of it has to be done with hard work. And if you look at the globalization of wine, we're not just competing against California wineries, like it was twenty years ago—now it's opened up to the world market. In the 1980s, imports went down as low as 13 or 14 percent [of U.S. wine sales], but now it's at least 30—and look at the pricing pressure they've put on. The good thing about a global market is that it shakes out the people who shouldn't be there, but you have to be a very skilled producer to survive—especially in California, which has one of the highest delivery costs in the world, what with labor, land, environmental mitigations, and the three-tier system.

"That's why you have to have professionals," Benziger concludes, "not just Uncle Joe, Aunt Susie, and Little Johnny anymore. So how do you determine how to bring in the *right* family members to continue the company's success without pissing off your really good employees? In the old days, primogeniture was what happened—the oldest got it all, and everybody else worked for them. That's the way it worked in Bordeaux. But in Burgundy it was the opposite, which is why Burgundy is chopped up into all these little pieces. If you have a stockholder situation, it's cut-and-dried—it's pretty much all determined by corporate law. But this is where family businesses crash and burn."

The local precedent for Benziger's concerns—the event that he had earlier described as "one of the scariest things" that had ever happened to him—was the sale of Fetzer Vineyards by the company's eleven sibling co-owners. Since 1992, when this occurred, several of the Fetzers had (after the noncompete clause of their sale agreement expired) started their own wineries, mostly in Mendocino County. John, the eldest, had Saracina; Dan, the youngest, had Jeriko; Patti had Patianna; Bobby (who died in a whitewater rafting accident within weeks of my meeting with York and Benziger) had Masut, a biodynamic vineyard and cattle ranch; and Jim, who had originally enticed York into viticulture, had Ceago Vinegarden in neighboring Lake County.

In 2005, I paid a visit to Ceago with York, Benziger, and the French biodynamic guru Nicolas Joly, who was passing through Northern California on his way from France to Australia. I had previously met Joly during one of his Return to Terroir/Renaissance des Appellations events—showcases of organic and biodynamic wines, with the loquacious French crusader serving as inspiration and impresario. The day before the New York tasting, I spent two hours with Joly at a Midtown Starbucks getting a dose of his passion and charisma.

A square-framed, good-humored, bespectacled guy in a blue button-down shirt and Birkenstocks (conveying the countercultural ex-corporate banker that he is), Joly told me that, after getting an MBA from Columbia in the late 1960s, he'd done military service in Quebec and then traveled through South America on foot, living on a dollar a day. He'd returned to work in Manhattan for Morgan Guaranty, but while banking taught him "the language of economics, which is necessary today, it didn't fit my deep aspirations. It was not my life—not the resonance I was looking for. So, in my free time, I went to the library to learn to make goat cheese. I would leave New York on Friday night in my old station wagon for the Adirondacks, then walk two hours with a tent by the full moon, watching nature. In the U.S., there is a fabulous richness of space—in France, the only place you have space is sailing on the sea."

In 1977 Joly decided to retake the reins of his family's estate: Coulée de Serrant, which, having been planted in the twelfth century by Cistercian monks, was being benignly tended from afar by his aging mother. Initially accepting the advice of his local agricultural adviser, Joly began applying pesticides and fertilizers, which enabled him to make more money by reducing his workload; after two years, however, he noticed that not only did the vineyard have fewer bugs, but the soil had also changed color. "I had the feeling I was destroying my place. You don't think about the system of life when it's all around you; you think it will always be there. But chemicals cut the vine off from life forces, and without the assistance of microbial organisms, no root can feed itself on the soil. After weed killers, you need chemical fertilizers, which have salt, so then you need to force water into the vine, and it begins to lose its resistance to disease. It's a fabulous marketing trick to get farmers stuck in this system."

During this period, Joly chanced across a book about biodynamics in a market in Paris. At the time, France had only three winegrowers subscribing to the practice, but Joly was inspired by Steiner's effort "to bridge the gap between the quantitative visible world accessible to our senses and a qualitative, more subtle world which is the source of life." He experimented with biodynamics on a small section of his vineyard, and as he relates in his book *Wine from Sky to Earth,* "Little by little, I saw nature being reborn. . . . Ladybugs and other insects returned among the vines—but this time, each of us was conscious of their presence. The estate had escaped a very great danger."

Converting the remainder of Coulée de Serrant to biodynamics during the 1980s, Joly "didn't talk about it because I didn't understand what I was doing." He started speaking in 1995, and since then he has become the leading voice of the international movement. A week before our meeting, he told me, he'd been in Italy; a month before that, in Cuba converting a tobacco estate ("The taste of cigars has gotten too heavy because of the chemical influence"); and two months before that, on a rice plantation in Japan consulting for a sake producer ("Rice is a plant that is strongly influenced by moon forces"). He asked reimbursement only for his travel expenses, the better to give people "a process of thinking whereby they can discover the originality of where they are." Cheese, oysters, and vegetables, he said, are all capable of expressing terroir. Reblochon from the Alps, however, is an example of a cheese that—despite enjoying AOC status—had "lost its taste" because the cows eat imported hay. "The ham of Parma is processed in Parma, but the pigs are raised in China. To this I'm saying no."

Joly explained that "each country has originality in terms of heat, light, liquid, and earth—wherever you are, those four elements work differently. An appellation is like a form of dress: In Bolivia they dress one way; in France they dress another way. If you put two painters in a landscape, you'll get two different paintings—and each *cépage** also catches the geography in its own way. Vines do this through two things: the roots and soil; and the leaves and climate. But weed killers destroy microorganisms, so the roots can't establish themselves—it's like a painter who has no arms or hands. It used to be that chemicals stayed on the outside of a plant so you could wash them off, but now scientists have developed systemic poisons. Sap is related to the sun through chlorophyll, so chemicals are like putting dirt on a window. The taste of wine, and its aging capacity, are all related to the sun—if you interfere in that relationship, an appellation can't express itself."

I found that Joly could go on indefinitely until I interrupted him to change the subject, at which point he would agree to shift gears and then go on indefinitely again. (This is not a complaint; the only people journalists dislike are those who don't talk *enough*.) Among the topics he addressed at Starbucks were homeopathy, physical matter, and electronic frequencies, all of which are, of course, related. "When people laugh about homeopathy, I ask them if they have a cell phone. When you call Japan, how much matter are you using? Homeopathy definitely has an effect on plants; when you take energy out of the jail that is matter, they grow bigger with weaker solutions. Cartesians say the less matter, the less effect, but energetic people say the opposite. Life can act on a physical level or on an energetic level; when matter is too hard, life cannot stay—it moves toward a more archetypal level. We die physically, but not energetically—death doesn't exist except on the physical level. If an animal dies, the beauty of its shape and matter

* Grape variety.

280

will fall apart—where are the forces that have been making bones or hair? Could we use them in a more intelligent way? Dr. Benveniste's article about the memory of water was ridiculed, but he said that everything that's alive has a frequency—you can put it on a CD, send it all over the world, and it has the same effect. He says we can register the frequency of Roundup° and use it without the chemical. But it would be dangerous to use the frequencies of poisons. We've already been polluting at the physical level; could we start polluting at the energetic level? *Biodynamie* is bringing people to an understanding of the energetic world, so we have a duty to look more closely at how magnetic frequencies are affecting life. But if you use them without consciousness, you could be opening a very serious situation."

If, as Alan York had told me, the director of the Santa Barbara Botanical Garden had cut Alan Chadwick off in 1968 because he was "too outside," I wondered what he would do with Nicolas Joly in 2010.

I arrived at Ceago Vinegarden before Joly, York, and Benziger did, so Jim Fetzer took a few minutes to show me around. A handsome, square-jawed, compactly built guy with blue eyes and a full head of white hair (not unlike York's), he had been the original instigator behind Fetzer Vineyards' move toward sustainability in the 1980s—the family member who recruited organic farmer Michael Maltas to create a five-acre biointensive garden, which Brown-Forman maintained as a tourist attraction after it bought the company.† "That's a guy who really knows how to make money," York told me of Fetzer, whose new brainchild in Lake County was a 163-acre, $150 million biodynamic agricultural spa on the northern shore of Clear Lake—according to Fetzer, the oldest natural lake in North America, and in fact a century-old resort location sometimes called the Bass Capital of the West. As that title might indicate, the character of local tourism has historically tended toward the RV and bait-shop variety, but Ceago was taking things to a different level with its winery, vineyard, tasting room, olive groves, fig trees, lavender garden, sheep ranch, restaurant, villas, condominiums, hotel,

° A commonly used herbicide.

† Brown-Forman sold the property in 2010.

health spa, and boat dock, all built on a former walnut ranch and endorsed by the Sierra Club as a model of sustainable development. The idea was to create a resort that would show people how their food was grown, and a consequent agricultural exemption had enabled Fetzer to begin construction without a building permit. "This county's great," he enthused when the other visitors arrived.

"It's one of the good old counties," Benziger affirmed. "They want development."

"They want to work with me," Fetzer agreed. "I have unlimited water rights grandfathered in from the lake. There's a lot of algae and mercury, but the fish are low in mercury—I guess heavy metal sinks to the bottom."

Fetzer escorted us inside the compound, into an open-air banquet room with a wood-chip floor and enormous hearth stoked with a roaring fire. He said the adobelike walls of the building were made of Rastra, an insulating, nonflammable mix of cement and recycled foam. (Not all the wood was recycled, however—that would have been twice as expensive.) A skilled heavy-equipment operator, Fetzer had done much of the construction himself, just as he had at his family's first winery and later at McNab Ranch. "If I didn't do this, what would I do?" he wondered aloud.

"In France, they say that to know yourself you have to write a book and build a house," said Joly. "Your house is the clothing of your life. Each house shape has a wavelength or frequency. My house is old, so it feels the past—there have been 874 crops of vines there since monks built it in AD 1130, and I'm sure the monks are still there. From that point of view, the past is useful. We think we're very important, but we're just bringing a wheelbarrow of dirt to something that's already a very big hill."

Lunch, served in the open-air banquet room, featured Ceago wines and biodynamically raised lamb. Passing around a pitcher of water, Fetzer said it came from a well, not from the lake. "Tap water is the single biggest cause of cancer and death," he added.

"The water we drink is so sterile, the immune system doesn't get challenged," said Benziger. "That's the reason there are so many allergies and autoimmune diseases."

Joly said that the best water in France comes from the Massif Central. "Vichy is a drama," he added.

Soon we were joined by the Ceago winemaker, Javier Tapia Meza. Upon tasting the winery's sauvignon blanc, Joly asked him why it was sweet. At the risk of disclosing a trade secret, Meza said, "I let it [the fermentation] stop."

"Let it?" Joly asked. "Or stopped it?"

"Stopped it."

"How?"

"With the temperature."

"And then you filter?"

"Yes."

"You are destroying the wine."

I looked around at the group, which constituted the inner circle of Joly's U.S. following—those who carry the biodynamic wine banner most proudly and publicly. Having made a commercial killing in the American way—via the mass market and megaproduction—Fetzer and Benziger had since reinvented their companies to reflect an inarguably Earth-friendly ethos; but even though Benziger included filtering among the eraserlike influences that "wipe out the fingerprints" of the land, he and Fetzer were (unlike their European mentor) still fighting for survival in the dog-eat-dog world of critical acceptance and consumer preference. Like it or not, as New World winemakers, they were bringing a wheelbarrow of dirt to another wheelbarrow of dirt.

"Making wine for the consumer is the opposite of the AOC," Joly went on. "Real beauty doesn't need cosmetics. The more you screw nature in the farming, the more you have to work it out in the cellar."

"You have to filter to stop ML," Benziger said in defense of Meza.

"Add one gram of a sulfur a week," Joly suggested.

"That works until you put the cork in the bottle," said Benziger.

"You cannot strip the character of the wine!"

"Well," Benziger insisted, "if you do it carefully—"

Joly didn't wait to hear the rest. "If I carefully kick your ass," he told his American acolytes, "I am still kicking your ass."

S OON AFTER THE turn of the twentieth century, Randall Grahm's tightrope act on the edge of propriety met with an unamused response from, shall we say, inside the box. In 2001, the Cardinal Zin brand was banned by Ohio's Alcohol Beverage Control board, whose labeling code forbade any "advertisement or representation portraying pictures of . . . children [or] religious subjects"—thus disqualifying, it seemed, the priest on a bottle of Bonny Doon zinfandel. In response, the artist Ralph Steadman wrote:

> Just what is it that liquor regulators are there to regulate? Do they not know that the Catholic Church has claws? That they are also guilty of gross hypocrisy and blasphemous misconduct in the name of all that is sacred? They drip with obscene opulence while two-thirds of their followers worldwide live in poverty, and worse, must provide the world with as many children as they can manage to swell the ranks of Catholics everywhere. . . . Spoilsports never give up in their quest to deaden the human spirit. To quote Nietzsche: I can only believe in a God who can dance. Well, cheers to that! If God is watching he is also laughing at those who peddle their piety like a blunt weapon. He may also feel sad that his creation of a thinking man turns out to be such a miserable experiment.

Closer to home, Grahm's old suitcase-clone program also came back to bite him. Since she told the tale so well on her Web site in

December 2001, I yield to the British wine writer Jancis Robinson, master of wine:

One day in the 1980s Randall Grahm, California *cépagiste* and the most quotable man in the world of wine, came back to his Bonny Doon winery from a trip to the southern Rhône Valley, opened his suitcase and found some vine cuttings in it, as some determined, but arguably antisocial, growers of difficult-to-obtain grape varieties are wont to do wherever plant quarantines are in force. He believed these cuttings to be Roussanne, planted them at Bonny Doon in the Santa Cruz Mountains and blended the result with some Marsanne (that had gone through the official California vine source program at Davis) to produce a quite delicious, scented, full-bodied white wine he called Le Sophiste.

In 1994 these Roussanne vines succumbed to the dreaded Pierce's disease (now apparently moving inexorably north through California's vineyards with potentially catastrophic consequences). Grahm took cuttings and planted them in the Chequera vineyard in Paso Robles. The wine they produced was not so exciting here and was labelled simply Bonny Doon Roussanne.

Rich Kunde of Sonoma Grapevines, one of California's most important vine nurseries (and an extremely useful early barometer of varietal fashion), had also acquired some cuttings from Randall Grahm's original Roussanne vineyards. Grahm says he gave them to Kunde in exchange for some other plant material. Since Grahm is a tireless searcher after varietal novelty, the only guy to take California Malvasia Bianca seriously for example, this seems highly likely. Grahm also claims he specifically asked Kunde not to propagate these cuttings, presumably so as to avoid awkward questions about their provenance.

Whatever the true circumstances of the transfer of plant material from Bonny Doon to Sonoma Grapevines, Kunde nurtured and multiplied the cuttings and sold them on to various growers all over California. One of them was Chuck Wagner Jr. of the famous Caymus Vineyards in the Napa Valley, who in 1994 bought thousands of them for his Mer Soleil white wine vineyard in Monterey.

Wagner is a friend of John Alban of Alban Vineyards in Edna Valley, who made his name by planting vines by the name of Viognier, then almost unheard of in the state, in the late 1980s (although Joseph Phelps was the original California pioneer). On a visit to the Monterey vineyard in 1998 Alban took a look at Chuck's young Roussanne vines and told him, them's not Roussanne, they're Viognier.

It was at this point that all hell, or rather farce, broke loose. Wagner sued Sonoma Grapevines for millions of dollars in view of his supposed future lost earnings of the high-end wine he planned to make with the Roussanne. Meetings with lawyers took place and expensively extended themselves and the result is that now Kunde is suing Grahm.

The great joke here is that approximately one wine drinker in several hundred, if not thousands, could describe the characteristics of Roussanne. If anything, Viognier is a far better known and more glamorous variety which, I would have thought, could be sold at a higher price than Roussanne. . . . Other California growers who bought the mislabelled Roussanne from Kunde are more relaxed, and will simply rename future vintages of the wine, presumably including the one that won local "best of class" in the California State Fair.

Kunde eventually settled with Wagner, apologized to Grahm, and—having also gotten entangled in a lawsuit about an infamous "black goo" fungus that afflicted California vineyards in the late 1990s*—sold his company. Wagner proceeded to loose his lawyers upon Grahm, who was subsequently threatened with another suit by his own insurance company if he didn't settle, which he consequently did. Robinson, citing other examples of mislabeled grapes and wines, concluded that "more than anything, they should serve to remind us that it is what's in the bottle that's important, not what's on the label.

---

* "These organisms have been around from day one," Kunde told *Wine Business Monthly*. "The difference is we have doctors and lawyers planting vineyards today."

Though perhaps we should all have smelt a rat when Grahm labeled that original wine Sophiste: 'one who reasons with clever but fallacious arguments.'"

As it happened, within a few months Robinson would team up with Grahm on one of his most notable PR stunts. Owing to his exasperation with conventional wine closures—specifically their susceptibility to "cork taint," the moldy-basement smell conferred by the chemical TCA (short for 2,4,6-trichloroanisole)—Grahm had begun using Stelvin screw caps on Bonny Doon wines, a risky move in a tradition-laden industry that associates corks with quality and screw tops with jugs. As Grahm would write, "We had to create acceptance for this technology, or we were quite literally screwed." Hence, he and Locke devised the idea of a lavish Funeral for the Cork to be staged in New York's Grand Central Station, complete with a cork sculpture of a corpse in a coffin (RIP "Monsieur Thierry Bouchon") delivered by hearse, accompanied by a dirge, and eulogized by Robinson. It was augmented by a dinner inspired by Joris-Karl Huysmans's 1884 novel *A Rebours* (sometimes translated "Against Nature")—a work that, Grahm opined at the event, "is amazingly funny and creepy at the same time," addressing as it did "the perils of an extremely jaded sensibility, of connoisseurship taken to its ultimate extreme." At one point in the story, the narrator, having become temporarily impotent, invites his friends to a funereal dinner in which all the courses are black; *et voilà*, Grahm's New York repast included black mustard-scented uni, miso-glazed black cod, black mole-roasted venison, a salad of "dark and bitter greens," and chocolate tortoise. The food was supplemented by two vintages of Le Sophiste, eight of Old Telegram, and seventeen of Le Cigare Volant, some with black ribbons tied around their necks indicating that they were the last bottles of their vintage.

This event, which was conceived mainly to attract media attention, succeeded in the extreme. "The wine press has been truly captivated by this development," Grahm reported in his fall 2002 newsletter (acknowledging that he had "personally fanned the flames whenever possible by describing the cork industry as a 'dinosaur with 3½ feet in the tar pit,' which tends to wind writers up"). Thus encouraged, he followed up in January 2004 with *Born to Rhone,* a four-hour rock opera accompanied by a six-course meal, all staged in a circus tent by the Teatro ZinZanni company on San Francisco's Embarcadero at a cost of $200,000. Featuring a team of high-wire acrobats, a contortionist, a juggler spinning fluorescent hoops, a naked white-painted woman, and green-painted servers sporting antennae, the plot revisited young Don Quijones, now portrayed as a Beverly Hills–reared orphan and "international *terroiriste*" who, after escaping from Soledad Correctional Training Facility, is abducted by aliens in Napa Valley on a flying cigar. The production's thirty-two "highly barbed, anti-Napa, anti-establishment, pro-Rhone varietal" (in the estimation of the *San Francisco Chronicle*) songs, all of which mimicked the music and lyrics of classic rock standards, included "Big House Rock," "Little Soucoupe (You Don't Know What I Got)," "Monster Grenache," "Roussanne," "That Old-Time Pomerol," and "Why Don't We Do It in the Rhone?" The overall thrust was expressed in "Leader of the Pac Rim":

> Wine critics were always putting him down (down, down)
> They said his tannins weren't sufficiently round
> (Whatcha mean when you say that his tannins weren't round?)
> They told me his market research was bad
> And were sure that Stelvins were only a fad
> That's why I fell for the Leader of the Pac (rim, rim).

Grahm has since said that the Bonny Doon marketing mania of this era represented "the playing out of an obsessive itch for recognition and approbation (especially in light of the tepid reviews Parker and the *Spectator* were giving us at the time)." As he wrote in his spring 2001 newsletter, "It seems that I have most likely (and most unfortunately) burned all bridges with Mr. Parker." Then, in an oddly penitential moment, he lamented, "This puerile attitude—I can do it myself, I don't need any help, thank you very much—is not one that I can continue to indulge if the business is to continue to prosper."

The same newsletter, however, contained the following bulletin:

We were recently informed by the *Wine Spectator* in a tear-stained epistle that we were not being invited to participate in the 2001 New York Wine Experience, despite our attendance for the last 12 seasons. It seems that their selection policy had recently changed in the direction of more rigorous reliance on numerical ratings and our wines had in the last year failed to match the stratospheric, rarefied altitude of some of our high-flying colleagues. Our Department of Sales Prevention and Anti-Marketing leaped immediately into action and generated the following missive. . . .

There followed a bureaucratic form letter requesting that the magazine reconsider its decision, including fill-in-the-blank spaces for the date, name of the publisher, and publication being addressed. If this didn't succeed in getting the point across, Grahm followed it up a year later with "A Perfect Day for Barberafish," a parody of the J. D. Salinger story in which, in this instance, the subject's mother laments her son's earlier remark that he'd "rather have a frontal lobotomy than a Laube in front of me.

"If he wants people to start thinking about Cigare Volant as a *serious* wine again, he might just think about *that* the next time he makes a comment about Mr. Parker's girth," the suicidal vintner's mom goes on to note. A year later, however, came *The National Vinquirer*, Grahm's twenty-four-page parody of supermarket tabloids, containing a story titled "Noted Wine Critic Explodes":

Said Mr. Parker's friend and colleague, Pierre-Antoine Rovani, who was dining with Mr. Parker at the time of his explosion, "Robert was enjoying a very sexy and hedonistic moment in the meal just prior to the unfortunate occurrence. I am definitely planning to include the explosion of Robert in my 'Most Memorable Personal Dining Explosions of 2003.' Offhand, I would give the explosion perhaps a 96. It was great, no, very great, very explosive and continued with a long and sustained finish. Now I don't wish to quibble but I would have liked to have seen perhaps a little more hysteria, screaming and vomiting from the female diners for it to rate a perfect one hundred points. Yes, there was mayhem and screaming, but I really expected just a little bit more from an explosion of that magnitude. However, it would be accurate to report that there were literally gobs of fruit as well as gobs of poor Robert just about everywhere."

The lyrics in "Born to Rhone" were filled with inside jokes about the wine business, tailored to resonate with the attending audience: Bonny Doon wholesalers from around the country, a group whose attention Grahm now needed more than ever to garner. At that point there were 3,500 wineries in the United States (compared with only 1,000 in 1981), but the ever-proliferating number of producers was represented by a shrinking number of distributors—an apparent paradox that *Practical Winery & Vineyard Journal* referred to as "a perfect storm." Since the repeal of Prohibition, alcohol sales in the United States have been conducted through the so-called three-tier system, in which producers are allowed to sell only to wholesalers, who distribute the product to retailers. This framework, which—among many other things—increases the price of the product by mandating the inclusion of a middleman, is further complicated by the fact—also the legacy of Repeal—that each state has its own laws governing sales and distribution. As a result, regional wholesalers have been the channel through which wine flowed throughout the country, with the nominal advantage to wineries that such relatively small distributors could devote a reasonable amount of attention—that is, promotional effort—to the limited number of brands each one handled. By the early 2000s, however, most of these smaller companies had been bought out by bigger ones, reducing the total number of wholesalers by a staggering 90 percent: Where there had been 2,500 distributors (more than twice the number of producers) when Grahm founded Bonny Doon in the 1980s, by the mid-2000s there were 250—one-fourteenth the number of bonded wineries.

The eight-hundred-pound gorilla of this world was Southern Wine & Spirits, which, since its 1968 founding in Miami, had increased its reach to thirty-seven states from coast to coast, employing a workforce of ten thousand. The prime dictum of the consolidated corporate environment is to "move product"—and the easiest products to move, of course, are the most widely known and readily available. Ergo, the wineries that get the most attention from big distributors are the biggest ones. By contrast, small or midsize wineries are pretty much left to fend for themselves, and as time has gone on, more and more such modestly scaled producers, unable to generate enough capital to advance their wares, have been sold to corporations that already own several wineries (as well as beer and spirits producers, which have higher profit margins) and, as a consequence, can streamline costs by consolidating resources. Any such winery's decisions on matters pertaining to style and production are subsequently made at corporate headquarters, where *more* tends to be a synonym for *better*. The prime retail target in this contest isn't the Beverly Hills Wine Merchant or Spago's, but Safeway, Costco, Outback, and the Olive Garden.

Though it appears axiomatic that this world is "competitive," it isn't according to at least one definition associated with that word. "Competitive is when you have a sense of something being better quality," says Roger Boulton of UC Davis, "but competition has been squashed by distribution, because getting on a shelf is more important than having a good product. Market access is controlled by a handful of people, and how you manage and position your business to get on a shelf is very different from how you develop your winery to make the best wine possible."

"The dirty secret about the wine business is that wines are not bought and promoted strictly on how wonderful they are," Grahm elaborated to me one day. "Obviously it's an advantage if a wine tastes good—it's better than tasting bad—but wines are largely promoted by how many marketing dollars are provided throughout the various tiers of distribution. Big companies have a lot of money available to schmear on things like incentives—for example, if a salesmen sells *x* number of palettes, he'll win a TV, or a car, or a trip to Australia. Wineries pay special allowances to wholesalers, which they can pass on to lower customers' prices temporarily, or simply pocket the money to make a bigger profit. Or to incentivize retailers: If this restaurant sells a given number of bottles of this syrah, they get a magnum of something or other.

"In the old days," Grahm went on, "if shop owners liked the wine, they bought it. But now, from the wholesaler to the retailer to restaurateurs, everybody's got their hand out: 'What are you gonna give me?' We're buying allegiances, not earning them. There's an uneasy dynamic tension that exists between suppliers, distributors, and end users—you get suppliers forming alliances with chains, whether it be Costco or somebody else, so that they can exercise maximum pressure on distributors to get them to lower their margins. It's power politics—everybody's trying to grab the money, knowing that they need each other but not wanting to give anyone else any more power than they absolutely need to stay alive.

"It's all become so cynical." Grahm sighed. "It's like we're just playing pretend that we're in the wine business. When big distributors come to visit, they don't even want to taste the wine—they just say, 'No, thanks—let's talk about depletion allowances.' Corporate is not even the word. It's a machine—a widget, numbers and dollars. When I started, I could more or less create my own reality—play by my own rules, design my own game, make the wines I wanted to make, and get people to sell them for me. As a practical matter, I could make the weirdest, funniest oddball wines—French colombard chaptalized with honey, or the crypto–cold duck experiment La Canard Froid—and there would always be some lovely, soulful, passionate distributor somewhere who was willing to humor me. But even just in the last few years, consolidation has changed the rules of the game. Now those distributors don't exist, by and large—they've all been either bought out or put out of business. If I go to a distributor now and propose an unusual wine, they just look at me like: 'Are you kidding? It's an interesting idea, but we could only sell twenty cases. Why bother?' 'But what about the relationship we have? We're partners!' 'No; we wish you luck, but we're not interested—though we'll be happy to buy your Big House, your Cardinal Zin, or your Pac Rim Riesling.' The mindset of large distributors is simply: *Grow.*"

John Locke recalls that whenever Grahm returned from visiting big distribution houses, "We would all be on suicide watch—he was an inch away from ritual seppuku. He thought they were unaesthetic commercial money grubbers who only knew about sell sheets and Parker scores. He had to rely on them for Big House, but the guys who could sell Big House couldn't sell Cigare." This conundrum was compounded by the fact that Grahm "intuited that Cigare wasn't going anywhere—I couldn't get growers to work with me to improve it, and I didn't have money for vineyards and couldn't get it. So I decided to concentrate on less expensive wine like Big House to make money—in my rudimentary grasp of economics, I thought that if I grew the business, it would eventually reach a sweet spot. I didn't understand all the implications of growing a megabrand—that I'd actually have *less* money then. In an environment where brands are predicated on growth—sometimes huge growth—they suck up all the oxygen. Even a rapidly growing brand is a double-edged sword—distributors like to sell them, but then there are pressures to hit sales quotas, so you have to keep feeding it because wholesalers focus on it. It's a vicious circle: The more you sell, the more you sell. And as a brand grows, the product inevitably gets skinnier and skinnier. It's the Hershey bar formula: Just use fewer almonds. And people are only interested in a wine to the extent that it appears to be hot—so much of what we do is the sizzle, which takes a tremendous amount of marketing energy. It wasn't enabling me so much as *disabling* me—I felt like I was on a merry-go-round and couldn't get off. And even then, we still weren't large enough to have clout, or small enough to have *recherche*. We still give a shit about quality, whereas wineries our size and above are generally pretty atrocious."

In the period and market to which Grahm is referring, a pair of elephantine gorillas held sway over the American wine world. One was the notorious Two Buck Chuck, produced by the Bronco Wine Company—the same outfit that, through its distribution arm, run by Joe Franzia, had helped establish Glen Ellen as the cheap wine of choice in the 1980s. Despite or because of successes like that, the Franzias' statewide operation, Classic Wines of California, was eventually beset by competitors like Southern, which, upon gaining a foothold in California, could apply nationwide clout to demand exclusivity from the likes of Glen Ellen and Robert Mondavi. After Classic had built up and surrendered enough clients in this fashion, the Franzias decided to take a different tack.

The boom of the 1990s had a downside, which history could have predicted. Again and again, ever since the 1870s, upturns in the wine business had inspired frenzies of overplanting, which eventually exceeded demand and littered the landscape with vinous corpses. The Franzias, who had been in the California wine business for a hundred years, took advantage of this in the 1990s, buying bankrupt properties at bargain-basement prices in Central Valley. In this way, Bronco soon became the biggest winegrower in the state, controlling more than thirty thousand acres of vines whose juice was funneled into wines that the Franzias distributed themselves, allowing Bronco to keep prices as cheap as the dirt in their vineyards, which would otherwise have been used to grow carrots. The brand names of the bottled products were similarly acquired and repositioned, albeit from more prestigious places—for example, Napa Valley.

One such brand was Charles Shaw, founded in 1974 by an investment banker of the same name. Having studied business at Stanford and done financial work in France, Shaw had fallen in love with Beaujolais and subsequently bought property in St. Helena, in the heart of Napa Valley. Obtaining cuttings of Beaujolais's true gamay grape (California's "gamay beaujolais" is actually a clone of pinot noir, whereas "Napa gamay" is Valdiguie, an inestimable French variety) from Georges Duboeuf, the best-known producer of Beaujolais, Shaw built a Nantucket-style house and turned a hay barn into a winery where his grapes were vinified, true to Beaujolais tradition, by carbonic maceration.* So picturesque was Shaw's setup that it served as a location for *Yes, Giorgio,* the 1982 movie featuring Luciano Pavarotti riding in a hot-air balloon and singing "I Left My Heart in San Francisco."

Unfortunately the dollar was so strong at the time—and the franc so weak—that authentic French Beaujolais could be had in the United

---

* Fermented whole, without crushing, in an environment deprived of oxygen, to emphasize fresh, fruity flavors.

States for a third the price of Shaw's. After he went bankrupt and got divorced, Shaw's house and winery were auctioned off on the Napa courthouse steps for $1.6 million. However, his eponymous, ostensibly worthless brand name remained up for grabs, succumbing to the clutches of Fred Franzia for the sum of $25,000.

Though his brother Joe was considered pushy, Fred was known as the bad boy of the business. Relishing his role as a thorn in the side of the superpremium world, he was fond of proclaiming that no wine was worth more than ten dollars even when sold in a restaurant. He embellished this claim in 1993 with a felony conviction for conspiracy to defraud, admitting to disguising low-grade grapes by scattering the leaves of more expensive ones over the top of a picking bin. Bronco, pleading no contest to misrepresenting about a million gallons of wine in the late 1980s and early 1990s, paid a fine of two and half million dollars; Franzia himself, who was fined $500,000 and ordered to give up the presidency of the company for five years, was still allowed to oversee Bronco finances as the company went on acquiring such place-specific brands as Estrella, ForestVille, Rutherford Vintners, Napa Ridge, and Napa Creek.

A 1986 federal law had prohibited wine brands from promoting the geographic locations on their labels unless 85 percent of the grapes arise from those same appellations. More than a hundred labels, however, were grandfathered in under the old rules—including, as it happened, Rutherford Vintners, Napa Ridge, and Napa Creek. After Franzia acquired them, their wines originated decidedly elsewhere, so they could be made and marketed much more cheaply than those actually grown in Napa, where grapes cost ten times as much.* This inspired the Napa Valley Vintners Association, which had worked long and hard to secure its place at the pinnacle of American winedom, to lobby the state legislature to pass a law forbidding such misleading practices. Citing the 1986 federal law, Franzia challenged its constitutionality in court, asserting that, despite their brand names, the grape sources of his wines were identified elsewhere on their labels. A court

---

* To be fair, Napa Ridge wines had also been made from non-Napa grapes under the company's previous owner, Beringer.

of appeals ruled in Bronco's favor, but in 2004 the California supreme court reversed the decision.[*]

Meanwhile Franzia built a 92,000-square-foot plant at the southern end of Napa County, capable of bottling eighteen million cases of wine per year—twice the total annual production of all other Napa Valley wineries combined.

Although it originally came from Napa, the Charles Shaw brand, whose name contained no geographical associations, probably wouldn't have contributed much to the legal conflagration. Perhaps for that very reason, the contrarian Franzia kept it under wraps until 2002, when he made a deal to sell Charles Shaw wine exclusively through Trader Joe's discount stores, marketing it for the ridiculous price of $1.99 per bottle. Made with full benefit of contemporary technology, the wine—in any of its various varietal forms, from cabernet to chardonnay to sauvignon blanc to merlot—was a poster model for modern enological legerdemain, winning awards and inspiring critics to declare it superior to much more expensive wines (though some critics opined that special bottlings were concocted for competitions). A slew of apocryphal stories sprang up, one holding that the brand consisted of wine dumped on the market by an airline that couldn't use corkscrews after September 11, 2001. The "Two Buck Chuck" moniker was coined in an Internet chat room by a Trader Joe's employee, but when another winery started using the same nickname, Franzia threatened to sue. Thus promoted by word of mouth, Two Buck Chuck was a wine seller's dream, taking off with virtually no advertising and acquiring the aspect of a cult. By 2004 Bronco was selling six million cases of it, which was said to make it the fastest-growing wine brand in American history.

All of this would have been singularly impressive if not for a similar family story that was playing out at the same time. A Sicilian native named Filippo Casella, after spending several years as a prisoner during World War II, had immigrated to Australia in the 1950s. He worked as a farmhand until 1965, when he planted vineyards in New South Wales to grow bulk grapes for big wineries. As Australian wine came

[*] In January 2010, the U.S. Supreme Court declined to hear the case.

up in the world (owing not least to Robert Parker, who liked the ripe, concentrated character of the country's trademark variety, syrah—aka "shiraz"—especially as expressed in the warm Barossa Valley), the Casella family—who had no international contacts, nor experience with bottled wines—developed ambitions to sell wine in America.

Through the Australian Wine Commission, the Casellas connected with W. J. Deutsch & Sons, distributors from White Plains, New York, whose most important client was Georges Duboeuf, the Beaujolais producer who had helped Charles Shaw. With the fading of American enthusiasm for Beaujolais nouveau—the bubble gum–like wine sold within a month of its making as a celebration of each year's new vintage—Deutsch was seeking new import clients, so he agreed to distribute the Casellas' wine in exchange for 50 percent ownership of their brand. The first attempt—Carramar Estate, a premium product introduced in 1999—fell flat, causing Filippo's son John to offer to buy back the inventory and dissolve the distribution partnership. Deutsch just told him to try again.

Casella had developed a theory: Most people didn't like red wine because its tannin and acid make it taste like black tea without any sweetener. Adjusting the latter upward and former downward, Casella defined his goal as a wine that would appeal to 85 percent of potential consumers without offending the other, more sophisticated 15 percent. The resulting product was an ideal wine for the American market: simple, soft, rich, full, fruity, and familiar to palates reared on ketchup and Coca-Cola.

There was still the problem of a name and label. As it turned out, the latter was supplied by one Barbara Harkness, a graphic designer whose marketing company—"Just Add Wine"—was in the business of creating brands. The Casellas' marketing director, John Soutter, met Harkness at the Sydney airport and bought three of her designs on the spot, including one with a hopping marsupial on a black background, suggestive of aboriginal art. The Casellas found the image elegant, understated, and classically Australian, and in searching for possible names to accompany it, they looked up *kangaroo* in a textbook. In a description of the related rock wallaby, they discovered the species's

Latin name, *Petrogale xanthopus,* with its vernacular nickname in brackets—[yellow tail]. To "underscore the wine's lack of pretension," they printed it exactly that way on their label.

If timing is everything, the release of [yellow tail] in the United States coincided with several crucial circumstances. To Jon Fredrikson, the wine-industry analyst who had advised Leo McCloskey about evacuating from the Santa Cruz Mountains, the label's brackets and lowercase type subliminally suggested e-mail. Australian movie stars—Mel Gibson, Nicole Kidman, Russell Crowe, et al.—were in the process of seducing America, so Wine Australia subsidized Casella to invest in bush hats and oilskin jackets for salespeople. Deutsch's $24 million marketing campaign overlapped with the fact that the Australian drinks giant Southcorp had just been acquired by Rosemount, which turned over Southcorp's American distribution to its own wholesalers, leaving scores of regional distributors with gaps in their portfolios. Deutsch made sure that decent margins existed at every tier in the price structure, causing salespeople to take an interest.

Since the Casellas bought most of their grapes from other growers, and the Deutsches had trans-Pacific shipping costs to pay, the bottle price of [yellow tail] was more than twice Two Buck Chuck's: $6.99 per bottle. On the other hand, it could be sold in all kinds of stores other than Trader Joe's. The first American orders for [yellow tail] in 2001 amounted to 60,000 cases. By the end of that year they had increased to 225,000; to 1.2 million in 2002; 4.2 million in 2003; 6.5 million in 2004; 7.5 million in 2005. Midway through this dizzying trajectory, [yellow tail] was already the number one imported brand in the United States, outselling all French wines combined. In 2006 it surpassed Sutter Home as the number one supermarket brand, with its shiraz as the bestselling red. None of this was lost on the competition, which, between 2004 and 2007, introduced more than four hundred new table wine brands into the American market; of those, almost one in five had an animal on the label—a marketing trend known as critter wines.

In a curious way, the [yellow tail]–Two Buck Chuck phenomenon of the early 2000s mirrored what had taken place twenty years earlier with Glen Ellen and Kendall-Jackson. Those two brands—also launched within a year of each other, in late '82 and early '83—had taken off in a way that, for their time, was equally dramatic. Like [yellow tail] and Two Buck Chuck, they also occupied separate niches in the overall price hierarchy—but in 2006, [yellow tail] cost the same as K-J had in 1986, while Two Buck Chuck sold for less than *half* the 1983 price of Glen Ellen. Moreover, this new wave of buying was based much more heavily on red wine than the first one had been in the 1980s, when Proprietor's Reserve white and Vintner's Reserve chardonnay swept the continent. All of this reflected the fact that, since 1990, imports had doubled their U.S. market share from 13.2 to 27 percent. That, in turn, was part of the biggest change of all: For the first time in history, Americans were drinking as much wine as beer.

In that context, a debate arose within the wine establishment. One side lamented that low-price interlopers were damaging the premium market, enticing ignorant, gullible consumers to "trade down" to cheaper plonk. (This faction included the "bunch of whiners" whom Fred Franzia ridiculed in his battles with Napa Valley.) The other side, overjoyed that Americans were drinking more wine than ever before, held that this could only result in positive things for the industry—new converts would inevitably trade up as they grew more familiar with the product, and all boats would rise.

Not surprisingly, Randall Grahm adhered to the whiny point of view. "People who start out reading Grisham don't move on to Joyce," he opined. Nevertheless, as a winery owner who had started out at the same moment as Glen Ellen and K-J—but on a more rarified plane—he now found himself, two decades later, competing with their crass contemporary equivalents. For the former figurehead of the New World Rhone revolution, this was especially galling in the case of [yellow tail], which occupied the same price category as Grahm's Big House brand.

"The Aussies have been waging a hugely successful war for the hearts, minds, palates and wallets of the Anglophonic consumer with their shiraz, so-called," he wrote in a 2002 Bonny Doon newsletter. "They have clearly shown that nurture wins out over nature, at least at the cash register." He went on to provide "a little primer" on antipodean (that is, Australian) shiraz—or "A.S."—versus proper (po-dean) syrah—or "P.S.":

P.S.: Fundamental expression of the wine is elegant, feminine, and stylistically closely aligned with Burgundy.
A.S.: Stylistically inclined with raspberry motor oil.

P.S.: Primary growing area rich in cultural history, dating back to Roman times.
A.S.: Region settled primarily by ex-convict population.

P.S.: Alcohol typically 12.0 to 12.5 percent.
A.S.: Do not open bottle in presence of open flame.

P.S.: Capable of expressing terroir for a French person.
A.S.: Capable of instilling terror in a French person.

P.S.: Often find detectable presence of minerality.
A.S.: Marked by lack of minerality, substituted by palpable presence of big tits, sorry, that would be big chips.

P.S.: The wine celebrates the unique characteristics of the vintage.
A.S.: The wine is palatable every goddamn year.

P.S.: Commercially iffy. Who can pronounce the names of the appellations, much less remember which years are the "good" ones, which ones the dicey ones?
A.S.: Commercially successful. Who can resist charming marsupials and/or brightly colored labels?

"Commercially iffy" was also an apt description of Bonny Doon. By 2006, it ranked as the twenty-seventh-largest winery in the United States, producing 450,000 cases (as compared, for example, with number-four Bronco's twenty million); but as Greg Brady, who arrived in Santa Cruz that year to become Grahm's general man-ager (migrating from Robert Mondavi after that company was sold to

Constellation), told me: "Bonny Doon grew successfully from every angle but one: business profitability. The company created a niche and differentiated itself, and it grew the business, but did it at the lower end. The single-vineyard designates never had big volume—and if you think you want quality, you're sourcing fruit for a different reason. Rejects from DEWN went into Big House, but then Big House took off—and once you're in Costco, they want more volume. The grape sourcing for Big House was higher than for what people wanted to pay [for the wine]—Randall had long-term contracts [with grape growers] that were too pricey, so he wasn't making big margins but still had to invest in a sales force and spend a lot of money to move the brand. He put a lot of dollars behind Big House in terms of depletion allowances, incentives, and end-of-aisle displays but didn't monitor the dollars, so after a while distributors had $44 applied against each case of Cigare. He didn't focus on selling his high-priced wine, so the brand was footballed around at different price points.

"You can't be both big and fine," Brady concluded. "Mondavi showed that: Woodbridge grew, and the high end suffered. You can be both if you're not using the same name, but otherwise the public doesn't know the difference. In the industry, 'Bonny Doon' became crazy labels and middling quality."

"I don't know anybody who's successfully been a boutique and a populist at the same time," Jason Lewis agrees. "Bonny Doon got so large that Randall wasn't a winemaker anymore—he was just a marketing guru. In the beginning, Bonny Doon *was* Randall, but after a while that [association] ceased to exist except for the DEWN connection and this guy who showed up at festivals.

"I had a teacher at UC Santa Cruz who made an analogy between Marx-Lenin-Stalin and Jesus-Peter-Paul," Lewis reflects. "The first guy is the idea man; the second guy is the implementer; and the third guy is the enforcer. Randall never made it to the third stage—he grew into an empire but never really had control of it like Jackson or Franzia. They were more methodical."

Considering the frustration inherent in this state of affairs, it's not surprising that Grahm's crowning literary achievement was born during this period. This was *Da Vino Commedia: The Vinferno* (by "Al Dente Allegory"), an epic three-part parody of Dante's *Divine Comedy*, written in intricately rhyming verse and beginning with the confession:

> Midway through a bonny career I had plied,
> I found myself lost, not in a copse of new wood,
> But rather, I awoke to grasp that I had put a great dream aside.
> The vast portfolio of labels, brands, had once seemed all to the
>   good,
> As one might sire a score of loyal scions, sons,
> Who would see to their old man in his doddering decrepitude.
>
> A career of witty *étiquettage*, bonny mots, and outrageous
>   puns,
> A true love of the biz that I could hardly feign,
> *Après tout*, in sum, it had been a superlative run.
>
> Yet I found myself at dusk midway up a great calcareous
>   mountain,
> When I was seized with angst to my deepest core,
> And the most feverish visions invaded my brain.

There follows a sixty-page tour of the Nine Circles of the vinous Underworld, comprising (in descending order) Limbo (pre-*Spectation*); Espousers of Gracious Living; Winemaking Consultants; Wine Technologists; The Avaricious (Wine Conglomerates); Manufacturers of Colmated Corks, Natural Corks, and Synthetic Cork-Like Closures; The Vine-Olent; Wine Marketers; and Treachery. The narrator's guide, standing in for the poet Virgil, is André Noblet, late cellar master of Domaine de la Romanée-Conti, who provides commentary on the tortures to which each class of sinners is subjected. Wine-country lifestyle enthusiasts, for example, are doomed to circular passage on a never-ending Whine Train, forced to drink domestic chablis while their livers are pecked by screaming eagles. In the Fourth Circle, Clark Smith, condemned to perpetual thirst, is seen whacking the bottom of an upside-down bottle "Which (owing to its stickiness) poured out not a single drop. / Noblet explained, 'It is not wine but a catsup-goo. / Concentrators on earth never knew when to stop.'" Leo McCloskey is also sighted, though a "translator's" footnote observes, "The poet does not specify Leo's punishment; it may be posited that he is permitted to drink but one whine for all eternity, inasmuch as his work on earth conduced to that consequence."

Toward the end, the author reveals:

I then beheld among the *zinners* a most familiar face. . . .
I now observed my own keening self, the paradigm of disgrace.

I'd always imagined that there would be ample, nay, infinite
     time. . . .
Enfin, I was but a mere whinemaker, with a clever product line.

This meditation on mortality sprang from several sources. In 2003, while visiting Carcassonne in southern France, Grahm awoke with a "searing" pain in his neck—the result, a local guide admonished him, of sleeping in a hotel whose beds were pointed in the wrong direction. ("The French are into geomancy," Randall reveals.) Grahm had been plagued by neck stiffness throughout his life, but when the pain persisted after he returned home, he consulted a doctor who told him he had a compressed disc. Heat therapy, stretching, and chiropractic work failed to cure it, so he visited a San Jose neurosurgeon who took an X-ray and MRI that "looked like the World Trade Center after it got hit by the plane." His spine was shown to be infected (a condition known as osteomyelitis, which also afflicted Mickey Mantle's legs), causing it to deteriorate and threatening him with paralysis. The next day Grahm entered surgery, where a piece of his pelvis was fused to his vertebra to replace the missing bone mass.

Other than the geomantic awkwardness, the only reason Grahm could fathom for this problem was the possibility of an unsterile acupuncture needle. ("You're not supposed to get infections in your neck," he points out.) While recovering from the operation, he spent weeks on an IV antibiotic drip and had to wear a halo brace around his head for three months, during which he was clothed in a gown that made him look "like a deranged New Testament prophet." He also turned fifty, which underscored not just the brevity of his life span but also the declining applicability of his enfant terrible status. Finally, there was another new factor that would threaten to make a grown-up of any *Puer aeternus*: The previous year, Grahm had become a father.

This turn of events resulted from something that had eluded Randall for so much of his life: a committed domestic relationship. His accomplice in the enterprise was one Chinshu Huang, a no-nonsense native of Taiwan who had come to the United States to study business and subsequently met Randall on a dating Web site. Their eventual daughter, Amélie, might thus be said to constitute the ultimate DEWN/Pacific Rim product: a semisweet international blend released as a one-time-only offering. Grahm had no plans to subject the project to technological manipulation, however, seeing as how "when you're a parent, what you say and what you do have to be the same."

In 2002 Bonny Doon had begun to farm its Soledad grapes biodynamically—a regimen that, like child rearing, dictated to Grahm that the practitioner be "totally congruent to yourself and your ethics." Considering his documented interest in chi gong, feng shui, and acupuncture, his receptivity to biodynamics wasn't all that surprising, but in light of his checkered history, some observers were skeptical about his commitment. One notably unconvinced onlooker had this to say in an essay titled "Is It Doonsday for U.S. Biodynamics? Randall Grahm's Faustian Deal," anonymously posted on *The Caveman's Wineblog*, a Web site maintained by Bill Zacharkiw, sommelier and wine columnist for the *Montreal Gazette*:

> Twenty-five years in the business and now Grahm is suddenly uber-organic? . . . If you close your eyes you can almost imagine the zany labels his propaganda machine is now developing . . . the self-proclaimed pitchman for Stelvin screw caps is about to screw over the category of biodynamic wines. . . . He is the Madonna of the wine world, riding the crest of a fad. Randall is reinventing himself to satisfy a short-term market gain at the expense of a worldwide movement towards a greater appreciation of Rudolf Steiner's work. . . .

Will Randall, the erring seeker, use his depraved advertising to promote jug wine as biodynamic? Will he willingly trade on the wisdom of biodynamics for short-term market share? If so, he has apparently sold his soul to Mephistopheles. . . . But for right now it's too early to see if this tale has a moralizing end, with eternal damnation for the foolhardy venturer.

Indeed, as he continued to turn out hundreds of thousands of cases of Big House, Cardinal Zin, and Pacific Rim, Grahm was forced to recognize the karmic split that characterized his business, image, and soul. "I have a finite numbers of years to accomplish something, and I don't really want to be remembered as a great marketer or popularizer of screw caps," he told me in 2006. "I want to be spending time in the vineyard, not schlepping stuff in Indiana. I don't want the responsibility for making so much wine—I've risen to my level of mediocrity. I'm in over my head." When I asked what he planned to do about it, he said: "I know exactly where I want to go: small, focused, distinctive, and necessary." He finished by telling me to watch and wait.

Lo and behold, within two months it was announced that Bonny Doon had sold the Big House and Cardinal Zin brands to the Wine Group, slashing production by more than 90 percent, from 450,000 cases to 35,000. This divestiture would reduce the number of wines Grahm made from thirty to about eight, and his staff would be cut in half. He would maintain ownership of Pacific Rim,* but its management would be independent and headquartered in Washington State.

"What's left is Cigare and the grapes we grow at Soledad," Grahm told me in the wake of the sale. "Everything must go. Unless we can grow the grapes ourselves or get them farmed biodynamically, it doesn't work in our program."

* Pacific Rim was later sold, in January 2011.

L EO MCCLOSKEY AND I are meeting a few people for dinner at a trattoria in downtown Sonoma: Mark Lyon, Sam Spencer, and Chris Silva of the St. Francis Winery, which has also been working with Enologix. Notwithstanding the *Spectator*'s recent 75-point score on its merlot, since signing on with McCloskey the winery has received a 92 on its Anthem Meritage blend and 88 on its Sonoma County chardonnay, a thirty-thousand-case wine whose ratings had fallen into the doldrums. "Chris Silva is a former business-litigation attorney," McCloskey tells me. "He wants to know how to formalize quality. He finds that winemakers are gooshy—if they say they're going for terroir, he'll just say: 'What's *that*?' He knows that when something isn't a number, smoke comes into the room and winemakers take advantage of that."

Silva turns out to be a fit-looking fortysomething with a loud voice, brutal handshake, and crisply pressed shirt bearing the St. Francis logo. A fifth-generation Sonoma County native, he married the granddaughter of the winery's founder and (although they've since divorced) is now president and CEO of the company. "People are a lot happier around wine than they are around attorneys," he explains as we sit down.

"I like attorneys," Spencer says. "I don't have any problem with them."

McCloskey pours the evening's first beverage from inside a brown bag—a rich, buttery but well-integrated white that tastes like chardonnay without artificial implants. Turns out that's because it's a white

Burgundy: a $182 Vincent Girardin Chevalier-Montrachet Grand Cru, which got a 95 from critic Stephen Tanzer and a 92 from Enologix. "There's an essential oil that's twice as high in French white Burgundy as it is in California chardonnay," McCloskey reveals.

Next comes a bottle of Bordeaux from Château Palmer, which got a 95 from Parker. Just before it's poured, we're joined by Leo's wife, Susan, bearing a sealed envelope that contains the wine's Enologix Index. Upon tasting the wine, she scrunches up her face. "Ooh," she says. "I don't like it. It's too tannic and bitter."

"It's Style Three," Leo agrees without opening the envelope. "I'm gonna guess 1200 tannin and 182 complex anthocyanin. It's not a 95-point wine—it's an 89- to 90-point wine, with a .48 quality index."

I also get an Old World hint of *Brettanomyces*. When the Enologix chemistry is revealed, the index is .44 with 1283 tannin and 150 complex.

"Parker has a higher tannin threshold than Laube," Lyon observes. "His palate is a bit more Bordeaux-like."

"He has less taste buds than Laube," says Leo. "Laube is more sensitive. But both of them like complex anthocyanin."

"They're both driving the direction toward ripeness," Lyon agrees.

"I have friends on Wall Street who won't buy wines that score under 100 in Parker," says Spencer.

"I know many restaurateurs who feel the same way," says Silva.

"There's a calculus to what makes somebody buy a bottle of wine," says Spencer, "but until you pull the cork, you can't even know whether you agree with Parker."

"It used to be a gold medal at the L.A. or Orange County Fair," says Lyon. "Now people can go on the Internet and do a Web search for a 'Sonoma County chardonnay over 90 points and under twenty dollars.' Until we released our '01 chardonnay, everybody at the winery was nitpicking about it—there was this problem and there was that problem. But after it got 90 points from the *Spectator*, there were no more problems—I was a genius."

This sentiment is bolstered among the participants by the next bottle: Lyon's Sebastiani Secolo Meritage, an oaky blend of cabernet sauvignon, merlot, and malbec from Sonoma and Alexander valleys.

"That's the best wine of the night," McCloskey says upon tasting it. Silva is positively carried away: "Beautiful! Superb! Congratulations!" he gushes. "You are a very talented winemaker."

Silva's contribution is the St. Francis Pagani zinfandel, a 90-point Parker darling and typical contemporary zin. Exploding with hot, syrupy flavors that clamor for attention, it's an apt corollary to a slogan that Silva has printed on the winery's harvest T-shirts: GO BIG OR GO HOME.

After conferring with the restaurant's owner, Leo says it's been proposed that we buy a bottle from the house list. The owner has even offered a suggestion, which arrives in another brown bag. When the wine is poured, however, it smells like seawater.

"I know what this is," Spencer declares after tasting the wine. He thinks it's from a local zinfandel producer that has been widely criticized for selling out to a big corporation, though the winemaker still uses old-fashioned redwood fermenters on some of his high-end wines.

"They put paraffin in them," Spencer reveals. Others pinpoint the flaw as trichloroanisole or TCA—the chemical that commonly plagues corks but has also been found to pervade whole wineries. Lately Laube has been "outing" companies that he identifies as having this problem. "Laube is a TCA posse," says Lyon.

Assuming a constabulary role in Laube's absence, Leo confirms: "This is tank TCA."

It turns out that Spencer was right about the identity of the winemaker, who happens to be one of McCloskey's critics. Therefore, as a control, we order another bottle of the same wine, which turns out to taste fine—as a matter of fact, it's the best-balanced wine we've had so far, neither overly oaky nor flagrantly show-offy, simply a suitable complement to food.

"What you see is what you get." McCloskey shrugs, characterizing the wine as "rustic and natural."

The last bottle is Sebastiani's flagship: the Cherryblock cabernet from a forty-year-old vineyard located inside the Sonoma city limits. At 1012 tannin and 188 complex, it constitutes an Enologix grand slam: Style Four with a .95 index and a 92 in the *Spectator*. This is McCloskey's ideal: sweet, luscious, polished, and suave, less a "wine" in the classic sense than some kind of cosmic comfort beverage (with a correspondingly celestial price).

Basking in the glycerine glow, Silva announces how honored he is to share a table with the present company. "The wine industry is very collegial," he remarks.

"Are you kidding?" Spencer asks. "I find it very competitive."

"It's mean-spirited underneath," says McCloskey.

"There's a lot of grousing and bitching about other people's success," says Spencer. "I don't hear anybody saying, 'Hey, come on in. The water's warm.' Maybe it's my personality, but as soon as people perceive that you're serious, they clam up."

"There are too many winemakers," McCloskey suggests, "and entrepreneurs aren't very collegial. Nobody would expect the heads of Silicon Valley companies to be collegial."

"I like competition," Lyon puts in. "I think Chile and Argentina are going to make us better."

"The consumer has never been in a better position," Silva concurs. "It's awesome—it's rock-and-roll time in the wine industry. The pressure's on like it's never been before."

"I love pressure," McCloskey muses. "I love the hunt."

"There are two kinds of people on a battlefield," says Silva. "The quick and the dead. We'll look back thirty years from now and say, 'What an exciting time!' Wineries are motivated not by passion, but by survival."

"I'm sick of hearing about passion," says Spencer. "People have been bullshitting for so long that it's become a general policy in the industry. Anyone who tells you they haven't used spinning cone is lying through their teeth. If people walked the tightrope they say they walk, they'd cellar one drinkable vintage out of every five.

"Winemakers like to mythologize themselves, but the emperor is buck naked across the board," Spencer concludes. "What's going on now is a healthy flushing of the toilet. It's going to be a drenching current, and all but the truly serious will get washed away."

"Here's my formula for the future," McCloskey reveals as we drive away from the restaurant. "I'm windsurfing or riding my bike, and my employees are here making winemaking better. My goal is to make my customers self-sufficient so that metrics alone can solve all their problems. Ultimately I'll be replaced by customer-management software. I'm now creating a thousand documents that include all my domain knowledge, so customers will be able to log into my Web site, track quality from grapes all the way to bottled wines, and see where value is being added or taken away. The revolution I'd like to be credited for one day is like the modern idea of architecture, where you can design a building on a computer before you build it. The old way is the French wine farm; the new way is mass production. But I'm using information technology to manage the wine farm in a way that formalizes and replicates quality—*that's* the front of the curve."

Revisiting the debate that closed our dinner—"Is the wine industry collegial or cutthroat?"—McCloskey says, "The reason the industry isn't as strong as it could be is that people don't get together and do something for the common good. Other industries don't allow the media to control the money. We need a producer-based ratings system like Pricewaterhouse, Dun and Bradstreet, or J.D. Power. The French equivalent of J.D. Power is the Appellation Contrôlée system. Europeans have been doing numerical quality for years—they have triple-A butter, double-A butter, different grades of beef and lamb. Quality has always been a metric, the purest form of which is dollars.

"In Napa Valley," McCloskey says, "I think many producers will end up doing what they do in Bordeaux. There will be different levels of quality—luxury, premium, ultrapremium, and consumer, similar to first growth, second growth, fifth growth. You'd need five to ten grades to make a region fly, but it would be a money tree. Right now, things are too confusing for the consumer—we should strengthen our appellations so that only certain varietals can be used with those names. In the U.S., we always want to do whatever we want to do, but the French don't. As an ecologist, I can see that some plants work better in some areas—everybody wants hardwoods from tropics, not from the Arctic, but here we have grapes planted in the south that should be in the north and vice versa. We as producers still have a chance to come clean and publish what we know—that this region is number one for this variety, and this one is number one for another variety. We already know what the best regions are. The Stag's Leap area is *not* a first growth of Napa Valley, for example—it isn't a homogeneous enough pocket, so it only produces high-quality wine in itsy-bitsy, tiny little lots. Oakville is number one. Rutherford is number two. It's possible to grade Napa within itself, and also to grade regions against other regions. So admit that Carneros [in far southern Napa and Sonoma Counties, on the shore of San Pablo Bay] is not a great region for cabernet—it's better for pinot noir. But also admit that Carneros is only a second growth of pinot noir—the first is somewhere in western Sonoma, the Russian River, or maybe the Santa Rita Hills near Lompoc. Right now, if somebody said that, they would be sued, because it gets in the way of somebody else's sales shtick. Every American salesperson can say anything he wants, and the American Way is for everybody to say they're number one. But somebody should *want* to be number two—that would be a nice position to be in, like with Hertz and Avis. In Bordeaux, Château Lynch-Bages does fine as a fifth growth. In France, someone who's a fifth growth saying they're a first growth would be sued, *because legally they're not.*"

But how exactly would such a system be established here in the land of the free?

"The government could come up with a model to classify all the appellations based on weighted average price and volume. It could be done in many ways: price times score, or a basket of scores. Or use the state of Massachusetts—they track the scan data of what a product sells for. So, say, if your score lowers to 85, your price would also go down. That would force pressure on stakeholders and critics—if a critic's scrutability is called into question, the government could set up another rating agency."

And just what kind of producer-based PricewaterhouseCoopers, Dun & Bradstreet, J.D. Power and Associates–like wine-rating system might that be? "Why reinvent the wheel? Parker's already got something that the consumer wants. Why doesn't he purchase Enologix? Or put it inside the *Wine Spectator*—that would make it into something between the French appellation system and *Consumer Reports*. It would be trustworthy because it's a hybrid—you could even sell producers software on how to improve their scores. Right now winemakers have no protection, because the system allows wines to be scored subjectively, with a single person doing the tasting. This would eliminate errant scores, and wines would get the ratings they deserve. Eventually we'll have an intelligent system, and I would love to be that company."

McCloskey locks the door to his Mercedes and opens the door to his lab, his mind growing larger all the time.

PERHAPS THE MOST emblematic evidence of Randall Grahm's change of life, after unloading Big House and Cardinal Zin, was the selling of his Porsche Carrera and the return to service of his 1972 Citroën, which had spent much of the previous year in a repair shop. With 300,000 miles on its odometer (Grahm guesses; the display has only five digits), the venerable Gallic vehicle, possessed of directional headlights and hydropneumatic, self-leveling suspension, helped to keep his daily existence in a constant state of uncertainty—intermittently overheating, refusing to start, and leaking hydraulic fluid, thus reconnecting him to the seat-of-the-pants adventurism that characterized his career in the 1980s, when he'd obtained the automobile. All of this, apparently, was forgivable in return for the privilege of driving "the world's coolest car."

More discernible to most Bonny Doon customers was an overhaul of the company's labeling philosophy. Vanished now were the fanciful names and cartoonish images that had fomented a legion of imitators, helping to populate store shelves with such non–Bonny Doon wines as Cleavage Creek, Dogs Bollocks, Fat Bastard, Goats Do Roam, Marilyn Merlot, Screwed, and Suxx. In their place—on Grahm's Ca' del Solo wines, anyway—were still-not-very mainstream photographs of sensitive crystallizations, a marketing stratagem pioneered by Domaine Leflaive in Burgundy. Although the concept was admittedly arcane (and at least one dubious Bonny Doon distributor thought that, more than anything else, the petri dish–shaped image resembled a condom), Grahm considered it worthwhile "even if it just sneaks into the consciousness of the consumer, causing him to ask, 'Is this something I should be thinking about?'"

In any event, the new labels served as a signal that something basic about Bonny Doon had shifted. "The old labels were just too much marketing showmanship," Grahm explained. "Don't get me wrong; I love whimsy. I *adore* whimsy, but it's a fine line, because you also want the labels to be reflective of the winemaking. I don't want them to be ahead of the wine, or a distraction from the wine. I want them to be *referential* to the wine—to be less flashy and to introduce an element of gravitas. Maybe I'm just going through this phase now where I have to put on my quasi-serious hat and don't have to be so clever, but can just be lovely. I'm trying to communicate with the public—to tell them I've grown up, that I'm not fooling around and using weird chemicals and putting words like 'New and Improved' on the label. It's probably 99 percent in my imagination and just goes over everybody's head, but I actually want the product to be new and improved."

Toward that end, the labels also now included a full disclosure of ingredients used in the making of the product in the bottle (as per the suggestion of Nicolas Joly)—for example, "biodynamic grapes, sulfur dioxide, indigenous yeast, bentonite." The new regime foreswore commercial yeasts, organoleptic tannins, artificial color enhancers, gelatins, and enzymes (except for the latter on botrytised dessert wines). "It's sort of like keeping kosher," Grahm said. "You can't really tell the difference, but enzymes lead to the harder stuff—with enzymes go tannins go gelatins." Micro-ox and oak chips, however, were still part of the program. "Untoasted chips impart zero oak character, but you get the benefit of anthocyanin, and it protects the wine from oxidizing. The closest thing I can analogize is if you could turn your stainless steel tank into a wood-sided tank for a short period of time." As for MOX, "If used discreetly, it's very benign—the oxygen relieves stress on the yeasts and helps the wines structurize. It's like arthroscopic surgery: If wine is sitting in a barrel getting reduced, you can splash it around, but you might not get the reactions you want. With micro-ox you can do a measured empirical amount, and if done correctly, it's essentially not much more than a slight exaggeration of naturally occurring process." If this sounds like rationalization, Grahm eventually concurred—within a few years he had abandoned micro-ox too.

The other big goal of the new regime was the hunt for potential vineyard property (aka "Search for a Great Growth in the New World") where Grahm might grow grapes in such a way as to make an "original" wine—"not just another good wine, or pleasing wine, but a wine that the world really needs." The minimum requirements for this were (1) a cool enough climate, but (2) long enough ripening season, with (3) adequate rainfall for dry farming, but (4) not so much as to leach the soil of minerals, especially (5) limestone. The most important criterion was less quantifiable: "mojo"—that is, a sense that "the site really wants grapes," for which the requisite research was "meditation and prayer." In his secret fantasy life, Grahm's ideal was "Ridge fucking Monte Bello"—a vineyard that, he admitted, he wanted to "rape and plunder" (albeit admitting that "that level of envy is not attractive").

Bearing all this in mind, throughout 2007 and 2008 Grahm went on countless Realtor dates. He found a pair of interesting places in the mountains near the town of Bonny Doon but later reported that negotiations had broken down because the owners were in "deep space." He dug some backhoe pits on the northern edge of Santa Cruz just off the Pacific Coast Highway—at a spot where an acre of pinot noir had actually been planted and ripened—but found the soils "not so interesting." Later he reported that "amazingly, in between things, I may, emphasize the *may* . . . may have found an appropriate site in the Santa Cruz Mountains to plant a grenache/syrah vineyard and build a winery," but the conditional language turned out to be well chosen, as nothing was heard of this site again.

A few months later, Grahm visited a property in Paso Robles that had "tons and tons and tons of limestone, nice exposures (southeast), likely adequate rainfall for dry farming, climatically mild during summer and cold winters (good for disease control)." However, the fact that it was in Paso Robles—a place of which he was not overly fond—put him in mind of an old Jewish joke:

"That's a beautiful diamond you have, Madame."

"Thank you—it's the Feinberg Diamond."

"The Feinberg Diamond?"

"Yes—it comes with a curse."

"What kind of curse?"

"Mr. Feinberg."

That February I rendezvoused with Grahm at yet another site— an undeveloped mountainside east of Los Gatos, on the north side of a two-thousand-foot-high ridge that Randall described as "a mirror isomer of Monte Bello." The access route was a one-lane road which, like his avowed object of desire, wound upward through woods, pastures, and open space, eventually depositing me at a cluster of farm buildings patrolled by a pair of terriers and their Appalachian-style owner, who directed me to turn around. I complied and, following the first fork to the top of a tortuously twisting dirt track, eventually spied Grahm, his manager Greg Brady, and a pair of Realtor/sellers, one wearing a dark beard and canvas Ben Davis coat, the other a black fleece vest and coiffed silver hair.

Looking around at the vegetative matrix of oak, bay laurel, manzanita, and madrone, Grahm was in the midst of observing: "Obviously the amount of rainfall here is nontrivial."

"It's about the same as Felton and Ben Lomond [in the Santa Cruz Mountains]," said the guy with the beard. "It's twice what they get in Los Gatos. It's also ten to fifteen degrees cooler in summer than the valley floor, but it's drier—you don't get fog on your windshield."

To go even higher, we piled into a pickup truck, which, after gunning and fishtailing its way another several hundred feet uphill, deposited us at an overlook with a stupendous view, a 180-degree panorama stretching north and east across Silicon Valley and San Jose to the San Francisco Bay. Far below was the original site of Almaden Vineyards.

"I just find this so sexy," Grahm said, looking more at the mountain itself than at the view. "There are so many soil types." The topography, however, was as forbidding as the pedology was alluring. For vines to be planted and cultivated here, the property would not only have to be cleared but terraced—a fearsome financial proposition. Standing on the edge of the vertiginous slope and recalling the site on Empire Grade that turned out to be poisoned with lead, Brady said: "This makes Locatelli look like a piece of cake."

"An architect friend of mine says that the only real building material is money," Grahm mused. Not long thereafter, though, he began to despair at the expense of emulating an Old World–style *vin de terroir* in the New. "The land might not be as expensive, but with labor costs, clearing, planting, trellising, developing water and roads and infrastructure"—a package of tasks that added up to expenditures of $35,000 to $50,000 per acre—"you have to spend almost as much as you would doing it in Burgundy."

Not long afterward, Grahm had T-shirts printed with the adage: IN ORDER TO MAKE GREAT WINE, ONE MUST THROW AWAY THE IDEA OF MAKING A PROFIT.

In April 2008, Grahm sent me an e-mail: "My entire program/life is now up in the air. I am beginning to think that I should expand my search for vineyard land beyond a 50-mile radius of Santa Cruz and perhaps consider the Old World as part of the grid. It does in fact stand to reason that there may well be more appropriate soils and climates in the O.W.—at least for pinot noir." In this context, he acknowledged "numerous implications to simply taking off and relocating to France from the standpoint of current business, current family, etc., so this program does need a little more fleshing out."

Toward that end, Grahm made plans to visit France and Italy that summer. As he went on to explain:

I don't understand—likely never will in this lifetime—why Burgundy expresses pinosity unlike anywhere else in the world. But you just don't (or at least I don't) get anything like it in areas that are relatively close geographically, climatically, geologically—Germany, Austria, Loire, Jura, Alsace, Val d'Aosta, Trento, etc.—so it is obvious that there is something very, very subtle (undoubtedly multifactoral) that happens in Burgundy that doesn't seem to happen anywhere else. It had occurred to me that if I were to consider planting pinot noir outside of Burgundy, rather than focusing primarily on Burgundy and trying to figure out what they do, it might make more sense to try and find a few examples outside of Burgundy that somehow seem to capture pinosity and see what sort of lines of comparison might be drawn with the real deal.

In the midst of this meditation, at the Oliveto restaurant in Oakland, Grahm chanced to taste a pinot from the Roero district of Piemonte that "was damn, damn good and somehow seemed to capture that quality of pinosity that was eluding me in all the other continental examples I had recently tried. . . . I hope to see this guy in early July, poke around and see if there is any more evidence to support my hypothesis."

As it happened, I had a trip to Europe scheduled for the same time—not to Burgundy or Piemonte, but to the Loire Valley, which Grahm also planned to visit. I thus succeeded in rendezvousing with him, his partner, Chinshu, and their five-year-old daughter, Amélie, one afternoon in the town of Mareuil-sur-Cher in Touraine, where we went to visit Clos Roche Blanche.

This small, unassuming estate might be offered as the epitome of what Grahm—American winemakers in general—pine for when they contemplate the Old World. The owner, Catherine Roussel—a friendly, graying woman in jeans and sandals, who had a charming habit of stifling a smile with her hand—had been born on the property, where she represented the fifth generation of her family to reside. First planted to grapes by her great-great grandfather in the nineteenth century, it still produced fewer than three thousand cases of wine per year; mainly known for sauvignon blanc, Roussel and her winemaker-partner Didier Barrouillet also raised chardonnay, gamay, cabernet franc, malbec (known here as cot), and pineau d'aunis (aka chenin noir, a mutation of chenin blanc) on fifty acres around her century-old house. The north wall of the building (which was made of limestone, aka *tuffeaux*) was sculpted with images of grapevines: roots at the bottom, trunks midway up, leaves and fruit bordering the roofline. This seemed consistent with the biodynamic regimen that Roussel and Barrouillet had once practiced, but Catherine said they had since abandoned it, partly because they "didn't want to be part of a movement."

"I respect it," she was quick to add. "Didier and I are interested in nature. But we are agnostic—we don't like churches. Maybe we are too Cartesian—there were too many things we didn't understand."

"We didn't believe it," said the wiry, well-tanned Barrouillet. "It only works if you believe it."

"Like everything in life," Grahm remarked.

We went out to see the vineyards, which were situated on a sloping plateau overgrown with tall grass. Although the property was no longer biodynamic, it was still farmed organically. "I don't know what's natural," Catherine said, "but we could detect traces of pesticides in the wines. So now we have flowers instead—we like big ones for bees and insects." She mentioned a study by Miguel Altieri, an agroecologist from UC Berkeley, that recommended mixed plantings every fifty yards for pest control. "It's the only study of this kind," she said, "and it was done in Napa Valley."

"*Quelle ironie!*" said Grahm.

Higher on the hill were the cot vines, a hundred years old and extremely gnarly. Roussel said yields averaged 1.5 tons per acre—a number that, in California, would be considered financially untenable. Like the house, the underlying soil was limestone—which perhaps led Randall to ask about pinot noir, a variety that is sometimes grown in Touraine. Roussel said she didn't like it. "Didier wanted to plant it, but I said no."

Grahm shook his head in disbelief—to the extent that he was able. He was carrying Amélie on his shoulders and, owing to the organic surroundings, sneezing every thirty seconds. On the way back toward the house, we paused at a limestone cave where Barrouillet made the wine; Roussel said it had taken three laborers several years to excavate it by hand. All the winemaking was now done by gravity: A press was positioned above the cave, through whose roof a hole had been drilled, enabling juice to flow down into the tanks. The walls and ceiling were covered with mold—a common sight in wine caves, though comparing this one to those in Napa was like comparing a '72 Citroën to a late-model Porsche.

Back at the house, we succumbed to the inevitable and tasted a few wines. "*Très particulier,*" Grahm said upon smelling the pineau d'aunis. "Spicy!" The inky malbec, by contrast with the pale pineau, was extremely tannic—a prime candidate for micro-ox, though somehow the subject didn't come up. The sauvignon wines hummed with mineral acidity in both of their in-house incarnations: "Cuvée Number Two" and "Cuvée Number Five." "It's called Number Five because it reminded Didier of Chanel Number Five," Catherine said. This reminded Randall of a story about two prisoners who were locked up for so long that they didn't repeat jokes—only numbers. "One would just say, 'Twenty-six,' and the other would respond, 'You crack me up!'"

As we lingered around the table, Amélie started exploring the floor, crawling around on the rug between the legs of Grahm's chair. "What is my girl doing now?" Randall asked in mock bewilderment, prompting giggles from below. "I have a *crazy* girl." It wasn't exactly invisible that he adored his daughter.

As we got ready to leave, Catherine recommended an organic restaurant in Véretz, on the south bank of the Cher River between Bléré and Tours. Caravaning in two cars (Grahm's was actually a van), we made it to Véretz without mishap but failed to find the restaurant—so, stopping to confer, we agreed to drive back through town, looking for it as far as the city limits.

After I backed up and turned around in an alley, I had to speed up to catch Grahm's van—which, to my surprise, kept on going out of Véretz. Eventually we reentered the previous town, where the van sped ahead through the twisting streets as if Grahm knew them by heart. At every turn I saw the same knife-and-fork sign for a restaurant, leading me to the conclusion that Randall must have remembered another place to eat in Bléré.

Finally the van pulled into what looked like somebody's backyard (albeit with barbecue smoke nearby). Since there was no place for me to park, I simply stopped in the street and waited with the engine running. When the passenger door of the van opened, a man I didn't recognize got out. Where did Randall pick that guy up? I wondered. Then the driver emerged, staring at me as if to ask why the hell I was following him.

Suddenly I felt as if I'd been doused in the face with water. The driver wasn't Grahm—although the van looked a lot like his, it wasn't. Somewhere back in the streets of Véretz, he'd given me the slip.

"You need a drink," Grahm said when I told him what had happened. I finally found him and Chinshu and Amélie at an outdoor restaurant in Véretz next door to the organic one, which was farther west than we'd first looked—and also closed. Randall had reportedly pulled a second U-turn in Véretz as planned, but did it by leaving the main road just before I came by. In other words, his vanishing act hadn't been intentional—but as it turned out, its abortive character had a wider application. Instead of continuing on to Burgundy and Piemonte as originally intended, he was cutting his trip short and returning to California, where Bonny Doon was now "in contract" with the owners of the property in San Juan Bautista.

A month before Grahm's departure for France, the Texas developers had broached a proposal to subdivide the property—still hoping to build houses on part of it but offering to sell 265 acres to Grahm. He and his general manager Greg Brady had subsequently tendered a successful offer of $4 million,[*] which was followed by many months of due diligence, starting with several backhoe pits. Grahm called the results "enormously encouraging," as they exposed sizable pockets of limestone and deep, well-fractured clay "seemingly ideal for dry farming." There remained, however, many questions on other issues, such as water, earthquakes (the San Andreas fault passes directly through San Juan Bautista), and, perhaps most pertinently, finance. Which is to say that the period when this all took place was late 2008, during the worldwide economic collapse that Grahm had taken to calling "the demise of Western civilization."

"The real challenge these days isn't making wine but selling it," he e-mailed me in early 2009. "We will have to be very, very clever in the coming year." Alas, this seemed an indication of how solvent he still wasn't. Although it was widely assumed that, since his big-brand divestiture, Grahm now had enough money to do whatever he wanted, the major goal he had achieved was alleviating $17 million of debt. "We have enough money to do some interesting things, but we're not exactly lighting cigars with fifty-dollar bills," he told me. One of

[*] Deduced through detective work and neither confirmed nor denied by Grahm.

said things was the Cellar Door, a new café next to the Bonny Doon tasting room—the result of not only Randall's longstanding fantasy of owning a restaurant, but also a place where his wines might be "better comprehended," that is, consumed with food. There were also things like severance packages for employees who hadn't survived the downsizing, so when all was said and done, half the price of the new property would still have to be financed by a bank loan, and *all* the money for developing it—clearing, grading, planting, trellising, road development, winery construction (whether with earthquakes or without)—was supposed to come from Bonny Doon profits, of which there were currently few. "With the exception of just a few markets, notably New York and Northern California, there does not appear to be any pulse at all," Grahm said. "Even wines I think are absolutely great are a struggle to sell."

Brady told me, "Coming in, I thought there was a strong business [in the brands that Grahm retained after the sale], but now, after increasing prices and eliminating discounts, I've seen they're not as strong as we'd like—growth hasn't been what any of us thought it would be. Part of it was a lack of understanding about how much those brands were mixed in with Big House. When you have products that are very difficult for people to pronounce the words—well, let's just say that Randall's voice and philosophy and approach are directed at a small subset of the population. He does a very good job of speaking to the people who understand him, but he also needs to speak to the people who don't."

Indeed for most of the contemporary wine-buying public, Bonny Doon's reputation was fuzzy at best. "It's going to take a while to undo the image we established," Grahm acknowledged. "It's almost like we're a start-up now." In a consequent effort to shed light on his operation, he did something previously unthinkable: took out a double-truck advertising spread in the *Wine Spectator*. Admittedly it wasn't your typical ad; an eighteen-panel comic strip titled "Doon to Earth," it portrayed him as a graying, ponytailed pitchman who, after reeling off some of his greatest PR hits (the Lone Ranger cover; the Funeral for the Cork) and presenting a candid chart of Bonny Doon's plunging

Spectator scores, spent most of its verbiage on an earnest explanation of himself and his company. ("We're into some pretty cool, esoteric stuff, as we focus on the holistic health of the vineyard, try to understand the deeper organization of the wine and encourage its fullest expression in our growing and winemaking practices.")

In the commercially pressurized atmosphere, Grahm also admitted to recent nightmares about a certain wine critic in Maryland. For the first time in his life, he went to see a psychic, asking about—among other things—the name Robert Parker. The clairvoyant consultant closed her eyes, thought it over, and reported from the netherworld: "He's angry because you were once vying for the same woman, and you won."

In light of the lack of fiduciary reinforcement, Brady was increasingly dubious about committing to San Juan Bautista. But Grahm, desperate to shed his history as the "boy who cried everything," saw it as his last best chance to create something of value. Considering the proximity of the bell-tower scene in Hitchcock's *Vertigo*—filmed in the town of San Juan Bautista—he was determined "not to look down," and so, on April 7, 2009, he signed on the dotted line, and the next day a thousand goats began removing brush and fertilizing the soil.

A month later, I met Grahm and his biodynamic adviser Philippe Coderey for a seemingly significant ritual: the spring burial of cow horns filled with ground silica, aka Preparation 501. It was a gorgeous spring day—warm, sunny, and cloudless, the hills still glowing in the wake of winter rains. The landscape was actually greener than the Bay Area to the north, an indication of its climatic temperance. As I arrived, a swallow darted by on the breeze and a northern harrier hovered nearby, scanning the ground for prey.

Grahm was late to join us, as the morning had presented him with a rare opportunity: He'd been a guest on the *Oprah Winfrey Show*, connected from Santa Cruz via Skype. The broadcast featured a "group" tasting of Bonny Doon wines, with participants offering comments from hither and yon—Skype CEO Josh Silverman from London, a couple named Cheryl and Don from a Virgin Airlines flight at

35,000 feet, and Grahm from a harshly lit, subterranean-looking location in California. In light of Oprah's commercial clout, in advance of the broadcast, Wally's Wine and Spirits had stocked up on every case of Le Cigare Volant available in L.A., alerted to the opportunity by Randall's mother, Ruthie.

As the segment commenced, Grahm claimed that he used Skype to communicate with distributors around the country, decreasing his need to travel. None of the guests was a hard-core wine buff, so, as the five-minute-long event unfolded, it bore the character of a tutoring session, with Randall peering into the camera and offering pointers on wine tasting, as he might if some of his parents' friends were visiting his winery. When Winfrey noticed him swirling the first wine—the 2008 Ca' del Solo Albariño—in his glass, she said, "I didn't know we swirled whites—only reds."

Randall explained that all wines need oxygen to breathe.

"I always thought those people swirling whites were being pretentious," said Oprah.

"Hardly," said Randall.

"When can we sip?"

Randall directed her to sniff the wine first. "What do you smell?" he asked.

"A little fruity . . . ," she said tentatively. "A little oaky . . ."

Silverman singled out citrus. "Good call," Randall said.

"What's next?" Oprah asked. The answer was Le Cigare Volant Rouge, which the hostess duly swirled, gripping the glass by the bowl and humming free-associatively, "Swirly, whirly, dirdy, birdy . . ." Finally, after sipping, she uttered the word that any producer of anything longs to hear from her mouth. "Love," she said. "Love, love, love."

"Lovely," Randall sighed.

"Don't you like this, Josh?" asked Oprah.

"It's fantastic," Silverman said.

"The third wine is what?"

Randall introduced Le Vol des Anges, a dessert wine whose name means "The Angels' Flight."

"I am not a fan of dessert wines," Oprah divulged.

"You're killing me, Oprah," Randall responded.

"I never make it to that part," said Oprah. "I get stuck in the reds. But this is a lovely one—it's not too sweet."

"Not cloying in any way," Randall rushed to confirm.

"It's very light for a dessert wine," Cheryl said from the plane.

"I'm not a dessert wine fan either," said her companion Don. "But I enjoy it. So I like it."

"See, Josh?" Oprah said. "Another use for Skype we hadn't thought of."

"I'm just excited about a man who gets to drink wine for a living," said Silverman.

By the time he got to San Juan Bautista, Grahm had already deconstructed the episode. Having gotten up early to participate, he worried that he'd looked like "death warmed over," and he was discomfited that Winfrey had rushed him from one wine to the next. He was naturally pleased that she liked the Cigare but annoyed that she'd dissed dessert wines in general by saying she liked his better than others. "That's like saying, 'Normally I don't like Jews, blacks, or Hispanics, but. . . .' It seemed as if everyone was just trying to be polite."

Grahm was wearing a broad-brimmed felt hat and the same long-sleeved brown Bonny Doon T-shirt he'd worn for the TV show. Coderey was wearing a Nike T-shirt that said JUST DO IT. As he and an assistant readied the horns, Grahm and I went on a walking tour, which, in light of the varied topography, amounted to a moderate workout. Randall said he'd recently seen a mountain lion on the property, which seemed to certify the unsullied nature of the place, in addition to manifesting (in his mind) the "great southern leopard" he'd described in the *Vinferno,* even though in the original work it was meant to represent Southern Wine & Spirits.

We came to a stop on a low, northeast-facing knoll that was reportedly underlain with limestone—a prospective location, in other words, for pinot noir. "One of our consultants said that San Juan Bautista is too warm for pinot," Grahm said. "It's not Champagne, that's for sure, but it's cooler and foggier than Calera, and I like Calera. It tastes like pinot. Frankly, I don't know that this is a good spot for pinot, but I planted pinot once thinking it *was* a good spot, and it sucked.

"This is me trying to talk myself into the fact that I'm not going to grow pinot here," Grahm said as we continued uphill, "but I *will* plant pinot—even if it's just one acre. Even if it's just one vine. In the end, this might just be a beautiful piece of property to leave my daughter with a single pinot noir vine on it."

As we climbed, we obtained expansive views of the broad, flat Pacines Valley to the north. "Our geomancer and feng shui consultant was very excited by some things here," Grahm said. "He liked the nearby peaks and, very importantly, it's a portal to the South [end of San Francisco] Bay. He wants us to orient the building north toward Silicon Valley, where the prosperity is. You want to be open to prosperity—or at least I do. I don't know about you."

Pointing uphill toward an open ridge with light-colored soil, Randall said, "Up there in that shaley area is where we'd plant reds. Probably we'd have to irrigate, but maybe not; maybe I'll plant grenache on its own roots and see what happens." The road cut beside us exposed a bank of bare earth, from which the roots of native flora protruded. "I think you could dry farm here," he observed. "See? Those roots are at least six feet long."

Eyeing the soil, he added, "There's an adjacent property here that has adobe clay. The guy built his house from adobe bricks; maybe we could get him to make some vessels from it." This notion was apparently inspired by the wine artisans of northeastern Italy and Slovenia, known for techniques that take "natural" winemaking to extremes. Josko Gravner of Friuli, for example, macerates indigenous grapes like ribolla gialla in clay amphorae buried in the earth, *à la* ancient Greece. "I tasted a 'white' wine from the Veneto the other day that was made from tocai friulani," said Randall. "It was fermented on the skins, aged in amphorae, and bottled with low or no sulfur. It was orange and nutty. I could have said, 'No way,' but I'd rather try and understand it. Like with Gravner: I personally can't stand the wine, but I want to be open to styles and ideas that are outside of my comfort zone—to get inside his head and say, 'Dude, talk to me.'"

As we turned back toward the meeting place, Grahm went on: "At some point growing up, you decide that you're going to be a suit or not a suit—corporate or not, military or not. Gravner is at the funky end of the continuum. The other end of which is proper chardonnay/ sauvignon blanc with cultured yeast, controlled temperature, standard clones—bright and recognizable, like meeting someone in a suit. You can be confident that he isn't going to murder you, as opposed to someone with dreadlocks down his butt. In *that* case, you can say, 'I'm going to try and get to know this person' or not, but to me the interesting wines are the outliers—the ones that behave differently from the others, the ones you don't like or don't know. In David Foster Wallace's essay 'A Supposedly Fun Thing That I'll Never Do Again,' about a luxury cruise, he genuinely tried to understand how other people see things. That's what I wish of Parker—that he would be more empathic. That he could say, 'I don't understand this, but I'm trying.'"

Eventually we reunited with Coderey and followed him to a southwest-facing slope where he'd chosen to bury the horns. The idea was to put them in a place with maximum sun exposure, seeing as how silica (as opposed to manure, which is associated with the earth, gets buried in the fall, and is used to aid fertility) consists of "condensed sunlight" which, after spending six months underground, would be dug up and distributed on vines to promote growth and ripening.

"Only 3 percent of a plant's needs are from the soil," Coderey said. "97 percent is from the sun." Preparation 501, he explained, is used to "transform sunlight into matter."

"I don't know if you can make the case that it transforms energy into matter," said Grahm. "What kind?"

"With a vine, it's the shoots," Coderey said.

"That's carbon."

"It happens through photosynthesis," said Coderey.

"How would a scientist think of it?" asked Grahm.

"I'd rather look at the plants than listen to the experts," Coderey said.

We trudged up the slope and, upon reaching a suitable spot, stopped to dig a hole. Doing the honors, Grahm went at the soil with a pickax, creating a shallow depression in which Coderey arranged a half dozen horns stuffed with milky slurry. Then he covered them over with dirt and marked the spot with a stake.

This seemed momentous indeed—the first celebration of spring, season of rebirth, in the place that represented Grahm's own renewal and hopes for the future. At long last, he was putting his money—and actions—where his mouth was. I asked what he was feeling on this historic occasion.

"I'm still thinking about Oprah," he said.

I F THE GLOBAL wine business is a war, the Great Recession that began in 2007 affected the North American industry in the way that an improvised explosive device affects a rolling Humvee. After seventeen straight years of growth in which the dollar value of U.S. wine sales had tripled, shipments declined in 2009. It wasn't that Americans stopped drinking wine; rather that they drank cheaper wine, tapped into their personal cellars, and went out to eat less often. Restaurant wine sales thus declined, while in-store sales of bottles under $15 rose, and those over $15 fell. Hardest hit (if a downturn in a bottle price of $100 can evoke sympathy) was the luxury sector led by Napa cabernet, which was popularly described as "dead in the water"—another way of saying that collectors who had spent years on cult wineries' waiting lists suddenly received exclusive offers of limited allocations. Meanwhile, Napa real estate values decreased by 15 percent, and grape prices plunged even further, with cabernet fruit selling for $2,000 to $3,000 per ton as opposed to the $3,500 to $5,500 it had previously commanded. As banks became shy, refinancing grew more difficult, and defaults on Napa wine properties quadrupled.

In Sonoma County, Jess Jackson's company—now called Jackson Family Wines, encompassing about three dozen wineries—laid off 170 employees (a fifth of its workforce), although Jackson himself was ranked by *Forbes* as the 397th richest person in the world with a net worth of $1.8 billion. (In a sign of the times, $2.2 billion had made Jackson only number 432 two years earlier.) He was now reported to spend most of his time in Kentucky overseeing his new passion for horseracing, becoming the majority owner of the 2007 Horse of the Year, Curlin—which won the 2007 Preakness Stakes and Breeders' Cup and 2008 Dubai World Cup, helping establish him as the highest-earning Thoroughbred in history—and 2009 Horse of the Year, Rachel Alexandra, the first filly to win the Preakness in eighty-five years, which Jackson planned to breed to Curlin.

Meanwhile, back in Sonoma, Sebastiani was sold for a reported $47.5 million, which was considered a bargain compared with what it might have brought a year earlier. In Sebastopol, Clark Smith sold Vinovation to a Napa company called WineSecrets, avowedly in order to devote himself "to clarifying the marketing of American wines by chronicling the flavor signatures and their natural and human sources for our 310 AVAs"—a task he set about performing for the Web site *Appellation America*. When it went out of business a year later, Smith began writing a monthly column on "Postmodern Winemaking" for *Wines & Vines,* where, among other things, he echoed Leo McCloskey in calling for appellation-based wine marketing in California.

Not every wine company was on the ropes. The seven biggest, led by Constellation and Gallo, increased sales by seven million cases in 2009. Cameron Hughes, the *négociant* who visited Vinovation while I was there, made out—to use the words of David Ramey—like a vulture, reblending and labeling high-end wines that had been dumped on the bulk market and marketing them under anonymous names (for example, "Lot 146") at prices between $12 and $22. Hughes's director of winemaking—a position that involved negotiating with growers and producers not only in California but also in France, Spain, Chile, and New Zealand—was Sam Spencer, who "pared back" his Spencer Roloson brand but continued to employ Enologix in assembling blends for Hughes.

Although McCloskey's customer base came from the sector supposedly suffering the biggest losses, Enologix experienced an upturn in business in 2009—a hint of the urgency at large in the luxury division. In the face of the storm, McCloskey advised his clients to lower prices by 15 percent and "overdeliver" on quality, acknowledging anew that California wines exist in a market economy—a lesson he'd first learned at Felton Empire during the recession of the late 1980s, which caused him to "get off any discussion of my personal view" of what constituted a worthy wine. His customers would have to cut prices considerably more than that, though, to match the $18 that Robert Mondavi (now a Constellation subsidiary) was getting for its 2006 Oakville cabernet, a wine that scored 90+ in the *Spectator* and *Advocate.*

"We're now witnessing the biggest change since the boom began [in the late 1960s]," McCloskey told me in 2009. "Wineries are the last to know what's happening to them, but a series of spokes are coming out, and the future of the small wine industry is at risk. Word is that a third of California wineries are not viable—the fine-wine industry now is big corporations, and large companies are commodifiers. I know the chemistry, and wines today from regions and producers that are known to make crap all of a sudden are big and red and all the same. People might say it's because of Enologix, but it's not me; there's another force, which is being exposed by the recession. When wines reach a state of oversupply and are relatively the same, the only difference is the price."

In monitoring the fortunes of California's two flagship grapes over the previous decade, McCloskey had developed a rule of thumb. "When there are a hunded thousand acres of a variety in the New World, there's commoditization of it. Chardonnay was the first example—in 2001 its market price collapsed and never recovered, and now there's no such thing as flagship chardonnay. Pinot noir still has an elastic price point because it's planted at the lowest volume—there are only twenty or thirty thousand acres. But now cabernet acreage is even larger than chardonnay's, so after the recession is over, I think Napa cabernet will continue to sell for $18. Eventually it will split into two categories: $18 to $22, and $45 to $58."

McCloskey still clung to the belief that cabernet would remain California's claim to fame—but perhaps its only one. "As I look backward, the well-laid plans of my generation haven't panned out," he said. "We made the claim that our wines were stylistically equivalent to Europe's, but Mondavi's 'fumé blanc' thing didn't work out; today New Zealand is the sauvignon blanc leader. And the New World Rhone claim didn't work out; Australia won that. My peers in the seventies were philosophical ideologues, but what happened was that ideas weren't enough. The market has a sense of things now, and it's just going to become keener and keener."

As it happened, McCloskey has a son who had recently graduated from college with an engineering degree. Between working for Northrop Grumman on the F-22 and F-35 joint strike fighters, Alex served what might seem a somewhat contradictory summer apprenticeship at Live Power Farm in Covelo—a direct descendant of Alan Chadwick's gardening gospel crusade, raising biodynamic crops and plowing fields with horses instead of machines. Not coincidentally, Leo read Michael Pollan's *The Omnivore's Dilemma*, which—together with the effects of the recession, corporatization, and commodification—bolstered his belief that the American wine industry should be regulated, as it is in Europe.

"My entrepreneurial nature makes me bridle against rules, but at some point the American approach is not useful in agriculture. In the long term, it would be better to get away from this market economy where your labors are just a function of the price and you're only as good as your last batch of wine. What's missing is protection of the land—we should see our wine regions like we see national parks: Napa Valley as the Yosemite of cabernet. Burgundy and Bordeaux are no longer capitalizing their land—they've been paid for hundreds of years, so there's no speculation or bubble, and people can focus on the hundred- or two-hundred-year job of making quality wine. But in this country we're still entrepreneuring—the American way is to try and finance your entire wine company by consumer dollars *and* make a profit *and* drive a Porsche. [British wine writer] Gerald Asher once told me that this generation was going to spend its entire life capitalizing wine companies that would be owned by their descendants. Finally, after the farm gets paid for, it will be stable, and you'll have a company that survives just by selling wine."

This called to mind that other ex-resident of the Santa Cruz Mountains who (except for the Porsche) was still earnestly engaged in all of the above. Amid the upheaval, Bonny Doon's downsizing continued apace, exceeding even the lean-and-mean framework that Randall Grahm had envisioned postdivestiture. He now compared his company to *Monty Python and the Holy Grail*, in which so many of a knight's limbs are amputated that he's reduced to head-butting his foes. The appendage Grahm was most committed to keeping was the new property in San Juan Bautista; least was the Ca' del Solo vineyard in Soledad, which was duly sold—a turn of events that Grahm said made him "neither glad nor sad. It was losing too much money; we're still hoping to buy the grapes for another couple of years if we can." In the meantime, he dismissed his general manager Greg Brady and winemaker Jillian Johnson, hiring Jason Jardine from Rhys to perform both of those jobs (supplemented by Bonny Doon's former vineyard manager Nicole Walsh, recently returned from a sojourn in New Zealand). Within a few months, however, Jardine was also gone,* his cellar duties assumed by Chantal Forthun, the winery enologist.

Amid this internal chaos, Grahm's public profile seemed to be reascending. In fall of 2009, the University of California Press published *Been Doon So Long: A Randall Grahm Vinthology*, a compilation of his creative output over three decades—mostly writings, poems, and parodies from the company newsletter, but also the lyrics from *Born to Rhone*, an illustrated history of Bonny Doon labels, and "Earnest Speeches and Sober Essays" from more recent years. To plug its publication and his other enterprises, Grahm joined the social-networking site Twitter, which revealed itself as a natural outlet for his restless wit, need for attention, urge to express himself, and potential for distraction. Within months he'd amassed 400,000 followers (and become much harder to get hold of) as he took to posting 140-character bon mots at a rate of a dozen per day, simultaneously acknowledging that such activity "is making us more sociopathic and narcissistic," is "probably more dangerous than masturbation, slightly less than crack cocaine," but on balance is "leading us all to hell in a handbasket." Among his followers was the Bordeaux estate Château Palmer, which he likened to "being followed by the Louvre or Miles Davis."

Meanwhile, in San Juan Bautista, fences were being built, wells drilled, and cover crops planted, though the introduction of grapevines

---

* In 2010, Jardine was named president of Flowers, the highly regarded Sonoma Coast chardonnay and pinot noir producer, after the Huneeus family acquired a managing interest in the company.

was on hold until wine sales increased. Nevertheless, Grahm predictably overflowed with ideas for his new sandbox. On the alluvial flats where the soil was deep, he planned to plant whites, musing that he was "pretty crazy about grenache gris these days" and also "interested in Friulani grapes." Unlike almost every grapevine planted in the world today, these would not be cultivated on trellis but rather traditionally head trained or raised overhead on pergola to increase the humidity of their growing environment. At the property's highest elevations, on top of a ridge that was being cleared of chaparral scrub, he intended to install grenache—the heartiest and most drought-tolerant of Mediterranean varieties, capable of withstanding wind and the dessiccation that results from it.

As for syrah, Grahm said, "While I love it, I'm now thinking that a moisture-constrained site is probably not best for syrah if one is truly serious about trying to match the variety to the site, rather than force the site to conform to what you wish it to be." This was concomitant with his announced desire "to subordinate my own will, ego, fantasy, or desire to make the wine *I* want to make and make the wine the *site* wants to make." Perhaps harking back to his own upbringing, he elaborated, "You might want your child to be a doctor, but if the child plays music all day, maybe it should be a musician. And if this place just wants to make weird-ass dessert wines—or, God forbid, cabernet— so be it." After vexing himself with the implications for Le Cigare Volant—which he hoped to produce as an estate *vin de terroir,* with all the grapes grown on a single property—Randall had had a middle-of-the-night revelation that it didn't *have* to be an homage to Châteauneuf-du-Pape; rather, the wine's composition might evolve in deference to its new source, perhaps as a pan-European blend combining the likes of grenache, tannat, and sagrantino (the latter "a killer grape from the Montefalco appellation in Umbria, said to be the grape highest in polyphenols, though tannat might give it a run for its money").

"People used to say to me, 'God, this wine is just like Châteauneuf-du-Pape!'" he recalled. "I would say, 'Well, that's sort of disappointing—why don't you just go get some real Châteauneuf-du-Pape and save us all a lot of trouble?'" In any case, he still hoped to farm the site without irrigation—maybe even plant the vines on their own roots rather than grafting onto domestic rootstock, theory being that ungrafted vines root more deeply and aggressively for water. This would tempt fate in the form of the phylloxera louse, a risk about which he said, "When you ask the question, you learn more about the person answering than you do about the question. Some say, 'We're all gonna die, we're all gonna die, we're all gonna die'; others say that if you're in a remote site and don't import soil and are careful with your nursery practices, you'll probably go a long way before you get it. The true-believer lunatic fringe would say that you might get it, but if you're biodynamic it won't be a problem."

Would all of this add up to an "original" wine? When it came to that question, Grahm was hatching other schemes that might qualify as his most off-the-wall ever. "I'll tell you the weirdest thing I've been thinking. A guy from the California Native Plant Society approached me the other day in a coffee shop and asked if I'd ever made wine from *Vitis californica* [the indigenous grape of California]. I've made wine from *Vitis lambrusca* [the indigenous species of North America]—isabella, clinton, noah, and ives, which were generally obnoxious as wines but quite interesting as brandies. Maybe I should rustle up some *Vitis californica* and make a garbage canful. A guy in North Dakota makes wine from native grapes; he barrel ages it, and it's actually quite good."

The wildest idea of all, though, was to plant vinifera grapes from seed—a nonstarter practice among vineyardists because, as with human reproduction, it doesn't duplicate a parent precisely. "Instead of identifying desirable qualities and reproducing them, you're scattering the genetic information," Grahm explained. "You're also getting [the DNA of] all the funny aunts and uncles and cousins." As a result, grape growers typically graft a bud or cutting from an existing vine onto a species of phylloxera-resistant rootstock known to possess certain growing characteristics—shy or vigorous, drought-tolerant or thirsty—so as to produce an exact clone of a desired grape which performs predictably. Grahm, however, had developed the notion that more "octaves and resonance" might be attained from the genetic diversity of grapes grown from seed—an idea he'd first conceived to amplify the "harmonic" of the pinot family (noir, blanc, and gris), but had since taken even further. He now proposed to collect the pollen of different varieties that prove felicitous in situ, mix the lot with random emasculated vines from the same property, and plant the seeds that result from these unions, giving birth to entirely new, unnamed grape varieties which, fermented as one, would create a unique product that "tastes like the site itself."

The time frame—and patience—required for such an experiment would be daunting. By itself, the painstaking process of pollen collection would require a pair of tweezers, a magnifying glass, and about an hour per grape cluster; the resulting vines would take years to produce wine, any one example of which "would be lesser than a wine we know, but all together would be greater" (in theory). In the end, the process would amount to a kind of meshuga massal selection* by gusto-Darwinian trial and error. Leaving aside Grahm's track record on long-term experiments, he acknowledged that he "would need to talk to a mathematics person to make sure it's done right," and that the economics of such an enterprise were "beyond ruinous—somewhere between research and sheer folly, so impractical and labor intensive that it would qualify as charity or good works." Nevertheless he felt it contained the potential to make a "real contribution" to New World winegrowing—a synthesis of nature and human ingenuity that could result in a true *vin de terroir*: a wine that, by definition, could not originate anywhere else.

"There he goes, doing something different again," McCloskey said when I told him about Grahm's latest ideas. "The way to be successful is to *do one thing well*." To which Randall responded, "I'm not sure I'm capable of refuting Leo, especially if he who ends up with the most money at the end of the game is right. Certainly, as far as the clock is concerned, I don't have time for too many more major shifts. I've basically got one shot, so I'm hoping that, with my intelligence and will and good fortune, I'll figure it out. At this point, for me, doing it is more important than doing it perfectly. I used to make fun of people who farmed for lifestyle, but I kind of get it now—I think it's a totally

---

* The practice of empirically choosing the best vines from a vineyard to propagate new ones.

reasonable thing to do, as opposed to trying to be perfect, and not deriving any enjoyment out of the world unless it *is* perfect."

In any case, since the Totally New Terroir Wine project would, of economic necessity, occupy a minor role in the new enterprise, there remained the existential dilemma of which traditional grape to plant first. Mulling his options, the erstwhile Burgundian admitted to feeling like the cartoon of a forty-year-old woman who says, *"Oh my god—I forgot to have children!"* "Oh my god," he concurred. "I forgot to make pinot!" While contemplating that seemingly eternal issue, he chanced to witness a genuine oracle on U.S. 101. "I was coming back from Santa Ynez, and my head was spinning: *Rhone or pinot? Rhone or pinot?* And I swear to God, right then a Mercedes convertible passed me on the right with a license plate that said PINOT."

And so it came to pass that, in April 2010, on a northeast-facing slope with limestone subsoil, in a region that, in his heart of hearts, Grahm suspected was probably too warm for pinot noir, he planted, on their own eighteen-inch-long roots, at intervals of two feet by three feet—a "claustrophobic" spacing pattern known as *plantation folle* or crazy planting, an especially apt moniker if you aspire to avoid irrigation in a place that receives no rain during the growing season—the first vines of what he envisioned as his final estate: a half acre of pinot noir.

"It's just something I have to do," Grahm said, and Faust himself probably couldn't have explained it any better.

Acknowledgments

Many people gave generously of their time talking to me for this book. First and foremost, obviously, are Randall Grahm and Leo McCloskey, who allowed me into their worlds and minds without making any attempt to affect the eventual outcome. Such accommodating and unguarded behavior, required for authentic journalism, is increasingly rare in a world of totally orchestrated PR.

Like Randall and Leo, but on a lesser scale, most of the people who indulged me are identified (though some didn't want to be) in the book. Among those who aren't quoted directly, however, are winemakers Michael Havens, Ehren Jordan, Tony Soter, and Dick Ward. Dick's partner at Saintsbury, David Graves, was the person who originally brought it to my attention that 1981 was a "node" when many influential wineries were founded.

Besides my old pal Paul Draper, David Noyes and Carl Djerassi mined their memories about the early days of Ridge Vineyards for me, while wine broker Alexia Moore and sommelier extraordinaire Larry Stone (formerly of Rubicon, more recently of Evening Land) shared their many decades of experience in the California industry. Deep in the background where librarians dwell, Axel Borg of UC Davis and Robert Zerkowitz of the Wine Institute tirelessly fielded my requests for elusive facts and figures. Gladys Horiuchi of Wine Institute also helped with arcane details.

In the literary/journalistic department, Laura Hagar of *North-Bay Biz* and Dean Robinson of the *New York Times Magazine* originally enabled me to examine Enologix in print—a task abetted by my

339

former *East Bay Express* colleagues Gary Rivlin and John Raeside. At the other end of the process, copy editor Shelly Perron contributed valuable fact-checking and tolerated my enthusiasm for em dashes. I'm very grateful to the patient and professional team at HarperCollins, with special thanks to Emily Walters, Kate Whitenight, and Lee Cochran.

Unfortunately, my longtime agent Fred Hill passed away in February 2011. I will always be grateful for his interest, support, and high standards—a tradition ably continued by Fred's partner in the agency, Bonnie Nadel.

Finally, a heroic quartet stands out as an ongoing source of assistance and advice. Two of these individuals, who have been my friends and allies for a quarter of a century, are on the dedication page. Bill Strachan has edited all of my books at four different publishing houses; if he hadn't taken an interest in this one (to say nothing of many others), it literally wouldn't exist. Meanwhile, my longtime mentor and surrogate big brother, Joel Peterson of Ravenswood, continues to serve as a good-natured sponsor and sounding board, sustaining me (to say nothing of many others) in ways from the enological to the existential.

The other two are relationships of slightly shorter duration but equal aid and loyalty. Josh Greene, editor and publisher of *Wine & Spirits*, not only read the manuscript and offered his expert observations but stands as a beacon of taste, values, and ethics. Those same qualities and more are present in my in-house editor, Leigh Lightfoot, whose sharp but loving eye is enhanced by a reluctance to consume any wine over 13 percent alcohol.

Index

Baxter, Al, 148
Beard, James, 56
Beaujolais, 294–95, 297
Beaulieu Vineyards, 20, 59, 146, 147, 229
Beauregard, Jim, 77, 79, 127, 169, 177
Beeswax Vineyard, 82–83
Beltramo's, San Francisco, 92
Bennion, David, 74, 75
Benveniste, Jacques, 88, 281
Benziger, Bruno, 92–100, 226
Benziger, Joe, 255
Benziger, Mike, 16
  at Beltramo's, 92
  and biodynamics, 248–56, 275–76, 283
  and Ceago, 281–83
  and competition, 225, 226, 232, 276
  and corporate consolidation, 233, 277
  and Enologix, 20
  on family businesses, 276–78
  and Franzia family, 97–98
  and Glen Ellen, 94–100, 225–26, 233, 245, 248, 254, 271–78
  and Imagery Estate, 255, 273
  and Park, Benziger, 92, 93
  at Stony Ridge, 93–94, 95, 237
Benziger family, 95, 210, 226, 276
Bergen, Candice, 42–43
Beringer, 99, 171, 178, 225, 295n
Beringer Blass, 15
Bertolli ranch, 128, 130
Beverly Hills Wine Merchant, 40–52
  author's visit to, 48–52
  clientele of, 41–43
  Grahm employed by, 40, 44–47, 50–52, 63, 126
Bien Nacido vineyard, 119
Big House:
  and Ca' del Solo, 82, 195–97
  label of, 197

name of, 10, 195
and Parker scores, 293
production of, 10, 118, 196, 199, 257, 322
and profitability, 301
sale of, 10, 155, 156, 305, 313
Bindi Quartz chardonnay, 265
biodynamics, 245–56
  and Benziger, 248–56, 275–76, 283
  and Charter of Quality, 252–53
  and crystallizations, 160–61, 162
  "Farming for Flavors," 275
  and Fetzer, 248, 281–83
  and fundamentalism, 254
  Grahm's interest in, 10–11, 86, 117–18, 124, 158, 161, 181–83, 304–5, 335
  and Joly, 279–81
  preparations, 87–88, 249–50, 251
  and quantum mechanics, 89
  and Steiner, 86–87, 159–60, 245, 248, 250, 254, 279, 304
  and uniformity, 251–52
Bird, Harry, 93
Bize-Leroy, Lalou, 241
Blue Nun, 40, 42, 92
Boggs, Lilburn, 58
Bonny Doon (town):
  environmental factors in, 28, 127
  founding of, 74
  neighbors in, 130, 141, 195, 236
  wineries in, 6, 77
Bonny Doon winery, 117–25, 155–63, 193–200
  biodynamics in, 117–18, 124, 158
  blended products of, 10, 118, 129, 133, 196, 198–199, 242, 259
  bonded, 129
  and Cellar Door café, 155, 322
  in decline, 6, 84, 235, 300–301, 322–23, 332–33
  and DEWN, 121, 198, 301
  and distribution, 134–36, 155–59, 290

Nietzsche, Friedrich Wilhelm, 284
Nixon, Richard M., 42
noah grape, 196, 335
Noble, Ann, 66–68, 70, 151–52, 217
  Aroma Wheel of, 66, 152

oak chips, 124, 183, 258
Oakville Winegrowers, 311, 331
Ohio, Alcohol Beverage Control in,
  284
Old Telegram, 9, 137, 140, 142, 287
Old World:
  artificial watering illegal in, 7
  Grahm's travels in, 238, 239, 317–23
  growing the brand in, 257–58
  New World vs., 31–32, 56, 131–33,
    187, 235, 331, 332
  traditional practices in, 32, 70–71,
    74, 78
Olmo, Harold, 57
Oprah Winfrey Show, the, 323–25
Opus One winery, 202
O'Rear, Harry, 110–11
Ough, Cornelius, 57, 65
Overstreet, Dennis, 41–52, 97
oxidation, 214, 215
oxygen:
  and tannins, 221
  and volatile acidity, 12

Pacific Rim Riesling, 197, 257, 305
Pagano, Janet, 64, 206
Pahlmeyer winery, 204, 206
Painter, Brooks, 170
Parducci vineyard, 174, 229
Park, Benziger & Co., 92, 93
Parker, Robert M. Jr., 16, 19, 193
  discontinuing reviews of Califor-
    nia wines, ix–x, 240
  Grahm described by, 12, 139, 240
  100-point scoring system, ix, x, 3, 15,
    159, 186, 202, 204, 288–90, 307
  influence of, 3, 15, 23, 24, 51, 103,
    104, 105, 107–8, 139, 140, 187,
    201, 203, 297, 307

taste preferences of, 103, 105,
  184–85, 203, 208, 241–42, 258,
  297, 327
Pasteur, Louis, 81
Pavarotti, Luciano, 294
Penn & Teller, 193, 241
Pepe, Emidio, 122, 124
Pepi, Robert, 227
Perrier Jouet, 147
Perrone, Osea, 74
Peterson, Richard, 229
Peterson, Tom, 60
petite sirah, 23, 148, 196
petit verdot grape, 103
Phelps, Joseph, 20, 55, 132, 134,
  147, 202–3, 286
phenolics, 8, 165–67, 189, 191–92,
  209, 214, 215
phenols, 19
Phillips, R.H., 152–53, 182, 183, 210
photosynthesis, 327
phylloxera epidemic, 132, 249, 335
Pierce's disease, 6, 85, 235–36, 285
Piesporter Goldtröpfchen, 42
pigato grape, 161
pinot blanc, 171
pinot meunier, 196
pinot noir, 20, 82, 130–32, 170, 171,
  182, 189, 219, 222
  and Châteauneuf-du-Pape, 131–32
  as gamay clone, 294
  Grahm's interest in, 9, 11, 65,
    67–68, 119, 127, 128, 130–31,
    158, 179–80, 183–85, 236,
    325–26, 337
  and market price, 331
  sur lie aging of, 122, 123
Pio Cesare, 171
Pirio, Dave, 21
Pollan, Michael, *The Omnivore's
  Dilemma*, 332
Pollard, John, 77–78, 169
polygons, decahedral, 124
polymeric pigments, 80, 189, 192
Pouilly-Fuissé, 42, 264